Sovereignty Unhinged

Sovereignty

DEBORAH A. THOMAS AND JOSEPH MASCO,
EDITORS

Unhinged

An Illustrated Primer for the Study
of Present Intensities, Disavowals,
and Temporal Derangements

DUKE UNIVERSITY PRESS
Durham and London
2023

© 2023 DUKE UNIVERSITY PRESS
All rights reserved
Printed in the United States of America on acid-free paper ∞
Designed by A. Mattson Gallagher
Typeset in Minion Pro and Antique Olive Std
by Westchester Publishing Services

Library of Congress Cataloging-in-Publication Data
Names: Thomas, Deborah A., [date] editor. | Masco, Joseph,
[date] editor.
Title: Sovereignty unhinged : an illustrated primer for the study
of present intensities, disavowals, and temporal derangements /
edited by Deborah A. Thomas and Joseph Masco.
Description: Durham : Duke University Press, 2023. | Includes
bibliographical references and index.
Identifiers: LCCN 2022028307 (print)
LCCN 2022028308 (ebook)
ISBN 9781478019084 (paperback)
ISBN 9781478016441 (hardcover)
ISBN 9781478023715 (ebook)
Subjects: LCSH: Sovereignty—Social aspects. | Social
structure—Political aspects. | Affect (Psychology)—Political
aspects. | Affect (Psychology)—Social aspects. | Politics and
culture. | BISAC: SOCIAL SCIENCE / Anthropology / Cultural
& Social
Classification: LCC JC327 .S647 2023 (print) |
LCC JC327 (ebook) | DDC 320.1/5—dc23/eng/20220906
LC record available at https://lccn.loc.gov/2022028307
LC ebook record available at https://lccn.loc.gov/2022028308

Cover art: Lochlann Jain, *Reach for Luck* (detail), 2019.
Pen and ink, 56 × 76 cm. Courtesy of the artist.

Contents

Acknowledgments

As is the case for all edited volumes, these essays appear together now after a long and collaborative push. We initially convened at the 2015 American Anthropological Association meeting in Denver, under the auspices of a double panel titled "What Sovereignty Feels Like." We were interested in bringing together a range of scholars who were trying to think sovereignty beyond political economy and beyond conventional models of self-determination, and instead in relation to affect, emotion, and the senses. We hoped that such an interrogation would lead us to understand something new about our contemporary conditions, and about the ephemeral and nonlinear way sovereignties might surface and circulate. We were so energized by our gathering that we continued to think together. Thanks to the Marion R. and Adolph J. Lichtstern Fund at the University of Chicago, we had the opportunity to convene in Santa Cruz at Danilyn Rutherford's beautiful compound to flesh out our own essays and to brainstorm toward an introduction and intervention. There, our conversations were supplemented by fantastic food and extraordinarily bracing body surfing! And as we continued our work together and the collective condition worsened with the rise of authoritarianism, climate disruption, and a global pandemic, its purview also grew as we invited additional interlocutors and additional modes of expression.

We are grateful, of course, for the patience, diligence, and brilliance of all the contributors represented here, and for the support and guidance of Ken Wissoker, Joshua Gutterman Tranen, and Chad Royal at Duke University Press. We also want to thank the University of Chicago and the University of Pennsylvania for financial support toward publication subvention. Most importantly, we thank all those who have engaged us in study—both those who have moved on and those to come—for continuing to inspire us to imagine other worlds, and to work with us to bring them into being.

Introduction
Feeling Unhinged

JOSEPH MASCO AND DEBORAH A. THOMAS

Prodigy is, at its essence, adaptability and persistent, positive obsession. Without persistence, what remains is an enthusiasm of the moment. Without adaptability, what remains may be channeled into destructive fanaticism. Without positive obsession, there is nothing at all.

—Lauren Oya Olamina in Octavia Butler, *Parable of the Sower*

The words in the epigraph to this chapter, penned by Lauren Oya Olamina, the protagonist of Octavia Butler's *Parable of the Sower* (1993), constitute the first insight from "Earthseed," the emergent text that guides the movement she seeks to bring into being, a new mode of survival on an increasingly unstable and violent North American continent. *Parable* is set in 2024, now less than one year from the present, but thirty-one years from the original publication date right at the end of the Cold War, a moment well into the crack epidemic, heading toward the peak of prison-industrial capture, as scientists began to frantically alert the world to the coming climate disruption, to no avail. *Parable of the Sower* chronicles the destruction of society as we know it—the endgame of the mass suffering wrought by the various exclusions of capitalism, colonization, and nationalism—and the pilgrimage of Lauren, and those she meets, toward a self-reliant togetherness rooted in a philosophy grounded in the principle of change. Lauren herself is afflicted by "hyperempathy," an "organic delusional syndrome," the result of her mother's drug addiction while pregnant with her. As Lauren describes her condition: "I feel what I see others feeling or what I believe they feel" (12). In a world that has already become undone, hyperempathy is a constant and painful burden for Lauren, a vulnerability that drives her to imagine and pursue the possibility of building a less violent social order elsewhere, perhaps farther north on the Pacific Coast, perhaps off world. Throughout *Parable*, we follow Lauren's motley crew as they fend off the miserable, the homeless, and the wretched who would kill them for food or supplies or weapons, and as they avoid those who have been ingesting a new drug that causes them to set fires (Butler's icy recognition of the increasing number of people in American life who have no interest in building or preserving anything at all). Lauren's group moves along the Pacific Coast northward as they attempt to get outside of the normative violence of a broken economy and failed national security state to create something new and outlandish. We are interested, in this volume, in exploring the possibilities and limitations of that new and outlandish world. We have no interest in the restoration of prior conditions or nostalgia for past times but rather focus our attention on the challenges of enduring violent present conditions and building meaningful social connection in the midst of rebounding forms of trouble.

The contributors to this volume came together to probe a series of questions: What is the political ground of the present? What is its horizon? How do we imagine sovereignty in languages other than action, agency, and control? What insights does affect, as a lens, give us in thinking through moments when something that feels like sovereignty occurs, or is felt to be absent? How do we avoid the political and historical capture that makes one complicit with a problem rather than creating the conditions of possibility to confront it? We wanted to more fully understand the ways sovereignty is lived and enacted in the realm of everyday practice, and the ways in which this might reflect an aspiration for a new arrangement of our normative understandings of the spheres of both the geopolitical and the interpersonal. From a range of vantage points, the essays included here take seriously the affective dimensions of these practices and aspirations in order to illuminate the epistemological, ontological, and transnational entanglements that produce a sense of what is possible—politically, economically, and socioculturally—in a post-9/11 militarized world infused with the violence of global capital, with accelerating climate disruption, and with resurgent racisms and exclusions. We are interested in the afterlives, and the new lives, of twentieth-century notions of states, activism, and agency, and in how twenty-first-century ideas about citizenship, relationship, and responsibility are being reconfigured in unpredictable ways. As ethnographers, we are also curious about what different forms of scholarly expression are necessitated by our changed condition—often cast as postpolitical, neoliberal, or late industrial. In such a deeply troubled era, how might scholarship work to transform rather than reiterate existing ideas about self-possession and awareness? What new genres of investigation or care, of writing or visualizing, are needed to engage living within the giant problem spaces otherwise known as economy, security, ecology, or politics?

We have called this volume a primer as a way of signaling our ambitions but also acknowledging our limitations. *Primer* has several connotations. In one context, it refers to the short nucleic acid sequence that constitutes the starting point for DNA synthesis, the molecule that begins a polymerization process. In this sense, a primer is a catalyst, the impulse that allows for the creation of something new. Primer is also that first coat of paint, a preparation that prevents overabsorption and the development of rust, that improves the coverage and lasting effect of the second coat, which is the main event. But a primer is also an elementary textbook that serves as an introduction to a subject of study (Harney and Moten 2013). Our project then is provisional and hopefully catalytic, a first approach that also points to a vast field of future study. But our field of study here is also speculative and hard to grasp, oriented toward the modes of feeling and anticipation that constitute the experience of navigating troubled times. In terms of social theory, it is counterintuitive. If one were to read a classic primer on sovereignty, for example, one would expect to see references to Hobbes, to the Treaty of Westphalia, to Wilsonian notions of democracy, and perhaps to figures like Weber and Schmitt.[1] These texts tell the story of sovereignty through the lens of the executive; they have an investment in making the figure of sovereignty a special entity, a singular form, often stacking race, class, and gender in a specific historical configuration (as Sylvia Wynter might put it, constituting a genre of the human via both hierarchy and exclusion).

Anthropologists have been compelled instead to explore the more diffuse, uncertain, complex ways people experience sovereignty and the challenge of navigating both uncertainty and survival. Stimulated by Michel Foucault's biopolitics, Giorgio Agamben's notion of bare life, and Deleuze and Guattari's rhizomic networks of force and possibility, political anthropologists have borrowed from political philosophy the conceptualization of sovereignty as domination, but have reframed this in terms of process and practice, more as performance than product (Hansen and Stepputat 2006). In doing so, they have been attuned to the entire universe of other concurrent processes, the intensifications of agency, the regimes of care and engagement, the temporal and spatial derangements that are not recognized traditionally as forms of sovereignty but that are, in fact, where most of us are living most of the time. We thus present analyses of sovereignty *unhinged*—unhinged from master narratives, unhinged from normative disciplinary frames, and unhinged from pragmatic developmentalism and utility. We are asking about what happens when the autonomous, rational subject is no longer the starting point of analysis (or policy, or transformation), and when we begin instead from the energies, excesses, and ambitions of being out of order, dislocated, even hysterical or mad.

This unhinging of sovereignty rests on a different theoretical lineage, one in which international relations, political economy, and the management of populations feature less prominently than embodied and phenomenological approaches to Being, and one in which violence has been central to its exercise and performance (Mbembe 2003). We ground this lineage within historical-ideological and onto-epistemological phenomena that produce whiteness, maleness, and Europeanness as the apex of humanity (Wynter 2003), the epitome not only of transparency and universality but also of determination and causality (Ferreira da Silva 2007, 2017). In other words, we begin with an understanding that, having defined itself as universal reason and absolute perspectivity, the interior humanity against which all exterior Others are compared and measured (and found wanting), Western European empire inhabits the expression of sovereignty, the conquest and disavowal of what Édouard Glissant (1997) has called "relation" (the basis of the right to opacity and the foundation of freedom), not only within Europe but also throughout the postcolonial world.[2] This sovereignty is obsessed with security because its conquest, cannibalism, and disavowal of exteriority are never seamless nor complete. It requires constant work to install a singular concept of the human and a world order based on property relations, and this work is always potentially undone by that which fails to recognize it, by that which refuses it in intentional and unconscious ways.[3] Put differently, the Euro-American logics of sovereignty are both delusional and crazy-making, demanding a singularity of life out of a vast multiplicity, creating and then naturalizing hierarchies that function only through dehumanization and exclusion.

If this is our baseline, confronting our contemporary condition requires a formulation of sovereignty that resides outside the normative parameters of perfectible governance, one that is rooted not in Being or History but in nonlinear temporality and nonutility. We take our cue here from Georges Bataille ([1991] 2017), who felt that sovereignty should be grounded in immediacy rather than future thinking, consumption rather than production, and the desire for nothingness rather than attachment. For Bataille, the

Masco and Thomas

early twentieth-century anthropology of noncapitalist societies provided important keys to thinking about relations between subjects and sovereigns. He was particularly compelled by ethnographic representations of the potlatch, as these appeared to him to counter the exigencies of mercantile (and industrial) capitalism whereby labor was oriented to future accumulation, for Bataille a form of both literal and figurative slavery. Through an unproductive sharing of wealth—and by "unproductive," Bataille means a wealth that is not accumulated for future gain—both the sovereign and the subject experience the primacy of the present, the miraculous excess, and the festival of life. Death, in this view, or the release of the fear of death, is the ultimate sovereign experience, and the states of laughter, sadness, rapture, anger, ecstasy, intoxication, horror, disgust, fear, magic, and eroticism all represent affective encounters with a nonexceptional sovereignty. To refuse conventionally iterated sovereignty for Bataille's sovereignty "*in the storm*" ([1991] 2017, 342) is therefore to seek a life "*beyond utility*" (198) and beyond the engulfment of recognition. What he called the "*human quality*" should not be sought in the language of either democratic rights and responsibilities or socialist collectivity, but in the one "who refuses *the given*" (343).[4]

This iteration of sovereignty abandons the world of projects and eschews the expectation embedded within the temporality of the future anterior or the notion of progress or the politics of recognition. In disrupting the disavowals and deferrals that undergird imperial Being, it creates the conditions for meaningful forms of life by nullifying the normative relations that uphold Being as the ground of subjectivity and governance. This is particularly resonant throughout the so-called postcolonial world, where, as Achille Mbembe has argued, we continue to deal with a form of governmentality in which "sovereignty consists fundamentally in the exercise of a power outside the law" (2003, 23). There is, of course, a long list of scholars who have critiqued the *post* in *postcolonial*, and who have limned the continuation of imperial relations of domination, even as these have shifted over time. While this scholarship ordinarily laments the failure to remake formerly colonial relations from the ground up, Yarimar Bonilla (2015, 2017) has suggested that exploring enduring forms of nonsovereignty should instead provide grounds for new theoretical and political openings. "The notion of a sovereign state, and its attendant sovereign individual who speaks and acts autonomously," she writes, "is thus giving way to the recognition of the non-sovereign nature of most social relationships—political, intimate, and affective—all of which require brokered and negotiated forms of interdependency and a relinquishing of autonomy" (Bonilla 2017, 333). Indeed, if the practice of sovereignty must lie in nonutility, then its aim cannot be the seizure of state power, but instead its refusal and abolition through what Savannah Shange has called a "messy breakup," a "rending, not reparation" (2019, 4). In other words, agency and sovereignty are not the same thing, which opens up the conceptual space for ethnographic inquiry explored in this book.

Paying attention to affective intensities, the spaces in which nonutility thrives, refusals of the terms of recognition, and moments of flagrancy is our way of getting at the unhinging we seek to identify, a way of thinking beside and beyond presumptions of possessive individualism, and a way of siding with Nietzsche's madman. Thinking sovereignty in relation to affect rather than the ways we've been given (ways that have made possible certain imaginations but foreclosed others) offers a conceptual space for analyzing historical formations as dynamic, and as simultaneously constrained by the institutions, economic realities, and political conceits of different eras. We are interested, then, in the spark of self-possession that feels like sovereignty and offer here a variety of vantage points—the necessary first draft and hopeful catalyst—for an emerging ethnographic methodology of current conditions.

An earlier generation of scholarship on affect was oriented toward thinking about what mobilizes people to act, identifying the prepolitical animation that moves people to care about something and activate attention, care, politics. That was the moment of the AIDS crisis, the aftermath of the first US invasion of Iraq, the post–Cold War moment of globalization, theorized in both romantic and destructive terms (Staiger, Cvetkovich, and Reynolds 2010; Ahmed 2004; Sedgwick 2003; Massumi 1993). As we've settled into a normalized kind of neoliberalism, trade blocs are gone, China is ascendant, and the United States is simultaneously withdrawing from global alliances and intervening in new ways via covert actions. All are affected by the sheer social force of information technologies and finance capital. We are one generation into the demobilization of a more radical historical vision of inequality. Platforms like #MeToo and the Movement for Black Lives have overcome some normative social silencings, yet the proliferation of presentism buries a deeper understanding of why things are the way they are. Too often the call to crisis is merely an effort to reestablish the very conditions of possibility for that violence (as Donald Trump might put it, to make "America White Again") rather than a way to assess foundational logics, structures, institutions, or ambitions (Masco 2017).

How, for example, should we parse the affective intensities and challenges of a summer like that of 2020, in which unprecedented public protests against anti-Black police violence took over US cities that were also in

Masco and Thomas

lockdown under COVID-19 pandemic protocols, creating loss of jobs and evictions while in many regions of the world people were also navigating the challenges of extreme weather events—involving heat, hurricanes, and fires? What are the techniques of survival in such a multiply-threatening moment, the forms of self-activation that Lauren Berlant (2007, 759) would have called modes of "lateral agency," not sovereignty, where agency "can be an activity of maintenance, not making; fantasy, without grandiosity; sentience, without full intentionality; inconsistence, without shattering; embodying, alongside embodiment"? In other words, when does exhaustion produce zones of personal and interpersonal creativity, modes of engagement that matter to managing the compounding dangers and stresses of the moment, which in so many cases lead to forms of self-sacrifice?

In response to the current twenty-first-century moment, the affects we explore here aren't explicitly instrumental. Most of our contributors feature a problem that people are not going to be able to solve, and each chapter considers how people manage that state of being (abject, captured, or fatigued, but also creatively attempting to create new worlds, or to move within violent orders of being). Our focus is on bringing affect, agency, and politics into a more nuanced relation than has been conventional. We are asking readers to be caught, as all the subjects in the book are caught, without an easy answer about what the effects of a particular political moment can be. How, for example, can one solve the violence of capitalism or imperialism (or the multigenerational fusion of the two in what Karuka [2019] has called "shareholder whiteness")? Individuals are, instead, always inside these problems working with all available resources to navigate the resulting turbulence while also seeking opportunities for positive world making or more provisional modes of relief.

Affect, on its own, is not a political project of any kind. As Jessica Winegar shows us in chapter 1, moments of collective euphoria might actually do political work, but this doesn't necessarily lead to the consolidation of a new disposition, and it may, instead, reveal the limits of intensity (psychically and physically) as people become literally exhausted. The upside-down temporality and bodily adjustments in Purnima Mankekar and Akhil Gupta's essay also generate new forms of imagination and wonder (chapter 5). And sometimes the steamroller of the corporate NGO might not actually reach its expected destination, as Arjun Shankar demonstrates in chapter 7, and the lunch ladies negotiating vulnerability at every level can unexpectedly keep their jobs. The deranged spatiality and temporality of late modernity enables these fatigues, innovations, hopes, and surprises, and ethnographic attention to them helps us to understand which parts of these derangements people are negotiating at particular moments, and how they theorize and act on them. As Bonilla puts it in chapter 4, the world is filled with preexisting disasters that new emergencies ride on top of—the earthquakes come after the hurricane in the midst of a pandemic in Puerto Rico, leaving the vulnerable even more so or, at times, allowing those most experienced in emergency conditions to lead the way to a different dispensation.

The contemporary context points us to the contingency of local action, one in which our current concepts like endurance and precarity, though evocative, are not sufficient. Affect, as we present it, reflects the capacity to act and be acted upon (in the Arendtian sense) but not with a particular telos (Berlant 2007). In a way, then, we also want to imagine new forms of agency without knowing what they will look like, without relying on the neoliberal idioms of choice and resilience (Evans and Reid 2014). How might we understand possibility as simultaneously emergent with perception, limit, strength, opportunity, and loss? How can we see the mechanisms by which these possibilities are shared or transmitted, but not always consciously? We want to foreground unpredictability in everyday life today, the inability to predict or map effects with the kind of precision and dogma that post-structuralists may have felt was possible. We are trying to map the possibilities of some sort of collectivity that could come into being, some kind of world making that has also to do with the recuperation of vulnerability in relationality, of engagement without possessive individualism, of lives lived in the tangle of preexisting modes of violent relation. Following Lauren Berlant (2016), we are interested in recognizing the broken modes of sociality that are informed by dominant projects of militarism and capital while also attending to how individuals come to navigate social orders with diverse projects, expectations, and techniques but with little expectation of control or mastery. If we take "What does sovereignty feel like?" rather than "What does sovereignty look like?" as our organizing question, we put a microfocus on instability, on undoing, on the ways sovereignty encompasses different (sometimes divergent, sometimes convergent) intensities and temporalities, and therefore on how people are experiencing a moment or condition; we don't assume this is knowable without doing the investigation.

Our primer (part investigation, part first-layer methodology, part affective recruitment, part provocation for future study) is thus designed to elicit an approach, rather than an endpoint, mode, or theory. This method helps us find where to locate the ground to which we want to move, and to live in and through the everyday with attention. We seek a method that helps us see five hundred years of European modernity and the West as a project of exclusion that might always have been otherwise, that leads us to appreciate the condition of our condition without resorting to totalizing narratives (of revolution, of science, of imperialisms, of Afropessimisms, of Anthropocenes). We strive, instead, for a way to sit in uncertainty and still engage in forms of nonteleological world making that have an unpredictable range of affective possibility. As a result, we are inclined toward the spheres of the intimate, messy, and chaotic, and toward the everyday rather than the eventful (Das 2006). We attend to the quotidian enactment, refusal, exhaustion, and consolidation that characterize moments in a duration of political life.[5]

> I mean he's like . . . like a symbol of the past for us to hold on to as we're pushed into the future. He's nothing. No substance. But having him there, the latest in a two-and-a-half-century-long line of American Presidents make people feel that the country, the culture that they grew up with is still here—that we'll get through these bad times and back to normal.
>
> —Lauren Oya Olamina in Octavia Butler, *Parable of the Sower*

In this quote, Lauren Oya Olamina is speaking about their new president, Donner, an advocate of state privatization, of short-term thinking and a narrow pursuit of profits, a law-and-order executive that promises new jobs and opportunities but delivers workers into toxic spaces, violent labor relations, and racisms but who also signals a still present (if objectively barely functioning) federal state. The continued existence of a president, an individual occupying the position of chief sovereign and thereby maintaining a connection to the more robust nation-state politics of the past, reminds Lauren of a world committed to a social contract based on the lost assumption about an ever-improving collective future and security. But she is clearly skeptical, drawing our attention to Donner's supporters' illusory sense of progress and perfectibility, challenging their belief that the "normal" to which they strive to return is indeed desirable, that it isn't itself fatally flawed, constituted through a series of disavowals of the processes that have been the foundation of the modern world—imperialism, colonization, genocide, and plantation-based slavery. Writing in the wake of the Reagan-era political realignment, Octavia Butler was all too aware of the vast populations inside the United States being readily abandoned by the neoliberal turn, aware of the hollowing out of civic society and infrastructures in support of wealth consolidation and expansive militarism, well aware of false nostalgia for a United States that could be imagined as uncontested but only for those implementing Jim Crow, native dispossession, and extraction regimes.

Thus, we work in *Sovereignty Unhinged* to challenge political, economic, and psychic orders that protect some while leaving others to negotiate advancing necropolitical disorders, exclusions, and abandonments. These are the disavowals that produce the themes that commonly permeate the essays in this volume. We are confronted with out-of-joint temporalities and radical disjunctures; palimpsestual dislocations and compressions; gaps, lags, and emergent relations. We are also facing difficult spatial reckonings, reorderings, and hauntings, with unpredictable movements and claims-making across both real and imagined boundaries. And we are forced to contend with the realm of the body and the meanings attached to its physicality, management, performativity, and limits. In *Parable of the Sower*, these tensions are viscerally explored as Lauren is violently forced out of her fragile gated compound and out onto the open road, walking the dangerous route from the loss of one community to the almost impossible founding of another. Following Butler's attention to the circuits of empathy and violence, change and crisis, capture and choice that inform Lauren's hazardous journey, we have grouped our chapters under the pull of opposite impulses: "Capture/Escape," "Breaking/Making," "Exclusion/Embrace." Each section explores how modes of collective identification, labor, and subjective experience are activated and experienced against the contingencies of social dis/order. Each chapter tracks from a distinctive perspective the destabilizations and intensities informing how individuals navigate the simultaneity of violent conditions while maintaining a focus on the always available potential for positive world making.

We feature Lochlann Jain's artwork, which not only undoes normative understanding about self-possession but also offers a visual register of nonsovereignty focused on the project of breathing. Jain's *The Lung Is a Bird and a Fish* project details the modes of biological capture in an industrial age that links organisms via the increasingly vexed necessity of respiration. Jain offers us an illustrated exploration of industrial life itself, focusing on the promise of good air, easy respiration, reliable breath. Jain links the laboratory animals whose bodies are mobilized by researchers to understand compromised breath (from asthma to emphysema) to the concentrations of airborne toxicity that index race and class with ferocious specificity. As Alison Kenner (2018) has detailed, the terrors of an asthma attack create a haptic of environmental reasoning, a mapping of the spaces, interiors, weather conditions, and season that shut down breathing in a painful seizure. "Breathers," as Tim Choy (2011, 145) would remind us, are a class of living beings that are linked via the ways that air distributes harms unequally and represent the ultimate revolutionary class. As Kenner shows, asthmatic attunement requires learning urban space via constrictions in breath and deploying science (i.e., the inhalers that Jain shows are developed via animal bodies in laboratory tests) and new kinds of self-knowledge (i.e., practiced forms of holding the body and controlled emotions and thoughts, as one tries to move through a sudden spasmodic loss of breath). Breath is a nonsovereign necessity, producing contemporary derangements linking the bad smog days in Delhi and other global cities to specific neighborhood conditions of toxicity to climatic disturbances on hemispheric and even planetary scales.

Via art and research, Jain connects basic scholarship on oxygen to the development of laboratory practices that create choking animal subjects, to innovations in gas and chemical warfare that target breath itself (see also Sloterdijk 2009). In Jain's work, the suffocating subject is revealed as a fully modern achievement—nonsovereign, in pain, and linked inextricably, if unevenly, to other beings via science, warfare, and shared industrial atmospheres. Jain asks us to take account of the hidden connections between differently breathing beings, to see a shared relationality to destabilizing environmental conditions and to interrogate the contemporary practices that harm in the name of knowledge, profit, or power—themes that crisscross chapters in this volume. In this way, Jain, alongside Christina Sharpe (2016), attunes to the everyday challenge of respiration in our historical moment, of breathing in a world still infused with racisms, sexisms, and homophobias and structured by violent orders of policing and toxicity.

The first section of essays—"Capture/Escape"—attends to the messiness of revolutionary projects, the problem of historical violence, and the unpredictable aftermaths and by-products of nationalism. In it, Jessica Winegar, María Elena García, Deborah Thomas, and Yarimar Bonilla raise questions about the ghosts of imperialism, civil war, and revolution in relation to contemporary dynamics of normative sovereignty regarding regime change, the production of consuming rather than critically engaged subjects, and the replacement of local expert knowledge with state forensics designed to manage processes of death. Here we ask: What happens to revolutionary energies—the collective effervescence that can constitute a new social order—as they become coded into state institutions, policy, and policing? How does the promise of a radical break with the past become undone in the implementing of a new social order, often renewing long-standing violences within new languages, codes, and silences? How does feeling free secure the very possibility of sovereignty but also show its limitation in that it is so impossible to hold on to?

In formal state-based politics we show that ambitions for the unhinging of sovereignty are foundationally linked to psychosocial and affective distortions, fields in which the violence of political life is miscast as love, aesthetics, or silence via modes of either amplification, silencing, or forgetting. Jessica Winegar asks us to understand love for the leader, the euphoria of projective attachment for the very idea of a figure that could hold the promise of making a new political order out of the disappointment of a destabilizing revolutionary moment. The overdetermined affect Winegar finds for the newly installed President Sisi—a kind of collective love suffused with erotic desires and misrecognized hope—is a register of the unstated fear of a world without a strongman, a world where violence is no longer organized via recognizable parties and politics, instead of a revolution, a constant unraveling. The promise of Tahrir Square in 2011, the euphoria of overthrowing a dictatorial regime, enabled an intensity that people want to maintain but with new attachments and misrecognitions as the brutality of a new political order secures power. Winegar tracks the polarities of love and disgust that follow in Egypt, modes of affective displacement that have the intensity of revolutionary energy but no longer organize the spark of revolutionary political demands.

Love, here, is not primarily the sustained commitment to others that Octavia Butler's Lauren seeks to cultivate in a violent world, despite her hyperempathy for other people's pain, but rather a mode that overrides and resists the violence of the present. Similarly, María Elena García explores, in chapter 2, the recent production of a Peruvian cuisine for international connoisseurship, a seemingly depoliticized love of flavor and taste that politicians and public figures turn to as a way to change the narrative, to move away from political unrest and decades of conflict to focus on foodways as a form of togetherness. García shows how the entry of Peruvian cuisine into the global marketplace offers a powerful way for Peruvian elites to launder and erase Indigeneity while also riding on its foundational aesthetic forms. A Peruvian nation focused on aesthetics and markets emerges in her account that can no longer imagine a speaking role for Indigenous people in the national narrative; instead, Indigenous subjects are offered up as mute witnesses to the repurposing of their foods for an international consumer. But here the derangement is doubled, as cuisine offers a positive image of Peru, a desirable commodity form that can compete with other international culinary regimes at an aesthetic level and thereby offer a compelling multicultural portrait of the nation, but it does so by repurposing and commodifying Indigeneity itself, rendering it an apolitical domain of taste, texture, and color. Love, here, is deeply connected to political erasure, to a branding operation that uses Indigenous aesthetic forms and symbolism to remake the national image as tasty, not unequal; as cosmopolitan, not divided; as safe, not violently contested.

The propaganda of history as enabled by violent erasure also informs Deborah Thomas's chapter, which traces the relationship of death and sovereignty in a garrison community in West Kingston, Jamaica. Connecting US War on Terror policing practices in the hemisphere with the *longue durée* histories of colonization and the plantation in Jamaica, Thomas asks about forms of "nonsovereign death." Here the state's ability to kill is matched by the state's ability to forget and erase, leaving residents of a garrison violently attacked by state authorities with unacknowledged dead loved ones, with haunted relations to space and place that are informed by the long histories of the plantation, racial and gendered codes of violence, and colonial modes of spatial control. Unpacking the ongoing negotiation of a 2009 extradition order from the US government that led to a police assault on a historical garrison community, Thomas asks how those caught in the aftermath understand their relation to violence itself, how ghosts of the long dead inform those recently killed, and how the (post)colonial state continues to inform contemporary life in Jamaica, rendering some lives nonsovereign and expendable in the wake of the plantation, but also capable of and invested in vast community mobilizations, diverse modes of interpersonal care, and complex memory work. Here, affect and memory are archival projects, stored in individuals as they negotiate violent state projects that demand official forgetting and complacency. In this way, Thomas asks where the plantation continues to reside, where the logics of imperialism are stored and felt, and how individuals come to rely on complicated forensic practices in search of memory, community, and repair.

In her reflection on the multiple emergencies in Puerto Rico, Yarimar Bonilla asks us to consider preexisting disasters, meaning the legacies of past violent events as well as the ongoingness of structural abandonment across economy, politics, and social exclusions. For people living on an island experiencing not only ocean rise due to polar ice melt but amplified hurricanes due to petrochemical emissions, the question of how to identify the cause of crisis is rendered simultaneously corporate, imperial, and planetary. Bonilla assesses the intersubjective experience of long-term neoliberal austerity measures in the ongoing aftermath of hurricanes, earthquakes, and a global pandemic in Puerto Rico—showing how impossible it is to sort out cause and effect in the midst of a multifaceted emergency.

Demonstrating that there are no "natural disasters" anymore in a world destabilized by global warming, global capital, and US imperialism, she contemplates the tactics and survival challenges for those living in a state pushed into failure—focusing on exhaustion rather than resilience, commitment rather than abandonment, living on rather than surviving.

Between the first and second sections lies Leniqueca A. Welcome's visual intervention. Photocollage, for Welcome, has become both a modality of refusal and an invitation to looking otherwise. Through collage, Welcome conjures ethnographic insight from uncertainty, witnesses without laying bare, and offers new possibilities through juxtaposition, while also respecting the opacity of her interlocutors (Glissant 1997). With *Wading in the Thick*, she presents four collages that grapple with life and death, and with the afterlives of death, in ways that upend the forensics of surveillance and capture. The images here, in their intentional nontransparency, offer thick forms of ethical relation; they are moments in a conversation among the producers and consumers of the images and the images themselves. They encourage viewers to feel rather than identify; they incite confusion; they disrupt normative expectations about time, space, and agency; they enact repair. Paired with textual ethnographic snapshots, the collages are not illustrations but juxtapositions that invite us to perceive askew, to experience the asymmetries of life, love, and attempts to be recognized as human.

> God can't be resisted or stopped, but can be shaped and focused. This means God is not to be prayed to. Prayers only help the person doing the praying, and then, only if they strengthen and focus that person's resolve.
>
> —Lauren Oya Olamina in Octavia Butler, *Parable of the Sower*

Our second section—"Breaking/Making"—seeks to limn the complexity of being in and counterimagining the possibilities of the current economic moment, confronting the lived contradictions of laboring in a globalized world, suffused with the violence of petrochemical and financial capital, and related forms of war. In this late industrial moment, where supply-side logistics organizes geopolitics via unequal markets that both distribute climatological insecurities on an unprecedented scale and make employment a provisional condition tied to foreign profits, derangements and dislocations abound.

The task of navigating both opportunity and abandonment in the highly contingent spaces of temporary workforces and deindustrialized labor is the subject of Purnima Mankekar and Akhil Gupta's contribution in chapter 5, which follows the enthusiastic but upside-down world of service call centers in India. Here, the arrival of new kinds of jobs in call service centers for multinational corporations whose customers are largely in Europe and North America offers an exhilarating opportunity for workers but at an unusual price. Inverting their lives to work in the time zones of customers on different continents, the pleasures of high-tech jobs (involving not only pay but also daily connections to people located all over the globe, with all the imaginative possibilities energized by overcoming time and space in this manner) are gained. However, the job also requires many to give up normal access to family and friends at home, to a life organized by local rhythms and established time horizons.

Perversely, life in the call center after a few years can produce a feeling no longer of radical mobility but of stuckness for those who have not risen in their career position but also have traded away the continuities and connections to local family and friends. Mankekar and Gupta identify an affective force of possibility that call centers can unlock for individuals, a freeing of the imagination which nonetheless requires constant negotiations of "being out of joint." Being out of joint is an increasingly collective condition in the twenty-first century. This forces individuals into a daily negotiation of social, environmental, and economic disorders and their compounding effects—creating a modern subject that is neither sovereign nor in control but rather one that attempts to navigate both physically and psychically a wildly contingent world and its distributed violences—and does their best every day to make it work.

Sovereignty as interdependence (not freedom) is the theme of Jessica Cattelino's contribution, chapter 6, on the settler state conditions of the Everglades, a region crucial to Indigenous worlds that is undergoing massive transformation due to the combined forces of global warming, tourist economies, and water demands from urban centers. Underscoring the multiplicity of Indigenous sovereignties, as well as the continuing paradox for native communities negotiating state and federal law from "domestic dependent nation" statuses, Cattelino considers how the Seminole Tribe of Florida navigates radically shifting legal and ecological terrains. She explores the rise since the 1980s of both casino gambling and a new water politics that force multiple, constantly troubled sovereignties to be mobilized in the same territorial region, constantly in tension, mobilizing for good relations. For the restoration of the Everglades—that unprecedented attempt to sustain its ecological form even as erosion and ocean rise threaten to submerge the entire region—activates all claims, making land and water rights increasingly contingent, though vital, formulations that try to moderate the flows of water and earth.

In short, Cattelino invites us to try, just try, to be sovereign over water, the irresistible flow that enables life itself, and to do so from within a politics of good relations toward the earth. In the hyperviolence of the settler colonial state, now magnified by the force of global warming, which promises to push all coastal communities underwater in the coming decades, Cattelino offers the startling proposition that true sovereignty resides in dependency: that is, in collaborations across political lines and in support of a vast set of more than human relations that constitute all the forms of life, both on and in between water and land. How to define and act in support of ethical community relations under conditions of massive ecological transformation is an ongoing challenge for those navigating the violent and long-standing settler colonial legal paradox; it is also an increasingly urgent collective project in the twenty-first century, as the atmosphere heats, the ice melts, and the oceans rise.

In the turbulence of ecology/economy, these once seemingly separate domains are now fused via the historical work of petrochemical capitalism, bringing formally into question the viability of the Euro-American commitment to creating futurity. What are the tactics of survival, the modes of flexible reaction and counterreaction to radically destabilizing conditions, the ways of staying sane and active as one is bounced, struck, or hijacked by the combined force of petrochemical economies, superheated ecologies, and national politics? Here, we need Arjun Shankar's ethnographic engagement with the lunch makers in a school in Advisandra, India, local women paid by the state to make sure each child in the school has a good hot lunch (chapter 7). A modernization project tied to the intimacy of food, the hot lunch program provides a classic social contract between citizens and the state—life support via institutional organization. But here, Shankar's ethnography troubles such a claim: the cooks have not been paid in months (and are barely making it when they are paid), and a proposal to outsource the food contract to a Hindu religious organization threatens to replace them altogether. The contradictions of the Indian state—as the largest democracy, as well as a quickly neoliberalizing state that is also number one hundred on the Global Hunger Index—leave children in the most precarious of positions. Thus, the lunch makers are at the fulcrum of multiple national projects—both mobilized and expendable, as contracts get written and rewritten. But the new food contract requires standardized lunches, and the roads that allow the school to be connected to these larger national projects are not yet built. Shankar follows the lunch makers as they navigate the turbulence of national infrastructures, religious projects, and national promises, tuning into the affectively charged and gendered modes of concern, of capacity, of imagination that allow the cooks to carry on, with or without pay, despite a lack of job security—but with the very real pleasure of feeding schoolkids, feeling sovereign by being together for others over their stoves.

Labor is transformative of far more than psyches and imaginaries. As Alex Blanchette demonstrates in chapter 8, on the embodied forces of the twenty-first-century factory farm, workers are physically remade through contact with the pig. Closely examining the effects of repetitious slaughter-house work in an industrial hog operation that organizes millions of ani-mals in the United States, he considers the emergence of a system for the maximal extraction of value, from not only the pig but also the worker. The inability to standardize the pig's body perfectly for human consumption, despite decades of trying, means that the slaughterhouse cannot be fully mechanized. Instead, it needs the expert craft of people assigned to work the human/animal interface. The speed and volume of this factory system forces employees to work well past the limits of the human body. "Break-ing in," as Blanchette shows, is simultaneously a conceptual and embodied process for workers, as they learn not only the techniques of working with pig bodies but also to endure the transformation in their own bodies—as hands, fingers, and tendons are worn down and remade to match the haptic feel of the animal. The slaughterhouse exposes a brutal and explicit necrop-olitics via an instrumentalization of biological essence on a mass population scale. The dream of the perfect factory, fully automated and without any waste, is relocated here to the cuts and repetitive stress injuries of workers, who have found ways to value each cut as a mode of self-sacrifice to worker security. In this way, Blanchette reveals how the bodies (of both pigs and people) are captured by an industrial concept that seeks maximal extrac-tion at every stage, remaking the conditions of life, for living, and for death.

These are also the themes that Lochlann Jain explores in his contribution on the multispecies politics of breathing, which sets up our final section.

> It's no small thing to commit yourself to other people.
>
> —Lauren Oya Olamina in Octavia Butler, *Parable of the Sower*

Our third section—"Exclusion/Embrace"—explores how we think about in-dividual capacities in political moments in ways that are not naive in terms of the stakes, and that explore what it takes to mobilize through fatigue, exhaustion, and frustration. It grapples with the problems of knowing and not knowing, capture and refusal, and it seeks to hack political liberalism within anthropology and beyond. What would happen if we were to suspend the logics of otherness that inform anthropology, that are organized under what Trouillot (1991) called the savage slot and what across the twentieth century became area studies? What if the historical moment of the early twenty-first century creates problems and lives suffused with violent collective conditions that can only be lived as isolated beings? An unhinged anthropology would not mobilize difference as a way to study normative centers, metropoles versus peripheries, small-scale cultures versus national ones, seeing the vast range of ideas about the world as containers that stack in relation to one another—like the perfectly ordered world of supply-side logistics. Such a project would tune into radical difference that demands to not be understood and ordered, refusals of such an absolute kind that they move outside of language. They might also focus in on explicit forms of identification that disavow collectivity, that produce massive harm to both self and world and do so with illiberal glee.

Here, Octavia Butler's notion of hyperempathy figures the problem directly—marking a special kind of connection to the pain of others. Lauren's agony at seeing others in pain, and the literal indexing of another's bodily suffering to her own, signals the capacity for a full identification with another person, an absorbing on sight of their state of being and a sympathetic harmonizing with them via the physical act of sharing, not removing, their pain. But Butler does not allow so complete a recognition: Lauren's hyperempathy is marked as her "perception" of other people's pain, rather than an identical incorporation. Thus, it is felt but imagined, real but also staging the question of how much an individual can know another person, of how empathy actually works, and of how much solidarity in difference is actually possible. For our purposes, Butler's notion of hyperempathy poses the question of sharing and investment across radical difference but without full understanding. Might an unhinged sovereignty be located in being unknowable to others, in a life without recognition? We explore in this last section the modes of self-awareness in conditions of derangement that nonetheless affectively inform something like hope, unpacking some contemporary logics of negative deferral while seeking the infrastructures of mobilization that have the capacity to shift the world.

The inescapable derangement of US racial politics is explored in Kristen Simmons and Kaya Williams's "mixtape for America," a narrative and

Masco and Thomas

musical experiment that explores the vibrational forces of activism and survival in the time/space of institutional racism (chapter 9). It offers an ethnographic reflection on being caught in the dangerous moment of anti-Blackness and Indigenous dispossession, finding white supremacist formations across universities, urban landscapes, and racial justice protests. Instead of advocating for a revolutionary project that allows a perfect release from the foundational violences of the American political project, they focus on the affective intensities and musical soundtracks that allowed them to endure. Simmons and Williams explore what it feels like to be under a sign of erasure, as well as the way that music offers the constant invitation to fugitivity and a shared vibe. Here, music is more than a lifeline—it is a way of thinking with others, maintaining memory, and recognizing political struggles as harmonically collective. Music is also, of course, a means of calming and enlivening one's nervous system—of adding energy or soothing frayed nerves. From Standing Rock to the Movement for Black Lives, from Chicago to New Orleans to Nevada, Simmons and Williams consider the qualities of atmosphere—from the moment of easy breathing with beautiful others to the loss of breath that can come from the police boot or the university administration or the seminar table. By adding a soundtrack to everyday life, Simmons and Williams assert how music can transform the all-too-frequently broken and racist everyday into something life affirming, even exhilarating, infused with shared potential.

Danilyn Rutherford begins chapter 10 by asking provocatively, "What if the other others—the ones beyond the pale of citizenship and even humanity—were actually rulers of the realm?" This might mean that those who refuse recognition, who remain stubbornly opaque, non-hail-able, have a mysterious power, one we might call sovereignty. For Rutherford, the bad subjects, those who do not respond when called, can be found everywhere. Her chapter considers the frustrations of colonial explorers in Papua New Guinea when their first and absolute display of power—the shooting of a gun (then an unknown technology in the region)—turns out to be of no interest to locals. Papuans simply refuse to connect the killing power of the gun to the Dutchman to the state and to empire in the logical chain of colonial power—a spectacular form of nonrecognition, the unwillingness to be in awe or, as Rutherford puts it, a decision to "turn their back" on the Dutch explorers' message. Rutherford then considers the sovereignty of those who cannot talk, of those disabled and in need of constant physical care, who nonetheless generate a social field around them evoking pleasure as well as shifting political outcomes. Providing a series of ethnographic encounters between her daughter, Millie, and state representatives and classroom teachers, Rutherford considers Millie's effect on people; that is, her nonspeaking yet affectively charged effectivity. She limns the experience of a subject who cannot be hailed in reliably intelligible ways but who nonetheless shapes the world, linking speaking subjects through their uneasy efforts to confront a radical otherness who nevertheless extends compassion, care, and love. Here vulnerability, not control, is creative, generating social relations and modes of address that are not captured in language—showing that Millie's self-ownership, her performance of a radical opacity as Édouard Glissant might put it, opens up the possibility of different orders of being, multiple worlds within worlds, and surprising modes of collectivity within alterity based on social commitment, love, curiosity, and care.

But if the social order is organized not only by so-called possessive individuals, by the gun-toting officials, but also by vulnerable subjects whose ambitions are difficult, if not impossible, to decipher, then what is ultimately collective about a historical condition? Joseph Masco asks this directly, assessing the state of US politics in 2018, right at the middle of the Donald J. Trump administration, at a moment when claims to a collective belonging (across race, gender, class, and immigration lines) were being undermined in particularly violent ways by the state. He asks what is the condition of our condition, interrogating the forms of collectivity and exclusion that have always informed the American project but that are being recontextualized by changing conditions in the twenty-first century—across finance, militarism, and the environment. The strident calls for white hegemony in the Trump era, the attacks on inclusion and democracy itself, are indexed to radically shifting material conditions in the United States and efforts to maintain an exclusionary nationalism. He shows that, while the United States maintains unprecedented financial and military power, pain—psychic, economic, physical—has extreme new metrics that amplify foundational violences, creating an ever deadlier circuit.

Asking why the United States in the twenty-first century has not only the world's most incarcerated population but also the most drugged, in chapter 11 Masco considers how it is that collective life has been so thoroughly hacked by narrow political and class interests that are avowedly antidemocratic. In such a world of escalating pain and abandonment, illiberal desires can be weaponized, a way of doing double injury to the collective life of people and the idea of governance itself. The failures of the state to deal with deindustrialization, boom-and-bust capitalism, and global warming while pursuing permanent warfare has created an intensified dynamic around race, gender, and citizenship that Trump exploits under a logic of theft. Masco considers the arrival of a "suicidal whiteness"—that is, one that embraces the very projects that collectively injure (guns, petrochemical capital, tax breaks)—in the name of protecting an imagined superior racial status. Acknowledging the masses of injured, sick, and addicted bodies in the twenty-first century, the chapter considers the intense psychosocial investment in a whiteness that not only refuses a politics of equality but that readily encourages the destruction of the world rather than change. In this way, Masco considers the structural emergency of American life. His assessment of the United States in the fall of 2018, a period of seemingly maximal danger across many social conditions, marks also a moment before the emergence of COVID-19; that is, a short time before a global pandemic would systematically amplify every existing deadly relation. What, then, might be the affective and embodied forms of the emergencies still to come, the ones in formation but not yet in sight?

> All that you touch,
> You Change.
>
> All that you Change,
> Changes you.
>
> The only lasting truth
> Is Change.
>
> God
> Is Change.
> —Octavia Butler, *Parable of the Sower*

In *Parable*, the center of Lauren Oya Olamina's Earthseed gospel is change. In our view, change requires accountability. This is not the accountability of double-entry ledgers, so central to the imperial project (Carby 2019) and capitalism (Poovey 1998), but an accountability that resides outside the normative parameters of perfectible governance, and emerges from affective recognition and hope. It is not the logic of insurance, which emerges out of bought and sold bodies (Ralph 2015), but rather the commitment to the possibilities of solidarity and even love for strangers. Hope, here, is not rooted in progress and perfectibility, but is an everyday practice of care and attention, an emphasis on the specificities and complexities of particular times, places, people, and relations. This moves us into uncertainty and outside of both the liberal and illiberal narratives of counterrevolution. It moves us into a jazz fugitivity, as Michael Ralph argues in his afterword, an improvisational politics that refigures the value of life and reorients the temporality of breath. Our investments here are in the present, but we understand that futurities condition the present in ways that often determine affects of sovereignty, freedom, love, loss, and possibility.

As we move beyond a political economy frame to attend to the psychic and affective dimensions of historical experience, we are interested in how a notion of sovereignty gets activated and deactivated over the course of a lifetime and within the struggle of the everyday. We are making historical legacies multiple, thus embodying different political valences. We are attempting to model a way to engage long histories of violence through a notion of daily practices and commitments in order to demonstrate the moment-to-moment deployment of these forms of violence and people's agency in trying to build new worlds. And in thinking through relation, we argue that nothing is singularly local. Indeed, the forces that shape earthly conditions today—racism, militarism, financial capital, and carbon and other forms of toxicity—are planetary formations that inform individual lives with differing intensities and concentrations of both fast and slow violences. Thus, we make the body central in thinking about qualities of life and living to undo the concepts that can authorize ethnography, the modes of theory that flatten human experience by assuming rational choice, that deny the power of affective experience to determine the qualities of life or that reject the psychic complexity of social encounters. The kinds of sovereignty we are thinking through are produced and apprehended through sensory regimes that shape the forms of agency and self-formation that are possible at particular moments, and we believe that attending to these sensory or affective regimes begins to undo the "savage slot" (Trouillot 1991) mode of anthropological analysis. We explore the affective terrain whereby world making is evident, in the moments of attention that lock a body into a larger frame of reference that matters. And in the twenty-first century we know that people have phenomenal powers, altering the very composition of the earth, shifting the weather, changing the terms and qualities for life itself. *Sovereignty Unhinged* explores how individuals navigate and live in a world filled with fast and slow violences but also endless opportunities for reworlding.

Parable ends not with an Earthseed insight but instead with verses from the gospel of Luke (chapter 8:5–8), with the story of the sower: "A sower went out to sow his seed: and as he sowed, some fell by the way side; and it was trodden down, and the fowls of the air devoured it. And some fell upon a rock; and as soon as it was sprung up, it withered away because it lacked moisture. And some fell among moisture. And some fell among thorns; and the thorns sprang up with it, and choked it. And others fell on good ground, and sprang up, and bore fruit a hundred fold." What forms of affective recognition are we sowing today, and what forms of unhinged sovereignty might we reap from them?

Notes

1   See Getachew (2019) for a discussion of the incompatibility of these notions with the kinds of anticolonial sovereignties that were envisioned from the mid-twentieth century through the 1970s by (inter)nationalists like Nkrumah, Williams, and Manley.

2   See also King's elaboration of conquest as a conceptual frame, as "a milieu or active set of relations that we can push on, move around in, and redo from moment to moment" (2019, 40).

3   Here, we are thinking about refusal in two ways. First is its articulation by Black feminist scholars for whom refusal is a practice rather than an event, a creative, "nimble," and ultimately unpredictable modality through which subjects are, unconsciously and otherwise, "refusing the terms of negation and dispossession" (Campt 2017, 96) in which their lives are rendered valueless. Second is the sense of refusal proffered by Indigenous scholars and other anthropologists for whom refusal is somewhat more intentional (Simpson 2007, 2014). For these scholars, refusal marks a position of optimism and hope on the part of anthropologists' interlocutors, and a methodological limit for anthropologists themselves. It is "a political stance" and a "generative act"; "it is an effort, at least minimally, to redefine or redirect certain outcomes or expectations or relationships" (McGranahan 2016, 334). See also Ortner (1995b).

4   For more on rights as perpetuating relations of domination, see Hartman (1997).

5   In her theorization of "slow death," Lauren Berlant (2007, 757) resists the logics of sovereignty, writing: "We need better ways to talk about activity oriented toward the reproduction of ordinary life: the burdens of compelled will that exhaust people taken up by managing contemporary labor and household pressures, for example; or spreading-out activities like sex or eating, oriented toward pleasure or self-abeyance, that do not occupy time, decision, or consequentiality in anything like the registers of autonomous self-assertion."

PART I

Capture/ Escape

1

Love and Disgust
Sovereignty Struggles in Egypt's Uprising

JESSICA WINEGAR

The sun was setting in Cairo on February 11, 2011, and I was absentmindedly preparing macaroni and cheese for my four-year-old child while watching what had become constant coverage of the Egyptian revolution on television. Anyone who was in Egypt at that time will remember the ubiquitous hum, in houses and cafés, of the live feed from Tahrir Square on Al Jazeera and other channels, akin to that of the World Cup, but punctuated by songs, cheers, and chants, and often the rhythmic hammering of brick and asphalt to make defensive weapons. Suddenly, the newly installed Vice President Omar Suleiman came on the screen and grimly announced that Hosni Mubarak had resigned, and that power was being transferred to the Egyptian military. My partner and I hugged each other in excitement (in retrospect, ignoring the implications of the second half of that announcement) and grabbed our confused son in mid–macaroni and cheese bite and ran out of the apartment. Neighbors met in the hallways and in each other's living rooms in front of televisions, hugged each other, wept, cheered, loved. Many then headed immediately to a nearby traffic circle for a spontaneous celebration with more hugs and tears of joy. My family descended to the subway to head to Tahrir. Our metro car was packed with young people erupting in spontaneous and hilariously creative call-and-response chants celebrating victory against the regime. When we got to Tahrir, my son rode my partner's shoulders as we circulated the square amid the dense, vibrating crowds of celebrating families, homemade fireworks, hugs, and hoots. My little boy received numerous chocolates and kisses from random Egyptians excitedly telling him, "Raise your head up, you're Egyptian." This phrase was a new version of President Nasser's postindependence invocation to the nation the night he nationalized the Suez Canal in 1956: "Raise your head high, brother, the era of subjugation has ended."

This night with hundreds of thousands of Egyptians was, like the famous protests in the square for the eighteen days before, a deeply affective, embodied experience. We were bodies together in the square, in a kind of communitas—"an intense community spirit, [a] *feeling* of great social equality, solidarity, and togetherness" (Turner 1977; cf. Armbrust 2019). Egyptians expressed and created bonds of love for each other through chanting, singing, cleaning, sharing food and drink, treating wounds, hugging, and circulating in groups around the square to take it all in. We felt what Gastón Gordillo (2011) has called "resonance" with one another, a kind of vibration between bodies in the square that were there—bringing our energy together toward the climactic event of Mubarak's dramatic departure that night.

Just over two years later, on June 30, 2013, hundreds of thousands of Egyptians descended on Tahrir Square again, this time to call for the new president of one year, Mohammed Morsi, to step down. The square was even more full of Egyptian flags than during the 2011 protests, and many people were wearing the colors of the flag. The main stage featured speakers leading chants against the supposedly traitorous and animalistic Muslim Brotherhood, and many posters and signs featuring Abdel Fattah al-Sisi's visage. On July 3, Sisi, then minister of defense, quickly removed Morsi from office and jailed him.[1] Celebrations erupted in the square, but in contrast to those on February 11, 2011, these were accompanied by military jets, helicopters, and huge flag-colored fireworks. Talking about events on the line from Chicago with my friend Mona in Cairo, with whom I spent the famous eighteen days supporting the revolution (Winegar 2012, 2015), she said two things with breathless excitement that have stuck with me: "Jessica, you won't be afraid to come to Egypt again"; and "I think Sisi is really cute." A month later, a thousand of Morsi's supporters, who had gathered in two demonstrations at major Cairo intersections to oppose the coup, would be brutally murdered by state forces in the largest single-day massacre in the modern Middle East. Mona supported it, as did so many others with whom I shared that resonance in Tahrir. In just two years, the diffuse love for others that had been the medium for claims to everyday sovereignty had become a concentrated love for the sovereign ruler, fueled by disgust for his opponents among their fellow citizens, who were cast into a state of exception (Agamben 2005). How did the people of Tahrir come to support the resurgence of the military regime and the mass murder of their cocitizens? This question puzzles many Egypt scholars and analysts. An important part of the answer lies in Mona's words that day: fear of the Muslim Brotherhood, rooted, as I shall show, in disgust for them and love for the ruler.

In this chapter, I propose that attention to love and disgust can help us more fully understand what motivates, sustains, and suppresses sovereignty struggles in times of intense upheaval and social protest. These are liminal times when the sovereign power of the state is unstable, and when people experience heightened emotions.[2] Thus, studying affect, as that which "arises in the midst of *in-between-ness*, in the capacities to act and be acted upon" (Gregg and Seigworth 2010, 1) is key to ascertaining three aspects of sovereignty struggles: (1) how popular sovereignty comes to be a thing that people fight for; (2) how hegemonic forces (in the Gramscian sense) try to congeal the state's sovereign power; and (3) the shape of the "actually existing sovereignties" (Shoshan 2016, 123) that emerge through the process of upheaval. As the case of Egypt makes clear, sovereignty was never fully achieved. It is, rather, an ongoing struggle in the space of a fluid, nonbinary in-between. Affects that I gloss as love and disgust have been central to this struggle. While other scholars have productively examined anger and disappointment as key to politics in uneasy times (e.g., Greenberg 2014), I suggest that love and disgust are also useful to explore in relationship to sovereignty because of their ambiguous yet strong relationship to moral judgment and collective acts of boundary drawing—key bases of these three aspects of sovereignty struggles.

Love and Disgust as Political Affects

There is a defining tension in social theories of love as to whether or not it is positive or negative, and it is precisely this tension that makes it so central to these three aspects. Love has long been theorized, by Marx and others, as that which binds people against the powers of capital, providing an alternative sensory medium for social relations outside of property (Hardt 2011), and also against the violence of colonialism, capitalism, and racism (Dillard 2016; hooks 2000; Sandoval 2000). As I will suggest, this love is the kind that arose during the eighteen days of Tahrir Square—a "declaration" of love "as a sovereign way of being defined, spirited and powerfully marshaled" (Dillard 2016, 202) that Michael Hardt marks as properly political love because it "move[s] across . . . scales, betraying the conventional divisions between personal and political, and grasping the power to create bonds that are [at] once intimate and social" (2011, 677). Love was how

Egyptians drew sovereign boundaries around themselves and their bodies, and rejected the violence of the authoritarian state and the predation of the neoliberal regimes it enforced. Their declaration of love for one another, enacted through acts of care, affection, recognition, respect, commitment, trust, and communication (hooks 2000), was framed as the ultimate expression of what is right and good, in contrast to the morally corrupt and repugnant regime. Martel (2008) reads Hannah Arendt (1968) as saying that at some level, love is essential to the creation of a collective.

But Arendt's acceptance of the necessity of love was "reluctant" (Martel 2008) because she also recognized how it is too easily co-opted by individual, private will. She even called love "perhaps the most powerful of all antipolitical human forces" (Arendt 1968, 242, quoted in Martel 2008, 296). This is what Hardt calls "love conceived as a process of unification," the narcissistic love that is "the author of the most reactionary political projects" (2011, 677). Lauren Berlant (2011b) also issues a strong warning against viewing this kind of love as entirely ethical (or even love), because of its link to desire. This love is the "vertical love" that Massad (2013) argues characterized Arabs' relationship to rulers before the uprisings, and which I shall suggest was central to the hegemonic struggle of the Egyptian military to regain sovereign power after the uprisings. It was a love for a morally righteous bounded nation above all others, whose narcissism was not entirely absent in the eighteen days, and which later became isomorphic with love (*hubb*) for the ruler (Sisi), who became an object of desire, sexual and otherwise, and who spoke about love in many of his speeches.

Like love, disgust is a political affect similarly based on boundary drawing and moral judgment. It could be perceived as the opposite of love, although scholars writing on disgust have noted how it is often accompanied by a kind of intense, macabre fascination with its object (Livingston 2008; Menninghaus 2003; Vatan 2013). Indeed, it is the revulsion and fascination with the disgusting that make it a liminal affect, "epitomiz[ing] the dialectic of distance and proximity" (Vatan 2013, 29), and thus, I argue, ripe for sovereignty struggles in uncertain times like an uprising and its aftermath. Disgust signals both a broken boundary—something is too close that should not be—and an attempt to reinstate that boundary. As Vatan argues, disgust is a "forceful . . . gatekeeper that erects protective barriers to preserve the integrity of the self, the cohesion of a group, or the cultivation of an aesthetic ideal" (2013, 28). One could say that the Mubarak regime provoked a kind of disgust that partially drove people to protest in the eighteen days. In the years leading up to the uprising, it was not uncommon to hear Egyptians

Jessica Winegar

talk about the "disgustingness" (*qaraf*) of various actions of regime figures, of how they were treated in government offices, of the government's disregard and mismanagement of infrastructure that led to copious mounds of trash and sewage from burst pipes in the streets—garbage, shit, and urine being among the ultimate producers of disgust in the literature on that topic. But it was the grotesque images of bodies tortured and killed by the police and state security forces circulated by activists on social media that were the tipping point for many to turn wholly against the regime.[3] The struggle for political, bodily, and spatial sovereignty in the eighteen days was very much about drawing a boundary around the "Egyptian people" (*al-sha'b al-masri*), figured as clean and pure, and the regime (*al-nizam*), whose disgusting garbage was literally and metaphorically kept out of the square in highly symbolic acts (Winegar 2015). This was disgust as undergirding a set of actions to decontaminate society from the immorality of a rapacious authoritarian regime, which aligns with some philosophers' view of disgust as a positive moral judgment (e.g., Plakias 2013).

But like love, disgust is an affect on the edge of the properly ethical. Martha Nussbaum (2010), for example, argues that disgust's obsession with contamination renders it inherently suspicious, especially as the bodies and bodily acts of women and minorities have historically been figured as animalistic contaminants to the properly human. Certainly, as I will soon detail, regime figures' attempts to reassert state sovereign power from 2011 onward relied heavily on disgust as a mobilizing affect to exclude regime opponents from the body politic. Activists on the left all the way to Islamists were figured as disgusting, both physically and morally, in ways that legitimized mass state violence against them.[4] Of course, we find this tactic of sovereign power across a range of places and histories, from the colonial powers to the Nazis to the Hindu Right (e.g., Ghassem-Fachandi 2010).

Sovereignty in the Square: Love and Disgust

In the eighteen days, love for each other and disgust for the regime and its effects were primary ethical, boundary-making affects that motivated and sustained the protests. During that time and immediately after, many people described their experience in the square as "amazing" (*mubhir*), as "beyond the imagination" (*fu' al-khayal*), and often shook their heads, at a loss for words. What they affected and how they themselves were affected reflected a kind of unqualified intensity that was not always based on or reducible to signification (see Massumi 2002). The resonance between bodies in Tahrir Square was experienced but not explicitly referred to as love by the protesters. Indeed, naming it love may not quite capture this unqualified intensity, although some interlocutors did (see Malmström 2019, 49). What that time in Tahrir felt like was not limited to emotions; rather, it was a range of affects that exceeded the limits of discourse. The eighteen days were a kind of "time out of time," as Hanan Sabea (2011) so aptly put it. It was about "excising a slice of time out of the rhythm of the familiar (the ordinary and the known) and, through that rupture ... making it possible to imagine other modalities of being" (Sabea 2011). Yet it is so difficult to articulate that becoming through language. If grassroots sovereignty "feels like" anything, I would say that millions of people felt it in the square. What we experienced was a becoming of another modality of being (Biehl and Locke 2017). This was love that, in the Arendtian sense, serves as the basis of politics: an exteriorization of interior will; a love for who people are without objectifying what they are (Arendt 1968; see Martel 2008).

This *who* instead of *what* could be found in the communitas of Tahrir, in which people's individual faults and idiosyncrasies were accepted, and in which most social hierarchies and distinctions were nearly erased. The affective solidarity that was constituted through acts of care, sharing, affection, respect, and recognition was indeed an antistructure (as Turner characterized communitas) in that it, however temporarily and tenuously, reversed the sovereign power of the state. Citizen brigades overturned the everyday violence of a corrupt state when they engaged those of us waiting to enter the square with warm welcomes and friendly banter, rather than barking orders or deliberately ignoring the waiting crowds. They created straight orderly lines to ensure that everyone was respected and had an equal chance of entry, instead of demanding bribes. They refused entry to anyone who worked for state security or carried a weapon. People brought food and medical supplies to the square—distributing them and caring for the ill and wounded for free. In these ways, they reversed the decimation of public services and rejected the social inequalities greatly exacerbated by the state's neoliberal economic policies. They kept the square meticulously clean, in a literal and metaphoric refusal of the disgusting garbage that the regime had produced, and that had indeed been the regime (Winegar 2015).

But this sovereignty—over one's own body, one's social relations, and public space—was compromised. At many points in the eighteen days, the square was filled with many nationalist songs professing love for the nation, for Egypt. Kids, like my own, got their faces painted with the Egyptian flag. Itinerant sellers successfully sold hundreds if not thousands of headbands, scarfs, and badges emblazoned with the colors of the flag and nationalist slogans. The affect of love motivated people to participate in the protests and gave them strength to stay in the square in difficult conditions, but when it became encapsulated in discourse, commodities, and iconography, it was bound to the territorial-political entity of Egypt and no longer affect in the strict sense. It became signified by flags and other commodities for sale. Its narcissism was encapsulated in stickers being sold in the square, including one that read, "Egypt above everyone [*misr fawq al-jami'*]." While discourses and visuals of "love for Egypt" lent a symbolic focus for the protesters, they also had the potential to sever the uprising from allied movements around the world (e.g., Occupy and the *indignados* movement, the Hong Kong protests, the Tunisian uprising). They partook in the same nationalist frame as that promoted by state institutions. Thus, the sovereign feeling of intense, resonant love for each other was both a deeply embodied refusal of the state's sovereign power to maim, wound, and divide bodies from one another, and something that was available for appropriation by the state.

Indeed, that is what happened the very night Mubarak fell. Military tanks were in the square. People climbed on top and took celebratory photos with the soldiers, waving Egyptian flags. Chants of "the military and the people are one hand" erupted. People widely believed that the military saved the revolution. Over the next few weeks, pro-military nationalism came to dominate. A joke even circulated that the revolution would not be over until every child had their photo taken atop a tank. The staff at my son's day care brought all the kids to a military checkpoint one day and took a group picture of the kids holding Egyptian flags in front of the tank. They sent the photos home as gifts to the parents.

After Tahrir: Disgust for the Brotherhood

What followed was a tumultuous year filled with protests and state violence, during which the Supreme Council of the Armed Forces ruled the country. Weary of the military and former regime elites, the population voted Mohammed Morsi, the Muslim Brotherhood candidate, into the presidency in the spring of 2012. He certainly had many enthusiastic supporters, especially among religious conservatives following the Islamist trend, and among those who had benefited from the Brotherhood's social services in the areas of health, education, and food provision that had filled the gap left by the state's rollback of social programs in step with IMF and World Bank mandates. But many Egyptians voted for Morsi as a kind of lesser evil than the Mubarak-era candidate, Ahmed Shafiq, on the basis that the Brotherhood was independent of the regime, and in the hopes that perhaps the Brotherhood could grow into an inclusive party. Their hopes quickly dissipated as the Morsi government began replacing respected government employees with their own adherents, and sidelining their opponents and all alternative voices while writing a new constitution, in which it appeared that the rights of women and religious minorities would not be considered. The government's attempts to fix the economy mostly failed, in large part because the military (which owned a vast percentage of the nation's resources) blocked any major changes. As fall moved into winter, the constitutional crisis gave a focus to rising resentment of the Brotherhood, and protests erupted. The Morsi government handled the situation poorly, blocking all dialogue across the political spectrum, allowing Islamists to beat protesters and tear down protest encampments, and setting up counterprotest supporters who spewed vitriol against revolutionaries and Christians.

As the Brotherhood, and Islamists more broadly, launched moral judgments against anyone who disagreed with any of the government's actions, figuring them as un-Islamic, amoral, vulgar, unpatriotic, and so on, disgust emerged as a central affect for those increasingly unhappy with Brotherhood rule. Facebook and Twitter filled with expressions linking the Brotherhood explicitly with disgust (*qaraf*), figured as referring both to their bodies and to their ideas and practices. People wrote tweets or created Facebook groups with rhyming names like Enough with the Brotherhood, Enough with Their Disgustingness (Bala ikhwan bala qaraf) or I Am Sick of the Brotherhood's Disgustingness (Ana zahqan min qaraf al-ikhwan). In the press and in everyday talk, the Brotherhood (and Islamists more generally) were described as "disgusting" (*muqrifin*): smelly, rotten, vile, and boorish. A Facebook group emerged and quickly gained over a million followers with the (rhyming in Arabic) name I Am a Brotherhood [Member], I Am a Sack of Garbage (Ana ikhwan, ana maqtaf bi-widan), signaling that they were themselves smelly, disgusting garbage.[5]

Political cartoons and street protest culture at the time rendered the Brotherhood animalistic by portraying them as sheep. Sheep are widely viewed as stupid creatures, and of course are the prime choice for mass slaughter during the Islamic Eid holiday. One of the Arabic words for sheep rhymes with the word for the Brotherhood (*khirfan/ikhwan*), which of course made for lively, sing-along protest chants. Sheep marionettes and images depicting the Brotherhood as sheep appeared in protests, such as one I attended in Tahrir in May 2013. The image of them as sheep played on

Jessica Winegar

the widely spread and held view that Brotherhood members had no independent minds of their own and only did what the organization's *murshid*, or supreme guide, ordered them to do.[6] The direct relationship of sheep to disgust may be tangential here, though certainly in the writings on disgust, animals pose a particular problem because they are that which is too proximal—whose boundary with "us humans" needs to be maintained (Miller 1997). A cartoon of the era likening the Brotherhood to sheep not only portrayed them as mindless animals following their leader but also seemed to portend, or perhaps justify, the boundary making that would be necessary to enact their slaughter a few months later.[7]

After a year of political failures, Morsi had lost his popular legitimacy, and the Brotherhood came to be blamed for everything that was wrong in the country. The protests that started on June 30, 2013, also included expressions of sensory disgust with the Brotherhood, congealing, in the mass protest context, into contempt and anger. In various chants, the Brotherhood were called sheep, liars, and cowards and were accused of tricking people in the name of religion. As disgust operates to distance that which is too proximal, it undergirded chants like "They are not brothers, nor Egyptians" (*Mish ikhwan wa la masriyyiin*), which used the word for the Brotherhood (*ikhwan*) but recuperated it to mean brothers, that is, relatives, more generally.

After Sisi deposed Morsi, supporters of the latter built encampments in two major squares in Cairo. The largest was in Rabʿa Square in the middle-to upper-middle-class neighborhood of Nasr City; the other was in Nahda Square in front of Cairo University, closer to Tahrir. As the Rabʿa sit-in in particular grew over the course of six weeks, disgust discourses ramped up to a fever pitch. Pro-Sisi Egyptians criticized Islamists' manners, morals, and hygiene. A leaked video from the period shows the previous mufti of the republic, the highest religious figure, giving a long lecture to a large hall filled with military officials, encouraging them to disperse the protesters by any means necessary. Standing on a podium with the official, broadly respected, dress of the renowned Al-Azhar University, he said in formal Arabic, "We have to purify our city and our Egypt from this riffraff [*awbash*]. They do not deserve our Egyptianness. . . . We have to disown them." He then switched to colloquial Egyptian Arabic and said that the protesters were "putrid people. They smell [*nas nitna. Rihithum wihsha*]." Then back to formal Arabic: "Inside and outside." Surely some of the officials listening to this speech went on to commit the massacre shortly thereafter.

Of course, there are numerous cases throughout modern history when support for mass murders has developed, and indeed been cultivated, through processes of dehumanization and othering. But the Egyptian case is perhaps surprising because it happened just two years after a massive revolution against tyranny and state-sanctioned killings, and just a year after Morsi's democratic election. Here it is helpful to remember that for at least two decades, the Mubarak regime had primed the population to hate its main challenger (the Muslim Brotherhood) and indeed all Islamists, through state discourses that positioned Islamists as savage, disgusting, uncivilized, and un-Egyptian. The brutal show of sovereign state power in Rab'a drew on a history of demonization of Islamists but brought it to a whole new level. And it was, in large measure, justified through the cultivation, among large swaths of the population, not only of love for Sisi and Egypt but also of disgust toward the Brotherhood and toward the encampment itself.

Such judgments of the Brotherhood as disgusting were indeed very central to the legitimization of Rab'a, highlighting disgust as a key affect of sovereign denial. Even in light of a bloody massacre with dead bodies piled up, many Egyptians have remained disgusted by the Brotherhood, the main victims of that massacre. When I spoke with Sisi supporters during fieldwork a year later, for example, if the subject of the Brotherhood came up, they often flared their nostrils and turned their lips down as if they smelled rotten eggs—as did Mona when she and I met for the first time after the event. When we fought about it, she told me that I did not know what it was like to actually live among them, to have to drive around their disruptive sit-ins (Rab'a was not far from her house). She justified the killings by saying the army had no choice, that the protesters were all armed (they were not) and ready to destroy Egypt. In essence, they were not Egyptians, in her view. She held this view despite the fact that she, and indeed many Egyptians, had neighbors and relatives in the Brotherhood or in the broader Islamist movement. Again, one of the features of disgust is that it is an affect produced by a proximity that is not desired—proximity in the neighborhood, in the family, in one's religion, and in the nation.

Love for the Sovereign

To more fully understand how the mass murder of fellow Egyptians was accepted by large numbers of the population, we need to turn to Mona's other comment to me on the phone from Cairo to Chicago when Morsi was deposed: "I think Sisi is really cute." Paired with this disgust at another group's attempt to claim sovereignty was love for the nationalist sovereign power that the Sisi regime both promised and cultivated. Sisi's ascent in the sum-

Jessica Winegar

mer of 2013 from minister of defense to what many thought of as "savior of the Egyptian people" by launching the coup against Morsi was accompanied by a massive surge in what I term Sisiophilia, a word that captures the undercurrent of sexual desire in the love for Sisi, which is key to why Berlant (2011b) cautioned against love as a properly political affect. Mona and many others, like anthropologist Maria Malmström's interlocutors, became incredibly passionate about Sisi and talked about "having their country back" and having a "real man" in power. This was an intense feeling of sovereignty expressed through nationalist love for Sisi that proliferated in mass culture. It was a narcissistic, nationalist love that relied on masculine, military, and bourgeois aesthetic judgment. It drew on patriarchal family metaphors that had circulated in mass media for nearly a century, in which patriarchy was represented as "a form of love rather than an expression of authority grounded in compulsion" (Armbrust 2009, 253). This is why, I suggest, Sisi supporters did not recognize these feelings of love as contrary to what they fought for in Tahrir Square in 2011.[8] Sisi was not understood to be an authoritarian compelling obedience from his subjects. Rather, the love reflected a desire for a strong yet refined male savior, a good Muslim man, and a benevolent patriarch. And these characteristics were constituted, indeed substantiated, for many Egyptians by his clean-shaven image, the well-worn mark on his forehead from prostrating in prayer, his military clothes or business suits, and the soft tenor of his voice.

Both before and especially after the Rab'a massacre, love for Sisi was expressed in huge street banners, large gilded-frame portraits of him dotting the urban landscape, songs and music videos by some of Egypt's top musicians, political cartoons, television talk shows, Twitter hashtags, and Facebook groups. Many of these expressions used the word love (hubb) to refer to both Sisi and the nation as if they were one, and indeed Sisi's love for the nation was often framed as the basis of people's love for him. In just one of many examples, a song released after the coup but before Rab'a titled "We Love You Sisi" lauds him for "getting rid of the Brotherhood for us" and refers to him as a "respectable Egyptian," "the symbol of virtue," "son of the Nile," "one of us," "who protects all of us," and an "uncle" ('ammu, the word used for the father's brother, a man who symbolizes great power in the patriline).[9]

It became especially commonplace to describe Sisi's appeal in gendered terms. The well-known young poet Hisham al-Jakh, whose poem "Joha," released just prior to the uprising, was a scathing criticism of the regime, referred on national television to Sisi as a cock (a rooster, dīk). In discourses

1.1   Youth expressing love for Sisi at the 2015 Egypt Economic
             Development Conference. Sisi is in the middle of the frame.

like this one, Sisi was portrayed as a great model for all men and an object of swooning for women. A much-circulated video on YouTube and Facebook in the fall of 2013 shows a local television channel interview with dermatologist Dr. Amany al-Sayyid. In the video, she launches into a four-minute monologue about how much she loves Sisi. In rushed breathlessness, she says, "I'm the woman in all of Egypt who loves Sisi the most.... I loved Egypt because of him.... When I listen to him, I become amazed. He is an angel, not a human being. He is a miracle, and a gift from our Lord.... I stopped watching TV serials and movies and I only watch him now."[10] The expressions of love were not limited to women. Magdy al-Galad, the former editor in chief of one of Egypt's so-called independent newspapers, wrote with homoerotic overtones, "I want the president to hug me and kiss me." Bishop Boulos Ewidah of al-Zahraa church said, "I melt with ... love every time I see him."[11] During Egypt's famous international economic conference held in 2015, billed by the government as the beginning of the country's economic recovery, Sisi began his opening address to the attendees by softly uttering the phrase "Long live Egypt"—which was then chanted back at him by the audience. Then he asked the young men and women who helped with the conference to come up on the stage with him. They did so with great excitement and admiration, and one can hear phrases such as "Long live Egypt" and "We love you, I love you" in the crowd, with a sentimental selfie (figure 1.1).[12]

Jessica Winegar

1.2   Two young men in Tahrir Square with Sisi masks and poster. The poster has phrases such as "Long live Egypt" and "The army and the people are one hand."

Sisi himself also used the discourse of love very frequently in his speeches and comments to the media. In fact, love featured prominently as a way to claim national sovereignty from negative factors figured as external— most notably, terrorism and radical Islam. His message was: if we love each other and love Egypt, then we can stand together and defeat these threats. Sisi's incessant talk about loving Egypt, Egyptians loving each other, and how Egyptians had to love Egypt also served to distinguish him from the Brotherhood, who were framed as vile in their hatred for others. Indeed, a large part of Sisi's appeal also stemmed from his self-presentation as a civilized, moderate Muslim—marked by his prayer bruise, his refined suits, and his soft voice. His slow, gentle way of speaking especially contrasted with the loud voices shouting about the coup and infidels that emanated from the stage at Rab'a.

Finally, love was expressed through commodity circulation that iconically transformed Sisi's image into the nation, and an object of desire that could be possessed. Some could be used to adorn other commodities, from cars (bumper stickers) to refrigerators (magnets). Many could be worn so as to become one in narcissistic love for the sovereign, such as T-shirts and lanyard badges with his visage, masks of his face, and cologne marketed in his name (figure 1.2). Cologne signified the opposite of the bad smell attributed to the protesters. And if disgust is associated with purging what does not belong inside, literally and metaphorically (Menninghaus 2003),

1.3   Abdel Fattah al-Sisi's image emblazoned on expensive
chocolates. Photo courtesy of Maria Malmström.

then the chocolates in his image and the special sandwich called Sisi Mix
that was sold by different local shops mark desired ingestion of the sovereign (figure 1.3).

Conclusion: Actually Existing Sovereignty

I return to the question with which I began. Why did so many Egyptians,
who just two and a half years prior had initiated and supported a mass uprising against the regime, come to support that very regime's mass murder
of their compatriots? Part of the answer has to do with the affective state
produced by continued protests. For many, these were both enervating and
stressful. Many Egyptians came to see, indeed came to feel and sense, that the
protests and resulting state violence were disrupting all that they had fought
for—a life of dignity. When 50 percent of the population lives at or near the
international poverty line, one cannot even economically sustain two years
of protests, of disruption to income. The rise in everyday crime—muggings,
car jackings, and so on—also created a basic fear for safety in the streets. By
the summer of 2013, many were tired of the constant news of protest and
violence. In Cairo in particular, protests were seen to add to the already
omnipresent traffic jams in the city of twenty million. Sisi's promises of a

         Jessica Winegar

civilized future for Egypt, and his masculinist military aesthetic connoting stability, were indeed appealing to those seeking sensory calm.

As of this writing, the military regime is enacting unprecedented levels and forms of sovereign state power over bodies. The violence is still justified through the president's and state media lackeys' repeated proclamations of "love for Egypt" (*hubb li-masr*)—this is love that is much more captured by discourse and regimes of signification than the embodied love in Tahrir Square, although it was there too. The forms of sovereign state power justified by love include, of course, the Rab'a massacre, but also tens of thousands of political prisoners, hundreds of forced disappearances, and draconian press, protest, and electoral laws since.[13]

Love for Egypt is a key affect of alignment with state sovereign rule, just as it was central to creating solidarity in Tahrir. Disgust for the regime, including its garbage and torture of bodies, played a role in gathering people in Tahrir, just as it became a primary affect intensifying state sovereignty. In this sense, both love and disgust were key to how popular sovereignty came to be a site of Egyptian struggle and how hegemonic forces tried to congeal the state's sovereign power. Clearly the past years in Egypt have witnessed a complex struggle between these two sovereignties. Love and disgust have been two primary affective means of challenging and reproducing them. One might also think about love and disgust as being opposite sides of the same coin, and thus very close to each other in creating capacities to act and be acted upon. One can very easily flip into the other. What remains to be seen for Egypt is whether or not the love of many for Sisi will flip into disgust on a mass scale. But struggles for sovereignty are often lived between these two poles, in a gray area not easily encapsulated by discourse or signification.

These days, it is difficult for many of the most committed Egyptian revolutionaries to talk about what happened in Tahrir Square in 2011 without running up against the limits of discourse. The revolution did not turn out as they hoped, and they now vacillate between anger, sadness, resignation, feeling fed-up, disbelief, and disgust—disgust with the government, disgust with the Brotherhood who they think messed everything up in their one year of rule, disgust with other Egyptians for their support of Sisi. These emotions are partly affected by (in the affect theory sense of being acted upon) the state's struggle to strengthen its sovereignty. They also affect (in the sense of creating a capacity to act) a kind of solidarity when shared in group contexts—over drinks or meals, for example. Many of the revolutionaries have returned to their everyday lives—intending to, as some say, leave politics (*siyasa*) for a while and instead focus on their careers and personal matters. Many are in jail. A significant number emigrated to Europe and North America to escape the state's sovereign power once and for all. But those who can, still talk about 2011 and its still-unfolding aftermath. They write, tweet, post, teach, and make films about it. Lawyers work for the release of the jailed, for justice for the dead. A majority of Egyptians sat out the March 2018 presidential elections for a second term for Sisi, despite threats of fines for nonvoters.

This is what actually existing sovereignty looks and feels like. It is fragmentary, uneven, and consists of multiple temporalities, including potent memories and indeed affects of past achievements, and ongoing unachieved hopes that keep ideals alive. Nitzan Shoshan reminds us that Schmittian theories view the sovereign as "only sovereign to the extent that it attains this power of decision and remains a mere political contestant so long as it has not." He argues that "such an either/or conception of sovereignty, while it may work well for political theory, becomes muddled in the lived realities of actually existing sovereignties, which always remain both partial and contextually achieved" (Shoshan 2016, 123). Thinking of sovereignty in this way captures how many Egyptians live with these memories and hopes. It captures the porous and shifting reservoir of affect that can, in moments of protest and resistance large and small, affect events and other people and be affected by them. It allows us to see how the revolution has not failed, as so many pundits would have it. Rather, the concept of actually existing sovereignty emphasizes the revolution as an unfinished project (Biehl and Locke 2017). For that is what it feels like to so many in Egypt.

Arendt (1968) was extremely wary of how sovereignty struggles seek to bind, divide, and enforce mastery over plurality, connectedness, and freedom. Indeed, one can say that all sovereignty struggles are ethically ambivalent inasmuch as they involve what Fiona Wright, writing about Israeli activists' love for Palestinians, calls "affective entanglements" in which "the becomings of activism are closely linked to the sovereign power it exposes and challenges" (2016, 139). But at some level Arendt also recognized the necessity of such struggles for sovereignty—for, like love, they produce a kind of familiarity and a "will to dare to face the [potentially overwhelming, open-ended] future" with other people (Martel 2008, 303). Actually existing sovereignty is a necessary, ongoing, affective process without closure. To launch a totalizing discursive critique against this process would be to traffic in the sovereign logic of the regime.

Jessica Winegar

To close this essay, then, in a way that does not close the process, I quote Reem Saad, an anthropologist from and based in Egypt. These words were initially written for an article on revolutionary poetry, in response to attempts to close the sovereignty struggle by critics claiming that the revolution was not a real one. They emphasize Saad's affective participation in the eighteen days, the process of the sovereignty struggle, and how it is motivated toward the future. She still stands by these words, as she, like so many people in Egypt, lives and fights in the gray zone of actually existing sovereignty:[14]

> I use the term *revolution* here, although the 18 days in Tahrir do not fit any academic or analytical definition of the term. But I write this piece from a personal rather than an academic standpoint. I am a participant in the events I describe, and like many others in my position, do not see the time frame to which the term applies as the 18 days that ended with the fall of Mubarak. We use the term to denote a process that is far from over, and, perhaps like the poetry verses I consider, it is a mantra that motivates us to continue our efforts. In this sense, the term *revolution* does not describe past events but signifies an intention and a goal. (Saad 2012, 65)

Notes

1   The demonstrations were the culmination of the three-month Tamarrod (Rebel) initiative to gain signatures from fifteen million Egyptians opposing Morsi's rule by the first anniversary of his presidency—the number of votes that put him in office. It later became clear that Tamarrod was aided and abetted by members of the Interior Ministry, army, and police (see Ketchley 2017).

2   Armbrust (2019) provides a brilliant analysis of the liminality of revolutionary times in Egypt.

3   The middle classes were especially disgusted by the image of the beaten and bloody head of one of their own: Khaled Said, a youth brutally tortured and killed by police in Alexandria in June 2010 after he posted a video of policemen dividing up drugs from a drug bust to resell. The image of his head went viral and sparked mass protests that summer, just six months before the uprising.

4   This chapter focuses primarily on the Muslim Brotherhood, who are just one group along a spectrum of Islamist groups and leanings in Egypt. This diversity among Islamists was not often recognized by opponents of the Brotherhood, who lumped together all who wanted Islam to be the key source governing politics in the country.

5   The word used for the sack of garbage is the same one used to describe the large palm frond baskets carried by poor garbage collectors in the streets, and thus has a classist ring to it, unlike, for example, garbage truck or plastic garbage bag.

6   Notably, Morsi was not the *murshid* and was thus figured as a stupid president who just took orders from *murshid* Muhammad Badiʿ. A famous video of Badiʿ whispering in Morsi's ear during a press conference was widely circulated on social media in confirmation of this view.

7   Thanks to Lisa Wedeen for pointing out the complexity of this cartoon.

8   Of course, this is not to suggest that all Sisi supporters backed the 2011 uprising. Indeed, Sisi's rise was a great relief to Mubarak regime supporters.

9   "We Love You Sisi," posted on YouTube by topproblems, accessed May 20, 2022, https://www.youtube.com/watch?v=LRB6ppzHMvk.

10 The video was available on YouTube at https://www.youtube.com/watch?feature =player_embedded&v=-ohfdZjZI68 (accessed August 25, 2015), but has since been removed.

11 These comments are from a collection of statements at a now removed link on the Masr al-Arabia website, http://www.masralarabia.com (accessed August 25, 2015).

12 A video is available on Facebook at https://www.facebook.com/watch/?v =830937670322407 (accessed May 20, 2022).

13 As well as those killed in the other encampment in Nahda Square, who are often forgotten in the face of the sheer weight of Rabʿa.

14 Reem Saad, email communication, October 21, 2018.

2

Tasting Sovereignty
Love and Revolution in Peru

MARÍA ELENA GARCÍA

In 2011, in a world still untouched by COVID-19, PromPerú, the Peruvian state export and tourism agency, launched a promotional video to mark the international début of Marca Perú (brand name Peru) (Marca Perú 2011). In the video, *zampolla* (Andean panpipe) music plays in the background as a bus with the symbol of Marca Perú and the red and white of the Peruvian flag on its side drives down the open Nebraska plains.[1] The camera pans out across fields as the bus enters the main street of Peru, Nebraska. As it does, the video's narrator tells us that "every Peruvian, by the mere fact of being Peruvian, has the right to enjoy how marvelous it is to be Peruvian."[2] We are then introduced to this small town (population 569) as the narrator sets the stage. "Peru, Nebraska has a problem," he says. "They are Peruvians, but they don't know what that means."

The bus stops, the doors open, and the driver—none other than Gastón Acurio, Peru's most famous chef—announces their arrival. As Peruvian chefs, actors, musicians, surfers, and tourism promoters exit the bus, the narrator explains that their mission is "to be ambassadors of our country and read them their rights as Peruvians." One of the chefs then picks up a megaphone and, fist in the air, tells the town in Spanish that they are Peruvians and, accordingly, they have "the right to eat well." The video, which went viral overnight, documents the power of Peruvian food and culture. Educating North American Peruvians about their rights as Peruvians, these cultural ambassadors perform Peru for their compatriots in multiple ways. Most importantly, this was a powerful performance of national sovereignty and a reflection of the sentiment expressed in Peru today: Peru is not only in a different place economically, socially, and politically; inverting the common North-South story, Peru is now the one bringing civilization to the world.

This performance is particularly striking when we consider that only eleven years before this video was made, Peru was still reeling from the political violence and economic precarity that engulfed the country in the 1980s and '90s, due largely to a war between the ruthless Maoist-inspired Sendero Luminoso (Shining Path) and the Peruvian state. In the early decades of the twenty-first century, Peru became one of the world's leading culinary and tourist destinations. People traveled not simply to see Machu Picchu, they went to Peru to eat. Indeed, in this story of national resurgence, food has been central as hegemonic narratives emphasize the power of food as a social weapon that can heal the wounds inflicted by long histories of colonial violence, exclusion, and inequality.

This remarkable story of resurgence resonates deeply with many in Peru. Despite the intensification of social conflicts (particularly around extractive industries such as mining), political corruption scandals, and ongoing debates over the violence and authoritarianism of the late twentieth century, many Peruvians have fervently embraced the hegemonic narrative of a nation transformed "from terror to culinary destination" (Peru, n.d.). This is a story that celebrates what chef Gastón Acurio describes as the "beautiful fusion" of multiple cultural traditions and "races" (*todas las sangres*), of a country that finally recognizes the value of its unique racial, cultural, and culinary blend, and of citizens who, for the first time in decades, can proclaim love for their country and brethren, and are proud and happy to call themselves Peruvian. In other words, this is the story of Peru's gastronomic revolution.

This chapter calls into question the celebratory claims of this so-called revolution. Here and elsewhere I argue that, in fact, hegemonic discourses and performances of love, happiness, and inclusion obscure ongoing violence, particularly against Indigenous lands and bodies; that the gastronomic boom is simply another expression of the long story that is "the coloniality of power" in Peru (Quijano 2000; see also Lugones 2007; Cusicanqui 1987). I make this critique, however, understanding very well the seductive power of this story. I must admit that the first time I saw the "Peru, Nebraska" video I had a rush of nationalist adrenaline that instantly brought a smile to my face. Despite my best efforts to watch critically, and despite the video's problematic representations of cultural and racial difference, I remember a fleeting sense of triumph over the United States, as North Americans were now the targets of a Peruvian civilizational mission. Although I have lived

María Elena García

in the United States since I was fourteen years old, I remain closely identi-fied with the country of my birth, tied to Peru by relations of family and friendship. I am not above feeling the tugs of nationalist pride, even as I recognize that this is precisely what the Peruvian state, and the makers of this very well-produced video, want me to feel.

This video was part of an explicit political and economic strategy of national branding and marketing, one whose focus was on selling Peru to Peruvians at home and abroad. Importantly, it communicated not only that Peru was/is in a different place economically and politically. For Peruvians watching, Peru was also, and suddenly, in a different place emotionally. After decades of being seen as "less than," of being equated with violence and poverty, Peru was suddenly on the map. And Peruvians could and should be proud of being a global culinary destination, of having three restaurants included in the prestigious list of the World's 50 Best Restaurants, of being seen as a place and a people of taste and refinement.

Even critical viewers could be swept up in this nationalistic fervor. I remember vividly the wave of emotions, a mix of something like happi-ness and nostalgia or *saudade* for Peru. But there was something else. I was deeply moved and surprised when I felt the tears come. I don't know if it had to do with pride in being Peruvian, in the celebration of our food and our music; or if it was a feeling of relief, that we were no longer a people plagued by violence and despair. I caught myself and have since written very critically about this celebratory story of Peruvian conquest and multi-cultural positivity. And yet, I am still struck by the power of this particular story of Peru's rise from the ashes of war.

Affect, as Sara Ahmed writes, can be "sticky" (2010, 29). And the affec-tive power of the most recent efforts to resignify Peru, and *peruanidad* (Peruvianness), through food, sticks with me. As the late Patrick Wolfe (2013, 2–3) reminds us about the workings of what he terms "the settler complex," colonialism is about elimination, erasure, and dispossession; and it is also about affect. Dakota Sioux historian Philip Deloria describes Wolfe's work as revealing how "settler colonial binaries hide in plain sight, lodged in the affective structures of feeling that win consent and shape everyday life and that simultaneously offer opportunities for diagnosis, intervention, and resis-tance."[3] To return to my affected viewing of the Peru, Nebraska, video, to the tension between critiquing power and succumbing to it, I think this is perhaps what it means to struggle with gastropolitics in Peru today, to recognize the aesthetic, sensorial, and cultural hold that it has on so many people (myself included), but also to see it as a vast apparatus of power, consumption, and knowledge production that, to borrow from Jodi Melamed (2011), has the ability to "represent and destroy."

In the following pages, I want to explore the dark sides—and affective power—of culinary nationalism in Peru. More specifically, I want to explore what it means when Gastón Acurio states that Peruvians (and others around the world) must "fall in love with Peru," as he has done in countless interviews. What does it mean to love, and what does love do, in Peru's gastronomic revolution? I want to suggest that while dominant gastropolitical discourses and practices deploy love as shorthand for the celebration of racial and cultural diversity, national reconciliation, and social inclusion, I see instead a national culinary project that mobilizes love as a strategy that serves to reinscribe inequality. Love in this context amplifies and sustains state narratives of postwar reconciliation (narratives that also criminalize social protest or alternative visions of belonging) and works to reemphasize racial hierarchies and restore order.[4]

Backstories/Ghost Stories

I remember the blackouts. I remember playing cards by candlelight, never sitting too close to windows, learning to open our mouths when car bombs went off so our eardrums wouldn't burst. I remember the night my brother, maybe three or four at the time, sliced open his face, just above his eye. He had been playing, running, and hit the corner of a coffee table. I remember the flashlights, the panic, the worry over how to get to the hospital during curfew. And I remember the feeling I had the first time I saw Sendero Luminoso's hammer and sickle burning on the side of one of the hills of Lima, the way those eerie flames haunted me for years to come.

I don't remember the dogs. We were in Mexico City that early morning in December 1980 when people in Lima awoke to the sight of dead dogs hanging from lampposts. But I know that image, the photograph of one of those dogs, still hanging, about to be released by a police officer. That is one of the dozens of photographs included in *Yuyanapaq*, the photographic exhibit that accompanied the report prepared by the Peruvian Truth and Reconciliation Commission (CVR) (Comisión de la Verdad y Reconciliación 2004). I have seen this image so often that I could say that I do, in fact, remember those dogs. Their deaths can easily become entangled with memories of that time, memories of return despite the violence, and memories of rupture. In 1985, as war hit the streets of Lima more intensely, my parents decided we would not visit Peru again until that violence ended.

María Elena García

We would not return to the arms of my grandmother, to laughter with my cousins, to the smells and sounds and sights of the city I continued to think of as home. That same year, my family moved to the United States, a move I experienced as another radical and violent rupture.

I blamed Sendero. My parents, however, blamed General Juan Velasco Alvarado (1968–75) for having to leave their home in the first place.[5] For them, as for many others in Peru, the Shining Path was an extension of the disorder General Velasco had unleashed in the late 1960s and '70s. Narratives about Velasco emphasize the expropriation of lands, the redistribution of resources to landless farmers and poor migrants, and the nationalization of Quechua, events that many in Peru—particularly upper and middle-upper classes—remember as the beginning of the end of order, as the moment racial hierarchies were upended. These histories also have much to do with elite anxieties over what some have called the "Andeanization" of Lima. Eighty percent of Lima's population of over ten million is made up of migrants or the children of migrants, and Peruvians often conflate Velasco's rule (particularly his agrarian reform) and the war with Sendero Luminoso with the waves of Andean migration into the capital city (Altamirano Rua and Altamirano Girao 2019). While the military leaders that overthrew Velasco tried to undo much of his revolution, they were unable to stop a social transformation already underway. Andean people not only challenged power relations in the countryside, but also literally changed the urban landscape as they moved to Lima and created new informal settlements, usually called *invasiones* or invasions (Matos Mar 1984).

This is a time that is remembered powerfully, violently. Velasco is a ghost who lingers, who continues to haunt a nation. "Velasquismo is a traumatic, repressed phenomenon," writes Peruvian sociologist Gonzalo Portocarrero. "A history that is taboo. A ruin you do not visit. To speak of that period, of that figure, is disturbing and contentious. . . . To return to that moment in time is like descending to a dark and loud underground; a labyrinth populated by ghosts" (2003, 229). In late 2019, a Peruvian film about Velasco's agrarian reform unleashed some of those ghosts. Watching *La revolución y la tierra* in the theaters, a friend of mine told me, was unlike anything he had experienced. "People yelled, wept, applauded, and angrily stormed out." Very shortly after debuting, the film became the most watched documentary in the history of Peruvian cinema (*RPP Noticias* 2019). More than fifty years after his revolution, Velasco's ghost continues to elicit visceral responses; embodied expressions of rage, or vindication, depending on where you stand.

The politics of memory in Peru, as in most places, are fraught. A few years ago, I took a cab to the LUM, the Lugar de la Memoria, la Tolerancia y la Inclusión Social (Place of Memory, Tolerance and Social Inclusion), a relatively new museum dedicated to archiving memory and sustaining conversation about the times of violence in Peru, meaning the violence of the 1980s and '90s.[6] The address from the LUM's website did not register on Google maps, and the cab driver was confused and unsure where to go. I had been there once, before the museum's official opening, so I had a sense of where it was located. As we drove, the cab driver suddenly told me he remembered a big square building around the area I was indicating. "That must be it," he said. "I always wondered what that was. But why do we need another museum like that? We should look to the future, not to the past."

I was not surprised by the driver's lack of awareness of the existence of this new museum. His emphasis on moving on, looking toward the future and letting go of the past, is a common narrative in Peru, where despite the horrific impact of this violence on hundreds of thousands of Peruvians, many prefer not to remember. *Yuyanapaq* ("to remember" in Quechua), the photographic exhibit that accompanied the CVR's report in 2003, has been relegated to the sixth floor of what used to be the Museo de la Nación (now the Ministry of Culture), and is visited mostly by school groups, scholars, and some tourists. And the CVR's report—which emphasized Peru's colonial legacies and implicated sitting presidents—continues to be mired in controversy. This is the historical context in which the LUM operates. The museum was inaugurated in December 2015, but since the beginning of its conceptualization and construction (in 2009), decisions about how to represent this history have been the focus of many debates and discussions.[7] Despite these tensions, there would seem to be more space for discussions about Sendero than Velasco. Perhaps Velasco's ghost is harder for some to exorcise. Regardless, in the struggle over memory in Peru, there are many who still have little choice in what they can or can't remember (Del Pino and Yezer 2013; Drinot 2009; Falcón 2018; Milton 2014; Rojas-Perez 2017).

Casa Moreyra: Love and Restoration

I walked through the busy streets of San Isidro, one of the more exclusive districts in Lima, passing high-end boutiques and restaurants and searching for Astrid y Gastón's new locale.[8] Chef Gastón Acurio's renowned restaurant, the first in Peru to be recognized as among the World's 50 Best Restaurants, had recently moved from Miraflores (a wealthy neighborhood and popular tour-

María Elena García

ist destination) to this new space in the heart of San Isidro, an even wealthier district. I worried about finding it until I arrived. There was no way to miss it.

The restaurant, housed in the renovated Casa Moreyra, the three-hundred-year-old main house of the old hacienda in San Isidro, was stunning. The house stands on a glamorous avenue, between Avenida los Incas and Avenida los Conquistadores. It sits majestically across the street from a striking church, La Virgen del Pilar, which has its origins as the chapel of the old hacienda of the Moreyra Paz Soldán family, later given by the family to Catholic missionaries who used the property to create a new convent and rebuild the church in a neocolonial style. The restaurant is also walking distance from one of the more important archaeological sites in Lima, the Huaca Huallamarca, a pyramidal structure used by the Hualla and other Native peoples since approximately 200 BC.⁹ San Isidro pulses with the activity and wealth of a modern financial district, but one cannot help but feel the layers of history upon entering the almost blinding whiteness of the Casa Hacienda Moreyra.

As you walk up the steps into the foyer, you feel as if you are stepping into another moment in time. Quite a deliberate move, taking us back to the time of colonial grandeur, control over production, and perhaps idealized visions of good patrones (landowners/bosses) and orderly workers; before the time of Velasco's agrarian reform. As you arrive at the foyer, you are greeted by an elegant hostess who asks you graciously to wait until your table is ready. The tasting experience, which features either seventeen courses or thirty-four, begins with a few cocktails and appetizers on the terrace before you are escorted to the main dining room for what our hostess describes as "a taste of Peru, an embrace from Peru to the world."¹⁰ To me it felt like a bringing together of art, alchemy, and gastronomy. I was especially struck by two experiences. One, you can eat your alcohol. The traditional pisco sour was served on a plate, chilled, with a hint (in the form of a spray) of pisco. And the guinea pig, or cuy, arrived hidden, beautiful, never betraying the rodent it once was. The animal appeared in two small circular bits, and when you popped one in your mouth, it dissolved into air, with just a hint of the flavor of cuy meat.

Casa Hacienda Moreyra was designed and built in the mid-seventeenth century by Catalan architect Pedro de Noguera. The Paz Soldán family, a cornerstone of Lima's aristocracy, bought the Hacienda in the mid-1800s and remained in control of the property until Velasco's agrarian reform.¹¹ It was declared a historical monument by the state in 1972. Acurio's decision to move his flagship restaurant to this specific space speaks volumes. This is a project of reclaiming ownership, restoring order, and rewriting history.¹²

For one, he has literally inhabited a national monument of Peru's pre-Velasco glory, a significant symbolic move. What Peruvian anthropologist Enrique Mayer says about haciendas in general applies well to Casa Moreyra in particular: it "evokes not only the land but also a world of refined privilege. It associates a family surname with a place.... The memory is also fused with a building, the casa hacienda, constructed on an imposing place as the exclusive domain of the family and guests" (2009, 77). Haciendas were one of the key institutions of Spanish colonialism. They were vital not only for their political and economic role but also for reproducing a colonial social order. As Mayer puts it, "The hacienda was a place where traditions were kept, continuity with the past was affirmed, privilege was underlined, and refinement was cultivated. It was an intensely private world with sharply defined boundaries and rigidly enforced patterns of exclusivity" (2009, 78). It is one of the striking features of the coloniality of Latin America that haciendas are unapologetically aestheticized and even romanticized today (see, e.g., Garayar et al. 1997). Astrid y Gastón's webpage is illustrative of the Peruvian and arguably hemispheric fascination with the grandeur of colonial times. The website provides a description not far from Mayer's: "Casa Moreyra was always more than a place of residence. Its significance in history is linked to its original rural role rather than to its current palatial beauty. It was a center where all types of activities came together and took place: first the economic ones and then the social, cultural and religious ones."

The house is more than a house. And while the house serves various functions, the economic role is the one most emphasized. The website recalls that the hacienda's eight thousand hectares of cropland formed part of "the great pantry of Lima." Those days of rural glory, however, came to an end. And while he is never mentioned, the ghost of General Velasco Alvarado haunts this history as well. "During the twentieth century," the site tells us, "due to urban expansion, these properties were divided and they eventually disappeared. Lima began to rely on distant pantries and the few hacienda houses that remained were removed from their original role, and they started to be confused with common houses or urban mansions." Even if there is no direct mention of agrarian reform or expropriation, Peruvians reading this history are well aware of what is meant by "the eventual disappearance of these properties."

Gastropolitics works to obscure the resentment and racial antagonisms commonly expressed about Velasco's reforms. It does so in part by reframing them as echoes of the past that are replaced by the love between city

María Elena García

and country, the recognition and inclusion of Indigenous others. But it does this through strategies that in fact work to reestablish orders felt to have been upended by Velasco. This is a significant undertaking, as Velasco evokes a visceral rage and disgust in many Peruvians. Consider the following statements:

> They took my grandmother's hacienda because of this idiot who believes in giving the same to everyone . . . instead of giving opportunities so that everyone can achieve their goals by virtue of their effort and hard work. [It was a mistake] to give land to so many ignorant Indians who don't even know how to manage an hacienda.

> Velasco gave them machinery and seeds, land, etc., and what did the Indians do? They sat on their arses and let the machinery and seeds go to waste. . . . They went back to their mountains, to their coca, and continued to breed more children and more poverty.

> [Velasco] was a fucking Indian, a cholo, because of him the cholos fucked up Lima, the city was made 100% by Europeans and now it's a disaster full of combis [public transport vans], filthy markets, Indians begging in the streets and other shit. . . .

> Velazco [sic] . . . stole your parents' land with that agrarian reform bullshit, as a consequence of that your forefathers (antepasados) migrated to Lima, that is to say, they invaded Lima to work as servants and that is why we need to put up with this invasion of darkies (cobrizos) that we see now in Lima with all their delinquency, thefts, gangs, and corruption. (quoted in Drinot 2017, 103, 107)

These statements speak to the ways race and Indigeneity in Peru are deeply embedded within racial capitalist and neoliberal ideologies. And as Peruvian historian Paulo Drinot notes, many Peruvians understand the agrarian reform "in terms of its supposed consequences for the social and racial makeup of Lima, arguing that it contributed to the wave of migration from the highlands to the capital, which, in turn, radically transformed what was until then [imagined as] a largely criollo, or white, city" (2017, 103; see also Gandolfo 2009; Martuccelli 2015; Parker 1998b; Protzel 2011). These are responses that make clear the affective legacies that accompany memories about this time, generations after the reform. Even for those too young to have experienced Velasco directly, the reproduction of the rage of the propertied classes has, for many, become something of a family tradition.

Indeed, these comments are eerily similar to those members of my own family have made. To this day, they talk about Velasco as a *resentido social* who took land and property away from those who knew how to manage it, turned the country into a backward, underdeveloped nation, and, most significantly for them, upended clear social orders. A *resentido social* does not only mean that one carries a "chip on their shoulder" (as Mayer translates the term) but that one resents the entire system and hopes to disrupt the established order of things.

In many ways, Velasco embodies an extreme version of what Sara Ahmed (2010, 30) calls "affect aliens," those others who disrupt the structures that reproduce hegemonic social orders. The legacies of Velasco's agrarian reform are contested, but there is no question that, as Portocarrero puts it, Velasco's rule was "the most audacious attempt in the history of Peru to contain social antagonisms" (2003, 231). Enrique Mayer writes that Velasco "completed the abolition of all forms of servitude in rural estates, a momentous shift in the history of the Andes, akin to the abolition of slavery in the Americas" (2009, 3).[13] The comparison with the abolition of slavery illustrates the momentous impact this government had on Peruvian society.

As I describe more fully later in this chapter (and elsewhere), with the support of a network of state and private actors, Acurio has successfully renarrated Peru as a happy nation, that "multicultural nation reimagined as a space of peace and love, where 'fellow feeling' is translated into a feeling of fellowship" (Ahmed 2010, 49; see also García 2021). He has done this in part by trying to minimize the ghostly presence of Velasco—by trying to replace hate and resentment with love, affection, and tolerance—and Peruvians love Acurio for that. This is a powerful love, one that responds ferociously to any slight, any hint of critique (García 2013). Gastón (as Peruvians call him) is Peru's savior, the son who returns to his country of birth after studying and living in Europe, despite the uncertainty that awaits him, in order to "give back." He serves as the quintessential example of one who sacrifices for his country.

Significantly, in this story, Acurio is clearly positioned as the figure of *el buen patrón*, that feudal figure who laid down the law, and the benevolent patriarch who took care of "his" workers. In interviews, many (including public intellectuals, chefs, state representatives, and Indigenous producers) referred to Acurio as "el patrón." And in his role as one of the principal proponents of the alliances between chefs and producers promoted by the gastronomic revolution, he too positions himself in this way, even if implicitly.[14] Here, it is worth noting a significant echo of Velasco's moment that

María Elena García

can be heard in Acurio's revolution. Velasco's speech on June 24, 1969, announcing his agrarian reform, is perhaps one of the most famous speeches in Peruvian history. It ends with the sentence that, as Paulo Drinot notes, has come to define not only the agrarian reform but the whole Velasco government: "We can now say to the man who works the land [*hombre de la tierra*], using the immortal and liberating words of Túpac Amaru: 'Peasant, the landlord (el patrón) will no longer eat from your poverty!'" (quoted in Drinot 2017, 97).

Acurio turns this on its head. In reworking this idea, he seems to be saying that feeding the "landlord" (the globalized elites of today rather than the feudal elites of the past) will in fact bring prosperity, and the ability to produce, to rural farmers. With only a bit of exaggeration, one might say that the new revolutionary message is, "*Hombre de la tierra*: feed the *patrón*, feed yourself." This is the idea behind the chef-producer alliances: chefs in Lima commit to buying directly from producers in rural regions of Peru, and in that way not only support farmers economically but showcase them and their best products as the protagonists and the engine necessary to keep the revolution moving, and to keep world-class restaurants operating. Of course, the caveat is that producers are expected to be grateful for the support of their new *patrón*. Thus, the gastronomic revolution—not Velasco's revolution—is in fact what will liberate them, by anchoring them to working the land and returning to the imagined benevolent relations of the feudal past. Actual market relations may be very different, but discursively, the imaginary of the present moment is one that turns Velasco's revolution upside down.

Moreover, the historical narration of Casa Moreyra, and the website more generally, also does important work in revisioning agrarian (and racial) relations and social hierarchies in Peru, and in Lima more specifically. After a brief introduction to the significance of the Casa Hacienda, Acurio notes that its history begins even before its construction, and the website then takes you to a timeline that begins in 1000 AD (when the "lands that were part of the Hacienda de San Isidro were irrigated by the Huatica irrigation canal, what is now Avenida Camino Real") and goes directly from that moment to 1538, three years after the founding of Lima.[15] With only a few stops along the way, the history of Casa Moreyra ends in 2014, with the arrival of Astrid y Gastón.

Without spending too much time on this periodization, a few observations are warranted. First, in a thousand years of history, Native peoples simply never appear. Even before the arrival of the Spanish, the only historical fact that merits attention is the fact that there existed an "irrigation canal." Who designed and built the canal is rendered unimportant and irrelevant. Similarly, while the catacombs at Casa Moreyra would seem to signal the presence of slaves on the hacienda, there is no mention of the entangled histories of slavery and haciendas in Peru. Second, the entire decade of the 1980s, when the war between the state and leftist insurgents was terrorizing large parts of the country including Lima, is avoided completely. The late twentieth-century events include the declaration of the house as a national monument (ironically in 1972, during Velasco's government) and the fact that the house was the site of an important continental gathering of architects and designers in 1999. The house is a time capsule that emerges effortlessly in the sixteenth century, passes through several aristocratic hands, is a witness to the founding of Lima and Peru, and is untouched by the violence of the centuries. The house is literally a monument to the glory of an agrarian and elite world that gave birth to the City of Kings, Lima. It is a bridge between feudal and neoliberal worlds. Astrid y Gastón's move to Casa Moreyra makes a powerful statement. By reclaiming, restoring, and rewriting this old hacienda's history, Acurio and his collaborators carefully craft a story of return: a return to the imagined colonial grandeur of the City of Kings, to the time before waves of rural migration "stained" the city and "destroyed Lima's monumental patrimony" (Gunther 1992; Parker 1998a).[16] Most importantly, this is a story of return to the time before the chaos of the agrarian reform and the violence of Sendero Luminoso, the story of a renewed Peru made possible by the love and hard work of chefs, producers, and other happy citizens. In his role as the benevolent *patrón* who supports producers as they return to lands as laborers, but working for others, Acurio produces an image of a humane and multicultural capitalism, that is without racialized rage or resentment. If, as Peruvian anthropologist Enrique Mayer (2009) suggests, the agrarian reform is made up of "ugly stories," gastropolitics offers instead beautiful stories of Peruvian love, inclusion, and success.

Mistura: Love and Recognition

As in earlier years, in 2015, Apega—the Peruvian Society of Gastronomy— organized a training workshop during the culinary festival Mistura for participating agricultural producers. This included producers from almost every region of the country. The workshop took place in the early morning, before the festival opened its doors. It was a cool spring day as producers arrived and settled into their seats in front of a large outdoor stage. After they waited for over an hour, the workshop began with a performance by a clown. Much as

María Elena García

one might do with children at a birthday party, the clown joked and laughed, eliciting audience participation. He performed for about twenty minutes, ending with a song called "El baile del gran vendedor" (The dance of the great seller). Taking over from the clown, a festival organizer whom I will call Carlos led the rest of the workshop. His focus as he addressed the approximately eighty men and women present was on three main points: the importance of presentation, cleanliness, and discipline. "Gastronomy is a display case," he began. "You need to make yourselves attractive so the consumer will fall in love." To do this, producers were told, it is necessary to bring to the surface "the magic of your origins" (la magia de su origen) and to offer "pretty, happy faces" (rostros bonitos y sonrientes) to consumers. As Carlos spoke, images of "happy faces"—all brown, all smiling widely, all wearing colorful hats—flashed on the screen behind him, clearly as examples of what to emulate. Carlos then talked about funds Apega had set aside to "beautify markets, produce stands, waiters; to beautify the presentation of the producer and the product."

Taking a break from speaking, Carlos then introduced an organization (created and supported by Apega) called BPM (Grupo Buena Práctica de Manipulación, or the Good Food-Handling Practices Group),[17] which would teach producers how to best present themselves as clean—how and why you use gloves, aprons, and hair nets, how and why you wash your hands—because, he said, "delicious and healthy food can only be possible with good and clean presentation of person and product." Later, during an interview, he told me that the workshop's focus on hygiene is particularly important as "we must teach them to be clean so they can have a healthy life; this is the mark of a healthy life." Finally, Carlos turned to the importance of rules and discipline. Transitioning from the previous discussions about presentation and cleanliness (and invoking religious doctrine), he reminded all present that being at Mistura is a great opportunity for them, but that they must remember that there are rules. In fact, he said, Apega has a pamphlet that describes the "Ten Commandments" for producers, commandments that would help them sell "better" at Mistura and other agricultural fairs. As one of the many festival workers handed out the small colorful pamphlets, Carlos emphasized a few of those commandments: "always have happy, smiling faces," "always have good, clean presentation," and "always have orderly products and stands."

Mistura, arguably the central stage for showcasing Peru's gastronomic revolution, began as a relatively small culinary festival in 2008, but grew quickly into the largest culinary festival in Latin America, with close to half a million visitors at the height of its existence.[18] Elsewhere I have discussed and critiqued the representation of Mistura as a multicultural and socioeconomically diverse haven where, as Apega's website put it, "differences are left at the door" (García 2013, 2021). For the purposes of this chapter, it is worth noting that for many in Peru, Mistura symbolizes a national ideal. Consider the words of Alexander Chiu Werner, a specialist in digital marketing writing in the pages of the business and economics daily *Gestión*, for whom Mistura stages a multisensorial version of the country, one that allows you to see, hear, and taste an "integrated" and "inclusive" Peru:

> Mistura is not a gastronomic festival to eat tasty dishes but rather a place in which you will live and taste for yourself the mixture that is Peru: from the agricultural worker of the farthest countryside to the cook who lives in the city. Mistura could be summarized as a space where you encounter the Peru that you want to see, feel and taste: an integrated Peru, inclusive, happy and proud. . . . The consumers value a brand that satisfies you as a person, that teaches you and offers an emotional connection that goes beyond commercial exchange. (Chiu Werner 2012)

This description resonates with Acurio's interpretation of this festival:

> Perhaps Mistura is the fiesta we have been waiting for; where our emotional independence finally has arrived and together we can celebrate our ability to conquer the world. May the campesino be lauded much more than the chef that is featured in the famous magazine. May the most famous restaurant have a smaller clientele than the man on the street corner selling *anticuchos*. And may no one be bothered by the other, but instead may all help all, may all celebrate all, may all embrace all. From Peru we are helping demonstrate that our cuisine contains weapons more powerful and, of course, less bloody, that can contribute to a world where justice and pleasure, ethics and aesthetics always go hand in hand. The dreams of Mistura are large. History is just beginning. (Acurio in Pérez 2011)[19]

Importantly, Mistura is also the principal stage for showcasing the gastronomic revolution's commitment to supporting Indigenous producers, described as necessary for Peruvian gastronomy, as the "first link in the Peruvian food chain" (Valderrama 2016, 31; see also Apega 2013; Ginocchio Balcázar 2012). But Mistura, and gastropolitics more generally, promotes the fiction of "the happy Native," a version of what Silvia Rivera Cusicanqui has called "*el indio permitido*," the authorized Indian.[20] As is by now well known, this term refers to the subject position that emerges in the context of neoliberal (or settler-colonial) recognition; when states "actively recog-

María Elena García

nize and open space for . . . indigenous presence" (Hale and Millaman 2006, 284).[21] As I argue elsewhere, however, "the authorized Indian" has been replaced by the figure of "the happy producer," a figure who represents an authorized subject who bridges the feudal hacienda past and the neoliberal market future (García 2021). And as was made clear in the vignette that began this section, this subject is expected, and trained, to be clean and docile, and to reflect Peruvian multicultural diversity—Acurio's beautiful and happy fusion—in appropriate ways.

At the end of Apega's workshop, Gastón Acurio took the stage and spoke to the producers present. This is how he began:

> First, I want to welcome you to Lima, the city that for centuries has turned its back on you, that for centuries did not know how to acknowledge that it was thanks to you that all our days were happy ones, because those dishes that our mothers prepared were possible only because of the marvelous ingredients that you provided, product of great effort, and from many early mornings when you woke up at dawn to produce. But it is never too late and today we are here in the city that finally learned how to recognize, and thank you, for the work you all have done to bring joy to the cities of Peru and today, begin to bring joy to the cities of the world.

Acurio warmly welcomed producers to Lima. And this greeting did not refer only to their specific trip to Mistura, but more generally, suggesting that they were now—*hoy día*—welcome in Lima, the city that for centuries had turned its back on them. Moreover, he told them the city was learning—finally, because it is never too late—to recognize and be grateful for their labor, without which Peru (and the world) would be deprived of the marvelous Peruvian ingredients that make cities happy. He went on to describe the current moment as one when the world had "discovered that it is diverse and [had] learned to enjoy the marvels of cultural and biological diversity." This is why, he said, Peruvian cuisine and Peruvian products were now recognized around the world as "something different, something unique, that enters the hearts of people . . . and make[s] consumers in the city and the world fall in love with Peru." This was an opportunity, he told them, and it was important to take advantage of that opportunity by any means necessary.

Acurio continued by describing the "millions of consumers waiting to buy these new Peruvian products," who wanted to purchase these products by paying fair prices directly to producers, because they knew that these products would be "good for their bodies, good for their spirits, good for the environment, good for society." "These are the economic values of today," he told them, and they "benefit producers, they benefit a country like Peru, a region like ours; they benefit a world that is more fraternal, more solidary, more peaceful." This is why, he told them, producers needed to "prepare themselves, improve themselves, without fear," so they could sell more efficiently. This is also why, he said, "we need to get used to mutually respecting each other and respecting the other is not pretending that others should understand us, but that we should understand them." He went on, noting that while producers might value all different kinds of potatoes— the big ones, the small ones, the imperfect ones, the ugly ones—they had to understand that there are consumers who want only the big ones, and so they needed to learn to respect that and to price their products appropriately. At the same time, he continued, chefs need to learn to appreciate diversity and to buy the entire harvest from producers, and learn how to use different products. "Diversity is a challenge to creativity," he stated.

Acurio began his concluding remarks by emphasizing the importance of this "dialogue" between the producer, the consumer, and the chef, and noted that "the good news is that this is a magical dialogue, because everyone benefits." Chefs benefit from the challenge posed by new products, and consumers benefit from eating these delicious culinary inventions. Producers, he told them, benefit because they know "the diversity of their harvest is valued, and they begin to learn too that there are minimum standards they need to comply with in order to build a solid and just commercial relationship." They benefit from the training they receive, from learning how to participate in the market; Mistura provides an opportunity to accumulate both economic and cultural capital. This is precisely one of the key dimensions of the "cunning of recognition," "its intercalation of the politics of culture with the culture of capital" (Povinelli 2002, 17).

Acurio's emphasis on dialogue is not surprising. As Charles Hale reminds us, "neoliberal multiculturalism is more inclined to draw conflicting parties into dialogue and negotiation than to preemptively slam the door" (2004, 18). Also significant is the reframing of social relations as "*magical* dialogue." As Jane Desmond notes in her discussion of cultural performance, "spectacle . . . replaces narrative, and with it the possibility of historical reflection. The social, political, and economic histories which brought performers and spectators together in the same space are either entirely absent, re-presented as nostalgia, or recoded as cultural or natural conservation" (1999, xvi). In this case, violent histories of discovery, dispossession, and marginalization are reframed as a dialogue that is equally beneficial for all those participating in it.

María Elena García

At this point, his voice increasing in tone and volume as he spoke, Acurio offered producers a powerful conclusion, eliciting whistles, strong applause, and a standing ovation from the crowd:

> Thus this is a virtuous circle in which chefs . . . finally have assumed our responsibility, understanding that we are in a privileged position . . . and because of that, because we are in magazines, and television, we have the obligation to become the ones who carry the voice of our agricultural brothers because they are far [away], working so that we may exist. We have the dream that one day in the near future, consumers will be able to celebrate the work of the small producer with the same emotion, energy, fervor, and care as the work of the chefs. And just as there are guides and rankings for chefs, there will also be guides and rankings for producers. We form part of a chain in which all of us have equal importance. [Today] marks the start of a new phase in which we all must work together so that in a few years we . . . can say . . . that our products are all over the world . . . thanks to you. And you will see how your children will be people with more recognition, more prosperity, and your lands, your towns will be more recognized and loved by the city that finally gave you its eternal thanks.

Even with these words on a page, one can sense the emotional momentum that was so palpable in that space, the feeling of being seen, validated, and vindicated. It was the kind of energy that one finds in sporting events, campaign rallies, and perhaps even charismatic churches. I was struck by the intricate tapestry Acurio was weaving, one that seemed to foreground repair (Lima will no longer turn its back on you), to celebrate a glimmering future of equality and respect between the country and the city, but that nonetheless was as far from revolutionary as one could be. What he was celebrating was not the transformation of relations but rather the importance of citizens knowing their place; this was not revolution but restoration. Acurio's civilizing project and vision for empowerment might seem to be at odds, but what Acurio's performance pulls off seamlessly is conveying a clear message about producers learning the rules of the game and knowing that if they follow them, the rewards for them and their children will be enormous. Left unspoken is what happens if producers dared not to heed Acurio and Apega's advice.

It is important to remember that Acurio's speech came after a two-hour mandatory training workshop directed at producers, a workshop that began with a clown leading the group of men and women in calisthenics before launching into his "dance of the great seller." Once the clown left the stage, Carlos introduced the various regions of the country that were represented by producers participating at Mistura, and then reminded those in attendance that they were not just representing their communities; they were representing a brand, Marca Perú. He addressed the importance of continuous training (*capacitación*) so producers could learn how best to "commercialize agro-food chains," "position their brand," and "sell to consumers." Every region should be linked to a particular product, he told them, which can then be promoted as part of the national brand. Tellingly, however, the rest of the workshop was not about marketing strategies or business plans or even specific forms of state support that could be offered to producers. It was focused on the "need to make [producers] more attractive so the consumer can fall in love." This has everything to do with crafting a particular subject: the Peruvian producer, one who is clean, culturally authentic, well behaved, and happy. And he is also a man.

It is striking how, discursively at least, there is a shift from the figure of the market woman, who had been at the center of concerns for regional elites and a generation of anthropologists, to a new subject, the male producer of the modernizing rural countryside.[22] The masculinization of modernity is, of course, an old idea. As María Josefina Saldaña-Portillo (2003) noted in her insightful reading of modernization theories of the Right and revolutionary visions of the Left, the subject of modernity is almost invariably masculine. Arturo Escobar (1995) has come to a similar conclusion in examining the ways in which development, as a set of discourses, also produces an ethnocentric and androcentric vision of the future. For Escobar, this is one of the many effects of the disciplinary power that comes with development. If this is true, then Mistura is simply the latest instantiation of such disciplinary modalities.

In his address to the workshop's attendees, Acurio simply needed to refer to the importance of "training and improving yourselves," "respecting the other," and "learning how to understand what the other wants." If you want to sell your products, to benefit from this network of commercial exchange, Acurio was saying, you need to be open to new challenges and participate in the market appropriately. Still, the tone was laudatory and the sensibility one of humility, support, and social justice. This is a familiar version of justice, of course, one that in this context centers chefs as, according to Acurio, they are the ones who have "the obligation to become spokespersons for our producer brothers." This can feel like a form of solidarity or even advocacy, and perhaps this was the spirit in which it

María Elena García

was intended. Nevertheless, these comments can also be considered part of an old Andean tradition that Ecuadorian sociologist Andrés Guerrero (1997) called "ventriloquist representation," in which Indians are spoken for by traditional elites. Landowners, political parties, local elites, and social scientists all profess to understand Indigenous needs and thus speak on behalf of "their" Indians. The voices of Acurio's brothers and sisters in the countryside remain distant here.

When I spoke with Carlos immediately after the workshop, he was gushing about Acurio's ability to "shatter frameworks" (*romper esquemas*). For Carlos, this was an entirely new approach to social inclusion. As we walked to his office for our scheduled interview, he told me Acurio had just delivered a manifesto: "He has launched a manifesto, a framework for policies that carries with it a revolution!" As we sat in his office, he leaned in and said, "You have to understand, he is a social innovator; he proposes new ways to see old problems." He continued, "For example, he says, 'You all are important; we are in a process of revalorizing your work, and you are the greatest exponents of cultural and biological diversity.' But at the same time, he says, 'We need entrepreneurs who know how to do business.' He makes them understand that it is not the case that I am going to accept anything that you want. They have to be serious. In other words, [Gastón] is a teacher: he explains possibilities but he also shows the *chicote*."

At the mention of the *chicote*, a whip used for hitting and disciplining animals and people, like those who worked the fields of *hacendados* before agrarian reform, my face must have betrayed my thoughts. Carlos stopped talking, looked at me for several seconds, and then, perhaps deciding that what my face registered was confusion, he explained, "The *chicote* is for hitting [El chicote es para pegar]." And then, restating this once more, he continued, "The *chicote* is an object for hitting. So [Gastón] says, 'I will buy from you but you must offer quality goods. You must be disciplined [*ordenados*] and comply with the deals you make.' If you don't, you can't participate. You can't benefit. In other words, he is not the typical paternalist. It is not that typical paternalism that says sure, do what you want and I will help you. No, no no. This [the gastronomic revolution] is not a handout [*asistencialismo*]. He is a good *patrón*." Once again, feudal, pre–agrarian reform tropes (*chicotes* and *patrones*) fold neatly into the neoliberal frameworks of the gastronomic revolution. In today's Peru, punishment for producers who do not comply with the gastronomic revolution's rules does not literally involve a whip, but it does mean exclusion from important market spaces, such as Mistura.

Despite claims of inclusion and equality, then, there is reason to be skeptical about just how much of that is being accomplished. Just after Acurio walked onto the stage to deliver his speech at the end of the producer-training workshop, two Andean producers, a man and woman, dressed in their authentic regional clothes, were hurried onto the stage with the great chef. They stood by his side as he spoke, as he answered questions, and as the crowd applauded, but they were never named and never spoke. The next morning, all of the major Peruvian newspapers carried the photograph of Acurio with these authorized figures, visually reflecting the chef's willingness to share the stage with Indigenous bodies.

Love and Fusion: Concluding Thoughts

Have we arrived? Maybe. It's true, we fought for a long time, but here are our young people, dreaming in peace. Celebrating without fear, grateful to be from Lima, children of all bloods. From Andean to coastal, from Chinese to Japanese, from Italians to Arabs, from Spaniards to Africans. Impossible love that our parents knew how to defend and make flourish. And here we are today, seeking to be free at last, telling everyone, among chili peppers and dressings, that you do not have to build walls but bridges.

—From Astrid y Gastón's website

In 2018, Gastón Acurio delivered a TED talk on love and cooking in Peru. In that popular talk, he makes the seductive argument that cooking at home can change the world (Acurio 2018).[23] He begins with a love story: the children of Cantonese and Italian families fall in love in the streets of the port city of Callao, Peru. Their families are against their love, so the young couple moves far away to make their new home. Romance gives way to disagreement in the kitchen; soy sauce and Parmesan cheese come into conflict. Over time, however, conflict yields to creativity. Old flavors from different worlds mix in new recipes. This, Acurio tells us, is how Peruvian cuisine was born, a product of "500 years of beautiful fusion," and of romantic and harmonious encounters among diverse peoples (Acurio 2008). And he continues, "Peru received millions of people who dreamed of a better world. But Peru did not receive them in ghettos. We did not separate them, but rather integrated them, joined them together. The message from Peru is clear: nothing bad can happen to us; only good things will occur when we embrace our diversity; and when in the kitchen we build bountiful bridges of love and peace" (Acurio 2018).

María Elena García

For Acurio, this story—of colonial encounters reframed as tales of love, of differences giving way to not just tolerance but national reconciliation—is the story of Peru. It reflects beautifully what Sara Ahmed calls "multicultural love," a form of love that produces the nation as "an ideal through being posited as 'being' plural, open and diverse; as being loving and welcoming to others" (2015, 133). And in this story, Acurio is the "good and tolerant subject" who lovingly identifies with and celebrates this multicultural nation (Salecl 1998, 4). For example, he begins his TED talk by positioning himself as a product of colonial encounters that move from difference and confrontation to unity in love: "I am Limeño, son of all the bloods, as you can see [gestures to his face]. My mother, daughter of the coast, aristocratic and viceregal, and my father, a son of the Andes, the Incas, from Cuzco. In my home, the Andes and the coast, historically confrontational, were united thanks to love, as happened to most people from Lima, descendants of the most diverse backgrounds: Africans with Amazonians, Japanese with Andeans, Chinese with Italians."[24] Here, the sexual violence of colonial encounters is represented as a story of impossible, defiant love. In the tasting menu for Astrid y Gastón in spring 2018, we see this quite explicitly. The menu, titled "Lima Love," tells the story of contemporary Peru, of a nation "celebrating without fear, thankful for being Limeños, children of all the bloods. Of Andeans with coastal peoples . . . of people from Spain with Africans. Impossible loves that our parents knew how to defend and flower." The first dish on the menu is called *La cama indecente, la del amor prohibido* (The indecent bed, the one of forbidden love).

Race and sex haunt Peru's gastronomic revolution. The commonplace descriptions of beautiful fusion, of the love between races that flourishes against all odds and, importantly, produces a uniquely Peruvian cuisine, culture, and subject, is in many ways nothing more than a rearticulation of *mestizaje*, that contested national ideology of inclusion prevalent throughout Latin America. Multiple scholars have written about the varying configurations, politics, and implications of *mestizaje* across the region, and what they emphasize is that the logic of *mestizaje* has been about state-sanctioned exclusions.[25] Even in the poetic renderings of inclusion, like Vasconcelos's famous idea of a "cosmic race" that upended the Atlantic consensus on white supremacy and racial purity, the project of *mestizaje* was nation-building homogeneity. If you were not mixed enough (i.e., too Indian or Black), then you were not a proper national subject. As Stutzman aptly put it for the case of Ecuador, *mestizaje* was the "all-inclusive ideology of exclusion" (1981).

Acurio has worked relentlessly to resignify *mestizaje*, noting that his formulation of mixture and fusion contrasts with older, pejorative understandings of what it meant to be mestizo. Take, for example, the description of some of his dishes, such as *Las causas cinco razas*, featured in his book *500 Years of Fusion: The History, the Ingredients, and Peruvian Cuisine's New Proposals*: "Five bloods run through the veins of the Peruvian of today, five great influences make up our cuisine. The Andes, with all its different cultures. Europe, that since the arrival of Pizarro has not stopped sending Spanish, Italian or French migrations. Africa, with its rhythm and seasoning. China, with its woks and ancient gastronomic taste. Japan, with its maritime vocation and great stylization. Five cultures perfectly assembled: may five *causas* pay them homage" (Acurio 2008, 195).[26] Perhaps one should not read too much into the incredibly reductive language of Andean, European, African, Chinese, and Japanese "bloods." Nevertheless, it is worth noting how this view of cultures flattens and caricatures centuries of imperialism, colonial violence, indentured servitude, slavery, and conquest. In their place, one finds the smooth language of integration and fusion.

My argument here is that in Acurio's formulation (and in that of the gastropolitical national project more generally), love does not just erase violence. It also serves as a powerful affective and political strategy that enacts violence on those bodies that don't conform to the borders of the newly drawn nation and its authorized subjects (Ahmed 2015; see also Ahmed 2004). Rather than thinking about love as antipolitical (following Arendt 1968) or even "properly political" (with the hope, following Michael Hardt [2011], that it might "create bonds . . . at once intimate and social" and transform us and our world), my reading of gastropolitical love resonates more closely with the work of theorists who call attention to love as an "unjust ethic" (Dave 2016), an affective force inseparable from histories of settler colonial erasure and dispossession (Povinelli 2006), and quite often intimately entangled with discourses and practices of violence and hate (Ahmed 2015; Govindrajan 2021). To return to Sara Ahmed's formulation of multicultural love, as she notes, the "identification with the multicultural nation . . . relies on the structural possibility of the *loss* of the nation as object. The multicultural nation can itself be taken away by the presence of others . . . by [those] who don't accept the conditions of one's love" (2015, 134, my emphasis).

Narratives that center Peruvian cuisine—and the nation—as the culmination of centuries of "beautiful, tolerant, and consensual mixture" and "forbidden love," as the reflection of a socially conscious, inclusive, and

María Elena García

loving community, are not just strategic political attempts at sanitizing violent histories. These are deeply felt national ideologies; they are embodied and sticky attachments that many Peruvians will fiercely defend.[27] "Love sticks the nation together," writes Ahmed. "It allows cohesion through the naming of the nation . . . as a shared object of love. Love becomes crucial to the promise of cohesion within multiculturalism; it becomes the 'shared characteristic' required to keep the nation together. The emotion becomes the object of the emotion" (2015, 135). But this is also why love, as she notes, can so easily become the conduit for hate (Ahmed 2015, esp. chapter 2). The love of nation is mobilized in order to police the affective meanings of that imagined nation, where those unauthorized subjects or "affect aliens" that dare to protest, or don't fit the gastropolitical figure of the happy, docile Native, are criminalized and deemed subversive, antinational, terrorist. Given the Peruvian backstory of violence and the very real and recent discourses of national security that tortured, disappeared, and murdered so many, love, in this context, can be terrifying. Ghosts are always lurking in the background, haunting this new multicultural love that of course is simply a reconfiguration of settler colonial orders.

As a cultural, economic, and political project, gastropolitics renarrates and reimagines the past as a path toward crafting a Peruvian future. The first few lines of Peruvian poet and journalist Rodolfo Hinostroza's book *Primicias de la cocina peruana* is instructive here. *Primicias* means "first fruits" and refers to the link between those first fruits and their future potential. Hinostroza writes: "This is the story of a successful culinary *mestizaje*, of the peaceful encounter of two gastronomic universes, one European, the other American, to produce a delicious and properly Peruvian cuisine. It is the most successful synthesis of the Indian and Spanish created in America, with the happy contributions of the Arab and Black female cooks who came with the conquistadores. . . . This encounter led to a cuisine that is delicious and original, singular and succulent . . . seductive and addictive, superior and distinct from all other cuisines of the region" (2006, 9). Note the language that describes the encounters of (at least) two worlds: peaceful, successful, happy, seductive. This is indeed a seductive framing that has shaped authorized state narratives about Peru as nation, people, and history. It has also obscured histories and futures of extractive capitalism and racial violence. Yet this hegemonic story is haunted by restless ghosts produced in large part by long histories of economic and racial inequality. In particular, the ghosts of General Velasco Alvarado's agrarian revolution and Sendero Luminoso's violent Maoism refuse to let go. In trying to exorcise these ghosts, the gastronomic revolution has attempted to create its own utopic vision of neoliberal futurity. But like other efforts to narrate repair, reconciliation, and multiculturalism, gastropolitics only serves to obscure what Jean Franco (2013) calls the "cruel modernities" that make up Abiayala (or the Americas) today.

Notes

1 Peru Country Brand, "Peru Brand: A Symbol Linking All the Country," accessed April 7, 2022, https://peru.info/en-us/brand-peru.

2 Unless otherwise noted, all translations are my own.

3 From the blurb of *The Settler Complex*, published as an edited book in 2016 by UCLA's American Indian Center.

4 As I argue in the following pages, Peru is a love story; a story like many others, where discourses and performances of love, inclusion, and recognition in fact mask the violence of white supremacy and ongoing colonial arrangements. But as with all stories, this one too is more complicated. There are many cracks in the gastropolitical machine; alternative voices, practices, and politics that emerge from those cracks; other ways of imagining, feeling, and living the present and future and past in Peru. While a fuller discussion is beyond the scope of this chapter, I explore these cracks and possibilities in García (2021).

5 For more on Velasco Alvarado's rule and the revolutionary government of the armed forces more generally, see Aguirre and Drinot (2017), and Drinot (2017).

6 Lugar de la Memoria, la Tolerancia y la Inclusión Social, https://lum.cultura .pe/.

7 This was even the case among activists and artists who were divided between challenging state-sanctioned histories of the internal conflict and accommodating exhibits to fit within socially accepted terms and understandings of the conflict (Jorge Miyagui and Mauricio Delgado, personal communication, June 2015; see also del Pino and Agüero 2014). On the politics of institutionalizing memory, see Drinot (2009), Feldman (2012, 2019), and Milton (2014, 2018).

8 Astrid y Gastón, http://www.astridygaston.com/.

9 This site is a testament to Indigenous histories in Lima prior to the city's founding, as well as their resilience in the face of dispossession and marginalization. There are dozens of *huacas* throughout the capital city, a reminder that Lima was built on top of and around these monuments. On the history of Indigeneity in colonial Lima, see Charney (2001) and Cogorno and Ortiz de Zevallos (2018).

10 In June 2015, when I visited Astrid y Gastón in its new location, diners had a choice between these two tasting menus. The restaurant has since changed

to include an à la carte menu and one shorter tasting menu that changes seasonally.

11 In a telling reflection of the patriarchal nature of Peruvian society, the name Casa Moreyra comes from Luisa Paz Soldán's husband, Francisco Moreyra.

12 I wonder, also, about the personal dimension of this move. The Acurio family was one of many impacted by Velasco's reforms. The family owned half of Maras, a region in the Sacred Valley near the city of Cusco that is home to famous salt mines and Moray, the archaeological site next to which chef Virgilio Martínez built his latest restaurant, Mil. According to one of Acurio's cousins (with whom I spoke in January 2020), their grandmother was among the first to fight against the expropriation of their lands in court, and she was able to regain some of their territory.

13 Velasco was deposed in 1975 due to increasing economic turmoil, unemployment, and political opposition. Military generals from the RGAF declared that Velasco's reforms had not achieved the ideals of the Peruvian revolution, and appointed Francisco Morales Bermúdez as president (1975–80). Moving away from Velasco's leftist approach, Morales Bermúdez declared the "second phase" of the revolution, which would include a reversal of some of Velasco's policies and lead to democratic rule.

14 This refers to an alliance developed between Apega, Conveagro (National Convention of the Peruvian Agro or Convención Nacional del Agro Peruano, https://conveagro.org.pe/), and ANPE (National Association of Ecological Producers or Asociación Nacional de Productores Ecológicos, https://www.anpeperu .org/). See Bohardt (2014), Ginnochio Balcázar (2012), and Kollenda (2019).

15 Astrid y Gastón, "The History of Casa Hacienda Moreyra," accessed April 7, 2022, http://en.astridygaston.com/history/. It might be too much to note that the web design firm that created this site and those for many other elite restaurants in Peru is called Buendía, which translates simply as "good day" but can also be seen as an allusion to the Buendía family, the fictional founding family of Macondo made famous by Gabriel García Márquez in *One Hundred Years of Solitude*. That novel, like this house, is premised on a nonlinear sense of time, where the violence of colonial and modern periods is impossible to separate.

16 Those familiar with Peruvian history will be aware of the "myth of old Lima," an idealized representation of colonial Lima as a beautiful, clean, and prosperous city constructed by writers, singers, and public intellectuals (see, e.g., Pacheco Velez 1985; Palma 1923). Among the fiercest critics of this myth is the Peruvian essayist, poet, and playwright Sebastián Salazar Bondy, who wrote his groundbreaking book *Lima la horrible* (1964), during a context of increasing Andean migration to Lima.

17 A more literal translation would be the Good Manipulation Practices Group.

18 Mistura was canceled unexpectedly in 2018. That year, Apega partnered with the Grupo Nexo Franquicia to create the Mistura Franchise. According to Bernardo Roca Rey (Apega's president), this would allow Apega to "export"

Mistura, and Marca Perú, to the world (Melgarejo 2019). That plan backfired, leading to accusations of financial mismanagement that coincided with the death of Apega founding member Mariano Valderrama. By late 2019, Apega had disbanded, and Mistura seems to be over. However, according to a few chefs with whom I have spoken, there are efforts to revive this culinary festival, though perhaps in a different form. The COVID-19 pandemic disrupted these efforts, and it is unclear at this point what the possibilities are for the development of another culinary festival.

19   *Anticuchos* are skewers made with marinated beef hearts.

20   On the "happy Native," see Desmond (1999), and Trask (1999). On the "authorized Indian," see Cusicanqui (2007), Hale (2004), and Hale and Millaman (2006). Almost without exception, images of racialized others in visual representations of Mistura and Apega-sponsored agricultural fairs show them smiling, laughing, and often dressed in ways that match up with idealized folkloric representations or racial tropes.

21   For important variations on this theme, see Hale's (2002, 2005) argument about neoliberal multiculturalism, Povinelli's (2002) "cunning of recognition," and Speed's (2019) formulation of the "settler-capitalist state."

22   On the figure of the market woman in the Andes, see Weismantel (2001).

23   As others have noted with regard to male advocates of "slow food," "returning to the kitchen," and "cooking in the home," a critical feminist reading of Acurio's push for a return to home cooking would emphasize nostalgia for a heteronormative "past" that relied heavily on the labor of women.

24   Gesturing to his face is telling. Acurio seems to be reminding viewers that he, too, is a product of all the bloods, a mestizo embodying this Peruvian fusion. Even as he tries to decenter his elite whiteness, however, Acurio can't help but note his noble lineage: he is the son of an aristocrat mother and of a father who was not "just" from the Andes, but from Cusco and the Incas, born of one of the largest empires in the history of the world.

25   See Appelbaum, Macpherson, and Rosemblatt (2003), Sanders (2014), Sanjinés (2004), Stepan (1991), Wade (2010, 2017), and Wickstrom and Young (2014). On *mestizaje* in Peru, see de la Cadena (2010), and Portocarrero (2007, 2013).

26   This text, a large coffee table book with spectacular photographs, offers a sweeping history of Peruvian cuisine, its principal ingredients and cultural influences. It also features Acurio prominently (the cover is a black-and-white photograph of his face), as well as plugging his principal restaurants by showcasing some of their recipes. The book was declared "Best Cookbook in the World" in 2008 by Gourmand World Cookbook Awards.

27   The place of food and taste here is not insignificant. As Ben Highmore writes, taste can be thought of as an "orchestration of the sensible, a way of ordering and demeaning, of giving value and taking it away.... [Taste is] the very basis of culture, not simply its system of values but the way that set of values gets under your skin and into your bones" (2010, 126).

3

Death and Disavowal

DEBORAH A. THOMAS

> In the wake, the past that is not past reappears, always, to rupture the present.
> —Christina Sharpe, *In the Wake*

If it is true that death mediates sovereignty, then we must ask what a sovereign death feels like. This is, perhaps, a question that is more easily answered in its inverse. A death does not feel sovereign when, for example, one's sister's body stays on the road for three days after she was shot by the Jamaican security forces while she was attempting to get to her church during a state of emergency in 2010. Or when bodies are thrown in mass graves in the nearby cemetery, or when they are left to fester on the street in the hot sun, or are burned in the public dump adjacent to the community. A death does not feel sovereign when one is called into the police station to identify two nephews who were killed in that same state of emergency, and one is unable to recognize them because their bodies are so badly burned. Or when, on emerging from one's home as the most intense period of the emergency is lifted, one sees bloodstains in the streets and bodies wrapped in sheets, when one can't avoid the stench of corporeal decomposition.

Or perhaps these are exactly examples of what sovereign death feels like within the context of a postcolonial political modernity forged through imperialism and plantation slavery. Philosophers and critical theorists have taught us that death is a political decision, and that modern sovereignty is characterized both by the right to kill or let live, and by the power to name the exception.[1] Many have also argued for the centrality of coloniality to political modernity, seeking to expose the inadequacies of both Enlightenment-era theorists of the political and their contemporary counterparts.[2] Among the latter, it is Achille Mbembe's (2003) elaboration of the plantation system as a "terror formation" that most explicitly brings together biopower, the state of exception, and the state of siege as a political constellation in which race is the foundational vector of otherness, creating a state of "necropower." The colonial world, for Mbembe, is the quintessential site "where sovereignty consists fundamentally in the exercise of a power outside the law," "where the violence of the state of exception is deemed to operate in the service of 'civilization,'" and where racial exclusion is geared toward the "denial of any common bond between the conqueror and the native" (2003, 23, 24). Black death, in these contexts, represents the essence of disposability, mediating the power of the sovereign and the racial, class, and civilizational hierarchies perpetuated in and through modernity, and therefore through Western democratic liberalism.

While death mediates sovereignty, it is also itself a form of mediation. For Georges Bataille, this mediation exists through the affect of fear, an anticipation grounded in an attachment to the future that "prevents man from attaining himself" ([1991] 2017, 218). This fear mediates the social worlds in which we create ourselves as persons and collectivities, and anthropologists have long had much to say about the ways death mediates life, providing windows into a society's most important organizing principles. This is evidenced not only by the vast literatures on funerary rituals and practices (e.g., Bloch and Parry 1982; Metcalf and Huntington 1991; Kaufman and Morgan 2005), but also by those who have examined the "political lives of dead bodies" (Verdery 1998) and the ways "the dead sacralize the land and endow it with historical depth, political significance, and symbolic meaning" (Balkan 2015, 26). Rituals surrounding death also establish an affective sphere through which we are called to bear witness not only to the life of the dead but to the conditions that structured that life, and that continue to structure the lives of mourners. Within Jamaica, these conditions include a complex (though not uncommon) set of class and racial hierarchies that operate through notions and practices of gendered respectability, and that undergirded the forms of anticolonial nationalism that became dominant in the mid-twentieth century. This is something I have written about at length elsewhere (Thomas 2004, 2011).

I am interested, in this chapter, in the relationships between death and mediation on two levels. On one hand, I want to understand something about how death is mediated within contexts of postcolonial political crisis. On the other, I want to think through death itself as a form of mediation,

Deborah A. Thomas

as a process that can tell us about the relationships among death, life, and death-in-life, and therefore about the disavowals inherent to Western liberal democracy—its foundations in imperialism, slavery, institutionalized inequality.[3] I want to do this in the same way that forensic examinations might reveal the truths about bodily harm. To do so, I want to explore the forensic responses to the 2010 Tivoli Incursion in West Kingston, Jamaica. By forensics, I mean to signal a form of assessment designed to establish consensus regarding protocols for evaluation and determinations of causality, and therefore ultimately the parameters of accountability surrounding both eventful and durational processes. If forensics are, as Michael Ralph has written, "a mode of inquiry concerned with who owes what to whom" (2015, 143), then to explore forensic responses is to imagine what meaningful forms of repair are available to us, even as we move toward the seemingly perpetual suspension of normal policing and the long-term use of extreme powers. To circle back to how we might think about these questions in the Caribbean, let me first embark on a short detour to Greece.

Death and Witnessing

Nadia Seremetakis's (1990) classic article about the performance of mortuary laments by Maniat women in rural Greece addresses them both in terms of women's self-reflexivity and as indicating something about the relationships between the self and the social within cosmological and material orders. Seremetakis is interested in what laments show us about how self and sentiment are mutually constituted through an antiphonic construction of pain, and in how they simultaneously produce both a juridical discursive field through which women bear witness to the life of the deceased, and a political strategy "that organizes the relations of women to male-dominated institutions" (1990, 482). Drawing from the Greek concept of antiphony, Seremetakis elaborates how witnessing and suffering for the dead conjoins the individual, social, and juridical spheres through emotional expression: "In Greek, the concept of *antifonisi* (antiphony) possesses a social and juridical sense in addition to its aesthetic, musical, and dramaturgical usages. Antiphony can refer to the construction of contractual agreement, a creation of symphony by opposing voices. It also implies echo, response, and guarantee. The term strongly infers dyadic, musical, dramaturgical, social and juridical relation" (1990, 492). Expressions of pain, for Seremetakis, are thus an alternative means to establish truth claims, particularly for those in conflict with dominant social orders, through the force of affect. They establish the conditions for, and manifestations of, a sovereign death, a death, that is to say, that recognizes the sociopolitical legitimacy of the deceased in life, and that therefore calls into question the normative parameters of what it means to be human (and, ultimately, a citizen) within a given space. Death, in this case, is a form of self-consciousness or, in Mbembe's limning of Bataille, "the most luxurious form of life" (2019, 69). Focusing on death, or, more pointedly, focusing on the forms of mediation that make a sovereign death, can therefore bring light to the various ways in which, and processes through which, this legitimacy has been disavowed.

In classic Caribbean ethnography, we see that life is similarly realized and recognized at the moment of the threshold of death. Zora Neale Hurston's *Tell My Horse* ([1938] 1990) is preoccupied with the rituals surrounding death and the constant appearance (and antics) of those who should be dead. She turns her most careful attention to those practices that are geared toward maintaining the boundary between the world of the living and the world of the dead. In both Jamaica and Haiti, she goes to great lengths to document the funerary rituals characteristic of each locale, tying them also to practices in other areas of the diaspora.

In Jamaica, Hurston tells us that when a person dies, "it is a rigid rule that the whole district must participate" ([1938] 1990, 40) in the ensuing rituals, called the "nine-night." She shows how every precaution is taken to make sure the death is a good death, with a good death being a final one. The body has to be prepared, with limes and nutmeg being rubbed on the deceased's nose and mouth, under the arms and between the legs; the body has to be fed, but never with salt, because salt will make the body heavy and unable to leave the world of the living; the body has to be placed in the coffin with its head atop a pillow inside of which have been sewn "parched peas, corn and coffee beans" (42); nails have to be driven through the cuffs of the deceased's shirt, the heels of the deceased's socks; the coffin has to be "lowered with proper rituals and patted to rest in the earth" and "a trail of salt and ground coffee" has to be laid "from the grave to the house door" (43); songs are lined out hour after hour. All of this occurs, she tells us, so that the "duppy" of the deceased—his ghost—would not return.

The duppy, one of Hurston's Jamaican informants tells her, "is the most powerful part of any man." "Everybody has evil in them," he continues, "and when a man is alive, the heart and the brain controls him and he will not abandon himself to many evil things. But when the duppy leaves the body, it no longer has anything to restrain it and it will do more terrible things than any man ever dreamed of. It is not good for a duppy to stay among

Deborah A. Thomas

living folk. The duppy is much too powerful and is apt to hurt people all the time. So," he concludes, "we make nine night to force the duppy to stay in his grave" ([1938] 1990, 43–44). On the ninth night after death, everyone in the district convenes at the house again, this time for singing and music and joviality, the goal being to give the deceased a happy send-off "'so that he will rest well and not come back again'" (48).

Elisa Sobo's ethnographic research in rural Jamaica documents the continuation of these beliefs into the 1980s. "The social world includes ancestors," she writes. "Their continued existence complicates obligation. No one ever disappears completely, and relationship tensions are projected onto the dead" (Sobo 1993, 265). Duppies, here, are active within continued networks of obligation that exceed the temporalities of past, present, and future. They "do not understand that they are dead and so," according to Sobo's interlocutors, "although they should settle into their graves and rest, they try to do the things they did in life" (1993, 266). The living, therefore, must enact a range of practices to ward off the dead, especially as they are often buried on "family land"—land that is held in common by all descendants of an original ancestor, who would have either purchased it or acquired it in another way during slavery or not long after emancipation.[4] As the culmination of the mortuary ritual cycle, being buried on family land solidifies the inalienability of the land, thus bringing together ancestral veneration, the sense of belonging to a place, the articulation of freedom, and "individual and collective identity and personhood" (Hume 2018, 131).

Moving from Jamaica to Haiti, Hurston noted that there, duppies are called zombies; they are the living dead, bodies without souls. Haitian zombies fascinated Hurston, and she was interested to find out why zombies, unlike duppies, were unable to rest. She was given many answers: "A was awakened because somebody required his body as a beast of burden. In his natural state he could never have been hired to work with his hands, so he was made into a Zombie because they wanted his services as a laborer. B was summoned to labor also but he is reduced to the level of a beast as an act of revenge. C was the culmination of 'ba' Moun' ceremony and pledge. That is, he was given as a sacrifice to pay off a debt to a spirit for benefits received" ([1938] 1990, 179). While the dead in this context were called on to continue to labor, she also reported that they were used as sneak thieves and, if we are to believe her informants, to marry off daughters. Ever the skeptic, however, Hurston was convinced that "if embalming were customary, it would remove the possibility of Zombies from the minds of the people. But since it is not done," she says, "many families take precautions against the body being disturbed." Zombies, being complete sovereigns in Bataille's sense, could never experience a good—that is, final—death.

As in Jamaica, Hurston proceeded to describe ritual practices surrounding death in Haiti: setting up watch in the cemetery for thirty-six hours after burial; cutting the body open, or just putting a knife in the right hand of the corpse, flexed "in such a way that it will deal a blow with the knife to whoever disturbs it for the first day or so" ([1938] 1990, 191); and even poisoning the body. She discussed Guede, the entirely Haitian, that is to say nonsyncretized, *loa*, who was known also to be a grave robber, among other things. And she reflected on the subtleties of using graveyard dirt to maim and kill. "Soil from deep in an old grave has prestige wherever the negro exists in the Western world," Hurston recounted. She surmised that this belief might have "come out of the ancestor worship of West Africa" (238), making it an "African survival" of sorts (239). In Jamaica, Haiti, and "wherever the negro exists in the Western world," the funerary ritual practices Hurston documented stemmed from a strong belief in survival after death, "or rather," as she argued, "that there *is no death*. Activities are merely changed from one condition to the other" (43).

This is an insight historian Vincent Brown shows is encapsulated by the Akan *adinkra* symbol "'Nyame nwu na mawu' (loosely translated, 'God does not die, so I cannot die')." In *The Reaper's Garden*, Brown's exploration of death and power in the eighteenth-century Atlantic world, he argues that the notion that the dead "played an active role in worldly affairs" reveals death as "a transition between the physical and immaterial states of being" (2008, 66, 4). In Jamaica, funerals revealed common cosmological orientations and generated a shared moral universe among slaves. By participating in funerary rituals, Brown writes, "they recovered their common humanity, they assumed and affirmed meaningful social roles, and they rendered communal values sacred by associating them with the dead" (2008, 65). Where Hurston documented early twentieth-century practices, Brown describes those prevalent in the eighteenth century, as people from a variety of ethnic groups met each other on New World soil, continuing old and developing new rituals designed to "send spirits properly on their way to the other world" (2008, 66), to make sure they had sufficient foodstuffs, tobacco, and drink to nourish them on their journey, and that they were spurred on by song and dance. These were the practices that would ensure a sovereign death and therefore generate the affective recognition that would sustain their communities.

People in West Kingston who lost loved ones during the 2010 incursion also conducted such rituals, forms of local expertise and care designed to

Deborah A. Thomas

restore their loved ones to the realm of the human, to mediate their "bad deaths" in order to prevent them from haunting the living, from transcending the normative spatial and temporal realms of conventional modalities of sovereignty. Ultimately, however, these deaths were also mediated by forensic science, a form of mediation that operated at a different scale. Forensics, in this case, enacted a mode of truth telling designed to address immediate events, while also generating a transnational infrastructure for assessing the broader contexts and histories from which these events erupt. Notably, this infrastructure also created the conditions for bypassing the state even as it worked through state institutions to address the effects of its own violence.[5] If duppies are ghosts who won't go away until they are adequately recognized through community-based forms of care and modes of accountability, what kinds of forensic expertise are needed to reckon the chains of causality and determine the parameters for accountability within a context in which state violence is one contemporary legacy of imperialism and plantation-based development?

The Forensics of Death

The examples of nonsovereign death I opened with were gleaned from audiovisual interviews recorded with West Kingston community members between 2012 and 2015, after the 2010 Tivoli Incursion in which the Jamaica Defense Force and the Jamaica Constabulary Force penetrated the community of Tivoli Gardens in order to apprehend Christopher "Dudus" Coke, a penetration that resulted in the death of at least seventy-three civilians. Coke had been ordered extradited by the US government in August 2009, and after a long and scandal-ridden delay, the prime minister of Jamaica authorized the attorney general to sign the order, and the military and police forces began to plan their operation.

Coke had been a key player in the transnational trade in drugs and arms, and was to stand trial in the United States for these involvements. He was also, however, don of Tivoli Gardens, and therefore central to the maintenance of the garrison system of politics in Jamaica, through which the relationship between an elected member of Parliament and a local leader mediates the flow of social benefits and job contracts from the government to the community in spaces where the state has otherwise abdicated its responsibility for those citizens living there. Of course, this flow of state largesse is dependent upon the reverse flow of votes at election time. Dons, within this context, become the center of local authority, political and economic life, social welfare, and cultural expression, and they are both revered and feared.[6] Coke was not captured during the week of the operation, but more than four thousand West Kingston denizens were detained under emergency regulations, the vast majority of whom were ultimately released without charge after having been "processed," a phenomenon that came to refer to having been fingerprinted and photographed, and having had personal details recorded (Amnesty International 2011).[7] The aftermath of the Tivoli Incursion, therefore, left residents to deal with the trauma of having experienced the uncertainties and violence of the week's events, and to attend to their dead.

Beginning in 2012, Deanne M. Bell, Junior "Gabu" Wedderburn, and I recorded approximately thirty oral histories documenting community members' experiences during the week of the Tivoli Incursion. These interviews, in addition to other materials—including the footage from the US drone that was overhead during the operation, archival film and stills of Tivoli Gardens, portraits of our interviewees and pictures taken by community youth during a workshop we ran with students from the University of Pennsylvania in August 2013, additional video from a guided walk through the community in January 2014, and emails and cables between personnel within the US consulate in Kingston and their counterparts in Washington, DC—form the basis for our film *Four Days in May*, and our installation *Bearing Witness: Four Days in West Kingston*.[8] The archives we developed offer a window not only into the historical and material conditions of life in garrison communities, but also into the sensory realms of death and its temporal effects and affects.

The state also developed its own archives. On June 2, 2010, residents of Tivoli Gardens in West Kingston, Jamaica, were invited to come to the local police station and community center to identify deceased loved ones based on photographs taken by security personnel. These photographs were compiled into a thick book and scanned onto a computer. When autopsies were eventually conducted (bodies having been stored in refrigerated shipping containers), the initial photo identifications by community members were cross-referenced with their loved ones' physical remains.

Errol Witter, the public defender at the time, requested access to independent forensic pathologists and ballistic experts in order to investigate the deaths in West Kingston. This was in part because crime scenes were not being protected in the immediate aftermath of the incursion, and there were reports that security forces were telling community members "that they should immediately clean their houses even if a person had been killed

Deborah A. Thomas

inside by the security forces and the scene had otherwise been undisturbed" (Amnesty International 2011, 24). It was also because fifteen badly decomposed bodies were being processed for burial without full autopsies three days into the state of emergency (Amnesty International 2011). Indeed, by June 15, 2010, at least fifteen postmortem examinations had been conducted without the presence of an independent pathologist, and seven additional bodies were in such an advanced state of decomposition that it would have been impossible to conduct such an exam (*Jamaica Gleaner* 2010c). This had occurred despite the prime minister's successful lobbying for assistance from the United Nations and other multilateral donors in order to deploy four forensic pathologists to Jamaica between June 14 and July 16, 2010. One of these four, Michael Pollanen (chief forensic pathologist for Ontario, Canada), in conjunction with the head of the Legal Medicine Unit in Jamaica's Ministry of National Security, established a protocol that was to guide the postmortem examinations, one that reflected international best practices and United Nations standards.

By June 17, however, Dr. Pollanen complained in a letter to the public defender that the postmortem exams he observed did not adhere to the agreed-upon protocol. In particular, he pointed out that while Dr. Dinesh Rao, then the acting director of the Legal Medicine Unit, was performing an exam in one room, his assistants worked unobserved in an adjacent room; that he couldn't keep accurate notes because exams were taking place too quickly and in more than one location; that by the end of the day, musculocutaneous dissections were not being completed "and the undersurface of the scalp and the brain [were] not examined for injuries"; that bodies were "piled in a heap on the floor of the mortuary" because there were not enough gurneys; and that stretchers used to transport bodies were "dirty and soiled in blood and decomposed tissue" (*Jamaica Gleaner* 2010a). Ultimately, Pollanen argued, "the agreed protocol did not have any significant practical influence on how the post-mortems were performed" (*Jamaica Gleaner* 2010a; see also Witter 2013, 50–52).

At that point, autopsies were suspended. A revised protocol was developed during a subsequent meeting between Dr. Pollanen, Dr. Rao, the public defender, and several senior government officials including representatives of the Jamaica Constabulary Force, the Ministry of Health, and the director of public prosecutions. This revised protocol would come to govern the conduct of all autopsies in Jamaica, "certainly those relating to police/military killings" (Witter 2013, 52). Over the following two months, autopsies were eventually completed in a "make-shift mortuary (a refrigerated metal shipping container)" on everyone whose death was attributable to actions taken during the state of emergency (Witter 2013, 54). Seventy-one autopsy reports were presented as evidence during the West Kingston Commission of Enquiry that had been appointed to investigate the events of May 2010, which began in December 2014.[9]

The conditions under which bodies were stored and autopsies performed raise again the question of what a sovereign death feels like in a postcolonial country with resources that are grossly insufficient to mediate death in an efficient, professional, and dignified manner. The Legal Medicine Unit of the Ministry of National Security has typically employed only two forensic pathologists full time, and these have traditionally been South Asian doctors contracted by the government of Jamaica. In a country with one of the highest per capita murder rates in the world (nearly 1,700 homicides a year in a population of 2.7 million), pathologists have to complete more than a dozen postmortems every day (*Jamaica Gleaner* 2010b), and only 5 percent of murder charges result in convictions (*Jamaica Gleaner* 2017). There is also no public morgue in Jamaica, despite repeated calls for one over the years. As Amnesty International reported, "Bodies awaiting post-mortem in the parishes of Kingston, St. Andrew, St. Thomas and St. Catherine continue to be stored in a private funeral home or in Spanish Town Hospital through special agreements with the state. However, both lack adequate refrigeration space" (2011, 24). Moreover, medical forensic and ballistic services in Jamaica rest under the authority of the minister of national security and the Jamaica Constabulary Force. In other words, there is no structure independent of government to enact investigatory services, services that are critical to the provision of impartially rendered justice. There have long been calls to change this situation. In fact, during the 2008–9 fiscal year, JA$200 million was budgeted toward the construction of a new state-of-the-art morgue, but because of Jamaica's fiscal problems these funds were redirected (*Jamaica Gleaner* 2010b).

Here is where Dr. Michael Pollanen, Canada's chief forensic pathologist, reenters our story. I had traveled to Toronto to interview him about his role as an external consultant and observer during the aftermath of the Tivoli Incursion. I wondered what it felt like to foreign doctors to enter such a chaotic scene, the result of a long history of entanglements with which they were likely not familiar. I was quickly disabused of the idea that this was a novel experience when Dr. Pollanen told me he had served in a similar role in other contexts—Haiti after the earthquake in 2010, Bali after the tsunami, Cambodia, Iraq—during what he called "mass fatality events."[10] Since World War II, but particularly since the 1980s, he explained, medicine and science were increasingly mobilized to support human rights claims, and thus forensic experts have worked in conflict and postconflict scenarios to support both judicial and humanitarian apparatuses. For him, therefore, what they encountered in West Kingston was "a very common scenario," particularly "in a tropical country, where refrigeration might be difficult, [and] bodies will decompose very quickly," but it was "relatively small as far as numbers of victims go." As elsewhere, he stated, the main goals were to treat the bodies with dignity, to establish protocols surrounding the proper collection of physical evidence, and to identify the victims.

Indeed, Dr. Pollanen argued, identification is usually the most critical issue on people's minds. He continued:

> I mean, people want to know what happened. Factually they want to know what happened too—I'm not suggesting that's irrelevant. But in fact, the most important thing usually in the end is identification. And that has been the driver of these two pathways [judicial and humanitarian] I told you about. Because if you take the pure humanitarian pathway . . . there are some missions which do not actually contemplate anything but identification, because the goal is really to provide the family with certain knowledge. I have met many families where they are plagued with doubt about the fate of their child, right? The mothers of the Plaza de Mayo are a good example of that. So from that point of view, the major, but not only, the major humanitarian variable is identification. . . . [We have] to make sure the identifications are scientifically sound, and therefore really have public confidence and the confidence of individual families.

Confidence, for Dr. Pollanen, emerges from doing "the appropriate level of engagement for the family," in order to attempt to mitigate the psychological damage of such a traumatic experience. Indeed, identifying loved ones whose bodies were eventually found in a refrigeration truck or on the street was one of the most difficult processes our interlocutors discussed when we recorded their narratives. And waiting for the autopsies to be conducted, they said, was excruciating. Dr. Pollanen acknowledged these phenomena and argued that engagement with families, in his opinion, occurs most effectively when the forensic scientists share a common cultural and historical frame with the victims. This is why he worked to establish what would become known as the G. Raymond Chang Forensic Pathology Fellowship, which is what he really wanted to talk about, and why he had agreed to our meeting.

"It was immediately apparent to me," Dr. Pollanen remembered, "within a day or two upon arriving in Jamaica, that the infrastructure for forensic pathology in Jamaica was low, in terms of facilities, in terms of human resources, in terms of expertise. Yet, [there was] enormous potential, enormous": "incredibly intelligent doctors, goodwill among the various participants in the criminal justice system, strong institutional partners in the government and in the University of the West Indies. It became immediately apparent to me that we had to set up an institutional collaboration to strengthen and grow and develop forensic pathology in Jamaica, and that's what we've done ever since." As a result of Dr. Pollanen's efforts, graduates from the Medical School at the University of the West Indies can now apply for a one-year clinical postgraduate training program at the University of Toronto's Centre of Forensic Sciences under his supervision. This program has been funded by the G. Raymond Chang family in Jamaica, which gave an initial JA$2 million donation in 2015, and an additional JA$2.25 million after the first two newly certified forensic pathologists returned to Jamaica in order to continue to grow the profession locally (*Jamaica Gleaner* 2017). For Dr. Pollanen, having local doctors respond to the forensic medical aspects of cases within the criminal justice system is exceedingly important: "When you want to develop a profession, a medical profession, the discipline of medicine, you have to develop the infrastructure, and it must be Jamaican. You can't . . . outsource it. It's something so embedded within the justice sector and medical system, you have to have Jamaicans doing it, or people from the Caribbean region, who have lived there and who have been educated there, to develop that as a profession." Because autopsies are "in service of the living" (*Jamaica Gleaner* 2017), he repeated, the forensic pathologists conducting them must be citizens in that community so that they can effectively mobilize science and medicine both to protect human rights and to develop the pathways required for effective juridical establishment of truth claims. The three doctors who have completed the fellowship, all women, are, in his opinion, "pioneers." They "will change the face of forensic medicine in the Caribbean region." Following this line of argumentation, a sovereign death is one that is mediated by doctors who are also compatriots so that their forensic rituals respect local forms of knowledge and expertise, while also building a transnationally recognizable (legal) infrastructure through which to address incidents of state violence.

Deborah A. Thomas

"Give us our dead boys, say residents." So screamed the headline of an article in the *Gleaner* on June 1, 2010. Residents of West Kingston had heard media reports that the bodies of relatives and friends who had been killed during the incursion had been autopsied the day before and therefore were ready for release from the Kingston Public Hospital and Madden's Funeral Home. "'But when we reach,'" one community member told the reporter, "'the people dem at Madden's tell we say the media was wrong and the autopsies would not be held today.'" Instead, they were told to give the officials present a photograph of their loved ones and their telephone numbers, and to wait for a call. Frustrated, this prompted one woman to lash out against the government. "'Me want to see who is going to put on green shirt or orange shirt and follow behind politicians after this,'" she said. "'The politicians dem put guns in the youth dem hands and then dem make police and soldiers kill the youth dem. We done with politics'" (Hall 2010). Here, this woman was referring to the colors of the Jamaica Labour Party (for which Tivoli Gardens has long been a stronghold) and the People's National Party respectively, and to the process of garrisonization over these past four decades.

This woman publicly stated what everyone already "knows," that it is not just community dons but also elected politicians who are responsible for the violent political partisanship and clientelism that has structured postindependence political life in Jamaica, and that garrison communities—those territorially rooted homogenous voting neighborhoods in downtown Kingston where political support has been exchanged for contracts and other social welfare benefits—do not merely mark discrete locales in Kingston, but also operate transnationally due to the ways they mobilize and mediate international trades in drug and arms. Despite two Commissions of Enquiry probing different aspects of the events surrounding the Tivoli Incursion, there was never a full and public airing of this history and its relationship to the political violence that has plagued elections in the country. Scholars like Christopher Charles have worked to demonstrate how party leaders mobilize hard-core political identities strategically, while at the same time denying, as he puts it, "the fact that in garrison communities, competitive electoral advantage is gained and political turf is maintained and old scores are settled through the systematic use of violence" (2004, 56). This remains one important disavowal that is foundational to our postcolonial condition.

The narratives we recorded with community members after the incursion also made legible the affective dispositions that are normative within garrison communities, dispositions that must also be confronted within processes of forensic humanitarianism. These encompass the requirement of submission to a set of dictating norms and forms of violence that include the suspension of critical consciousness, the simultaneous denigration of Blackness and its celebration in popular culture, the violent policing of movement, and the need to appeal to a leader for the provision of basic requirements. Community members did not explicitly articulate these dispositions when they narrated the events of May 2010. Instead, they appeared within the looping senses of temporality and racial reckoning they evoked (Does a policeman forcing young men to dance and sing under conditions of extreme duress know he is evoking memories of the Middle Passage?); through the difficult-to-parse relationship between surveillance and witnessing (Can a US drone corroborate survivors' accounts of violent actions by local police and military?); in relation to the complex chain of multiscalar political entanglements (Is our appreciation of politics one that always accounts for the various overt and covert dimensions of US interest?) and to a sense of trauma that is social rather than individual (Are narrative silences and occlusions evidence of a desire for opacity or a socialized response to danger?); and, finally, through a profound perception of misrecognition (Can non–garrison dwellers apprehend Tivoli Gardens residents as human beings in the fullest sense?).

The parenthetical questions I have listed here expose the kinds of disavowal that continue to actively frame political life in twenty-first-century Jamaica and, by extension, the postcolonial New World. We are loath to consistently recognize the continued legacies of slavery—and therefore racial degradation—as a foundational contradiction of Western liberal democracy; we do not often do enough to illuminate the various ways the US government actively asserts its own interests through economic, political, and military intervention abroad; we want to imagine that trauma is not ongoing and pervasive, an underlying condition to the perpetuation of historical and contemporary forms of sovereign violence; and we allow pessimism to occlude our vision of the ways people make life despite everything. These disavowals create roadblocks for an experience of sovereign death in Jamaica. Dr. Pollanen's fellowship, and his vision for creating a locally rooted team of forensic pathologists who can meaningfully tarry with the dead, is one vision of repair designed to deal with the exigencies of causality and accountability. But are there other forms of mediation that might challenge the ways political life is organized?

Deborah A. Thomas

Eric Klinenberg (2002) has offered a cautionary tale for those convinced of the transparent truth telling of a forensic approach to the body in moments of extreme violence or disaster. In his "social autopsy" of Chicago's 1995 heat wave, he shows how dead bodies became spectacular fetishes for journalists and, ultimately, for those concerned with how and why the over 730 people who died during the heat wave were disproportionately African American, elderly, and poor. Klinenberg argues that the deaths during the heatwave brought to light processes of urban marginality and insecurity, but that the political attention that was paid to the dead bodies refused to bring these issues into clearer public focus. "The bodies served," he writes, "as a double distraction from the sociological issues that the heat wave might have made visible: first, as commodified spectacles . . . ; second, as scientifically defined objects, in the narrowly medical attribution of the deaths" (Klinenberg 2001, 123). In other words, to determine, via autopsy, that the deaths of these bodies were related to the heat wave would be to find the city responsible for the forms of isolation and social inequality that would cause these sorts of death in some areas but not others.

At stake here is the issue of accountability, and as I have been hinting throughout this chapter, there is an important relationship to be parsed between mediation and accountability, especially within a context in which the declaration of states of emergency seems to be proliferating. In 2018 alone in Jamaica, prolonged states of emergency were in effect in the parishes of St. James, St. Catherine, and Kingston. These have compounded the special powers given within "zones of special operation" (ZOSOs, as they are locally termed), a new legislative designation in which extreme police powers are allowed in areas where "there are reasonable grounds to believe that due to rampant criminality, gang warfare, escalating violence and murder and the threat to the rule of law and public order," normal policing is not enough (The Law Reform (Zones of Special Operations) (Special Security and Community Development Measures) Act, Parliament of Jamaica, 2017). The designation as a ZOSO is for an initial sixty-day period, but this can be (and already has been) extended. Moreover, ZOSO designation is meant to entail some sort of focus on social and economic development alongside extraordinary policing. While there have been public discussions within the media about how and why ZOSOs and states of emergency now seem to regularly suspend normal police operation, and while questions have been raised about how the government will transition back from extraordinary powers to normal policing (*Jamaica Gleaner* 2018), there is widespread popular support for these tactics due to exhaustion and fear. Within this conjuncture, is there an equivalent to rural Greek women's laments, the means through which these women used their antiphonic public expressions of pain to create the possibility of juridical redress? What will mediate relationships among death, death-in-life, and life? And how will we recognize it?

Christina Sharpe has called this kind of death-in-life living in the wake. She argues that "while the wake produces Black death and trauma," Black people—"everywhere and anywhere we are"—nevertheless insist on life (Sharpe 2016, 11).[11] Zora Neale Hurston's attention to those ritual practices that are geared toward maintaining a boundary between the world of the living and the world of the dead should tell us, similarly, that there is something important to people about keeping death out of life. This is, in a way, the kind of "wake work" Sharpe (2016) is urging, the enactment of ethical forms of repair, recognition, and remembering. Living in the wake, then, requires accountability, an accountability that moves from forensics toward a public conversation that these various forms of mediation so clearly demand. This is what an empowering and liberatory sovereignty would feel like. It would feel like a dismantling of the disavowals so foundational to modernity, an autopsy of the West as we have come to know it. Do we have the courage to enact this kind of repair?

Notes

1   Of course, here I am referring to the work of Michel Foucault, Giorgio Agamben, and Carl Schmitt, among others.

2   Here, I am thinking particularly of Buck-Morss (2000), Césaire ([1955] 1972), Fischer (2004), Gilroy (2000), Mbembe (2003), and Scott (2007).

3   On death-in-life, see Holland (2000).

4   For more on "family land," see Carnegie (1987), Besson (2002).

5   This creates a different kind of context from the one James Siegel (1998) investigates within Indonesia, in which the local practices for assuaging ghosts lost their salience when the nation-state was made to take precedence over local familial patterns of authority and accountability, and when its power became reckoned through the figure of the "criminal" and its (in)ability to control it.

6   For more on political garrisons, see Gray (1991, 2004), Harriott (2004, 2008), Jaffe (2013), Munroe (1972).

7   Coke was detained and subsequently extradited on June 22, 2010. He stood trial in New York City and was convicted of racketeering and distribution of

Deborah A. Thomas

marijuana and cocaine in June 2012. He is currently serving a twenty-three-year sentence.

8 This exhibit was on display at the University of Pennsylvania Museum of Anthropology and Archaeology from November 2017 to October 2020.

9 The Enquiry presented a juridical forum through which sequences of events, chains of command, and forms of injury could be publicly discussed. The Commission of Enquiry hearings were broadcast on local television (and through online platforms outside Jamaica), and were open to the public, with the exception of only a few witnesses who requested to be questioned privately.

10 All direct quotations from Michael Pollanen come from an interview I conducted with him at his office in Toronto, Canada, on May 3, 2017.

11 See also Alex Weheliye (2014) on the ways Black life always exceeds the conditions of sovereignty that encompass it.

4

Pandemic Déjà Vu

YARIMAR BONILLA

In Puerto Rico, 2020 began with a jolt. January brought the onset of an earthquake swarm that rattled the southern coast, bringing homes and schools to the ground while sending emotional nerves skyward. In just one month, the local seismic network registered over 2,500 seismic events, with over 272 "felt events" of magnitudes between 2.0 and 6.4. Most of the quakes came in the wee hours of the morning. As a result, thousands found themselves sleeping in their cars, in tents, or on park benches, afraid to reenter their homes—that is, if their homes were still standing.

As with Hurricane Maria, the tremors were followed by political corruption scandals, mismanaged emergency aid, and failures within state agencies. Once again, locals were left to their own devices, forced to take recovery and community care into their own hands. While the Department of Education dithered in inspecting quake-damaged schools, parent groups and community associations began organizing homeschooling efforts and setting up donated tents for makeshift outdoor classrooms. While the central government stalled in delivering aid, caravans of citizens created traffic jams bringing emergency supplies to earthquake-impacted neighborhoods.

Eventually citizens became accustomed to the unstable ground. After all, Puerto Ricans are experts in resilience. Hurricane Maria taught us to live without electricity or running water. Then the earthquakes forced us to sleep in our running shoes, with our survival kits by the door. We've become accustomed to perpetual crisis and adept at managing state failure. Maybe because of this, when the COVID-19 outbreak began in March 2020, Puerto Ricans quickly treated it as yet another plot point in our compounding disaster.

Puerto Rico: tres años de historia.
Guía ilustrada.

4.1   Internet meme, "Puerto Rico: three years of
           history. An illustrated guide."

This feeling of layered crisis is perhaps most visible in the popular memes that began to circulate on social media in the wake of the pandemic. One example (see figure 4.1) features a book cover for an imagined illustrated guide to recent Puerto Rican history. It displays three emblematic objects: first, a gas canister like the ones used to fill generators during power outages after Hurricane Maria. Second, a backpack representing the survival kits that residents were exhorted to prepare during the onset of the quakes. And last, a surgical mask, the latest emergency object that residents are obliged to acquire in order to mitigate the latest existential threat.

Like many other forms of crisis and emergency, the COVID-19 pandemic is a socially produced event, driven not by biological forces or natural hazards, but by the deeply rooted social inequalities that shape our experiences of those hazards to begin with. The pandemic is thus also a disaster in the manner often described by anthropologists and other social scientists: a totalizing and disruptive event that reveals long-standing fragilities and creates new possibilities—both economic and political (Bonilla 2020a). Disasters not only destroy and damage; they also reveal. They peel away the blinders of habit and routine and cast new light on what might otherwise remain obscured.

In the wake of Hurricane Maria, some began to see Puerto Rico's colonial relationship to the United States in a new light. Across the States, many discovered that their nation was actually an empire. They felt outrage at the unequal treatment of the colonial citizens they never knew were their political kin. Even within Puerto Rico—where we do not have the privilege of forgetting our imperial ties—the true nature of Puerto Rico's colonial status was laid bare. For decades we had been told that the trade-off for our lack of sovereignty was the protection we received from the most powerful nation in the world. Yet after Maria, weeks turned into months and eventually years without the federal aid we had been gaslighted into believing would come.

The revelation of this political lie began long before Maria or even Trump arrived on our shores. During the Obama administration, the severity of Puerto Rico's debt crisis began to reveal itself, and our colonial status, long obscured by euphemisms and legal sleights of hand, was suddenly and crassly asserted. In lieu of a bailout, the federal government installed a Fiscal Control Board, funded by Puerto Rican taxpayers but accountable only to the federal government (Goldstein 2016). Caught in a political limbo with neither the protections of a state nor the fiscal sovereignty of a nation, we found ourselves unable to define the nature of our debts, the severity of our austerity, or the limits of our endurance.

When President Trump arrived in Puerto Rico, hurling paper towels in lieu of emergency assistance, many in the United States were scandalized. But in Puerto Rico, Trump's spectacle was simply an unvarnished symbol of the state violence that has underpinned our relationship to the United States since our acquisition. His tweets and stunts are but an extension of how Congress has long treated the administering of federal programs as colonial benevolence, rather than as a national responsibility (Bonilla 2018).

Perhaps this long history of imperial disdain and forced resilience prepared us for the pandemic, or at the very least paved the way for our lack of surprise at its mishandling. Long before testing kits were scarce and personal protective equipment was in short supply, Puerto Ricans had learned that they alone were in charge of their well-being. When Jared Kushner

Yarimar Bonilla

stated, in a White House briefing, that pandemic supplies in federal stockpiles were not meant for distribution throughout the fifty states but were, instead, meant for "us," many in the mainland United States wondered what he referred to (Mazza 2020). But in Puerto Rico we had already discovered the rhetorical figure of a federal government with its own set of needs, priorities, and logics that don't necessarily align with the desires of its constituents, much less the needs of the disenfranchised.

Puerto Ricans thus watched the many scandals that shook the nation during the pandemic with an eerie sense of déjà vu. When the USNS *Comfort* spent weeks virtually unused in New York City's harbor, Puerto Ricans immediately thought back to when that very same ship circled empty off our shores, even as local hospitals were overloaded and forced to turn away the sick (Schwirtz 2020). While many in the United States were appalled at the politicization of medical equipment and the ways in which Trump bragged about refusing to help governors who were not "nice" to him, we remembered all too well how he sparred with the mayor of San Juan while residents struggled without electricity, phone service, or running water (Marshall 2020). When mainland citizens were shocked to learn that stockpiled ventilators had gone to waste due to lack of maintenance, Puerto Ricans saw this as yet another instance of spoiled aid discovered in mysterious warehouses, abandoned airstrips, or rotted shipping containers on the vacant lots of party loyalists (Sanger, Kanno-Youngs, and Kulish 2020).

In Puerto Rico, some have speculated that COVID-19 has become the United States' "Maria moment," that is, the point at which residents discover that they live in a "failed state," with gutted infrastructure, inefficient state agencies, and a populace that emerged from the 2008 economic crisis with stark divisions between those who can manage to live through a hurricane, an earthquake, or a pandemic, and those who cannot (Packer 2020).

This might also be the moment in which Americans discover that the future is a canceled promise. Puerto Ricans, and many others across the globe, long ago realized that climate change, neoliberal austerity politics, the dismantling of social safety nets, and unsustainable global capitalism were heralding a troubling future. Long before Maria, young people in Puerto Rico were grappling with bleak prospects for even finding employment, much less for achieving a better standard of living than their parents. It is thus with deep cynicism that we view a headline from the *Wall Street Journal* (2020) lamenting the state of millennial graduates from top universities in the United States who, due to the COVID crisis, are now said to be "walking into a hurricane."

This feeling of déjà vu is not exclusive to Puerto Rico. Within the United States itself, what for some is a sudden crisis for others is simply the extension of an already existing state of insecurity. While some are only beginning to discover a negligent government capable of putting their lives at risk, residents of Flint, Michigan, entered the pandemic on the sixth anniversary of their still-unresolved water crisis. While many wring their hands over government officials who minimize the harm of a deadly virus, AIDS activists recall battling against the negligence of some of the very same politicians who are in charge of managing the current pandemic. As controversy swirls around the nature of a newly revalued state sovereignty in places like California, Indigenous communities wrestle with their decimated ability to manage their own affairs and care for their own communities (Rosenthal, Menking, and Begay 2020; Wilkinson 2019). And while some discover the limits of federalism in times of national emergency, others have long known that the United States is a federated empire structured precisely to ensure an unequal distribution of rights (Cassidy 2020).

The truth is that the pandemic is a disaster in the sociological sense: a sudden catastrophic event but also a revelation of failures, an episode that exacerbates already existing inequalities, and a moment of reckoning. Many across the globe are currently struggling with feelings of collective mourning and grief for the loss of loved ones, for the sacrifice of strangers, for vanished personal goals, projects, and plans for the future. For some this is experienced as a sudden crisis, while for others it forms yet another chapter in a larger narrative arc of shock, trauma, sacrifice, and forced endurance.

However, we must be careful not to romanticize this knowing déjà vu through well-worn platitudes about resilience that reduce the harm of repetitive trauma, the slow wear and tear produced by structural violence, and the risks that come with being deemed essential while being treated as expendable. Indeed, it is partly their overrepresentation as essential workers in industries such as health care, sanitation, and food service that has placed African Americans, Latinos, and other minority groups at greater risk of exposure to COVID-19. And it is their already constituted vulnerability that makes this exposure much more deadly.

In the context of Puerto Rico, the COVID crisis has been depicted in memes and other popular representations as simply the latest season of a long-running drama that has featured hurricanes, earthquakes, mass uprisings against government corruption, and years of austerity measures and colonial governance (see figure 4.2). Yet the way the pandemic is experi-

NETFLIX
presenta:

4.2   Internet meme, "Neflix Presenta: Puerto Rico se Levanta" (Netflix Presents: Puerto Rico Rises).

enced in this space of catastrophic sedimentation might offer some lessons to a world that now collectively faces a post-disaster future.

It is telling that two kinds of protest movements have emerged in the United States in the wake of COVID-19. On the one hand, there are protesters who long for a return to normal and resent how the lockdown has restricted their individual freedoms. On the other hand, there have been the historic uprisings for Black lives as well as demonstrations supporting rent strikes, demanding greater social assistance, and requesting more protective gear for essential workers. Thus, while some remain desperate to uphold exclusive notions of individual liberty, others are fighting for structural change and denouncing how both the risks of the virus and the burdens of the lockdown are unfairly distributed.

While some seek to narrowly circumscribe lockdown politics into false debates over individual versus collective rights, or social versus financial health, others are questioning the very terms of these debates. Across the many communities for whom COVID-19 arrived with the déjà vu of state violence, demonstrators have emphasized how gender violence, poverty, food scarcity, colonialism, racism, and austerity were already threatening community health, long before the arrival of the novel virus.

In fact, the very same day that armed protesters stormed the Michigan capitol with loaded weapons, activists in Puerto Rico carried out a "caravan for life" demanding increased testing, more government accountability, and greater social assistance for those struggling with food insecurity, domestic violence, and police brutality during the lockdown (Bonilla 2020b). Much of this work has been carried out by feminist and LGBTQ activists who have also been using the lockdown as an opportunity to educate residents about the rise of gender and transphobic violence, to denounce predators, and to seek justice for the victims of hate crimes.

These communities are also forging new ways of thinking about state obligation by pushing back on the scripts of coerced resilience that for so long have placed an uneven burden of care on individuals. Rather than simply accepting that they must work to flatten the curve, citizens are also calling on the government to raise the bar and provide an infrastructure and a social safety net that can protect us from future pandemics, disasters, and the crises endemic to pervasive health and wealth disparity.

Months after the onset of the pandemic, Puerto Ricans, like so many others around the globe, were precipitously ushered out of lockdown and implored to get back to the work of producing and consuming, even as rates of COVID-19 continued to climb. This was not because the state had taken the necessary public health measures; in fact, Puerto Rico remained dead last in terms of testing rates across the United States and its territories (Mazzei 2020). Contact tracing had yet to be properly implemented, and even basic statistical modeling and information sharing failed (Martínez Mercado 2020). However, as in other parts of the world, business owners were exerting pressure to get back to business, suggesting that employers were best equipped to ensure the health and safety of their workers—all while Washington debated immunity legislation to protect employers from litigation if they failed to do so (Werner and Hamburger 2020).

While both local and federal governments increasingly shrink from their responsibilities—failing at testing, tracing, and prevention—the burden of care is increasingly placed on individuals who have become the targets of both intervention and blame. However, the political effects of all this coerced resilience should not be underestimated. Hurricane Maria in Puerto Rico was soon followed by historic protests that led to the toppling of the governor who had mismanaged the disaster. Many involved in the

Yarimar Bonilla

protests cited as a motivating factor the awakening they experienced after the government failed to protect its citizens from infrastructural collapse and refused to account for its human toll (Walters 2019). If COVID-19 is indeed the United States' "Maria moment," it remains to be seen how nationwide protests and the collective awakening produced by state failures of care might open up new political possibilities and bring an end to the violent déjà vu.

Note

This chapter was originally published online as "Pandemic Déjà Vu" in *Public Books*, November 7, 2020, https://www.publicbooks.org/pandemic-deja-vu/.

Wading in the Thick

A Sovereign Encounter through Collage

LENIQUECA A. WELCOME

wade
verb
\ ˈwād \
waded; wading
Definition of *wade*

- to step in or through a medium (such as water) offering more resistance than air
- to move or proceed with difficulty or labor
- to set to work or attack with determination or vigor—used with *in* or *into*

thick
adjective
\ ˈthik \
Definition of *thick*

- having or being of relatively great depth or extent from one surface to its opposite
- close-packed with units or individuals
- viscous in consistency
- marked by haze, fog, or mist
- impenetrable to the eye
- extremely intense
- imperfectly articulated
- plainly apparent
- producing inarticulate speech

—*Merriam-Webster's Dictionary*

In the summer of 2016, during my first stint of fieldwork in East Port of Spain, Trinidad, I photographed three Black women who were workers for the Community-Based Environmental Protection and Enhancement Programme—a government sanitation initiative meant to provide low-income intermittent work.[1] The women, sitting under a shed sheltering them from the rain, agreed to share some of their stories with me and posed for the photograph during their stolen break. I mistakenly showed this image a few times in presentations early in my anthropological career. While all three women agreed to be photographed, two diverted their gaze, and the third looked directly at the camera with what I interpret as skepticism. This picture unsettles me, and this is why I previously chose to show it. I thought the dignity exuded through their refusal to fully engage with the lens, even in their relaxed postures, would act as a counternarrative (Campt 2017, 2019).[2] I thought it would be a visual rejection of the pathology, criminality, and deviance ascribed in local discourse to Black people in East Port of Spain and used to disappear the structural and extrajudicial violence performed by the state and police in the region. This image was to be the start of a visual archive that illustrates the history, effects, and affects of the sovereign violence enacted within East Port of Spain, the carcerality of the landscape, and the ways people refuse conscription. Yet, when I realized that I too, even with my best intentions, had captured these women with my camera and locked them in a flat representational frame with limited power to counter the hegemonic anti-Black visual field (Browne 2015), I refused to include this image in my research anymore. This would be the beginning of my exploration of how we could better employ images to bear witness (Thomas 2019) to both the perpetual transnational production of Black death and the battle for liberated Black life without replicating the imperial project of visuality aimed at ordering vision, disciplining bodies, and naturalizing history in service of the constitution of sovereign power (Mirzoeff 2011).[3] This exploration not only changed how, whom, what, when, and why I photograph but also led me to ongoing experimentation with collage as a visual methodology.

Scholars across disciplines have written extensively about the complexity of images and imaging in a world where the dominant gaze is white. They have documented both the long history of the use of visual racializing technology (from the eye to the camera) in the Western modern parsing, ranking, and fixing of a racial schema, with whiteness signifying the pinnacle of civilization, Indigeneity the embodiment of a savage priorness, and Blackness the marker of bestiality, and the countering efforts to see differently (see, e.g., Bruchac 2018; Cole 2016; Browne 2015; Weheliye 2014; Fleetwood 2011; Fanon 2008; Ginsburg 1995; Bal 1992). The "racially saturated field of visibility" (Butler 1993) produced by the hegemonic gaze complicates sousveillance, the production of counterforensic archives of violence, and the critical witnessing of any such archive, as it naturalizes casting Black and Brown people as demonic, aggressive, and threatening.[4] This preempts the public witnessing of state violence against racialized people (Feldman 2015) and the development of public empathy or grief (Butler 2016). Yet the same affective potency of images that makes them key components in the construction and institution of reality and its limits by power regimes also makes them apt apparatuses for projects that seek to challenge these realities in which violence is quotidian practice and to forge a world in which all people feel free.

Visual artists/scholars and social scientists have maintained that images have the potential to spur the development of a "civil contract," where those watching the image acknowledge complicity and forge a relationship with those featured, opening up the possibility for political action (Azoulay 2008; De Leon 2018); that images can be constructed to have texture that invites nonviolent relationships of touch and feeling despite histories of racialization and gendering that tend to impede such (Abel 2014); that imaging practice could be a space for collective healing, particularly Queer Black women's healing (Gary 2018); that images could be used for alternative re-memberings of the past to construct more fugitive archives (Kempadoo 2008); and that even the images meant for state surveillance and abjection contain quiet registers that sound refusal, demanding recognition of the sovereignty of the self in the face of sovereign (in the form of the state) domination (Campt 2017, 2019). In short, the visual sphere is a dangerous battleground (Mirzoeff 2011). Yet, acknowledging that images are affective objects, and that affective objects operating in the everyday at cognitive and visceral levels have the power to politically move people (albeit in different directions) (Thomas 2017, 2019), the productive question at hand is not, Should social scientists use images in their research given the risk?, but instead, How can we engage in the visual sphere in ways that structure more ethical interactions among producer, those reflected in an image, and audience? How might we use images to foster embodied encounters where we begin to understand our responsibility for one another, rather than simply laying subjects bare for another's quick gaze? In this vein, I offer collaging as a thick visual method rooted in an ethics of

Leniqueca A. Welcome

care and mutual sovereign being rather than one of representation, know-ability, and surveillance.

The use of the term *thick* as a methodological descriptor in the context of anthropology may immediately trigger an association with Clifford Geertz. In "Thick Description: Toward an Interpretive Theory of Culture" (in Geertz [1973] 2017) he asserted a need for thick description in anthropology, whereby the anthropologist would act as the authoritative symbolic interpreter and translator to provide a deep definitive account that unmasks one culture (generally non-Western) to another (generally Western). His was a thickness aimed at legibility. However, ironically, my visual method is more closely aligned with the ethos of John Jackson's (2013) thin description than that of Geertz's thick one. Much like Jackson's "thin description," or "flat ethnography" as he calls it, I seek to "slice into a world from different perspectives, scales, registers, and angles" (17), and collate these slices without providing a strict analytical roadmap of how to mine a complete comprehensive understanding of the world presented. I do this precisely because the aim is to invite the audience to read, feel, reflect, and recognize the effects of histories of criminalization and violence against Black people and their position in these histories rather than capture and represent subjects for another's gaze. Thus, rather than *thick* indexing an "ambition for full social knowing" (Jackson 2013, 13) the thick that qualifies my visual method is a spatiotemporal reference that gestures to my desire for these collages to forge an obtuse space that encourages slow, difficult encounter. *Thick* here is in the spirit of Édouard Glissant's (1997) concept of opacity. Similar to the way Sara Marcus (2019) conceptualizes Charles W. Chesnutt's 1901 novel *The Marrow of Tradition*, each collage aims to be a space of suspension like the hold of the slave ship, as theorized by Christina Sharpe (2016) and Hortense Spillers (1987), where linear time is at once inhabited, layered, and ruptured. Or perhaps more accurately, each collage is meant to be akin to a shoal as conceptualized by Tiffany Lethabo King (2019)—a liminal place that slows momentum, disrupts the normative, and offers time and space to reassemble the self on different terms.

The four collages I present below stand as a collection titled -scape.[5] Each collage contains elements of disparate still images produced within East Port of Spain and its environs during the period 2016–20 and archival images. The visual materials are juxtaposed together in what John Akomfrah (2018) terms "affective proximity."[6] My method involves intimate manipulation of the photographs such that my hand is unapologetically present in the final product, abdicating the role of objective documentarian. For each collage, I extract, transpose, hyperbolize, obscure, and layer fragments from several photographs to construct singular scenes that exceed the sum of their parts. While each raw image holds moments that easily pass unregistered in the constant movement of time, in the collage form, individual moments are suspended together in time to form a thick space the viewer must wade through to make any sense of it.[7] It is the suspension of time and the thickening of space that slows the audience down, allowing for productive dissolution of dominating realities, disagreement, dissent, the birth of new solidarities, and the crafting of alternate futures (King 2019; Marcus 2019). Each collage is paired with an ethnographic vignette from my research in East Port of Spain. The vignettes are not meant to be explanatory but instead are imagistic textual fragments that work in tandem with each collage, contributing to its thickness.[8] Through an encounter with the collages and the vignettes, I hope that audiences may register the breadth of structural forces and the range of feelings endured by the beings they are quick to dismiss and may develop the potential to feel, not for these people but in relation with them. These encounters fostered through a practice of collage are meant to contribute to the ongoing project of crafting a world of mutual sovereign being. This is a time and space where one is both a full self and selfless—where sovereignty feels like freedom to be as one chooses while refusing harm to another so they too may always be free.

Some of the signs within the collages will inevitably be broadly familiar as they fall within a globally circulating visual language that calls audiences to witness both the processes that seek to extinguish Black life and the refusal of these same processes. Some signs may resonate specifically with those deeply familiar with Trinidad's sociopolitical context, others only with people particularly intimate with the landscape of East Port of Spain. Some aspects of the collage are meant to be read cognitively, others only to be felt. These scenes are constructed in a way to encourage different levels and modes of engagement, but most importantly their thickness is meant to give pause through the ambiguity of what they present. These scenes invite endless revisiting and remapping and reassure those who encounter them only that they will never be sure of a comprehensive narrative. It is my hope that people will embrace the thick, wade through it, feel, listen, watch, think; that they will be unsettled and transformed by what inhibits them from easily moving on.

Leniqueca A. Welcome

Leniqueca A. Welcome, *-scape₁: Over-exposed*.

-scape₁: Over-exposed

"Our jury's first introduction to the case was through the prosecution. She opened by saying, 'It was a Diwali day. Diwali is a celebration of light over darkness. And on this Diwali day, it was a tragic ending for, for this family. Because here was the deceased sitting and playing All Fours [a card game] with his family and then he was shot and killed, basically.'"[9] It is a few months after Michelle finished serving on a jury for a case where a police officer was prosecuted for the fatal shooting of a young man from East Port of Spain, Trinidad. She heard about my research from a mutual friend and wanted to share her story because she still felt rattled by her experience as a juror. Michelle continues:

> At no point at all did we get a whole picture of what happened that night [of the police shooting]. You know, every day in court little bits of the story would be revealed to us, and we had to piece it together. The stories were so different [between the eyewitnesses called by the prosecutor and the police officers called to testify for the defense] that we had to determine what was the truth or what was the closest to the truth. And—I would say that the majority of us gave the benefit of the doubt to the police

even though there were discrepancies in both sides of the story. The people from East Port of Spain's discrepancies were put down to being because they were lying. And the police's discrepancies were put down to being because he made a mistake, you know, because of the adrenaline and the, you know, the kind of heatedness of the whole encounter.

Her labored breath as she speaks reveals her struggle with this admission. She continues:

Yeah, but I just—I felt like the East Port of Spain witnesses' errors in their statements had to do with an inability to average distances or a lack of understanding of particular questions. Whereas I felt like the errors in the police statements were calculated errors, you know, to—to pitch the story toward self-defense. So, it affected me, like psychologically, like, you know, I felt like mentally exhausted at the end of each day. And I had a very strong thought in my head that, you know, it's an embarrassment that this is the height of our justice system, you know, because it seemed pretty obvious to me what had happened, but we were relying on a kind of intellectual masturbation to kind of relieve someone out [of] their responsibility to the public in a sense. Like, like, I think that the cop shot the kid. Whether or not he intended to shoot him, he, I think he—he shot a man, the guy died, and I feel like a cop has a responsibility to the public. You know what I mean. At the end of the trial when we read the "no verdict," the defense looked very agitated to me. So I had the assumption after that, that the defense thought it was an easy win case for them because we were all kind of red-skinned Westy people [markers associated with affluence in Trinidad] who would—who came with our prejudices, you know. And I felt the general vibe was that there were prejudices. Did I tell you about the one juror who said that you're entitled to use "self-defense" in those areas?

She sees the frustrated look on my face. "Yeah—yeah," she responds emphasizing that someone did indeed make that statement. "I think if I wasn't there, it would have been 'not guilty.' Easy, easy, easy, easy peasy. And I think maybe the next jury [when the case is retried] will just say 'not guilty.' It's terrible. It's terrible. Yeah, boy, I don't want to do that [serve on a jury for a murder case] again." She takes a long pause. "You know, I felt like a failure at one point for not having had a verdict, but now I think it's probably the best outcome. I don't know if the police should be sentenced to life in prison for killing this kid either. I think, like, our police need a little more training to not be so aggressive—but maybe they have to be, you know. It's a kind of a take-no-prisoners mentality. But—yeah—I just . . ." Michelle's voice fades off as she too begins to contemplate whether the police are entitled to self-defense in "those areas."

-scape₂: Out of Order

It is 11 a.m. on October 19, 2018. I am sitting in a football (soccer) stadium in Arima, Trinidad, with approximately one hundred young Black boys, two US soccer envoys, representatives from the US embassy, and the founders of the Can Bou Play Foundation (a local sports outreach program). The sky is overburdened by clouds that carry the rains that will eventually contribute to massive flooding of the eastern half of Trinidad. The organizers understand they must proceed to the field with haste if the boys are to have their chance to play against the visiting professional players in a sports tournament organized by the US embassy and Can Bou Play (this is part of both organizations' anticrime initiatives). Yet the diplomatic speeches and photo-ops take precedence. The chargé d'affaires at the US embassy in Trinidad and Tobago addresses the boys of the MiLAT Programme first.[10] Distracted by the anticipation I share with the boys for the football games to start, I only catch bits of his address:

> We are your dedicated partners in the fight against crime, economic insecurity, and violence. . . . When you are ready, you should consider applying to college in the US. Our colleges want diversity, and you have an advantage because you already speak good English. . . . I like how you all respond, "Yes Sir!" I grew up in a West Point household and that "Yes Sir!" was a staple. . . . You guys are doing a great job. . . . When you get your phones back, let's rock. Follow us on Instagram @USinTT. . . . I'm not going to drop the mic. That would be a little bit too much. . . . You're doing great! Thank you for being here.

The speech finally comes to an end just as the rains begin. Realizing the speeches would most likely be the main attraction of the day with the field quickly becoming waterlogged, I settle in with the rest of the audience to listen to the other speakers on the agenda.

One of the founders of Can Bou Play steps up to the microphone after a brief introduction by the master of ceremonies that smugly reminds the US contingent that he scored the final header in the ninety-fourth minute in a

Inter1.2   Leniqueca A. Welcome, *-scape₂: Out of Order*.

game against Mexico, which prevented the US football team from qualifying for the 2018 World Cup. Though filled with pride at this small conquest of the United States on the football field, today the cofounder of Can Bou Play is working with the United States as an ally to alter the future of the boys gathered, in whom he sees himself. His speech begins:

> We [the members of Can Bou Play] come from a lot of different backgrounds. And we realized that we are role models within our community, and we didn't used to see anybody going back and giving back to their community. And we realize as role models, as current football players, we do still have an impact, and we wanted to take our experiences, our

know-how, our contacts, and bring them together and have a positive impact in the negative environment of Trinidad right now. You hearing a lot of violence, a lot of chaos going on, and we wanted some kind of positive change, and that's kind of one of the reasons we started the program. Since we started, we've been all over the country sharing our knowledge, mentoring, educating children just like yourselves who are not quite sure where they want to go—who are on the crossroads of one decision going, you know, the wrong direction or one decision going in the right direction. And we think that if you see people who come from the same environment as you coming and shedding a little light on where we come from, that you might make that right decision and go in the right direction. We all didn't come up with a silver spoon or gold spoon in our mouths. We all had to go through difficult times. We have all had to sacrifice, and you all will have to sacrifice things that you love, friends, family, time with them, in order to reach whatever goal that you want to reach. And I can say for this week, it's been a pleasure and an honor to partner with the US embassy with this sports diplomacy project because we have the opportunity to touch almost five hundred other lives within Trinidad and Tobago.

The crowd erupts in applause. There is more talking, more press pictures commemorating the event, and more downpours. The boys, however, never get to play their football games. Eventually they are bussed back to the residence quarters of the MiLAT Programme they are forced to call their temporary home.

-scape$_3$: To a Fallen Soldier

"I am sorry for your loss." I intend the words to fill the space between us, but the moment they escape my lips, a gentle breeze carries them away, over the sea. I immediately wish it had been someone else who assumed they could weave comfort from such a passive invocation—loss. Kareem's friend Akanni "Dole" Adams was not cast adrift in the darkness; he was shot a few weeks earlier by members of the Special Operations Response Team (SORT, an elite unit of the Trinidad and Tobago Police Service) because of his suspected status as a gang leader and alleged involvement in numerous crimes.

Kareem's eyes meet mine. "Do you want to see where it happened?" I nod my head in response to his question, and he leads me down the pier into a dark fisherman's locker. Standing in the locker, Kareem recounts the

Inter1.3 Leniqueca A. Welcome, *-scape₃: To a Fallen Soldier.*

day of his friend's murder. "I was working right over there." He points in the direction of a shed only a few feet away, then continues:

> My wife who was nearby call me on the phone and say, "You hear them gunshots?" She say it sounding real close, but when you live in these areas you have to be mindful of drive-by and thing. But I hear more gunshots an' I say, "Nah, something definitely wrong," I run out and I see people running, bawling, holding their belly. When I reach here [outside the locker where Dole was executed by the police], I could not even cry, I could not bawl, nothing. I was just frozen like I in shock or something. I see men lie down with gun over them.

Kareem later found out that Dole was sitting on a bench outside the fishermen's locker when members of SORT arrived and dragged him into the locker and shot him.

"Look, all the evidence is here," Kareem says as he turns on his cell phone's flashlight. He illuminates the bullet holes and bloodstains that corroborate his version of his friend's death, a version that differs radically from the police's story. The forensic tags next to two of the bullet holes catch my attention.

"How are there forensic tags *here*, yet the newspapers initially reported that Dole was killed during a shoot-out with the police at his home?" I ask naively.

Leniqueca A. Welcome

Leniqueca A. Welcome, *-scape₄: I've Got Life.*

Kareem makes a bitter sound, then quietly utters, "Does anyone care? All that matters is what the police say happened."

-scape₄: I've Got Life

It takes us five hours to arrive at Icacos, the southernmost point of the is-land of Trinidad: two hours in the hot yard waiting for the serially late or-ganizer of the day's activities and three hours on the cramped bus blasting decade-old dancehall hits, an irritation to the eleven teenagers from East Port of Spain present. Five hours, and here it is: a barren beach, cruel sun, and swarms of mosquitoes—a mundane landscape that mocks the long journey. But against a backdrop unworthy of them, Shay, Kai, and Brian mark their positions in the sand.

"Miss, we ready." I look up from adjusting the camera settings and I am silenced by the elegant lines of their bodies as their limbs cut through the thick humid air; their skin, decorated with glass beads stolen from the sea and specks of gold gifted by the sun; the lightness of their giggles that chase the sound of the waves.

"Miss, hurry up!"

Receive their offering before it is rescinded—witness this moment when their bodies are no longer tethered to the ground but not yet in full flight.

I press the shutter release. Knowing the image now exists in the world, they relax their forms. We engage in this ritual several more times; they dance on the beach, and they invite me to document it. As they glide, jump, and pose, they shed assumptions of their criminality, surveillance of their Blackness, and policing of their being. In true bliss, we craft an archive of their precious lives. How did we come to be on this beach? It all began with a project to combat more virulent images—archives that produce criminal life and ungrievable death. That day on the beach was the final session of a six-week photography and art camp for teenagers from East Port of Spain. We set out to make our own counterarchives to the mainstream construction of their selves and their community. Each session, through things said and unsaid, I was painfully reminded of the violence that haunts these children and the herculean task of making a world where their lives are understood as precious rather than criminal. *When will we have the world of which we dream?* As they danced and posed freely on the beach in front of me, I smiled at the realization that this world is both a time to come and a time already here.

Notes

Epigraph: Merriam-Webster, s.v. "wade (v.)," accessed February 13, 2021, https://www.merriam-webster.com/dictionary/wades; *Merriam-Webster*, s.v. "thick (a.)," accessed February 13, 2021, https://www.merriam-webster.com/dictionary/thick.

1 "East Port of Spain" refers to a dynamic geographic region within Trinidad consisting of several intrarelated mixed-income communities. Despite the rich cultural production, liberation movements, and prominent national figures that have emerged from the region, the area is heavily criminalized by the state, media, and bourgeois Trinidadian publics. This criminalization has only been further exacerbated by an increase in murder rates in the area since the early 2000s.

2 Tina Campt (2019) defines refusal as "a generative and capacious rubric for theorizing everyday practices of struggle often obscured by an emphasis on collective acts of resistance."

3 Here I refer to the type of embodied witnessing Deborah A. Thomas (2019) conceptualizes as Witnessing 2.0, which is a destabilizing practice of affective (rather than juridical) recognition of complicity, accountability, and love that may ultimately bring about transformational internal shifts.

4 Whereas *surveillance* typically refers to an omnipotent monitoring for social control of the masses, *sousveillance* is a term popularized by Steve Mann

(2004) to refer to a "hierarchal reversal" where ordinary citizens surveil the powerful as an act of resistance.

5   Though reproduced here at small scale for methodological discussion, the collages are meant to be displayed together as mounted canvas prints, each approximately 24 × 36 inches.

6   John Akomfrah coined the term "affective proximity" to describe his process for his experimental montage films. In Akomfrah's work, discordant elements are brought together and overlapped to create new meanings, allow multiple narratives to emerge, and allow for the possibility of migration from the moment one is in. His method has been highly influential to other Black filmmakers such as Arthur Jafa and Ja'Tovia Gary, whom I hope my own visual production will be in conversation with.

7   My use of *sense* here is deliberate. It is meant to emphasize my desire to cultivate a space for, and practice of, felt understanding rather than visual legibility.

8   Drawing on the work of theorists such as Roland Barthes and Walter Benjamin, Lisa Stevenson offers a more capacious definition of *image* such that the image is "that which express[es] without formulating . . . that which resists explanation" (2014, 12, 14). Stevenson thus puts forward the idea that image can be ethnographic method and writing can be imagistic, that is, open and unresolved, with an opacity that holds us.

9   These quotes are taken from an interview between the author and Michelle (pseudonym) in 2019.

10   The MiLAT Programme is a two-year, full-time residential mentorship program under the auspices of the Trinidad and Tobago Ministry of National Security. It is designed for "at-risk" young men between the ages of sixteen and twenty years.

PART II

Breaking/
Making

5

Affective Sovereignties
Mobility, Emplacement, Potentiality

PURNIMA MANKEKAR AND AKHIL GUPTA

Sangita had worked in a call center for the past five years, and, even though she was in her twenties, she was deemed a veteran because she had risen through the ranks. Hired shortly after she had completed her Pre–University Course diploma, she had been promoted to team leader, then to supervisor, and, when we met her in May 2009, was in line for promotion to the HR (Human Resources) section in her company.[1] Like those of other call center agents, her shifts were based on the time in the locations of the company's clients (for instance, processes catering to US clients were often scheduled in three shifts: 6:30 p.m.–3:30 a.m., which was the most desirable shift; 9:30 p.m.–6:30 a.m.; and the graveyard shift, 12:30 a.m. to 9:30 a.m.). Her relentless schedule left her with no time to follow her dream of going to college; sometimes, she said, she felt stuck in this job. Yet she derived great satisfaction from the fact that she was now able to support her entire family. Her father could retire from his job as a security guard in a garment factory, and her younger brother could finish his education and go to college, even if she could not.

Over the years, she had developed a host of health problems. There were months when she never got her period, and she also suffered from chronic back pain. She was deeply religious and regretted that she was seldom able to participate in the rituals her family followed or to enjoy other celebrations. She believed that this was a high price to pay, but, at the same time, she was aware that her work enabled upward class mobility, not just for herself but for her entire family—and as for many other agents we worked with, this mattered to her very much and was, in fact, one of the main reasons why she had sought a job in a call center. More significantly, she felt that she was now able to be a part of what she called a larger world, which was enchanting and frightening all at once. She said, "Now I don't just watch the world go by. I am a part of it. This is a new world. A scary world. And I don't know what lies ahead. But I am now a part of it."

Sangita exemplifies the complex forms of affective sovereignty that we witnessed in the lives and worlds of call center and customer service agents working in Business Process Outsourcing (BPO) firms in Bengaluru (formerly Bangalore). Experiencing both upward class mobility and a feeling that her dreams of going to college had been dashed, unable to participate in the everyday life of her family while at the same time feeling deeply obligated to their welfare, excited about her rise up the corporate ladder yet fascinated by (and terrified of) the new world that she was learning to navigate, Sangita confounds stereotypical representations of BPO agents as either neoliberal "cyber coolies" indentured to high-tech capital or empowered harbingers of a New India well on its way to taking its place in the sun on the global stage. What does affective sovereignty feel like to young people like Sangita?

We argue that in the world of call centers, affective sovereignty is deeply imbricated with the capacity for movement and mobility. However, for many marginalized individuals and communities, mobility is conjoined with emplacement. Rethinking sovereignty through affect entails theorizing how navigating the world not only implies mobility but equally involves processes of emplacement. Emplacement can entail feeling stuck. But emplacement can also mean feeling like one has a place in a rapidly changing world: hence, emplacement and mobility are neither dichotomous nor oppositional.

The informatization of the transnational service economy has generated the BPO industry, of which call centers are an important component (Aneesh 2015; Gupta and Sharma 2006; Mankekar 2015; Mankekar and Gupta 2016; Mirchandani 2012; Nadeem 2013). Jobs in BPOs demand mobility, fungibility, and highly flexible skills, and are contingent on the exchange of knowledge, information, and affect. Contact—whether physical or virtual—is central to the circulation of information and affect in this industry, with profound implications for the production of sociality and intimacy (Mankekar and Gupta 2016, 2017, 2019). Blurring the line between labor and leisure, affective labor entails new forms of imagination and aspiration for those working in what has been considered a "sunrise industry" in India.[2] These new forms of imagination and aspiration are inflected by our interlocutors' acute feeling of vulnerability stemming from being emplaced in a global service industry stratified by race, gender, and national location.[3]

Our fieldwork extended from 2009 to 2016, and conducting long-term ethnographic research enabled us to avoid synchronic snapshots of both workers and an industry that was rapidly shifting before our eyes. We sought to track how agents' conceptions of futurity were shaped by their affective labor over a stretch of time in which aspirations were sometimes fulfilled, and at other times dashed, over the course of their work cycle. And yet our intention was not to reduce the agents' lifeworlds to either their work cycle or the temporalities of labor and capital, but to explore the impact of multiple, often disjunctive, temporalities generated through the intersection of class, social obligations, religious affiliation, and discourses of national identity, gender, race, and sexuality.

In this chapter, we focus on how mobility and emplacement are coimbricated with ontologies of affective labor to produce specific kinds of affective sovereignties. Our interlocutors' ability to move across different borders— national, class, cultural, and experiential—formed the very basis of their affective labor. Caren Kaplan points to the freighted salience of the trope of mobility in contexts shaped by information technology and the digitalization of labor: as she puts it, "the rhetoric of cyberspace and information technologies relies heavily on the hyperbole of unlimited power through disembodied travel" (2003, 210). Kaplan insists that in contexts of high-tech capitalism, the self is not "released" from national (and other) locations but very much emplaced within them. Hence, the inability to be mobile along with processes of emplacement are equally fundamental to the labor and lives of BPO agents. We seek to untangle BPO agents' myriad itineraries of mobility: physical, as they make their way to and from work through a city that is winding down or asleep; virtual, as they engage clients in overseas locations; temporal, as they travel across different time zones to provide service to these clients; and social, as they struggle to inch their way up a slippery slope of class mobility.

The itineraries of mobility of BPO agents are refracted by processes of emplacement in spaces that are at once regulatory and generative: the cabs that transport them across an ambivalent, frequently hostile, city are simultaneously spaces of sociality and surveillance; even as they engage in virtual travel through their provision of services to clients all over the world, their movements within their workplaces are multiply monitored; and their precarious mobility up class hierarchies is regulated through affectively charged discourses of gender, sexuality, and community. As we will learn shortly, in some contexts, emplacement also entails being positioned in webs of relationality and affect. It is this looping back of emplacement and mobility that we wish to unpack.

Agents' affective sovereignties were shaped—shaded—by potentiality. We draw primarily on Agamben's complex discussion of potentiality, which shifts across his work. In *Homo Sacer* (Agamben 1998), potentiality is paradigmatic of sovereignty; to be precise, potentiality is actuated by the power of the sovereign to take a life. In this chapter, we do not concern ourselves with sovereignty that comes into being through states of exception. Instead, we turn to Agamben's (1999) essay *On Potentiality* to track agents' affective ability to navigate the unfamiliar and daunting worlds in which they found themselves.[4] The vulnerability of BPO agents—the ever-present specter of slipping down the ladder of upward mobility through losing their jobs, the slow accumulation of health problems the longer they work in this industry, their sense of being disconnected from daytime sociality—is precisely what throws their potentiality into relief. Agamben (1999, 177–78) argues that potentiality inheres in the "presence of the absence" of the capacity to act, that is, when subjects are faced with privation. Hence, potentiality exists in two modalities: the ability to act as well as not to act, or what he terms *impotentiality*. He adds, "To be potential means: To be one's own lack, to be in relation to one's own incapacity" (Agamben 1999, 182). Potentiality and impotentiality are, therefore, inextricable.

We thus conceptualize potentiality as subjects' ability to say "I could" rather than "I will"—the sense of agential capacity that shapes what affective sovereignty feels like. At the level of subject production, then, potentiality may be conceptualized in terms of affect, our ability to affect and be affected. As we have argued above, in the worlds of BPO agents, affect indexes a capacity for moving through and being emplaced in worlds that are frequently not of their making. Affect offers us a way to think of agential capacity in terms of potentiality, neither trapped in the sterile binary of domination versus resistance, nor understood as rational or instrumental action.

Given the rhythms of their labor, agents inhabited zones of temporal collisions and dislocations: their sense of sovereignty was refracted by a sense of time unhinged, a sense of time so fragmented as to seem dismembered. In what follows, we intersperse our analysis of these multiple, colliding temporalities with ethnographic vignettes to enact and evoke what temporal fragmentations and dismemberments felt like to our interlocutors and to us as ethnographers: we foreground how, like the dislocated temporalities that generate them, these affective sovereignties are unstable, fragmented, and profoundly contingent—a far cry from the sovereign subject enshrined by liberalism or the ensnared (or ostensibly self-caring) subject of neoliberalism.

Mankekar and Gupta

Delta Tech Park was built at the outskirts of Bengaluru in a peri-urban neigh-borhood called Green Meadows. We heard from several long-term residents that Green Meadows used to be a quiet outpost of the city: there were a few churches that served the Anglo-Indian community, a large mosque, a couple of small temples, and a warren of streets filled with small stores selling goods ranging from produce to furniture. For the most part, Green Meadows used to have a bucolic air: paddy fields lined the large lake that was the lifeline of the villages that surrounded it; cobras roamed the coconut groves that dotted the landscape while monkeys and parakeets screeched insults at each other. At the center of town was a midsized kalyana mandapa, a wedding hall where well-heeled Hindus celebrated the weddings of their children.

It is tempting to claim that once the IT industry arrived in Green Mead-ows, everything changed. It is true that the cost of land shot through the roof, with politicians and developers "persuading" villagers to sell their lands in order to build large tech parks, malls, and gated housing communities. Streets intended for modest traffic became perpetually, permanently, ensnarled in traffic. The city of Bengaluru, octopus-like, started to encircle Green Mead-ows. But it would be a mistake to assume that the IT industry took over life in Green Meadows. The spatiotemporalities of high-tech capital have had to coexist, and often collide, with those of religion, ritual, and kinship.

Other forms of life have reemerged.

These past few years, several temples have been built along the main street of Green Meadows, indicating both the irrepressibility of faith and the suc-cess of Hindu nationalist grassroots organizing. The big mosque on the edge of town has been repainted; it has acquired a larger, more powerful public address system, and groups of the faithful congregate regularly. And there are now no less than three kalyana mandapas in Green Meadows: wedding cer-emonies sometimes last several days, accompanied by music pouring out into the streets from loudspeakers hung on walls that attempt, entirely in vain, to contain the sounds of celebration, the aroma of feasts, and the flow of guests. These kalyana mandapas are a source of tremendous frustration to those who work in Delta Tech, especially those who have to commute in cabs that drive recklessly across town to get them to work, only to be stalled by the traffic and the swell of wedding guests outside their gates. In an industry where being unpunctual is likely to lead to the loss of a job or, worse, a contract, getting to work on time has become ever more uncertain.

The lake, so long the pride of Green Meadows, foams and froths at the mouth, much like a rabid dog: mysterious, enormous clouds of foam rise periodically from its surface to float onto the streets surrounding the tech parks, creating ever-larger traffic jams and making it still harder to get to work on time (Rao 2017). And, as if to reclaim their home, cobras have found their way into the manicured lawns of Delta Tech Park and the gated communities that are home to the CEOs and expatriate managers of the companies in Green Meadows.

If the mobility of capital and labor underscores the coimbrication of spatiality and temporality in the labor regimes and social relations of BPO employees, the stretching out of space is evident in the very name, Business Process Outsourcing, which indexes the range of long-distance services provided by Indian companies to corporations in countries like the United States, UK, and Australia. The labor regimes of the BPO industry also entail a stretching out and, simultaneously, an unhinging of temporality. As we argue later in this chapter, this resulted in a sense of time being "out of joint" (from Shakespeare; Deleuze 1995; Derrida 2006) for many of our interlocutors, which, in turn, enabled complex and contradictory forms of affective sovereignty.

What did working in BPOs mean to agents? We would typically begin our interviews with new subjects by asking why they sought jobs in BPOs. Invariably, in addition to mentioning that their high salaries far exceeded what their parents had ever earned or could even imagine earning, agents like Sangita, whom you met at the beginning of this chapter, would tell us that working in a BPO enabled them to feel they were part of an exciting new world. Many agents came from low-income families that had long been marginalized along axes of caste, class, and religion: we cannot underestimate the affective and psychic potency of the feeling that they (finally) belonged in this new world. Equally important was the fact that, in this sector of the economy, there were relatively few glass ceilings. If agents worked hard and exceeded the quotas given to them, they could aspire to rapid promotions and sometimes achieve them. Given the social positions of most of their families, the very capacity to aspire was intoxicating for many. But perhaps most significant was that BPO agents worked in environments that were less hierarchical than the workplaces of their parents and other family members because their firms had a relatively flat organizational structure. Agents, team leaders, and top management ate at the same company café: once again, the affective potency of this for some of our "lower-caste" interlocutors who, until now, had been prohibited by rules of commensality to eat alongside "higher-caste" people, cannot be underestimated. Apart from senior HR personnel, they all worked in cubicles in an open-office system. Most radical of all, while their parents and other family members addressed their bosses as "sir" or "madam," these young people called their supervisors and managers by their first names: formal equality, for so many who came from communities at the margins of caste, class, and religion, felt within reach.

Subject as they were to the vicissitudes of global capitalism, these jobs were by no means secure and may well be regarded as precarious. However, if precarity is, in the words of Anne Allison (2013), symptomatic of the evisceration of hope, our interlocutors had by no means lost hope in their futures.[5] On the contrary, despite the fact that many of them were chronically anxious about what the future might hold, they remained hopeful that they would not simply survive but would continue to ascend the ladder of upward class mobility, tugging their family members along with them. Indeed, in a national context marked by "jobless growth," where an increasing number of urban youth were either unemployed or underemployed and where rural youth faced increasing immiserization, our interlocuters felt they were lucky to have these jobs: it is difficult, therefore, to posit that they were subjects of a cruel optimism (Berlant 2011a; cf. Chua 2014).

Sovereignty and autonomy tend to be conflated in liberal discourses of individual sovereignty, but the affective sovereignties we witnessed among agents push against these conceptions of the autonomous subject. Equally, they defy monolithic and totalizing conceptions of neoliberalism whereby possessive individualism or the care of the self may have overridden or subsumed duty to family and community. In fact, agents' salaries and emoluments (many companies offered health insurance for parents and younger siblings, paid annual leave, paid medical and family leave, and other such perks) benefited entire families, and, for many, this was the primary motivation for taking up these jobs and remaining in them. Indeed, for these young men and women, affective sovereignty involved an ethical framing of their sense of being in the world, a feeling of being located and, hence, being emplaced in a fast-changing landscape.

This ethical framing emerged from their sense of duty to their families and loved ones. Contrary to ideas of autonomy or choice that undergird liberal notions of individual sovereignty, the affective sovereignty of our interlocutors emerged from a commitment to relationality, from being tied to them in deep and enduring ways through a sense of duty.[6] Some workers lived with their families; many others had left them to move to a city hundreds, if not thousands, of miles away: they rarely saw them either because of physical distance or because the temporality of their labor collided with the rhythms of family life, festivals, celebrations, and religious rituals. But whether or not agents lived in the same home as their family, and regardless of the fact that most of them rarely saw their family, agents felt deeply tied to their families and had a strong sense of duty and obligation toward them. Even agents who were estranged from their family continued to remit money home, and we came across several instances of agents who rushed home if a family member fell ill or died: in fact, a common reason for agents to quit their job was when a company failed to give them leave to visit a sick family member or attend a funeral or wedding. We do not romanticize or idealize our interlocutors' sense of duty or obligation to their families. For one, the discourse of duty often ran counter to, and constrained, agents' own desires for personal growth and professional success. Furthermore, this sense of duty could be oppressive and make workers feel overwhelmed from being pulled in too many directions (Mankekar and Gupta 2019). Nevertheless, it gave them an ethical framework that served as a map that they could turn to as they navigated landscapes that were at once familiar and unfamiliar, enticing and terrifying.

The growth of BPOs in India provides us with the opportunity to examine the coimplication of mobility and sovereignty on multiple registers. Globalization and transnationality are often assumed to bring national sovereignty to crisis. In both India and the United States, the outsourcing of labor has shaped discourses of national sovereignty in powerful ways. For instance, the Indian state has participated directly in the growth of the BPO industry by offering tax breaks to multinational companies to set up BPOs, and by establishing industrial parks and Special Economic Zones, or SEZs (Gupta and Sharma 2006). These state policies drew on the belief that national sovereignty depends on the growth of the economy: the assumption is that a strong economy will result in a modern, developed, and therefore sovereign nation.

The discursive conjunction of the growth of BPOs with discourses of national sovereignty was not restricted to government officials and politicians. When we began our fieldwork in Bengaluru in January 2009, the US economy was in the doldrums, and the contrast between the economic landscape we had left behind and the one that we were entering could not have been greater. Unlike the shuttered storefronts and desolate malls in California, stores, restaurants, and shopping arcades in Bengaluru were humming with activity: middle-class consumers were investing in homes and home furnishings; and retail and restaurant industries were booming. There was a sense of tremendous optimism in the air. In 2009, the government then in power was loudly proclaiming that India had "arrived."

Nor was this sense of national pride confined to politicians and upper-class elites. In fact, it was echoed by almost all the BPO agents we interviewed, a majority of whom came from low-income families. For these workers, class mobility had come very quickly and, for almost all of them, their own upward mobility was closely related to the upward mobility of India Rising. While working in a BPO offered unprecedented opportunities for earning salaries inconceivable to previous generations, apart from opportunities for personal growth and social mobility, it was the feeling that they were participating in the larger story of India Rising that was frequently articulated by our interlocutors: their aspirations seemed sutured to nationalist conceptions of progress, modernity, and sovereignty. As Rajath, a young man who had just started working in a BPO, insisted, "BPOs have allowed India [to] take its rightful place in the world. Now nobody can push us around." Thus, apart from opportunities for personal growth and social mobility, they felt that, by working in BPOs, they were performing a crucial role in a drama much larger than their own upward mobility or that of their families. In these discourses, BPOs and agents who worked in them were deemed directly responsible for not just their own economic progress but that of India.

On Mobility, Flight, and Feeling Stuck

Gupta's first meeting with Rajani was early in our fieldwork. A confident twenty-three-year-old, Rajani struck Gupta as a bit quirky. She had very strong opinions about everything: her work, the BPO for which she worked, the community where she lived, her neighbors. Rajani grew up in a small town not far from Bengaluru. Her family was lower middle-class and did not have many resources. But Rajani had long been enamored with the idea of becoming a pilot: she had dreamed of flying a commercial plane. However, the fees for flight school proved to be beyond the reach of her family. She toyed with the idea of taking a loan, but that was a risky proposition because, even with a diploma, it was difficult to find a job as a commercial pilot unless one had political or personal connections to bigwigs in the airline industry. So Rajani had settled for a job at a BPO.

By interesting (and somewhat poignant) coincidence, she was assigned to a process for a travel portal. As her luck would have it, this was a time when India's aviation industry was expanding rapidly. New budget airlines unleashed intense fare wars; as a result, one could purchase relatively inexpensive tickets to fly on brand-new airplanes. Rajani began to purchase tickets on these airlines and travel within India. On days when she didn't have to work, she would take the earliest flight out of Bengaluru on a plane that she had dreamed of piloting herself, spend the day in the destination city, and take the last flight back. She did this as often as she could—in fact, so frequently that she amassed a huge credit card debt. But she never stopped flying.

Rajani's love of flying illustrates the knotty relation between affect, aspiration, mobility, and emplacement. We resist the temptation to read Rajani's story as either a perversion of modernist ideals (the undisciplined BPO agent whose aspirations are out of sync with reality) or as a form of resistance to her emplacement and confinement by her job in a BPO. Rather, we see her mobility as allegorical of her refusal to stay in place in terms of class aspiration. Her imaginative world was shared by most of the middle-class and upper-middle-class people traveling on the plane with her, but their means perhaps exceeded hers. What might have been an inexpensive flight for other passengers was a very costly endeavor for her, but the fact that she persevered in the bodily pleasure of flying on different types of aircraft even when she could not afford it indicates the jagged edges of the temporality of global modernity that she embraced.

Of course, spatial and temporal mobility are neither gender-neutral nor immune to hegemonic discourses of race, class, and, in the case of our interlocutors, national location. Geographers like Doreen Massey (1994) have long posited that the mobility and immobility of women foregrounds how spaces are fundamentally gendered (see also Patel 2010; Mankekar 2015; Mankekar and Gupta 2019). Although physical mobility, the ability to traverse the city to do night work, was essential to working in BPOs, gender profoundly impacted the capacity to navigate space and time. Traveling across the city to do night work was particularly difficult for young women. For one thing, night work was often viewed with suspicion by neighbors, community members, and family members, who subjected these women to surveillance. Patel (2010, 3–4) argues that the nightscape is not a static geographic or temporal landscape: it is a dynamic, interrelational space, illustrated in the view of women as both a site and a source of contamination. Women who did night work were stigmatized. This had material consequences for them: sometimes landlords would refuse to rent apartments to women who worked in BPOs, who, because they did night work, were deemed to have a "loose character."

Then there were the very real dangers of sexual violence that these women faced by traveling across the city at night. The women we worked with frequently worried aloud about these dangers—not just from strangers but also from cab drivers and colleagues. These fears intensified after the widely publicized case of Pratibha Murthy in Bengaluru, who was raped and murdered in 2005 by a man posing as a company-employed driver. In addition, women who had migrated to Bengaluru from other parts of India, especially from the northeastern states, felt particularly vulnerable to sexual violence because they were deemed culturally and racially Other: race served to emplace these women in distinct ways. These dangers, and the stigma attached to women who did night work, were so acute that all the companies we worked with provided cabs or vans that transported their employees to and from work.[7] Companies maintained detailed logs of when and where women employees were picked up and dropped off. While these practices were ostensibly for the protection of women, like many protectionist discourses, they intensified their monitoring and surveillance. Even so, some women workers, despite being afraid to go out at night, used their work as a means to visit pubs and bars after work (see also Patel 2010): working in BPOs enabled these women to venture into spaces that, despite being dangerous, were full of enticement.

In addition to crossing normative temporal borders of the work day and challenging the borders marking out domains of respectability, agents engaged in a kind of virtual migration (Aneesh 2006), one that nonetheless led many to feel "stuck," especially if they had been working in call centers for over a decade. Although their labor moved across national borders, they themselves had to stay in place. After all, the expansion of outsourcing to the global South was a direct result of restrictions on the migration of foreign laborers to many advanced capitalist countries. These laboring bodies had to stay put—they remained in their countries because they were barred from migrating primarily due to their race, class, and nationality.[8] Capital required the fruit of their labor, but nationalist and xenophobic immigration restrictions made it impossible for them to live in these countries while they worked. Moreover, these workers' emplacement is what allowed their employers to keep their wages low relative to workers in the global North (Padios 2018; Vora 2015).

Unquestionably, our interlocutors' ability to speak English was a prerequisite to being hired in the BPO industry. Beyond that, their abilities to be mobile were driven by the potency of their aspirations to become BPO workers, make enough money to support their families, and ascend the occupational ladder of the industry: these aspirations were fueled by me-diatized discourses of upward mobility, globalized lifestyles, cosmopoli-tanism, and, in particular, representations of professional success in the IT and BPO industry.[9] We sat in on numerous job interviews with prospective call center agents, and it became clear that, second only to their ability to speak English, it was this drive to succeed, this fire in the belly, that made employers take note of them. As one HR person, Vineeta, informed us, companies looked for precisely this drive and personal ambition when they vetted potential employees. She added that they preferred to hire someone who came from a poor family and displayed a hunger to succeed even if their English was not perfect: this meant that they had staying power and would not complain about tough working conditions. "Give me someone who is trainable but comes from a poor family any day over someone who has the right accent and went to a fancy school," she said. "Such people will work hard and move up because they have no other options and because their families rely on them."

The young men and women with whom we worked were neither un-deremployed, nor displaying the inertia characterizing Jeffrey's (2010) in-formants in small-town Uttar Pradesh.[10] Yet there were many reasons why some of them felt stuck. While many of them had opportunities for promo-tions or for moving laterally from one company to another, their lives were full of anxiety and uncertainty: even though they felt they had made it, they were also painfully aware that they could lose everything if their company lost the process on which they worked or if the entire BPO industry tanked. They were profoundly conscious of the precarity of their fortunes. Those who felt burned out were often in a quandary, not least because they had become accustomed to the "high" of call centers. Sadia, a twenty-five-year-old single mother who worked for a multinational BPO, compared work-ing in a call center to an addiction.[11] She said, "You know it is bad for you in the long run, but it gives you a real high. The main problem is that the body cannot keep up with the work, and that is what is frightening." Sadia was one of many BPO agents who used the trope of addiction to explain why she remained in a job that was so exhausting.

Like many others, she worried that the unceasing pace of the work was unsustainable and could present serious challenges as she grew older. Sev-eral agents that we interviewed hoped to move to the HR divisions of BPO firms because they claimed that they loved the industry for all the excite-ment it offered. Others hoped that when they were too old to keep up with the pace of work, they could move to hospitality or other service industries.

They trusted that the soft skills and networks they had acquired would stand them in good stead. They argued that their primary accomplishment was that they now had confidence in their abilities and, especially, in their facility to deal with people from all over the world. Thus, for instance, Sadia had changed careers from the call center industry to event management because she felt she had acquired crucial social skills in her time at the BPO from interacting with overseas customers.

Like Rajani, many agents had aspirations that were "sticky" and endured, while other aspirations unraveled or had to be cast off. A job at a call center offered our interlocutors a different way of imagining the future. They aspired to becoming not simply middle-class but global citizens: many of them derived tremendous pleasure from inhabiting the new sensoria spawned by capitalist modernity and being introduced to new ways of being in the world. The technology parks where their offices were located were glass-and-chrome monuments to the promise of high-tech (post)modernity, which indexed what they believed were their roles in India's ascent to economic power. Our interlocutors learned to navigate new social and imaginative dream spaces when they browsed through the air-conditioned malls that nestle against many of Bengaluru's technology parks, purchased (or dreamed of purchasing) the clothes they saw on mannequins, tried out new cuisines in the teeming food courts, pursued new ways of navigating these newly formed landscapes of desire and aspiration, and explored new ways of inhabiting their bodies (Mankekar and Gupta 2019).[12] As we accompanied many of them to these malls and food courts, we were struck by the fact that working in BPOs had opened up new worlds of enchantment for them.[13] It is important to note that agents could rarely afford to purchase the commodities they gazed at in these malls; instead, the pleasure of malls lay in wandering through them. Furthermore, as we elaborate elsewhere, these malls functioned as pedagogical spaces in which call center workers learned to "do" leisure and, precisely through browsing these spaces of leisure, learned to perform affective labor—to this extent, the mall was an extension of the office (Mankekar and Gupta forthcoming; cf. Willis 2017).

But the ladder to upward mobility into the middle class, cosmopolitanism, and new worlds of enchantment was slippery indeed. Agents were all too aware that their jobs depended on their ability to meet, if not exceed, quotas at work. Additionally, from having to make a certain number of calls during their shifts, they had to ensure that they pleased their customers— this was now recorded in the form of CSIs, or customer satisfaction indices. Their futures seemed completely, irrevocably, dangerously entwined with the fortunes of an industry that was inherently mercurial, contingent as it was on the rapacious irrationalities of global capitalism. Regardless, they continued to show up for work: their aspirations and those of their families depended on it. Their aspirations referenced a forward-looking temporality and structure of feeling that was, at once, poignant, fragile, and suffused with enticing and terrifying possibilities. Aspiration, for agents, was indexical of their capacity to imagine otherwise and to this extent was generative of discourses of futurity: aspiration was about imagining a possible that may not have been probable. And our jobs as ethnographers entailed taking their aspirations seriously rather than dismissing them as false consciousness: instead of assuming that their aspirations were the product of the ruse of capitalism or neoliberalism, we recognized their affective force, particularly in a context where time had become out of joint.

These young men and women were acutely reflective about their positions in the global BPO industry. They spoke eloquently (and, to us and among themselves, volubly) about how they were paid substantially less than work-ers in advanced capitalist countries who did comparable work, and deeply resented that their employers were profiting from their low wages. Given that most of them were responsible for the financial well-being of not just themselves but their entire extended families, they had little choice but to show up at work every day, regardless of their exhaustion or feelings of burnout. *The main problem is that the body cannot keep up with the work, and that is what is frightening.*

They were extremely anxious that, as they grew older, their bodies would become less resilient to the rigors of their labor (Mankekar and Gupta 2019). Like Sangita, some of them were able to rise up the ranks to get positions in the HR sections of their companies. Failing that, like Sadia, they moved laterally to other service jobs in the hospitality industry and the event management industries that had grown after the liberalization of the economy. Some found jobs in banks or the retail sector. These were jobs with regular working hours, which, while more conducive to raising a family, struck many workers as lacking the glamor and buzz of working in BPOs. But going back to their hometowns or villages was not an option they were willing to consider for even a second, no matter how tired they were or how hopeless they felt. As one of them said to Mankekar, "It will be like going back in time. Who wants to ever do that? It is so slow back there." Even as they were exhausting, the tempo and the disjunctive tem-poralities of life in Bengaluru were addictive indeed.

One night Mankekar barged, or listened to, calls by Rohith, a young man who was highly regarded by his peers and his supervisors for being particularly adept at dealing with difficult customers. We recall that night to emphasize how, despite the arduousness and frustrations of his job, Rohith never lost his bearings; he displayed an unflinching ability to treat even recalcitrant clients with compassion; he wore his own dignity, like a soft but impenetrable cloak, around himself.

Rohith was working on a process outsourced by a utility company in the UK that was specifically set up to cater to low-income seniors (or pensioners, as they are called in the UK). Rohith was part of a team tasked with selling a discounted utility package that would enable potential customers to save money while also conserving energy. This was a hard sell for many customers, who were deeply skeptical that the discounts the company was offering were genuine. Mankekar sat with Rohith as he cajoled a customer that he was calling for the second time. Before he began the call, Rohith informed Mankekar that this customer was an elderly man who had asked him to call him back with more information about the discount. He added, "I've compiled this additional information for him, but I don't think I'll be able to clinch the sale even this time, no matter how hard I try."

Rohith's conversation with this customer took over thirty minutes. The customer asked him the same question over and over while Rohith repeated, with tremendous patience, the same information. The conversation meandered, jumping from one topic to another, with the customer sometimes asking about the utility package, at other times talking to Rohith about his children who had moved to Manchester, and at yet other times railing against the government then in power in the UK. It became apparent that the customer might have been suffering from some sort of cognitive decline, because he kept straying from one topic to another, often forgetting what had been said just minutes before. Every now and then he would raise his voice in frustration and would become querulous. It didn't sound like he was interested in the utility package at all. He just seemed to want to talk. He would get angry if Rohith brought the topic back to the package. The man lived by himself, and it was evident that he was desperately lonely. Yet Rohith never lost his patience and, at the end of the conversation, he asked the customer if he needed more details. After logging out, he turned to Mankekar with a gentle smile, pointing to his forehead, and said, "He is not all there. But there is nobody to take care of him, nobody he can talk to. I would never leave my ajja-ajji *[grandpa-grandma] alone. Ever. What is the point of working if you can't take care of your loved ones?"*

The outsourcing of labor to the global South in the past few decades has compelled us to rethink labor migration in terms of affective sovereignties by foregrounding the connectivities possible even when physical mobility is foreclosed by restrictions on immigration and racist and xenophobic labor policies. As Ahmed et al. (2003) and others have reminded us, mobility and immobility are related to privilege and marginality in complex ways. Our research has taught us that even when physical mobility is curtailed, the inability to move is itself productive of the formation of laboring subjects. Furthermore, we have been concerned with rethinking the scales of sovereignty by focusing on how they might intersect and, more fundamentally, with problematizing definitions of sovereignty based on unexamined assumptions about autonomy and choice. Gendered and racialized formations of spatiality and temporality profoundly shaped agents' abilities to be mobile and navigate the worlds in which they found themselves. Rather than doing away with the notion of sovereignty altogether, it may be much more conceptually and politically productive to think of how affective sovereignties are generated when subjects struggle to navigate worlds in which they find themselves. These are worlds that are suffused with opportunities as well as failures: affective sovereignties, therefore, emerge precisely in contexts where vulnerability and potentiality are inextricably entangled.

It is telling that, in the face of mass violence, ecological degradation, and excruciating poverty in so many parts of the world, anthropologists are rummaging through the rubble for signs of life that endure. Thus, for instance, Veena Das (2006) has asked what it is like to stitch a world together in social spaces shattered by violence, while Anna Tsing (2015) describes the mushroom that not simply survives but thrives in landscapes of destruction as it spawns resilient lifeways and modes of being in the world. The worlds in which agents lived and worked were not landscapes dominated by violence, despair, or destruction—or not yet, anyway. But, as we increasingly immersed ourselves in their lives, we repeatedly asked ourselves: How did they make a life and a world for themselves in the face of constant change, when the city felt as if it was spiraling out of control, when the industry on which they were reliant appeared volatile, and when their own aspirations seemed so fragile? What was it that endured when everything around them seemed to be shifting all the time, even when they, in some instances, felt stuck?

Mankekar and Gupta

Far from being automatons following a set script, agents frequently came across as creative—regardless of whether they followed their scripts or not. They had to think on their feet and come up with ways to coax recalcitrant customers, and often emerged from painfully tense encounters with their dignity and sense of humor intact. In addition to their physical and temporal mobility, their imaginative mobility and their ability to display empathy and relate to customers who lived several worlds removed from them—their ability to engage in experiential travel—was indispensable to their performance of affective labor. And for imaginative and experiential travel to occur, they had to transform themselves in intimate ways. Scholars and journalists alike have made much of the ways in which BPO agents adopt new speech patterns, accents, and, in some cases, new names and personas, but by the time we began our fieldwork the companies where we worked no longer demanded that agents take on new names or personas (cf. Aneesh 2015). Nevertheless, most workers had to inventively reconstitute their identities in ways that went beyond new names, accents, or personas. Many of them felt humiliated when they had to put up with racist abuse from overseas customers; most of them chafed against the multiple modes of surveillance to which they were subjected at work and in their families and neighborhoods; almost all of them spoke longingly about the family celebrations, birthdays, and religious celebrations they missed because they were either sleeping or at work. So what was it that endured despite all that they had to cope with?

As we have argued above, our interlocutors' affective sovereignty ensued from their embeddedness in relationships of duty and obligation: duty and obligation grounded them in a web of relationships that could be a source of strength, oppression, and, very often, both simultaneously. Their sense of duty and obligation provided them with an ethical framework: a map. We use the term *map* advisedly to foreground how these ethical frameworks of being in the world, in many ways, enabled their passage through landscapes that were enchanting, terrifying, and overwhelming all at once. As feminist scholars and activists have taught us, webs of duty and obligation can be exploitative and exhausting. And this is how they were experienced: for most workers, their affective labor did not end when they left the BPO. Even so, the ethical imperatives of duty and obligation gave them a way to place themselves within and navigate a rapidly changing world, even if that place sometimes felt claustrophobic and made them feel entrapped.

What is the point of working if you can't take care of your loved ones? The adoption (sometimes willing, but often coerced) of the discourse of duty as an ethical framework also foregrounds the multiplex subjectivities and identities of BPO agents: they were not just laborers but were also grand-children, children, husbands and wives, parents, older siblings, uncles and aunts, nieces and nephews who felt obligated to take care of their loved ones. Even though they were displaced from the daytime world, like many exiles, refugees, and migrant workers, they remained affectively bound to these worlds (Mankekar 2015). This sense of duty provided them with a sense of connectedness with a world beyond the BPO. Even though they were unable to spend daytime hours with family, almost all the BPO agents we worked with continued to provide for aging parents and grandparents. Many paid the tuition for their siblings, nieces, nephews, and cousins, hence offering them an opportunity to improve their prospects for the future: in these instances, their aspirations consisted of enabling their loved ones to fulfill their aspirations and dreams. Several of them helped pay off debts that their family may have amassed over the years; some undertook repairs to crumbling family homes; others contributed to the weddings, surger-ies, and funerals of extended kin. Their commitment to their sense of duty and obligation was a form of caring, even when they were estranged from family members, and the map generated by this ethical practice emplaced them in distinct ways. This sense of emplacement could make them feel trapped and stuck in place. Or it could potentially provide them with a sense of direction and, therefore, an ability to negotiate a world not of their own making, a chronotope where time was out of joint.

In some of the anthropological, sociological, and cultural studies schol-arship, call center agents have been referred to as "cyber coolies," given the relentless pace of their work and the inescapable fact of their exploi-tation for greater profits for multinational capital. Putting aside for now the genealogies of race and racialized labor in which it is embedded, this term foregrounds the ways in which BPO workers perform affective labor in highly exploitative conditions. Our task as ethnographers could there-fore have been easy: there was no dearth of data underscoring that work-ers were exploited and faced precarious futures. Certainly, over the course of our fieldwork, we compiled plenty of data on how hard agents worked, their state of perpetual exhaustion, and their frustration and rage about the racist abuse they sometimes experienced from overseas customers. In ad-dition, they frequently spoke of how stifling it was to live and work under the watchful eyes of supervisors, managers, and neighbors.

At the same time, we were constantly confronted with the vitality that seemed to endure in the face of the volatility of their lives. Every time we entered the shop floor (the room where agents had their cubicles) to barge (overhear) the calls they were making to overseas customers, we were swept up in a buzz that we could not ignore: the energy that swirled around the room was unmistakable, electrifying. Whenever we sat by an agent as she veered off-script to engage a difficult customer, we were struck by the creativity that leavened what was, in so many respects, the exhausting tedium of their lives. Agents were neither "clones" nor "dead ringers," as they have been deemed by some scholars (Mirchandani 2012; Nadeem 2013). Even when they had to engage in practices of impersonation (Mankekar 2015), we sensed an authenticity to their lives—something that endured despite the frenetic pace of their lives and the vertiginous nightscapes that they navigated as they made their way across the city. Still, we wondered: What were we to make of the fact that, despite not being able to spend time with family and friends, they remained tied to them through dense ties of duty, care, and loyalty? How were we to interpret the fact that their social lives, far from being evacuated of meaning, were rich, and their imaginative lives even richer? We learned to be attuned to ways of knowing that are also ways of sensing, and we sensed more than fatigue when we spent time with our interlocutors.

So how do we conceptualize sovereignty in such contexts? Having eschewed liberal notions of agency as something that sovereign subjects possess (or not, as the case may be), we have diverged from conceptions of power and exploitation shaped by a master-slave dialectic that assumes a binary between those who have power versus those who do not, or of the powerful versus the exploited and/or oppressed. We learned that there was no contradiction between the fact of their exploitation and the creativity that they brought to their work, or between their sense of claustrophobia and their sense of wonder about what the world had to offer (Deleuze 1990, 9). We had to retrain our ethnographic sensibilities to be attuned to those moments of opening, creativity, and dignity that we gleaned in the face of vulnerability and what was, undeniably, the tedium of seemingly unending labor.

And so it was that we turned to the concept of potentiality as that affective intensity that enables us to make a life in rapidly and constantly shifting circumstances. We revert here to Agamben's discussions of potentiality, according to which the ability to become a being—the process of becoming—is contingent on potentiality.[14] And contingency is critical to potentiality and, hence, to affective sovereignty. Potentiality does not index the essence of being human but is, instead, about one's emergence into being, and about the fullness of life rather than its reduction to bare life. As we learned through our fieldwork with BPO agents, potentiality is also about the capacity to imagine and to exercise imaginative mobility; potentiality inhered in their capacity to move across—and navigate—a world that was as enticing as it was anxiety producing; potentiality also entailed forming, or finding, ethical maps of duty and obligation that enabled them to navigate this world.

Disjunctive temporalities, aspiration, chronic anxiety, duty, excitement, burnout, enchantment: this heady mix of affective regimes, emotions, sensations, and feelings shaped agents' affective sovereignties. Despite our long-term fieldwork, our in-depth knowledge of the BPO industry, and our close tracking of the trajectories of our interlocutors, we would be hard put to predict what their futures held. But affective sovereignty, when refracted through potentiality, is precisely about not knowing the end point of agents' trajectories. Agamben reminds us that humans are made as such not through a moment of arrival but in the process of trying to get to an unknown and often unknowable end point: neither arrival nor the possibility of achieving one's potential is inevitable.[15]

Indeed, over the course of our fieldwork, we began to conceive of potentiality in terms of the ability to strive in the face of possible failure: potentiality was irreducible to arrival or success, much less to liberal or indeed neoliberal constructions of freedom or choice. Potentiality does not signal lack but, instead, evokes the presence of the possible; it is the zone of a presence which by necessity implicates its simultaneous absence. Moreover, potentiality is irreducible to actuality: it maintains itself as potentiality per se. Agamben argues that "human beings see shadows, they can experience darkness, they have the potential not to see, the possibility of privation" (1999, 181). This relationship between darkness and potentiality is crucial for our conception of the affective sovereignties of our interlocutors for whom potentiality inhered in the fact that they lived under the shadow of darkness. The ever-present specter of failure, of the vortex of depression and emotional paralysis, of the fear of losing their way in the new, unfamiliar worlds in which they found themselves—these forms of darkness engendered and shaded agents' sense of their potentiality.

We have insisted that potentiality indexes the capacity to navigate a world that is fascinating and terrifying in equal measure. If affect is a form of "intelligence about the world" (Thrift 2004, 60), our interlocutors reminded us that potentiality is an intelligence that inheres in the sense of one's place in the world. Massumi posits, "Potentiality is unprescribed. It only feeds forward.... Potentiality is the *immanence* of things to its still indeterminate variation, under way.... Immanence is process" (2002, 9, emphasis in original). Potentiality is itself an emergent quality of movement. Agents'

Mankekar and Gupta

ability to move was not driven by bodily intentionality; instead, their bodies were nodes in feedback loops in affective dispositions that congealed around regimes of labor, aspiration, and the worlds that they inhabited and navigated (Mankekar and Gupta 2019).

The lake, so long the pride of Green Meadows, foams and froths at the mouth, much like a rabid dog. As one of our interlocutors said to us, "Vulnerability is a good teacher. When we feel vulnerable, we learn to not despair, for to despair would be to drown in our fears." We have tried, therefore, to glean how fear and wonder, dignity and depression were part of the temporality of struggle for workers rather than a trajectory of movement toward a predetermined end point. We learned to ethnographically sense the ebb and flow of despair and wonder in agents' lives, and to how they sought enchantment, however ephemeral, in the face of crushing anxiety about their jobs and their futures. We set ourselves to the task of limning the shifting modalities of potentiality as contingent on their capacity to find their way through a daunting landscape. This was a world in which the ground beneath their feet seemed to constantly shift. This was a world marked by environmental degradation and pollution, traffic jams, road blockages, and speeding vehicles that crash and kill; of health hazards caused by the city's unthinking sprint into the "Future"; and of financial precarity and imminent job loss.

On Movement Out of Sync

When I think of my body and ask what it does to earn that name, two things stand out. It moves. It feels. In fact, it does both at the same time. It moves as it feels, and it feels itself moving. Can we think a body without this: an intrinsic connection between movement and sensation whereby each immediately summons the other?

—Brian Massumi, *Parables for the Virtual*

The opening pages of Brian Massumi's *Parables for the Virtual* foreground the intrinsic relationship between corporeality and movement in terms of its implications for social theory. Massumi pushes us to see movement as fundamental to affect: the unqualified, unnameable field of intensities suffusing our abilities to affect and be affected. He advocates that we "add movement back" into our conceptual frameworks for understanding social transformation (Massumi 2002, 3). While keeping in play movement's literality, we have expanded it to recenter the socius by tracing our capacities to engage spatiality and temporality in terms of mobility. At the same time, we have tracked how the capacity of workers to navigate the world was refracted by processes of emplacement: emplacement and mobility were coimplicated.

As we have argued throughout, movement, mobility and immobility, and emplacement involve not just spatiality but equally temporality. These regimes of temporality were neither universal nor transcendental; thus, rather than dismissing the phenomenological dimension of time, we have been concerned with how workers' experiences of temporality are themselves generated by specific regimes of affective labor. We are particularly interested in how subjects are produced when time becomes out of joint. Here, we are conjuring both Derrida's (2006) discussion of the nonlinear and antiteleological temporality of capital, and Deleuze's (1995) understanding of the disjunctive synthesis of time. For both Derrida and Deleuze, time becomes unhinged because it breaks regularity and order; it produces aporias; it generates the uncanny. This sense of temporality, a condition of our lives under capitalism, nevertheless opens up the subject to untimely forms of becoming.

For agents in Bengaluru's BPOs, time was out of joint in multiple ways. At its most obvious, as noted above, they had to work when their overseas clients were awake: given the time difference between India and most of these countries, they went to work when the rest of the city was asleep. Almost all workers complained that the demands of working at night had drastic consequences for their health and their social lives: thus, their spatial mobility entailed temporal disjunction. As one agent put it, she felt "out of sync" with the rest of Bengaluru, and particularly with her family and friends, because she had to work at night. Moreover, phenomenological experiences of temporal disjunction were themselves shaped by the *durée* or duration of labor: this went beyond time as experienced by the body to encapsulate how time enfolded upon itself to produce certain kinds of subjects (Bergson [1889] 2001). Our interlocutors made lives and worlds for themselves in a city that was now called the IT hub of the nation. This was also a city where the daily rhythms of life were refracted by temple rituals that overflowed into streets to disrupt traffic, calls to prayer from neighborhood mosques, and the raucous and joyful abandon of street festivals. Our ethnographic work with these young men and women underscored to us that this was a world of multiple temporalities that collided loudly, sometimes destructively, at other times in unpredictable ways, to create a sense of time that was so fragmented as to seem unhinged.

At the same time, our interlocutors showed us that affect entails the potentiality for interaction with other beings, and this generates a vitality that is immanent. Moreover, affective sovereignty inheres in relationality rather than the liberal delusions of autonomy and choice and thus defies attempts to be squeezed into the compartmentalized concept categories of resistance, compliance, co-optation, or refusal vis-à-vis capitalism, which, in turn, is deemed to penetrate sociality from the "outside" (Bear et al. 2015; Gibson-Graham 2006). An agent's ability to extend compassion to an elderly pensioner across physical and cultural chasms, to take flight while feeling stuck, and to persevere in taking care of their families even while they felt disconnected from their everyday lives powerfully foreground their capacity for living by a set of ethical practices forged in contexts of precarity, fear, burnout, and depression: here, rather than being unequivocally destructive, the unhinging of time is generative of complex formations of subjectivity. Their potentiality inhered in their recognition of persisting in acting, even when they did not always know the consequences of their actions, and of learning anew to respond to the worlds in which they found themselves.

Foregrounding potentiality in contexts where time is out of joint is critical to the conceptual and political interventions we seek to make. Seeking, and seeing, our interlocutors in terms of potentiality in the face of physical and emotional burnout seems to us to be particularly urgent at a moment when the neoliberal subsumption of life by capital is assumed to be imminent and inevitable, and where ecological degradation and "derangement" threaten the very possibility of life (Ghosh 2016; Tsing 2015). Seeking, and holding on to, their potentiality enables us to steer away from the violently reductive trap of narrating their lives in terms of a teleological narrative of the triumphal march of global capitalism. We thus push back against totalizing narratives about how neoliberal capitalism has purportedly swept across wide swaths of the global South to subsume the lives and worlds of all that come in "its" path.[16] In our conception of affective sovereignty, we also diverge from liberal conceptions of sovereignty vested in autonomous subjects.[17] We wish to track the unparsable, inextricably entangled sense of sovereignty—and what this sense of sovereignty might feel like—for BPO agents whose lives and worlds are shaped, in equal parts, by burnout and excitement, and by aspiration as much as fear. The complex lifeworlds of our interlocutors defy simplistic frameworks that would represent them solely in terms of their exploitation by forms of capitalism that are, nevertheless, irrefutably predatory.

We close by briefly reflecting on what it might mean to speak of affective sovereignties in a situation of heterogeneous temporalities and multiplex subjectivities in a postcolonial setting. Our point that time is out of joint for workers in the BPO industry emphasizes the fact that they are not simply reprising the story of European modernity or repeating the history of capitalist development. As a nation-state, India is not following a normative trajectory of development in which countries move from agriculture to manufacturing and finally end up in services. Development has not mimicked the trajectory of European nation-states with a time lag; what we witness instead is an economy that has largely bypassed manufacturing while maintaining high rates of growth, but where growth has not been accompanied by an expansion of jobs. The BPO workers are not part of a nation-state where "all boats are rising": they are unlike most of their fellow citizens in becoming middle class. Unlike the citizens of the industrialized world, they do not suffer from deindustrialization, nor does the working class suffer from Fordist nostalgia. The conditions in which they encounter global neoliberalism are thus quite different from their counterparts in the global North.[18] In underlining the disjunctural temporalities that make time out of joint, we wish to critically witness the aspirations and potentiality of workers, neither dismissing them for their naivete, nor treating them with disdain as people who insufficiently understand their own historical condition.

Notes

1   A Pre–University Course diploma is the equivalent of twelve years of schooling (also called "10 + 2"). Students receive a secondary school certificate after ten years.

2   Michael Hardt (1999) foregrounds the transformative impact of affective labor on social relations and politics (see also Vora 2015). Asserting that affective labor has always existed, he argues that its current position in relation to production has changed. He focuses on how the informatization of the economy—based on the continual exchange of information and affect—undergirds the preponderance of service sectors in postindustrial conjunctures, even as some countries in the global South like India continue to have mixed economies. The service sector spans activities ranging from entertainment and education to health care, finance, and customer service.

3   For important analyses of aspiration, particularly in the South Asian context, see Appadurai (2013), and Chua (2014).

4   In this essay, Agamben (1999) interrogates Aristotle's distinction between potentiality and actuality. Engaging that discussion is beyond the scope of our argument here.

5   Our theorization of aspiration is in dialogue with the work of Ghassan Hage (2003) on hope (see also Zournazi and Hage 2002; Miyazaki 2005; Zournazi

and Massumi 2002). On analytical distinctions between aspiration and hope, see Mankekar and Gupta (forthcoming).

6   We cannot engage here the question about whether BPO agents living in Bengaluru are more or less individualistic than young people in the West. We would prefer to give the last word on discussions about individualism versus relationalism to Sherry Ortner (1995), who, in a powerful essay, "The Case of the Disappearing Shamans, or No Individualism, No Relationalism," argues that such debates are mired in modernization theory, whereby subjects in "the West" are deemed to be more individualistic (and therefore more modern) in diametric opposition to those in "the East" who, by contrast, are defined in terms of relationality (and are therefore more "traditional"). We would only add that, in recent years, the master narrative of modernization theory may have been supplemented or, in some cases, replaced by totalizing metanarratives about neoliberalism, which is assumed to have transformed subjectivities across the globe.

7   It is important to note that women who work in BPOs are better protected than many other women who do night work—for example, sex workers or women nurses who do night shifts.

8   Asian American critique has long interrogated the significance of this apparent contradiction for the growth of capitalist modernity in the United States. For a sustained engagement with the simultaneous incorporation and exclusion of racialized laboring bodies vis-à-vis the nation-form, see Lowe (1996), Palumbo-Liu (1999), and Takaki (1998).

9   As part of the Information Technology–Enabled Services (ITES) industry, BPO jobs occupy an intermediate position between unemployment and underemployment on the one hand, and the software industry on the other. On those who come to Bengaluru and are unsuccessful in finding jobs in the IT industry, see Fuller (2011b).

10 BPO workers' feelings of being stuck contrasted sharply with those of some other young Indian men and women who have seen their aspirations dashed in recent years (cf. Chua 2014; Favero 2005; Jeffrey 2010). These youths had escaped to metropolitan centers like Bengaluru, a city that they felt was so full of energy that it seemed to be bursting at the seams, vertiginous, spiraling out of control. In the words of Jayashree, who had moved from Kochi, Bengaluru was hard to resist because "there is always something happening here. . . . In fact, there is too much happening. It makes me dizzy." Thus, they were neither waiting nor in limbo (cf. Favero 2005): their lives were marked by the temporality of acceleration rather than time-pass (Jeffrey 2010).

11 Interestingly, we came across several BPO agents who were single mothers: all of them lived with their parents, who helped to raise their children. These women indicated that the schedule of BPO work, which entailed working at night and being home during the day, enabled them to be present when their children were about to leave for school and when they returned in the afternoon. They frequently worried aloud to us about how the rigors of the double

day took a toll on their bodies. We address some of the effects of BPO work on women's health in Mankekar and Gupta (2019).

12 For a powerful analysis of the pull of commodity aesthetics in contexts of consumer capitalism, see Wolfgang Fritz Haug (1986). See also Mankekar (2004, 2015) for the erotics of commodity affect in postliberalization India.

13 Much thought has already been given to the relationship between capitalism and dis/enchantment—see, especially, the work of Weber ([1905] 2002), who underscored the relationship between capitalism, instrumental rationality, and dis/enchantment. In critical theory associated with the Frankfurt School, for instance, disenchantment is associated with capitalism and secularization and is deemed a necessary component of capitalist modernity; see, in particular, Adorno ([1946] 2001), Adorno and Horkheimer ([1944] 2007), and Benjamin ([1927] 2002, [1935] 2008). For critiques of the relationship between secularization and disenchantment, see Akeel Bilgrami (2014) and Charles Taylor (1994). Although we use the term *enchantment* in cognizance of its centrality to capitalist modernity (Benjamin [1927] 2002, [1935] 2008), engaging the relationship between secularization, instrumental rationality, and disenchantment is beyond the scope of this chapter.

14 In *Homo Sacer*, the condition of bare life or mere being arises when a human being is denied potentiality (Agamben 1998).

15 According to Agamben (1998, 1999), nonarrival occurs when biopolitics becomes so thoroughly normalized as to result in bare life.

16 We join with other scholars who wish to neither anthropomorphize neoliberalism nor construct it as monolithic, looking the same and having the same "effects" everywhere (for instance, Ferguson and Gupta 2002; Ganti 2014; Ong 2006).

17 Here we draw on Agamben's (1999) preoccupation with potentiality as part of a project of the retrieval of agential capacity rather than autonomy.

18 For this reason, we do not interpret their aspirations and potentiality in terms of "cruel optimism" (Berlant 2011a).

6

Sovereign Interdependencies

JESSICA CATTELINO

If I were to dump a bucket of water in the grassy front yard of the house I rented in the small city (population 6,000) of Clewiston, Florida, it could travel through a dizzying number of jurisdictions and territories in the subtropical Everglades wetlands before draining out to sea. One plausible path, according to water managers, would flow through the Clewiston Drainage District canals, which are managed by the South Florida Conservancy District as they cut elegant lines through Clewiston, a diverse agricultural quasi–company town where the US Sugar Corporation is headquartered. The drained northern Everglades wetlands are now agricultural fields and pastures, producing sugarcane, citrus, and winter vegetables. The Clewiston canals flow into larger ones operated by the South Florida Water Management District, a powerful regional agency that issues water permits, regulates use, and operates a vast system of canals, pump stations, and other structures across sixteen South Florida counties. The water managers who gamely modeled my bucket of water's journey paused at this point to say that the possible paths forward were "a little complex" and suggest that we start over from an easier point on the map.

Complex, indeed! The water might be pumped just north into Lake Okeechobee, the large inland lake managed by the US Army Corps of Engineers and the Water Management District that often is described as the "beating heart" of the Everglades. Or it could flow southward through cattle pastures and the vast sugarcane fields that stretch to the horizon, then on to the Seminole Big Cypress Reservation (population about 500), a rural and swampy reservation where the water would be managed by the

Environmental Resource Management Department of the Seminole Tribe of Florida. Then, continuing its way through gates and pumps and canals, it might flow into the Big Cypress National Preserve, or maybe instead through a Miccosukee Indian reservation and into the Everglades National Park before flowing out to sea. Along its journey of roughly 110 miles as the crow flies, the water would move past people fishing, scientists studying the treasured Everglades ecosystem, farmers pumping water off or on their fields, farm workers who have little political voice, and tourists enjoying nature. It would flow past (or through) cows, deer, alligators galore, turtles, fish, spectacular wading birds, invasive Burmese pythons, and other critters. And it would be governed by laws and guidelines set by the federal and state governments, the water management district and multiple drainage districts, the Seminole and Miccosukee governments, the National Park Service, and any number of other federal, tribal, state, and local agencies.

Water's flow, not unlike money's flow, makes it good to think with anthropologically because water connects people and polities, rendering them interdependent whether or not they want to be so. These interdependencies, and efforts to govern them, constitute everyday challenges to political autonomy and sovereignty. But they also manifest sovereign interdependencies.

Sovereignty—whether of states or subjects—is often defined by or otherwise linked to the conditions of autonomy and independence, including the affects associated with them. This is the case in scholarship, statecraft, and social movements alike. Ethnographic and historical attention to the day-to-day practices that constitute sovereignty, however, introduces a conundrum because actually existing states and subjects live, feel, and claim sovereignty in relation to others. Sovereignty "in relation to others" can refer to relations that augment sovereignty-as-autonomy—such as differentiation, decolonization, and resistance—or ones that belie it, such as negotiation, obligation, interdependency, and care. What does it matter that states and subjects live their sovereignty in relations of interdependency with others? And what affects does interdependency generate?

Empirically, the core claim of this chapter is both simple and, perhaps, counterintuitive: sovereignty, at least in large part, is achieved through, and lived as, interdependency.[1] This is interdependency more complex and felt than is recognition. This is demonstrated in two domains: market and legal integration, with a focus on casino gaming and water management. Sovereignty-as-autonomy is not an equal-opportunity view of the world, and dislodging its supremacy is, therefore, a political project. In what follows, I draw from feminist and Indigenous studies theorists alongside eth-

Jessica Cattelino

nographic examination of Florida Seminole casino gaming and Everglades restoration to examine interdependency in sovereign claims and practices. I argue that thinking about sovereignty as interdependency requires an affective pull away from the heady, gendered, and settler colonial triumphalism of autonomous freedom; instead, it pulls toward felt negotiation of and accountability to both human and more-than-human relations, as well as the institutional forms through which these relations are recognized.

Sovereign Autonomy and Interdependency

In scholarship and politics, sovereignty most often is measured along an axis that stretches from autonomy to dependency. A typical definition of sovereignty as "supreme political authority, independent and unlimited by any other power" (Alfred 2002, 460) derives in part from political and legal definitions grounded in Western natural law theories, which held the sovereign to be an unlimited (and, for some, divinely sanctioned) political power and authority over territory and law (Barker 2005; Bartelson 1995; Hinsley 1986).[2] That is, being sovereign has meant being autonomous, and insofar as a subject or a nation is not autonomous, it is not sovereign: autonomy is a condition and a measure. Critical analysis of sovereignty in anthropology and related fields frequently associates sovereignty with violence, seeing radical autonomy in the violence of the state and the subject (see, e.g., Hansen and Stepputat [2006] and other scholars engaged with Agamben [1998]). Sovereignty-as-autonomy is, however, consistent with some forms of relationality, insofar as it recognizes the importance of treaties and other international agreements as exercises in autonomous choice (think contracts).[3] Scholars of—and against—the politics of recognition (Coulthard 2014; Markell 2003; Povinelli 2002; Simpson 2014; Taylor 1994) since Hegel have grappled with the question of autonomy, showing that recognition is not simply an arms-length acknowledgment of an autonomous other but rather is productive of politics.

The dominant model of sovereignty-as-autonomy fits awkwardly with Indigenous sovereignty, whether regarding the relationships among Indigenous sovereigns or those between them and settler colonial polities. Indigeneity in the United States has been structured by dependency in a colonial mode, at least since the Marshall Court of the 1830s coined the term "domestic dependent nations" to characterize Indians who lived "in a state of pupillage" vis-à-vis the United States.[4] Although the form of domination that settler states impose on Indigenous polities is distinctive,

Indigenous sovereigns are not unique for their (only) partial autonomy. As Native American studies scholar Amanda Cobb (2005) pointed out, no modern sovereign exercises absolute sovereignty, and, in this, Indigenous sovereigns are no exception. Too few scholars and jurists have explored how Indigenous sovereignty can inform theories of sovereignty outside of Indigenous studies, or have taken Indigenous approaches to sovereignty as starting points for imagining new relations of obligation and reciprocity among a range of polities and peoples.[5]

Among political theorists, a key exception to treating Indigenous sovereignty as anomalous or failed was feminist theorist Iris Marion Young, who took Indigeneity as a paradigm for retheorizing self-determination. (Note that *self-determination*, in her use, corresponds closely to *sovereignty* as I am using it.)[6] In "Two Concepts of Self-Determination," Young criticized the prevailing view of self-determination as being "a circumstance in which the self-determining entity claims a right of nonintervention and noninterference" (2001, 26). Young drew on "feminist critiques of a concept of the autonomy of the person as independence and noninterference" to argue that the prevailing concept of self-determination "ignores the relations of interdependence peoples have with one another, especially in a global economic system." She argued "for a relational concept of the self-determination of peoples," with Indigenous peoples as her touchpoint (Young 2001, 26). For Young, freedom was not based on independence but rather on nondomination. The distinction is crucial, for it assesses not the mere fact of interdependent relations with others but rather the quality of those relations.

Feminist critiques have not only focused on interdependence as viewed from the perspective of disempowered people seeking liberation. Rather, they have shown the analytical and political importance of pointing out that seemingly autonomous dominant parties in sovereign relations are also interdependent and, indeed, much more fragile than they might at first seem to be. The attribution, including self-attribution, of autonomy to states (most often powerful ones like the United States) and individuals (most often men) depends on the obfuscation of their dependency on others, on less powerful nations, on women.[7] In "A Genealogy of Dependency: Tracing a Keyword of the U.S. Welfare State," political theorist Nancy Fraser and historian Linda Gordon (1994) assembled a genealogy of the political concept of dependency in the United States, especially in relation to welfare, and showed that the state of dependency has become increasingly devalued—and the term *dependency* increasingly pejorative—since

Jessica Cattelino

industrialization. This has had especially severe consequences for women, and it has relied on masking masculine forms of dependency. In the United States, structural relations of dependency are masked in the workplace (as "free" labor) and the so-called free market.[8] Evelyn Nakano Glenn (1992) and others in her wake have emphasized the interlocking gendered and racialized dimensions of domestic and service labor, showing the relationality and interdependence of white women and women of color, and from there arguing for feminist politics that guards against advancing the freedoms of some women (usually white and middle and upper class) at the expense of others (usually working-class women of color).

These scholars emphasized the political significance of the ideological efforts to separate autonomous from dependent social positions. Although not all feminist critiques of autonomy directly concern sovereignty, they usefully call attention to the way that valorizing autonomy and devaluing dependency distributes power and reinforces political and social hierarchies to the systematic disadvantage of women.[9]

Indigenous studies scholars offer a formally similar critique of the alleged autonomy (and masked dependency) of the settler colonial state. Settler state sovereignty is produced against, with, and through Indigenous peoples, as illustrated by national debates about reconciliation and coexistence in Australia, Aotearoa New Zealand, and Canada (Maaka and Fleras 2005; Povinelli 2002). Indeed, scholarship on settler colonialism has argued that the commonality among Anglo settler states stems less from their shared European legal and cultural history than from their colonial engagements with Indigenous peoples and resulting dilemmas and violences (Coombes 2006). That said, before jumping into settler state dependency, let me first emphasize that of course it is the case that settler state power constrains Indigenous sovereignty—Jean Dennison (2012) writes of the "colonial entanglement" of Indigenous sovereignty—and that Indigenous sovereignty is limited by settler colonial domination. But it is nonetheless important to identify the limits of settler state sovereignty-as-autonomy. As David Wilkins and Tsianina Lomawaima (2001, 249) put it, "The connections and interdependencies of the modern world deny the possibility of a self-contained, unfettered sovereign, but limited sovereignties exist all around us: United States of America, the individual states that constitute the nation, and the senior sovereigns, American Indian tribes who have called this country home for millennia." This line of argument had been developed by Vine Deloria Jr. In the 1979 article "Self-Determination and the Concept of Sovereignty," Deloria noted that even in European modern history, the developing concept of sovereignty masked the interdependency of nation-states: "In the technical language of the seventeenth and eighteenth centuries, sovereignty was the absolute power of a nation to determine its own course of action with respect to other nations. Treaties between the equal 'sovereigns' often disguised the fact of interdependence of European nations" (22). More recently and with focus on West Papua, Danilyn Rutherford (2012) calls attention to an aspect of colonial and anticolonial sovereigns' relationality and interdependency that deserves more attention: audience, in its multiplicity.

A focus on interdependence goes further than showing how settler states and other powerful sovereigns are partial and limited. It reveals that settler sovereignty is fragile, delicate, and destabilized on an ongoing basis by Indigenous sovereignty. Audra Simpson (2014, 22) calls this "settler precariousness": the ways that settler state sovereignty is shown to rely upon not only the assertion of territorial sovereignty over Indigenous lands but also the recognition by, and consent of, Indigenous citizens and sovereigns as such. Of Mohawk politics, Simpson (177) writes, "This is political life that, in its insistence upon certain things—such as nationhood and sovereignty—fundamentally interrupts and casts into question the story that settler states tell about themselves." As literary and Indigenous studies scholar Mark Rifkin (2009, 89) wrote of Indigenous sovereignty seen in light of US Indian policy, American Indian sovereignty is viewed as incomplete, as an Agamben-style sovereign exception, even as "continued Native presence pushes against the presumed coherence of the U.S. territorial and jurisdictional imaginary." As such, "the supposedly underlying sovereignty of the U.S. settler-state is a retrospective projection generated by, and dependent on, the 'peculiar'-ization of Native peoples" (91). Just as examination of gendered dependency shows the fragility of (masculine) gendered autonomy, so does examination of Indigenous sovereignty—in practice and in discourse—show settler sovereignty to be fragile, incomplete, and dependent (see also Sturm 2017).

Note that, while calling attention to interdependency, I am not stating what Indigenous sovereignty is. This is for several reasons. First, as many have pointed out (e.g., Barker 2005; Bonilla 2015), sovereignty is less helpfully analyzed as a thing than as a claim, project, or practice: sovereignty is not a universal ontology.[10] Second, Indigenous sovereignty is diverse and defies singularity.[11] Third, as a white settler scholar, I am not positioned to claim an ontological knowledge of Indigenous sovereignty. Critical theorist Aileen Moreton-Robinson, in the introduction to *Sovereign Subjects: Indig-*

enous Sovereignty Matters, wrote of Indigenous sovereignty not as something that could be defined singularly but rather as diversely manifested, and as embodied, ontological, epistemological, and "grounded within complex relations derived from the intersubstantiation of ancestral beings, humans and land" (2007, 2).

None of this focus on sovereign interdependencies is meant to discount or devalue autonomy movements. But it is worth distinguishing at least two forms of sovereignty-as-autonomy. The first is autonomous sovereignty that is claimed and enacted within a larger political theory and praxis of autonomy, in communities and polities where autonomy permeates the political and intersubjective fields. There, autonomy may flourish irrespective of domination. The second, and I suspect the more common, is sovereignty-as-autonomy movements and practices that seek to escape a condition of domination. In those cases, interdependence is domination, is oppressive. So autonomy movements are first and foremost about escaping domination, escaping harmful forms of dependency. In such cases, it is not apparent that the telos is in fact autonomy: instead, autonomy functions as the path out of domination, but the relevant polities and peoples and subjects, upon overthrowing domination, may well turn to other forms of interdependency as the good life, as freedom. They may choose different forms of deep relationality, not the rejection of interdependence in favor of autonomy.

Historian and Indigenous studies scholar Nick Estes (2019), when describing how water protectors at Standing Rock enacted a future of Indigenous liberation in *Our History Is the Future: Standing Rock versus the Dakota Access Pipeline, and the Long Tradition of Indigenous Resistance*, does not position that future-present of liberation as based in autonomy. When writing about the diverse Indigenous-led community joined in solidarity against settler colonialism and extractive capitalism, Estes returns again and again to kinship, solidarity, and good relationality as modes and models of freedom. The #NoDAPL camps "created a future in the here and now" that reconnected Indigenous peoples with the land and "capaciously welcomed the excluded, while also centering the core of an Indigenous lifeworld—relationality" (Estes 2019, 253).[12] Estes generally does not describe liberation as sovereignty, but throughout his account he connects freedom, sovereignty, and good relations. He tells the "history of Indigenous nationhood and political authority" for Oceti Sakowin as a "history of relationships," and he links the affirmation of "water is life" to "being a good relative" (21). Indigenous resistance, he writes, "defines freedom not as the absence of settler colonialism, but as the amplified presence of Indigenous life and just relations with human and nonhuman relations, and with the earth" (248). Estes cites Indigenous and feminist science studies scholar Kimberly TallBear, who criticizes settler liberal forms of governance and heteropatriarchal monogamy for producing bad relations, when the goal of relations among people(s) and among all relations, human and nonhuman alike, is to be good relatives. She wrote, "Making kin is to make people into familiars in order to relate. This seems fundamentally different from negotiating relations between those who are seen as different—between 'sovereigns' or 'nations'—especially when one of those nations is a militarized and white supremacist empire" (TallBear 2016, quoted in Estes 2019, 256).

Just as dominant economic theories of dependency mask the always-present structural relations of interdependency in the marketplace, so too does the obfuscation of dependency in political theories of sovereignty privilege a narrow but powerful conception of the autonomous nation-state or political subject. This excludes relations of interdependency that constitute political status and belonging. The remainder of this essay turns to an ethnographic register to show how, for American Indian tribal gaming and for environmental restoration, the political and material horizon of sovereignty is not (only) autonomy, but rather the assertion of political distinctiveness as the basis for a relationship of mutual obligation and sovereign nondomination.

Casino Gaming

In 1979, on their urban Hollywood reservation near Interstate 95 between Fort Lauderdale and Miami, the Seminole Tribe of Florida opened the first tribally operated high-stakes bingo hall in North America. This act launched a gaming revolution that soon spread across much of Indian Country, building American Indian nations' political and economic power even as it has exposed them to increased scrutiny in American law, politics, and popular culture. Forty years later, thanks to a radically transformed economy, Seminole citizens enjoy financial security after more than a century of struggle. Gaming and related hospitality ventures dominate the Seminole government's revenues and new investments: a massive hotel in the shape of a guitar opened in fall 2019 at the Hollywood Hard Rock casino resort, just north of where the old bingo hall still operates. The Seminole-owned multinational corporation Hard Rock International operates cafés, hotels, and casinos in seventy-five countries around the globe, and in 2017 the Seminole-owned Hard Rock Hotel and Casino Atlantic City opened in the building that once housed the failed Trump Taj Mahal casino.

Jessica Cattelino

American Indian gaming is paradoxical under the logic of sovereignty-as-autonomy. On the one hand, gaming has enabled the Seminole people and government to retake authority over aspects of their lives that had been challenged by dispossession and dominated by US federal control, such as housing, health care, education, and natural resource management. Such political distinctiveness represents hard-won and celebrated sovereignty-as-autonomy. On the other hand, Seminole economics and politics today rely on unprecedented forms and levels of interdependency, including market integration and tighter relationships with other polities. This seeming paradox is resolved by considering the ways that interdependency and nondomination constitute sovereignty, not despite but rather alongside autonomy.

Gaming revenues facilitate the autonomy of Indigenous nations and communities in ways that reinforce sovereignty. The Seminole Tribe of Florida now funds and operates health clinics, builds and regulates housing, manages natural resources, and runs a variety of government programs that once were operated under the federal Bureau of Indian Affairs and other federal agencies. Gaming revenues allow the democratically elected Seminole Tribal Council, through its budgeting process, to fund such programs more fully than ever, and also to autonomously govern and administer them under tribal, not federal, authority. Exiting federal control over the most intimate aspects of life—from medicine to the installation of kitchen appliances to the financial structure of families—is a major accomplishment described as such by Seminole research participants. Such a focus on autonomy is consistent with a long history of Seminoles' seeking to be left alone by settler government, and it is a reminder of the toll taken on Indigenous individuals and polities by the nearly two centuries of dispossession, new poverty, and US law and administration that considered/considers Native nations to be "domestic dependent" sovereigns and in a relationship of "wardship" to the United States (Barker 2005; Williams 2005).

Even as gaming has augmented the sovereign autonomy of the Seminole Tribe, however, it also has brought the government and people into new relations of interdependency with others, relations that support and augment sovereignty. These interdependent relations include but also go beyond market integration, as Seminole casinos and hotels rely on non-Seminole customers and employees, not to mention Wall Street financing. Over a decade ago, I observed something that has only intensified in the intervening years: gaming has increased the density and importance of Seminoles' collective and individual interdependent relations with the state of Florida, local municipalities, other Indian nations, and the federal government (see Cattelino 2008).

First, in the state context, the Tribe (as people call the Florida Seminole government) retains lawyers and lobbyists in Tallahassee to defend sovereignty rights and has played hardball with the state of Florida over a long-delayed compact agreement whereby the state guarantees to the Tribe exclusive rights to certain lucrative types of games, and the Tribe shares a portion of gaming revenues with the state. Although not as extreme, Florida joins states such as Connecticut in relying on income from tribal gaming compacts for fiscal health. In 2016, Indian gaming in the United States generated $1.83 billion in revenue sharing payments to federal, state, and local governments, on top of $36.2 billion in wages, with most jobs held by non-Native people (Casino City Press 2018). These relations with state governments and their citizens are a mixed bag, at best, when it comes to sovereignty. On the one hand, Indigenous nations enjoy a nation-to-nation relationship to the United States as fellow sovereigns, such that federal law regulating tribal gaming has compromised tribal sovereignty by compelling American Indian governments that seek the most lucrative forms of gaming to enter into compacts with states. On the other hand, gaming has afforded some tribes, including Florida Seminoles, unprecedented power in the halls of state government (see the following section on water for one example).

In local contexts, the Seminole Tribe enters into casino-related agreements with municipalities, for example over roads, emergency services, and law enforcement. In the casino era, dramatically more than before, Seminole officials and other individual citizens make local political contributions, join chambers of commerce, serve on the boards of South Florida nonprofits, and offer philanthropic donations to local causes. Philanthropy is especially significant as a reversal of charitable exchange, in a reorganized local field of power (Cattelino 2007, 2008). The Seminole Tribe has supplanted the US Sugar Corporation as the largest employer in rural Hendry County and, more generally, has become a major player in the local economies that surround its reservations. This is not unique: scholars document similar gaming-based local prominence, from boosting local economies in Oregon (Colley 2018) to reshaping regional tourism in the Great Smoky Mountains of North Carolina (Lewis 2019), while historian Alexandra Harmon (2010) turns to the archives to show how various forms of Indigenous wealth have unsettled local power structures since the early days of settler colonialism.

Gaming tribes increasingly participate in intertribal organizations and otherwise reinforce ties among Indian nations. These include trade groups (like the National Indian Gaming Association), business partnerships (e.g., in banking), buying-and-selling agreements to establish all-Indian casino supply chains, the Intertribal Agriculture Council, regional Indian rodeo associations, and any number of diplomatic relationships and political collaborations. The Seminole Tribe sends disaster relief to other tribes (and to neighbors like the Bahamas after Hurricane Dorian in 2019) and contributes to charitable causes in Indian Country. Individual Seminole citizens join trips for elders to visit other Indian communities, compete in intertribal athletics tournaments, and travel with their families and friends throughout Indian Country; they are able to connect to an unprecedented degree thanks to tribal social programs and to the per capita payments distributed to each citizen from casino revenues. To be sure, some such activities—such as the 1969 cofounding of the United South and Eastern Tribes, a nonprofit that advocates for regional Indigenous communities—predate gaming. And gaming has yielded not only new forms of collaboration and interdependency but also new forms of competition and hostility. For example, Brook Colley (2018) documents the tensions that arose when two reservation communities in Oregon created competing casino development plans. Nonetheless, gaming overall has facilitated efforts by nations to realize their sovereignty, in part through relations with one another.

When it comes to the US federal government, law is a key domain of Seminole sovereign interdependencies.[13] Since 1979, Seminoles have defended gaming rights through litigation. Simpson (2014) emphasizes two politico-legal processes that apply here: first, Indigenous peoples' engagement with settler state law is not solely a matter of being subject to it but also represents efforts on the part of Native nations to create and realize law and politics within the context of settler colonialism; and, second, examination of law—whether about Mohawk cigarette "smuggling" through their own territory that straddles the US-Canada border, in Simpson's case, or about blackjack and slot machines, in mine—shows the extent to which the settler state depends for its ongoing existence and legitimacy on (the consent of) Indigenous peoples. Since before gaming, as legal historians have argued (Harring 2002, 447), the coexistence of colonial and Indian common law has transformed each legal system. As anthropologist Jennifer Hamilton (2009, 2) writes, "Euro-settler systems of law developed in part as a response to settler encounters with indigenous populations." This process continues, and gaming has accelerated it.

Seminoles enact legal pluralism when they recognize, however reluctantly, both federal and Indigenous legal authority; the latter is grounded in the annual Green Corn Dance and the matrilineal clan system, and newly also in the year-round Seminole court. As Jim Shore, tribal general counsel since the early 1980s and the first Seminole to become a lawyer, explained to me of his work and how it relates to sovereignty: "I come from an old family, both sides. I know my language, the clan system, the dos and don'ts, and that's what got us here. . . . This is behind me. We can win all the battles against the white folks, but if we lose our tradition we are our own worst enemy—we'll defeat ourselves. We'll have just hollow victories [in the courts]." Without violating restrictions on outsider knowledge of clan-specific meanings and duties, it is possible to note that the Seminole clan system—which long had been the fundamental political system—is based on the interdependence of the clans, the partiality of knowledge that any individual in one clan can hold, and the responsibility to follow law. For decades, the Seminole Tribe of Florida resisted adopting a US-style judicial system of the type that good governance consultants are promoting throughout Indian Country. This may seem surprising, given that in the casino era the Tribe quickly adopted and adapted typical corporate risk management strategies, human resources practices, and other corporate management norms. What gave Jim Shore and others pause when it came to the court was the question of whether a standard American-style judicial system, even if guided by Seminole principles, could coexist with clan law principles and practices (which include limits on the legal authority of people from one clan over those from another). Perhaps counterintuitively, such concerns have not precluded the Seminole Tribe's participation in settler US and state courts. Many Seminole citizens, old and young, told me to understand gaming-related litigation as the continuation of Seminoles' legendary nineteenth-century military prowess, with today's warriors no longer on the battlefield but in the courtroom or at the negotiating table.

The Seminole Tribe of Florida has turned to federal courts to defend its sovereignty relative to state sovereignty. Under the 1988 landmark federal Indian Gaming Regulatory Act (25 USC §§ 2701–2721), if tribal governments wish to offer the most lucrative class of games of chance in their casinos (slot machines, blackjack, craps, etc.), known as Class III games, they must meet two conditions: (1) those types of games must be legal in the surrounding state (even if only in charity casino night fundraisers or with low jackpots); and (2) the Native nation and the state government must negotiate in good faith toward a gaming compact (most of which include revenue-sharing agreements). The second condition long eluded Seminoles because the state of Florida for more than two decades refused to negotiate a compact. (Meanwhile, the Seminole Tribe successfully built its gaming empire on Class II games, which include paper and electronic bingo and poker, while the state stood by and received no share of the revenues.) Frustrated by this failure of the state to abide by federal law, the Seminole Tribe sued the state in federal court. In 1996, the US Supreme Court, in the landmark federalism case *Seminole Tribe v. Florida*, ruled that the state of Florida was protected by sovereign immunity from suit by the Tribe over gaming, under the Eleventh Amendment of the US Constitution (517 US 44 [1996]). Although *Seminole Tribe* represented a serious defeat for Seminoles, the Tribe followed up by arguing that under this precedent the state of Florida, in turn, could not sue the Tribe for allegedly conducting unauthorized games. The Seminole Tribe won on tribal sovereign immunity grounds, and the US Court of Appeals opinion held that the case "demonstrates the continuing vitality of the venerable maxim that turnabout is fair play" (*State of Florida v. Seminole Tribe of Florida*, 181 F.3d 1237 1999, 1237).

Seminole Tribe may seem like a narrow case about sovereign immunity, and on one level it was that, but it was also a case that showed how Indigenous legal action in the twentieth century and beyond continues to reshape federal law, even under conditions of domination. Legal scholars regard *Seminole Tribe* as part of the Rehnquist Court's broader move toward states' rights, and as a moment when the lines of federalism were redrawn (Jackson 1997, 542). Indeed, this ruling affects not only Native nations but also state employees and others seeking to sue states in federal court, and it has shifted the ground of states' rights for all. The case is regularly taught in law schools for that reason (not as a federal Indian law case). As has been the case historically with regard to property, taxation, citizenship, and other fundamental legal principles, the legal actions and imaginations of Indigenous peoples have modified US law and sovereignty. It is a reminder that the law and sovereignty of settler states are unsettled by, and interdependent with, Native nations.

On the face of it, my focus on interdependency with various governments seems to run counter to Seminoles' pride in self-reliance and autonomy, in their ability to build houses they want to live in, operate a national economy, and educate their children in their language and on their own terms (Cattelino 2008). But these are not necessarily incompatible, either as structural relations or as feelings. Even as Indigenous claims to autonomy take real power and meaning from Indigenous political theories and against the historical backdrop of settler state paternalistic administration, they are coupled with practices and local political theories of interdependency that unsettle singular sovereignty and citizenship. And this is not unique to Indigenous sovereignty. I do not hold up Indigenous sovereignty as a model, since to do so would ignore the severe constraints of ongoing settler state domination. Nondomination remains a far-off goal, but it is one that Seminole and other Indigenous leaders, activists, and revolutionaries are enacting and pushing in the mundane work of everyday life as well as with more newsworthy activities, whether it was Seminoles' purchase of Hard Rock International or the 2016 and ongoing resistance at Standing Rock to the Dakota Access Pipeline. It is no coincidence that the latter involves water.

Water

Back in 2000 and 2001, when I was first conducting ethnographic research on Seminole sovereignty and gaming, I noticed that the tribal council had allocated significant casino revenues for water management. At the time, the Seminole Tribe had a Water Resource Management Department, and the tribal council was preparing to put down $25 million in matching funds with the US Army Corps of Engineers for the Big Cypress Water Conservation Plan, which would attempt to hold water on the reservation for wetlands restoration purposes (Weinberg 2002). Twenty-five million dollars is no joke, and this would be the largest-ever partnership between an American Indian nation and the federal government for the purposes of ecological restoration. During the same period, the Seminole Tribe of Florida became a partner in the Comprehensive Everglades Restoration Plan (CERP), which Congress authorized in 2000. This is the most expensive ecological restoration project in the world, and, along with other related projects managed by the South Florida Water Management District and the US Army Corps of Engineers, it aims to restore key elements of Everglades hydrology, water quality, and water supply and delivery. The Florida Everglades have, since the late 1800s, been reduced in size by half, and these unique and highly valued subtropical wetlands continue to degrade in the wake of drainage efforts. Meanwhile, South Florida counts eight million residents and continues to develop. Florida Seminoles, along with their Miccosukee relatives and neighbors to the south, are at the heart of some of the most expensive, scientifically interesting, and politically and socially vexed water issues in the world.

Through water we can learn more about sovereignty, Seminole and otherwise. When studying the effects of Seminole gaming, I documented the work of the Tribe's Water Resource Management Department and considered how they enacted sovereignty. They did so in law, insofar as gaming enabled the Seminole Tribe to assert its water rights and to craft and enforce its own water regulations under a historic 1987 compact reached with the state of Florida and the federal government (Shore and Straus 1990). Water managers also reinforced sovereignty materially, as they worked with reservation residents to provide flood control and drainage, irrigation, habitat protection for economic activities like cutting wood or for health like harvesting medicinal plants, along with ecological preservation and restoration. I could have stopped there, and it would have been a relatively straightforward case of building autonomous political power through gaming. However, department employees and a number of residents on the swampy Big Cypress Reservation told me that studying water management on the reservation alone was insufficient: to really understand the water and its stakes, I needed to look northward, to the non-Seminole farmers and other landowners from whose lands the water flowed southward onto the reservation. And so I did.

Water moves, and this is analytically significant for thought about political forms and processes. As anthropologist David Mosse (2008, 939) wrote, "water shares the complexity of land (from which it is rarely separable) as a medium of meaning and material relations, while adding movement and the dimension of time and process to the relationality that is inherent in space." Water respects neither property lines nor political borders. Water exerts force, and understanding and managing the force of water long has been viewed by American scholars and engineers as a matter of governance, and even, in the early days of American anthropology, as a scholarly justification for US settler colonialism (Schmidt 2017). Swamps and other wetlands long have puzzled US and other nation-state leaders, who struggle to build politics on shifting ground. Historically, water seasonally flowed southward from central Florida along a limestone plate, creating vast wetlands that covered the lower third of the peninsula and that today connect cities like Miami (which relies on the Everglades for water supply) to rural farmlands to Seminole reservations to expanding coastal suburbs.

Water politics and practices bring into being, and render understandable, sovereign interdependencies. It is tempting to add watery adjectives to the sovereign formations I study. Are they fluid, hydraulic, or liquid? Are the material forms that watery politics instantiate best described as wakes (Sharpe 2016), shoals (King 2019), or swamps (Ogden 2011), and under what historical and social conditions? Drain the swamp, politicians say. The analogies are tempting, but they can obscure more than they illuminate. Especially since the #NoDAPL movement, Indigenous and settler colonial studies scholars supplement their well-established focus on land with attention to water. In doing so, scholars revise and expand—not through analogy but rather by following water empirically—what counts as dispossession and how settler state power can be identified, analyzed, and diminished (see, e.g., Risling Baldy and Yazzie 2018). Since the early 1990s, Pacific Island studies scholars have led the theorization of Indigeneity and sovereignty in relation to water (e.g., Diaz 2015; Hau'ofa 1993; Ingersoll 2016). Epeli Hau'ofa (1993), in the classic article "Our Sea of Islands," reframed academic thought about Oceania by rejecting the prior focus on Pacific islands' smallness and remoteness to instead describe Oceania as a "sea of islands." Doing so shifted the focus to the vastness of Pacific Islanders' oceanic territories, and to the connections they maintained through known and trafficked watery territory. When the Idle No More movement spread through North America beginning in 2012, it was in part the resistance to Canada's assertion of sovereignty over waterways that galvanized Indigenous people to dance and occupy important places, both rural and urban.

When it comes to Seminole sovereign assertions to water, the 1987 compact set the stage for Everglades restoration. Back in the 1980s, residents of the rural, swampy Big Cypress Reservation, which is located south of Lake Okeechobee and between the cities of Fort Lauderdale and Naples to the east and west, had little say over their water. The US Army Corps of Engineers in the 1960s had dug a major canal, the L-28, through the reservation, with little to no consultation with the tribal government, much less with the Big Cypress residents whose lives and livelihoods would be disrupted. Soon, the water table fell lower and lower. Drainage alleviated flooding, to the relief of some reservation cattle ranchers and farmers. However, drainage remade the local ecology and brought negative consequences, including reduced access to plants and animals that sustained household economies and individual health. The impacts of drainage and related infrastructure were not limited to lowered water tables, however. Big Cypress residents recounting those years emphasized to me that they had lost control over their water, that others controlled them and their land anew. This was a new chapter in the long story of dispossession. The people who now determined how much water came onto the Big Cypress Reservation, when it came, and its quality included the state water managers who regulated water storage and flow through the canals that connected the lake to the reservation. They also included farmers to the north of the reservation who used public and private networks of canals to pump water off and onto their fields and

Jessica Cattelino

pastures. During wet summer months, Seminoles' northern neighbors sent water south, where it flooded the reservation. When farmers to the north needed water for irrigation during the drier winter months, they pumped water out of the canals and left the Big Cypress Reservation parched.

The Seminole Tribe could have sued over these and related concerns, and they threatened to do so, but in the end they negotiated a historic water settlement. The Seminole Water Rights Compact of 1987, which is the most significant American Indian water rights agreement east of the Mississippi River, guaranteed water allocations to the Seminole Big Cypress and Brighton reservations, established the right of the Seminole Tribe to govern water "as a state" under the federal Clean Water Act, established and empowered Seminole water policy-making procedures and governance mechanisms, and affirmed shared governance principles and regulatory protocols with the state of Florida. It also produced new and expensive forms of reservation bureaucracy, including land and water use regulations that some Big Cypress residents resent and resist.

The decision to reach a negotiated settlement that not only guaranteed rights but also established shared regulatory norms and practices was not reached lightly. When Jim Shore negotiated the compact for the Seminole Tribe back in the mid-1980s, he was less than a decade into his position as the first general counsel of the Seminole Tribe; he was also the first Florida Seminole lawyer. For Shore, the water compact simultaneously is about autonomy and the Seminole Tribe's connection to other, neighboring sovereigns. Thanks to the compact, Shore explained, "we are part of the system" and "have some say-so." Water itself demanded this sovereign duality of autonomy and connection. He continued, "We want to have our own regulations on-reservation, but not totally different than what they have, because water flows on- and off-reservation." There must be points of political and technical connection, insofar as water itself connects people(s). Water's flow shapes law, shapes regulation, and shapes how sovereignty looks and feels. In important ways, Seminole sovereignty reflects the qualities of the Everglades ecosystem. It was nineteenth-century Seminoles' use of the swamps that allowed them to survive brutal US military invasions and escape forced removal to present-day Oklahoma, and I frequently hear interviewees and speechmakers connect their sovereignty to their knowledge of the Everglades ecosystem.

Intergovernmental collaboration around water marks an important chapter in the twentieth-century shift on the part of the federal government from treating Seminoles with violence, hostility, and neglect toward increased cooperative negotiation. Make no mistake: this is an incomplete and complicated shift, and one that does not obviate but rather transforms settler colonial power. But it also emerges from and transforms Seminole power. This change has come, it must be emphasized, only after Seminoles had secured their water rights and achieved gaming-based economic and political power. Today, the compact guarantees a seat for the Seminole Tribe at the table of regional water management and Everglades restoration. Seminole representatives drive to the South Florida Water Management District headquarters in West Palm Beach for long technical meetings and political summits. Neighboring farmers now know that Seminoles have a unique right to water, whether they like it or not (views are mixed). The compact, when backed by gaming money and top-notch legal and technical teams, limits the power of federal and state authorities to govern water in an important and populous region.

Even so, it is a constant struggle to sustain Seminole sovereign authority over water. For example, the governing structure and technical failures of the Big Cypress Water Conservation Plan (the one for which the Seminole Tribe contributed $25 million nearly two decades ago) have greatly frustrated Seminole officials and staff, especially insofar as the Army Corps defaults to treating the Tribe as a local contractor rather than a sovereign partner. Sovereignty is tiring, is a struggle.

Everglades reclamation and restoration shed light on shifts from autonomy/differentiation to connectivity that more broadly characterized, respectively, the high-modernist statecraft of the 1900s and more recent shifts in rural state power in the United States. One of the major consequences of twentieth-century Everglades drainage was the compartmentalization of the ecosystem. The 1948 Central & Southern Florida (C&SF) Project, a textbook high-modernist joint federal and state undertaking to provide regional flood control and guarantee water supply to people and agriculture, reorganized the interdependencies that long had structured the wetlands. During two decades of massive construction, the C&SF Project built over one thousand miles of canals and levees (there are now 2,300 miles of canals) and installed pumps to move huge volumes of water through the system. The project, in the words of water managers, "compartmentalized" the region into functionally distinct zones for agriculture, water supply/conservation, urban development, and nature (the Everglades National Park had been dedicated one year before). Not only did the C&SF Project recategorize the waterscape; it also remade the waterscape and reshaped

Jessica Cattelino

political power through it. The northern reaches of the region, designated by the C&SF Project as the Everglades Agricultural Area, transformed into an agricultural powerhouse and unit of governance; the Everglades National Park became an international tourist destination and UNESCO World Heritage Centre governed by a major federal agency; the coastal areas exploded into metropolitan regions and powerful economic engines; while the water conservation areas remained vast but highly managed wetlands and, increasingly, political footballs. During the second half of the twentieth century, the distinctiveness of these zones was naturalized in law, planning, science, and public consciousness.

In recent decades, ecological restoration has aimed to reconnect the Everglades watershed. A major goal of CERP and related Everglades restoration is decompartmentalization, or "decomp" as most people call it. Decomp plans include backfilling some of the major canals, removing levees, and partially reconnecting the ecosystem, albeit while still managing it for flood control and urban water supply and while still abiding by legal settlements over water quality. Water managers have built a physical decomp model, and scientists are studying its projected impact. Generally, environmentalists cheer the plans, while many recreationalists, especially anglers, oppose it on the grounds that it will destroy major fisheries in the canals. Decomp requires undoing boundaries and barriers, both materially and in governance.

One of the principles that has guided South Florida water managers through these transformations is watershed governance. Policy makers and scholars around the globe recognize that water's qualities and uses fit poorly with prevailing forms of sovereignty. Over the past several decades, they have increasingly promoted "watershed governance," which coordinates governance within the lands that drain into a common body of water and aims to naturalize governance in alignment with an ecosystems model. This is described by geographer Alice Cohen (2012, 2210) as a "shift from political to hydrologic boundaries," though such distinctions blur in practice, and hydrology is hardly apolitical. Florida was one of the earliest developers of watershed governance when in 1972 the state created the South Florida Water Management District and its counterparts throughout the peninsula.

Indigenous water management can disrupt watershed governance. With guaranteed water rights under their compact, and with insistence on governing within reservation borders, the Seminole Tribe of Florida exemplifies a wider phenomenon whereby Indigenous sovereignty presents a profound and politically indeterminate difference within and against the boundaries of settler ecosystem governance. The idea of "dividing the American west into watershed-based constituencies," according to philosopher Jeremy Schmidt (2017, 93), originated with the anthropologist John Wesley. That origin, in the invasion and settler colonization of the US West, helps explain why Indigenous peoples do not fit well within views of watershed governance. As geographer Imre Sutton (2001, 251–53) discusses, tribal authority over water management fundamentally challenges the increasingly popular and global goal of watershed governance by asserting political difference that is territorially demarcated and realized. Watersheds and their governance, as Jeremy Schmidt and Nathaniel Matthews observe, rely on social as well as ecological solidarity, on "hydro-solidarity" (2017, 98). In this, Indigenous sovereignty can seem inconvenient, unnatural, antienvironmental, and in the way.

Environmental governance on reservation lands points to an important characteristic of watershed governance that often goes overlooked: the taking for granted of current distributions across space of environmental value and ecosystem functions. This is where environmental history and ethnography come in to illuminate how watersheds come into being and how they reproduce or unsettle the sociopolitical order of things. On the one hand, American Indian territories and peoples have been subject to disproportionate environmental destruction and injustices, as environmental justice advocates and scholars long have pointed out (Gilio-Whitaker 2019; Powell 2018; Sze 2018). On the other hand, many reservations have not been developed to the extent of surrounding lands, whether because of lender redlining, federal Bureau of Indian Affairs neglect or other forms of underdevelopment, or because Indigenous people and governments have protected their territories from the kinds of environmental destruction wrought by their neighbors. Therefore, environmentalists and state agencies often treat Indigenous lands and waters as biological preserves, as they take what Laura Kirwan and Daniel McCool call "the *last refuge* perspective" (2001, 266, emphasis in original). In a settler colonial irony, it is precisely because Indigenous people on reservations often have caused less harm to water and land than have nearby non-Indians that Indigenous communities face more restrictions, under federal law and in public expectations, on water and land use. The Seminole Big Cypress Reservation is home to endangered Florida panthers and other listed wildlife, so laws protecting those species disproportionately affect Seminole water and land use. Additionally, because reservation land is held in federal trust, Big Cypress Reservation residents are subject to a dizzying array of tribal and federal land use regulations. Watershed governance pinpoints reservation land for environmental regulation and protection, even as it idealizes jurisdictional continuity and homogeneity within a watershed. Watershed governance easily clashes with Indigenous sovereignty, making the latter seem like it stands in the way, is old school. The Seminole water compact highlighted interdependence and was forged through negotiation, on the one hand, while on the other hand its guarantee of water rights to Seminole reservations interrupts watershed governance with irreducible difference.

As Everglades water teaches us, sovereign interdependencies are of indeterminate political value. Water's movement challenges autonomous territorial sovereignty. But in this, water is not exceptional. Instead, it reveals a more general quality of sovereignty. Sovereignty is not only, nor even primarily, about autonomous authority over territory. Rather, it is in the play between autonomy and interdependency that sovereignty is produced and transformed. Rather than taking a side as if interdependence and autonomy were opposing positions, we instead should evaluate sovereignty by the measures of nondomination, as Young discussed, and good relations, as emphasized by Estes and TallBear.

By exploring the value and meanings of sovereign interdependency as nondomination and good relations, and by reducing the power and taken-for-grantedness of sovereignty-as-autonomy, we may be able to enact and imagine new and more just political futures. At the very least, we can endeavor to dislodge the sexist and anti-Indigenous entailments of sovereignty-as-autonomy. On its own, however, sovereign interdependency, whether with reference to economy or ecology, is neither a romantic alternative to nor a liberation from sovereignty-as-autonomy. Its affective field comes with no guarantees. Thus, identifying the conditions, including the feel, of justice in sovereign forms and practices remains an unending and contingent task. As Elizabeth Povinelli has suggested in a different context, the task is less to differentiate between dependency and freedom than to determine "which forms of ... dependency count as freedom and which count as undue social constraint" (Povinelli 2006, 3). That, in turn, is an ethnographic project, a creative one, and a practical one that people undertake every day, in South Florida and beyond.

Notes

1 Earlier versions of this line of thinking can be found in Cattelino (2007, 2008, chapter 6).

2 Most genealogies of modern sovereignty originate with Jean Bodin ([1576] 1992), who in the sixteenth century introduced the idea of "indivisible" sovereignty and conceived of sovereignty as located in a sovereign ruler (rather than a pope or Christian body) and as implemented through law. A number of writers since Bodin, including Harold Laski (1917), have criticized his monist theory of the state, arguing that pluralism is consistent with, and even intrinsic to, sovereignty. Even those critics of monism, however, still most often identify and measure political sovereignty by autonomy from (external) others. Another approach has been to theorize sovereignty in light of globalization.

3 Even those recent theories that highlight the role of the exception in structuring sovereignty—that is, the notion that the sovereign is simultaneously outside and inside the juridical order, as Giorgio Agamben (1998) suggests—take unitary sovereign orders as their unit of analysis. Agamben's analysis of sovereignty has been productive, but perhaps does more to account for US sovereignty than for Indigenous sovereignty. This is not just an empirical limitation. Rather, it is indicative of limits to Agamben's theorization of sovereignty.

4 In *Cherokee Nation v. Georgia*, most famously, US Supreme Court justice Marshall wrote for the Court that Indian tribes were "domestic dependent nations," that they were "in a state of pupilage," and that "their relation to the U.S. resembles that of a ward to his guardian" (1831, 30 US [5 Pet.], 16–17). The characterization of Indians as "dependents" subsequently limited their tribal sovereignty, placed conditions on their Indigenous and settler state citizenship, and inextricably linked their political authority to their economic dependency.

5 Partial exceptions are legal scholar T. Alexander Aleinikoff's (2002) constitutional analysis of tribal sovereignty, the US territories, and immigration and Thomas Biolsi's (2005) discussion of sovereignty and spatiality.

6 Young grants independence to sovereignty, but without working out the implications of the distinction. Ethnography compels me to apply her arguments about self-determination to sovereignty, and I wonder whether, in light of such evidence, Young would have subjected prevailing views of sovereignty-as-autonomy to the same critique as she applies to the concept of self-determination.

7 This analytical and political move resonates with Marxist feminists' insistence on robustly accounting for the social reproduction of labor within—not outside of—theories of capital.

8 Imagine if Agamben had considered this when analyzing the distinction between the oikos and polis at the foundation of his theory of the sovereignty, between "merely reproductive life" restricted to the home and politically qualified life, which is "born with regard to life, but existing essentially with regard to the good life" (1998, 2).

Jessica Cattelino

9   Similarly, feminist philosophers have pointed to the limitations of privileging autonomy in accounts of care, kinship, and politics; they have instead called for recognizing the constitutive role of dependency in subjectivity and polity (Fineman 2004; Kittay 1999; Tronto 1993). Some of these scholars are more attentive than others to the racialization of autonomy and of care.

10 Joanne Barker's (2005, 21) important introduction to the genealogy of the sovereignty concept emphasizes that sovereignty is not a definable thing. Thus, the scholar's task is to analyze the ways that sovereignty comes to matter in a particular context.

> What is important to keep in mind when encountering these myriad discursive practices is that sovereignty is historically contingent. There is no fixed meaning for what sovereignty is—what it means by definition, what it implies in public debates, or how it has been conceptualized in international, national, or indigenous law. Sovereignty—and its related histories, perspectives, and identities—is embedded within the specific social relations in which it is invoked and given meaning. How and when it emerges and functions are determined by the 'located' political agendas and cultural perspectives of those who rearticulate it into public debate or political document to do a specific work of opposition, invitation, or accommodation. It is no more possible to stabilize what sovereignty means and how it matters to those who invoke it than it is to forget the historical and cultural embeddedness of indigenous peoples' multiple and contradictory political perspectives and agendas for empowerment, decolonization, and social justice.

Barker continues, "The challenge, then, to understand how and for whom sovereignty matters is to understand the historical circumstances under which it is given meaning. There is nothing inherent about its significance."

11 Paul Nadasdy builds from ethnographic research on Yukon First Nation agreements with Canada to argue that sovereignty comes with certain entailments of the state—territory, citizenship, ethno-nationalism, and time/space—that cannot be escaped by Indigenous peoples' asserting and enacting sovereignty. He concludes that "in adopting a 'modern' (read: state-like) form of governance, Yukon Indian people are also compelled to adopt state-derived ways of knowing and being in the world. In this way, the Yukon agreements serve as extensions of the colonial project" (2017, 315). While I concur with Nadasdy's observations about the effects of bureaucratization and other aspects of state formation, I am less convinced than he of sovereignty's ontology.

12 He draws a contrast with the United States by noting that Lakotas and Dakotas named nineteenth-century extractive white traders "Wasicu": "the 'fat taker,' the settler, the colonizer, the capitalist. To be called 'Wasicu' was the highest insult. It meant that a person behaved selfishly, individualistically, with no accountability, as if they had no relatives." Importantly, the term "became synonymous with the United States, a nation that behaved as if it had no relatives" (Estes 2019, 97).

13 See Cattelino (2008) for a fuller discussion of law and interdependency.

7

Moral Economies, Developmentalist Sovereignty, and Affective Strain

ARJUN SHANKAR

Adavisandra is a village of approximately fifteen hundred residents located forty kilometers south of Bangalore city, South India's fastest-growing metropolis. The Bannerghatta forest curls to the northwest of the village, creating a visible, if illusory, separation from the city. When I first arrived in Adavisandra in 2013, three women from the village came to school each day to prepare midday meals, part of a program organized by the Karnataka state to make sure every child who went to a government school had a hot meal to eat for lunch. On this day, their meal was *raagi mudde*, a finger millet famous in these South Karnataka villages made into a large chewy ball, usually served with sambar, what those Anglophiles unfamiliar with the cuisine might describe as a "vegetable lentil stew." I watched as Bhagyamma, Parvatamma, and Jayamma, the three head cooks, made the meal in a small room, no more than twenty square meters, cluttered with pans, utensils, and plastic pots to carry water. The three women sat around a large steel pot, and Bhagyamma gently stirred the sambar as the other two women cut and threw vegetables into it, moving meticulously and taking their cooking very seriously.

Bhagyamma explained that they received only one thousand rupees per month for their work.[1] However, they had not received their salaries for over six months, a situation that was beyond desperate given each of their family situations. Bhagyamma was the best off. Her husband made a slightly more reasonable salary as a lorry driver, and so they were able to cobble together enough each month, though he left for three-week stretches at a time to do so. Parvatamma lived alone with her husband, a shepherd who made approximately five thousand rupees by selling adult sheep, a growth process that took about thirty days. Parvatamma's daughter had been married, and in order to pay the dowry they were forced to sell their land, which had left them with only their home and nothing else. Jayamma was struggling the most, as her husband had left her for another woman, and so now she lived alone with her two children in Adavisandra. Her son had opened up a ration shop in the village and was able to bring in less than three thousand rupees a month, making their lives barely tenable even with the income from her work at the school.

As the three women continued to stir the pot of sambar, Bhagyamma eventually told me, "It is difficult to lead a life. . . . In this age, only if we have income we can be all right. Otherwise it's a lot of trouble." The phrase reflected "the corporealities of poverty" that women living in rural places experienced every day (Nouvet, 2014, 83), a kind of global-rural common sense that life "in this age"—the age of neoliberal capitalist reforms, the age of agricultural disinvestment—was difficult to lead and a lot of trouble.

Still, the women all did their work with zeal, meticulously moving through the process of cooking and cleaning. There was real pride in their craft, and they told me, "We serve food and wash all the utensils and the kitchen. We keep it very clean. We treat it like our home. We come here and work. If we don't keep it clean, who will? What will people say then? That we are so dirty. How will we cook for the children?" Bhagyamma's statement explicitly referenced others in the community—"what will people say"—a gendered form of social collateral that influenced exactly how she and the other two cooks thought about their participation in the new economy created as part of the midday meal scheme (Schuster 2015). For Bhagyamma and the other cooks, the affective ties to these social relationships—feeling obligated, dutiful, clean, nurturing, and familial—created a different reason for working that could not quite be easily captured by the logic of salary, payment, and employment by the state.

On this day, before I had come to speak with these women, I had been talking to the school headmaster, who told me with great enthusiasm that they were seeking to move the school to a new, centralized midday meal scheme, administered by the nongovernmental organization (NGO) Akshaya Patra through a private-public partnership, a program associated with the Hindu religious organization ISKCON. When I asked the three cooks how they felt about this news, they were shocked, and then I was shocked, as it slowly dawned on me that they had not been aware that these already precarious jobs were actually in peril.

As soon as I mentioned this, they began to anxiously inquire as to exactly when it would happen: "When did the master say the ISKCON food would come?"

I had no answer to this question and muttered an incoherent response. Bhagyamma looked at me, visibly straining as she thought about what I had said. She then dismissed me without another word and silently moved back to the sambar, stirring it slowly and carefully. The other women, following her lead, also took up their tasks again. Whether or not their jobs would be lost, whether or not they would ever receive their pay, these were all abstractions completely out of their control and not worth straining themselves over. There was still the task at hand: to feed the children and to meet their obligations to those whom they cared about in their community, all of which gave their lives a sense of worth and dignity that could not be so easily stripped away by these future potentialities and which, however implicitly, unhinged the assumed total power of the state over their lives, their goals, their feelings, and their labor.

The Right to Food and the Paradoxes of the Developmentalist Moral Economy

Since the early 1990s, India has been nothing if not a place of paradox. On the one hand, it has been positioned as both the largest democracy in the world and the most ambitious advocate of free-market liberalization, boasting the largest number of billionaires while consistently maintaining GDP growth rates of over 6 percent and even as high as 10 percent during the early years of economic liberalization. Along with its economic development has come the massive infrastructural development of India's cities—hotels, highways, financial institutions, and world-class airports—symbolically marking India's ascension from an underdeveloped postcolonial nation to "India Shining."[2]

At the same time, India has faced, and perhaps facilitated, an incessant counternarrative, one in which it has been unable to make economic development trickle down to visible human developments in social sector areas such as education and health care. Instead, it has continued to be seen as a place of extreme social inequality, poverty, malnourishment, and illiteracy.[3] These continued assertions of massive inequality have facilitated a perceived crisis of sovereignty: How is the government to provide basic resources, especially to children, but do so in a way that facilitates accumulation as it has been institutionalized by the Indian government over the past forty years?

One response to the issue of malnourishment and child hunger came from the Indian Supreme Court, which, in 2004, established the right to food. It ruled in the case *People's Union for Civil Liberties v. the Union of India & Others* (2001) that the "Right to Food" was a fundamental right based on Article 21 of the Indian Constitution. Birchfield and Corsi write, "Drawing on constitutional precedent defining the Article 21 right to life as 'the right to live with human dignity and all that goes with it, namely, the bare necessaries of life such as adequate nutrition,' and a history of activist, human rights-oriented judicial interpretation of this Article, the Supreme Court in PUCL interpreted the right to life with dignity to include the right to food, thereby affirmatively incorporating the right to food—originally an aspirational Directive Principle—into Article 21 and transforming it into a justiciable and enforceable fundamental right" (2010, 16). The court's ruling was the result of major social pressures wrought by the Right to Food Campaign, which made the ethical argument that the government had a responsibility for food security and poverty alleviation. Such movements integrated globally circulating human rights discourses on dignity, which had been enshrined as a value in the Universal Declaration of Human Rights (1948), into the practical (or technical) question of how to solve the human problem of malnourishment and underdevelopment, which also, in turn, complicated any simplistic separation of government-led development projects from highly charged ethical debates (Bornstein and Sharma 2016; Mazzarella 2010).[4]

The ruling also highlighted, if not further facilitated, the emergence of biopolitically motivated "economies of care" (Ticktin 2006), including the continued NGOization of India's voluntary sector. In India, NGOs have proliferated at an exponential rate, numbering at minimum three million, but with some arguing that the number is actually over four million (Anand 2015).[5] These organizations have proliferated to alleviate social ills in education and health care as well as to manage the rural-to-urban migrations facilitated by economic liberalization's decimation of agricultural economies. These NGOs have run the gamut, from international NGOs whose primary headquarters lie outside India's borders, to national NGOs that work directly with the Indian government, to NGOs who refuse both corporate funding and government backing, choosing instead to function as independent advocates for ethico-political causes, like the right to food.

These care-and-compassion economies can stand in a complicated relationship with the state's economic development goals. In fact, the government viewed many human rights organizations as doing "antidevelopment work," claiming that by pointing out abuses of power, these organizations had caused 2 to 3 percent decreases in India's GDP over a five-year period (Bornstein and Sharma 2016, 76). In other words, these types of organizations seemed to challenge the singularity of sovereign power, especially in the articulation of moral claims that spilled in excess of the social relations and strategies to redress inequity (technocratic, monetized, unmarked, etc.) sought by the government. The fear was that sovereign moral legitimacy—defined as the state's claim to a monopoly on the legitimated determinations of right and wrong and how to rectify such wrongs—might have been "potentially undone by that which fails to recognize it, by that which refuses it in intentional and unconscious ways" (introduction, this volume).

As such, the national and state-level governments have been incentivized to forge NGO-state partnerships of their own. One such scheme created by the Indian government in the wake of the Supreme Court ruling was the Midday Meal Scheme, devised to make lunchtime meals at government schools free to children. The scheme provided funds for schools (1) to hire members of local communities in which schools were located and to buy the necessary resources to cook daily meals, or (2) to have meals shipped in by not-for-profit or private organizations tasked with cooking and transporting meals to schools. The decision to choose one form or the other has opened up debates that draw from the discourses of financial management—especially those regarding efficiency, standardization, and centralization—and has led to increased tensions regarding the reemergence of top-down governance.

In the state of Karnataka, especially in the areas surrounding Bangalore from which much of the ethnographic data for this chapter emerged, the primary supplier of centralized meals was Akshaya Patra, a national not-for-profit organization that supplied school lunches to over ten thousand schools all over India, with Karnataka being its largest consumer, with almost three thousand schools receiving the Akshaya Patra midday meals.[6] The organization states, "No child in India shall be deprived of education because of hunger. Today, through the partnership with the Government of India and various State Governments, as well as philanthropic donors, the organisation runs the world's largest mid-day meal programme. Built on a public-private partnership, Akshaya Patra combines good management, innovative technology and smart engineering to deliver a nutritious and hygienic school lunch" (Akshaya Patra 2008). Given its altruistic vision centered on the child, its direct reference to private-public partnership, and its idealizing of techno-managerial praxis, Akshaya Patra's project seems to fit the prototype for how developmentalist moral sovereignty ought to look. The organization's global notoriety had grown to the extent that even former US president Barack Obama sent a letter praising the organization in September 2008 for using "efficient and innovative business practices to scale up in a few years," ending by stating that the Akshaya Patra model of "using advanced technologies in central kitchens to reach children in 5700 schools" was "an imaginative approach that has the potential to serve as a model for other countries" (Akshaya Patra 2008).

An analysis of Akshaya Patra brings to the forefront the regimes of moral and ethical value associated with developmentalist sovereignty. Developmentalist sovereignty is one of the inheritances of the postcolonial nation-state, tethered to the affective intensity of being characterized as economically, politically, socially, culturally, and morally underdeveloped by the colonizer. In turn, the neurotic impulse to develop and progress has produced a form of internal colonialism that seeks to develop all those who are deemed underdeveloped by the state through totalizing strategies of neocolonial governance associated with modernity, liberalism, and salvation (the civilizing mission).[7] In this instance, developmentalist sovereignty places an excess value on centralized, efficient, scalable technocratic interventions and, in turn, takes these values as morally superior and therefore the only way of going about the work of helping Others. But these regimes of moral value are also intended to structure feeling, creating affective regimes by linking "affect with values" (Fassin 2012, 2) and producing hegemonic emotional registers that are tied to considerations of right and wrong emplaced by the state. From the perspective of the state, developmentalist moral sovereignty should completely foreclose on other competing affective moral fields, and citizen-subjects should totally internalize the state's version of how to participate in moral economies and how to feel about this participation.[8]

Unfortunately, for the state, people like the Adavisandra cooks still exist all around us and continue to move, grow, change, subvert, create, and relate in ways that exceed developmentalist sovereignty. Bhagyamma insists upon working in the kitchen, cooking meals for children, negotiating her interdependency with her fellow village community members despite the fact that these actions are not necessarily resulting in payment or mobility within India's developmentalist apparatus. Her relationships and the affects they produce are never purely utilitarian, merely about economic, atomized mobility or being recognized within the categorical moral imperatives of sovereign power. If anything, she is straining against these singular visions of how and why she should work in both explicit and less explicit ways.

In the rest of this chapter, I want to posit and theorize the concept of affective strain to get at how those who work in the moral economies unhinge developmentalist sovereignty. Attending to affective strain helps to showcase how the very acts of everyday living—the strain of movement, the strain of seeking mobility or keeping one's job, the strain of building new connections between places or maintaining one's connection to home, the strain of trying to do the right thing or figuring out what the right thing even is—constantly unhinge the predictions of developmentalist moral power. Strain, in one of its most common usages, implies the stress of the mind and body as they are pushed and stretched to an unusual degree or intensity; an embodied excess potential that is easiest to observe when it is converted and stretched to its limit as kinesis. Such strain can be quite painful in, for example, a strain of a muscle, literally the tearing that occurs when people stretch their bodies too hard against other forces, or, in other cases, the mental stress that might arise when people refuse the moral dogmatisms of those in power or when they fight to live dignified lives in the face of oppression. Oftentimes strain is recognized and noticed when it is directed explicitly as a critique of sovereign power, when potential energy has been converted almost too rapidly into kinetic energy. For example, the contradictions in developmentalist morality are clearly visible when juxtaposed with the protests, rights claims, and critiques of oppression that emerge in movements like the Right to Food Campaign discussed above, which may result in the loss of voice when people shout too loudly as they demonstrate in the streets or the rapid loss of physical fitness if they are considered enemies of the state and therefore thrown in jail, their bodily health completely devalued in logics of carcerality.

Strain may also be more subtle, less visible, a constant impact on the body that slowly erodes it or exhausts it. It might be about the ordeals of everyday life that create fatigue over time, like the constant mental stress the cooks experience as they deal with the fact that they will not be paid anytime soon. This type of strain can be about the everyday encounters and practices that may not be so overtly political but showcase how people persist and refuse despite this constant sense of precarity and the oppressive moralizing that seeks to render them responsible for their own predicaments and suffering. In these cases, choosing not to show strain, to go about life and continue to forge bonds that matter, might itself be an unhinging of sovereign expectation. If developmentalist sovereignty demands a moral purity toward its goals and at its behest—to see morality vis-à-vis a kind of antirelationality linked to individualism, autonomy, atomization, and so on[9]—going about the daily practice of cooking for children, as Bhagyamma and her colleagues do, despite the fact that their work is being compromised and rendered less valuable within the developmentalist moral economy, is a form of refusal that unhinges developmentalist sovereignty.

In these cases, affective strain emerges alongside another sense of the term *strain*, as a noun that connotes a bacterial or viral strain. In bacteriology, the strain of a bacterium is used to denote "the descendants of a single isolation in a pure culture" that have been artificially produced by scientists in a lab. In social Darwinist terms, this idea of the pure strain is articulated taxonomically as "an isolate or group of isolates of the same genus or species by phenotypic characteristics or genotypic characteristics or both" (see Dijkshoorn, Ursing, and Ursing 2000, 397). This articulation of *strain*, then, is about both stratification (separation of elements) and purification. These artificial constructions of intransigent imagined communities and racist moral hierarchies infiltrate and, quite literally, colonize the entire body politic. Indeed, as I will show, technocratic developmentalist visions reproduce hierarchies of purity that intersect with casteist Hindu ideologies, and the masculinizing and urbanizing of help work, all of which erase or demand the subordination of their binary impure opposites: the oppressed caste, non-Hindu, rural, and feminine. But these purist stratifications also rely on spread across all populations, that is, the complete and total colonization of people from these subordinated positions. For example, as I will show, they require that young men from these communities join help organizations and aspire to better wages and better lives for their families, even as they become enmeshed in the rhetoric of "doing good" that may actually require them to see themselves and their families as less valuable and less pure.

Despite the drive to moral purity within developmentalist sovereignty, those who labor as part of these economies continue to draw on their own embodied histories, which become the basis for forms of relationality that do not fit neatly into the prescribed purity politics of developmentalist sovereignty. This daily strain to maintain alternate relationalities through small acts that exceed sovereign expectation are the basis for other ways of being, claims of self-worth, and decolonizing ambitions. This is at least partially why the ideological singularity of the developmentalist vision as morally pure must consistently be imposed and reinforced: intimate, affective, embodied human relationships consistently strain against and unhinge developmentalist sovereignty's purity, legitimacy, and universality. At minimum, Bhagyamma's story reveals that her version of a feminist ethics of care is not limited to capitalist valuations of pure rational utilitarianism or blood-based purities of genealogical lineage. Instead, her sense of obligation emerges from a different idea of community, one that persists, refuses, and strains against the antirelational expectations of developmentalist moral sovereignty. Even the act of cooking *raagi mudde* is a unique form of embodied knowledge and the mere love for these tastes and styles of cooking strains against the kind of food practices and valuations imposed by Akshaya Patra, in, as I will show, the claim that sattvic meals, a brahmanic Hindu cuisine, are healthier and purer.[10]

Observing and thinking with affective strains focuses heuristically on relational potential, whether or not these potentials are valorized within the moral politics of what developmentalist sovereignty wants. If, for example, developmentalist affective regimes valorize hard work and perseverance, then exhaustion, disinterest, and persistence may all be the kinds of strain that unhinge its totalizing bootstrap morality in unique ways. If, in other cases, developmentalist affective regimes valorize individual productivity and atomized aspiration, then straining to hug loved ones, maintain embodied cultural practices, and care for community members may all unhinge its totalizing utilitarian morality. These actions may not be all that confrontational or even active, but instead are those affective potentials that emerge as always already unhinging sovereign foreclosure.

In the rest of this chapter, I excavate several examples of affective strain that unhinge developmentalist sovereignty. I begin by providing an ethnographic vignette focused on the Akshaya Patra factory and the truck drivers who transport meals from the Bangalore factory to villages all over South Karnataka. I draw from these interactions to underscore the kinds of affective strains that are generated when help work is centralized. If developmentalist moral sovereignty is associated with a paternalistic form of taking care of a large population, the flip side is the affective strain on those whose livelihoods are tied to this need to take care of Others, especially when they are not the managers of capitalist production, but constitute its labor force. In this section, I show how Akshaya Patra seeks to create a totalizing model of centralized cooking that reproduces affective fields that hinge on ideologies of purity and impurity. In turn, I show how truck drivers strain against their undervaluation as they seek upward mobility, challenging the colonization of their tastebuds and finding ways to live a dignified life. Following this exploration, I return briefly to Adavisandra village, to reframe the politics of developmentalist sovereignty for the Adavisandra cooks by showing how Adavisandra school leaders justify the entrance of Akshaya Patra meals through ideologies of rationality and irrationality, efficiency and inefficiency. In turn, the Adavisandra cooks strain to keep their jobs and articulate claims for collective redress of their grievances that unhinge the way

Arjun Shankar

that developmentalist sovereignty predicts they should or will react. Finally, I conclude with a few remarks about how the day-to-day affective strain of those who labor unhinges, whether purposefully or not, the persistent push toward total colonization at the center of developmentalist moral sovereignty.

The Factory

A few weeks after my chat with the Adavisandra cooks, on a cool Bangalore morning, I woke up at 3:45 a.m., straining to get out of bed and meet the demands of factory time. I dragged myself into a car with two of my research assistants, Sanjana and Supriya, and headed, bleary-eyed, to the Akshaya Patra factory, which sat at the furthest periphery of what has now come to be included as part of Bangalore city. It was hard to see at that time of morning, and we barely made out the green sign announcing our arrival at the factory site. During the day, one could see high up on a hill a large ISKCON temple on the same grounds as the factory. The temple stood as a stark reminder that this version of the midday meal scheme was tied to a Hindu version of charitable giving (Bornstein 2012).

By the time we arrived, it was clear that work was already underway. This particular factory site served meals to over nine hundred schools in the area, and in order for meals to get to every school site by lunchtime, work had to start before the sun came up. Time was recalibrated in centralized development initiatives like this one, straining to accommodate the burdens of scaling. As we entered the factory, we passed a huge fire that lit the final few feet in front of the factory, releasing smoke that rose up into the air and into the darkness. We passed through room after room of machinery, huge vats that would be filled with curries, vegetables, and sambars to cook. Through a large window we could see workers continuously mixing the food, dressed in blue suits with caps covering their hair and masks covering their mouths. They held their arms over the vat, and I imagined that this slow and steady stirring eventually tired them as their muscles strained under the constant, repetitive movement. Eventually the food would move step by step through the factory, a classic assembly line model of production, and into trucks to school sites all over the region, both into the center of Bangalore city and further out into the hinterlands that surround it.

In South India, the meals consisted exclusively of rice and sambar combinations along with a vegetable, a process of standardization that Akshaya Patra argued ensured that the food was cooked hygienically.[11] In this rendering, standardization was taken as an obvious social good, linked to an assumed improvement in health. The website outlined the rigid protocol by which quality was maintained in these meals, and the quality officer whom I spoke to at the factory expressed pride in these stringent standards. Quality had a twofold connotation: (1) as a gloss for "healthy, pure, safe"; and (2) as a gloss for a managerial methodology that built from Edward Deming's Total Quality Management (TQM), which was developed for postindustrial management initiatives like this one.[12] But standardization also reinforced a singular version of what meals should look like. If village schools made meals that reflected the very locally specific tastes of their children (in, for example, the aforementioned example of *raagi mudde*), centralized factories sculpted taste based on both what was easiest to mass produce and what had a perceived hegemonic cultural value. In this case, the rice-sambar-vegetable combinations constituted a sattvic diet, which were vegetarian recipes that did not include onions or garlic. Such recipes were ostensibly unmarked yet were quite obviously constitutive of brahmanic Hindu cuisine, implicitly mapping health onto already-existing Hindu caste hierarchies (*Churumuri* 2017). This implicit marking of value was even more clear when considering the demographics of Karnataka, in which almost 80 percent of the population eat meat and less than 5 percent are brahmins. Yet, by eating sattvic meals, children would imbibe these cultural valuations of who is and how to be healthy/unhealthy and pure/impure, literally through their consumption of food.

In turn, developmentalist centralization generated and emplaced religio-casteist affective fields in the very process of food production, distribution, and consumption. Most of the kitchen and trucking staff had come from Karnataka's villages and were from the Vokkaliga or Lingayat caste groups, two non-brahmin agricultural castes that dominated Karnataka state. These personnel knew that Akshaya Patra considered sattvic meals as more healthy and nutritious than what they might have eaten while at home, which were more similar to the meals cooked by Bhagyamma in Adavisandra. While they may not have explicitly mapped this healthy/unhealthy dichotomy onto caste, religion, and rural/urban divides, it was clear that they were expected to feel and comport themselves as if these kinds of meals would be better than whatever meals students would get in places that resembled where they themselves had grown up. Most importantly, they were aware that their own value was tethered to serving these meals: making meals that resembled those of dominant-caste Hindu food cultures was a known moral good, understood as a way of bringing exceptionally healthy values to poor populations who could benefit from them. And by doing this work, the staff was supposed to feel like

Arjun Shankar

they were moving up this religio-casteist hierarchy, participating in the project of uplift that previously might have been foreclosed to them. Whether or not they enjoyed the taste of these meals themselves, they were expected to feel a sense of worth when they became purveyors of these meals to others.

Yet, despite being tasked with delivering this sattvic food and even enjoying the sense of worth that came with this task, the truck drivers invariably contrasted these meals with the kinds of food they would have eaten in their homes in villages in Karnataka. In fact, some of the staff found the food bland and boring, and were nostalgic for the flavors they associated with their family homes. One of the truck drivers, Srinivas, for example, told me jokingly that regardless of the health value, he could never wait to go home and eat in his native place. Yes, he recognized that this food was "good for the children" and that he too would eat it without complaint, but his body could never quite experience it in the same way. He poked fun at the "purity" of the Akshaya Patra meals, laughing about the fact that health and spirituality always had to taste bad. The joke, as Jackson writes, is "a pleasure that pivots on people's stubborn recognition of their own continued worth despite external threats of devaluation and marginalization" (2010, S279). In this case, Srinivas's quip actually unhinges the attempt at developmentalist moral foreclosure regarding whose food should be consumed and why. In other words, Srinivas was straining against the brahmanizing of all his taste buds, embodying a position that would not be completely colonized.

None of the drivers made more than 8,500 rupees a month for their work, though of the four drivers we spoke to, some received as low as 4,500 depending on how long they had been with Akshaya Patra. Of this income, some went to taxes, and five hundred rupees went to lodging on the ISKCON campus. This, Srinivas told us, was the biggest benefit of his job: "To get a room for five hundred rupees in Bangalore city is most difficult." If Bhagyamma had deemed rural life difficult, life in the city was no less difficult for those on the margins who moved from rural to urban centers, unless, as Srinivas hints, they were able to join the developmentalist economy.

Srinivas had worked for Akshaya Patra for three years, and he was candid about why he joined it in the first place: "I was working as a security guard in Mantri apartments. When I saw the van going, I liked it. Children are being given food. I thought I should do this job. Wishing that I get salvation by doing this job, I joined." The Akshaya Patra trucks emerged here as a marketing campaign, but not necessarily as one might think. If initially the slogans, pictures, and financial dedications might be assumed to have been directed at the upper middle classes (i.e., those who might remember to donate to the organization), the campaign was also meant to strike at the heartstrings of those at the other end of this moral economy, that is, the rural or urban poor who might be seeking a job. These jobs carried with them implicit benefits because they were, by default, morally good. As Srinivas said, he might gain "salvation" by trucking meals to village children. He was therefore willing to take this job even though, as I learned later, he made less as a truck driver than he did as a security guard. Here, then, is another way that sovereignty in its developmentalist form relied on the linking of moral value to affects which, in turn, sustained the labor force for the moral economy. In this case, the production of a feeling of being saved in the work of helping others, which linked a kind of spiritual catharsis to the work he was doing, was the basis for Srinivas's continued interest in working in the development sector.

Srinivas continued, explaining that he had actually been hired for a supervisory role but soon after was demoted to the position of driver. He and the route boy who joined him on his journeys, Sanjay, discussed their situation together:

> SRINIVAS: When I joined, I was the supervisor. They canceled the supervisor post. So I started driving. The benefit is food and accommodation is available, so no problem.
>
> SANJAY: Even I was a driver before. But I did not have a vehicle, so I became a route boy here.
>
> SRINIVAS: Whoever comes to work here will have studied at least up to PUC [Pre–University Course diploma]. But the staff takes their pay on the basis of their service. So it's like, whether you are qualified or not, you get the same pay. They weigh everyone in the same plate.
>
> SANJANA: Do you have any chance of promotion here?
>
> SRINIVAS: No promotion, madam. On coming here as a driver, there are no opportunities for promotion.
>
> SANJAY: *We get the value a driver should get* . . . [emphasis added].
>
> SANJANA: What's the highest post here? Supervisor or what?
>
> SANJAY: There is no other post, madam. I am a driver, that's all. No supervisor, nothing. I have joined here as a driver. We can't do anything else. We cannot wish for higher posts.
>
> SRINIVAS: No, madam, we don't get anything as such. We might have a hundred problems with Akshay Patra; they might have given us a hundred troubles, but we cannot say all those things. What happens is . . . when I was working as a supervisor, I was forced to leave because they said they'll cancel the post. I did not like to leave, but it

was inevitable. After doing a higher-profile job, our heart won't agree to do a lower-profile job. In that condition, I could not leave the job and go jobless. . . .

If, on the one hand, driving for Akshaya Patra is meant to produce affects related to salvation, on the other hand, the day-to-day labor produced an affective field related to accepting one's lot in life. Here, Sanjay and Srinivas are expected to move in the world and through the organization with a kind of resignation to the impossibility of upward mobility because as drivers they get the "value that drivers should get." In this sense, the moral economies associated with Akshaya Patra reinforced affective fields that mapped occupation, class position, and status onto one another, which located the reason for immobility in those who were rendered immobile.

But even if developmentalist sovereignty sought to quelch the drivers' aspirations for mobility, Srinivas's aspirations could not be so easily quelched. As he himself said, his "heart" could not agree "to do a lower-profile job" after experiencing what it was like to be a supervisor and to be valued for his work. By mentioning his heart, Srinivas recognized that even if his mind, logic, and thought were telling him there was no possibility of mobility, his body would not allow him to accept it, pushing him to keep trying for something more. Srinivas was already wondering about his future after leaving Akshaya Patra: salvation or not, his heart could not allow him to imagine staying forever. He told me, "I want to have my own vehicle. A Sumo." The strain on his body would be worth it if he could keep going and prove to himself and others that it was just a stage in his mobility narrative. In the act of not accepting his lot in life, Srinivas was unhinging developmentalist sovereignty, which sought to make him feel that he should go about driving without aspiring for more and he should feel thankful for being allowed to participate in this righteous developmentalist economy.

He told us about his family as we drove toward his first stop on his route, a village some twenty kilometers outside of what has now been marked as Bangalore's southern edge:

SRINIVAS: My parents were laborers. We have ten acres of land. There is a bore well. I love being in my village and farming. But my parents said that they suffered enough, asked me to live well, and so sent me here. I don't like Bangalore in the least. I dearly wish to go to my village and do farming. The land is fertile. [But] there will be problems. So my father told me to go and work in Bangalore.

SANJANA: Now will you go back?

SRINIVAS: Yes, madam, there is a festival in my village. I will go now. It's a forty-five-minute journey. I can travel up and down every day, but it's just a risk.

SANJANA: Who looks after the land if you're not there?

SRINIVAS: My father looks after it.

If Bhagyamma and the other women's struggles in Adavisandra village provided one view of urban centralization, Srinivas's view from the factory provides another, equally related to the urban-rural nexus. In Srinivas's telling, the city emerged as the only means for mobility for those living in the village because India's free-market, urban-centric economic policies decimated rural areas, leaving agricultural life unsustainable for many who did not own large plots of land. Srinivas had been forced off his land by his own parents, who, like many in these rural peripheries of Bangalore, wanted nothing more than for their son to find some kind of success beyond the village. For those in Karnataka's villages, developmentalist sovereignty generates an affective field that assumes that mobility is found elsewhere, farther and farther from home.

But Srinivas missed his village, his traditional occupation, and his family, and he contrasted this longing with his dislike of the city. He was not the first nor the last young man I met who expressed these sentiments, many of whom would extend their critique of the city to speak of its pollution, congestion, and poor quality of life. Srinivas coughed while he drove, rubbed his legs, and honked at the congestion on the city streets, all of which punctured the story of where the good, the pure, and the valuable reside. At the same time, Srinivas remarked on the fertility of his land and strained against the notion that he should not or could not go back to his village. Whether or not capital accumulated in the city, beauty, clean air, and love were all still tied to his agricultural land.

There is no doubt that the strain of being kept from home was stressful for Srinivas. But the fact that he refused to be completely torn from home was the embodied excess that prevented the city, as the site for developmentalist sovereignty, as a place of growth and prosperity and possibility and production, from capturing him within its universalizing constraints. He awaited a moment when he could go home for his village festivals, to help on his family's land, and was willing to take the risk of heading back from time to time, even if it meant potentially losing his job. Here, developmentalist sovereignty has produced those actions which are deemed risky and those which are not, which are intended to tear people away from their closest relationships. But the fact that Srinivas was willing to take this kind of risk is the kind of affective strain that has the potential to unhinge developmentalism's requirement of unidirectional movements of people and value.

Returning to the Village

I head back to Adavisandra a few weeks later. On this day, I set about trying to figure out why, exactly, Adavisandra school had decided to shift from local meals to Akshaya Patra meals. Standing on the front steps of the school building, Purushottam Sir tells me authoritatively when I ask him why he is so enthusiastic about the Akshaya Patra scheme: "More than teachers, it will benefit parents, [the] public, and students. It's hard to find labor here. Sometimes what happens is . . . if all the responsibility is on them [the local villagers], they fear to take it. They see something on TV, or through some other media . . . then get scared . . . so when they get scared, they suddenly refuse to come to work. Here, we can't stop giving food because they are not coming to work. This is an everyday process. It has to go on."

I have listened to Purushottam Sir's words many times now, and each time I am taken aback at how easily he blames the Adavisandra community for the need for change, positing that those in the village cannot be trusted to do the work in school because they might not handle the responsibility. In a somewhat absurd line of reasoning, Purushottam Sir goes so far as to posit that those who live in the village are so feeble of mind that they might see something on TV and get irrationally scared, rendering them incapable of coming to work. The headmaster's views did, however, reflect a longer history of narratives about Indian villages, which has largely been seen through the lens of deficiency, backwardness, stasis, and superstition (Mines and Yazgi 2010). But by reproducing this narrative regarding the village, Purushottam Sir imagines its deficiencies in contrast to what he imagines will be the efficiency and predictability of the Akshaya Patra scheme. In Purushottam Sir's racialized reasoning, rural backwardness, incompetence, and naivete become the foundational basis for his argument about moving toward a new midday meal model that will be run by competent, urban managers. Here, centralized developmentalist reason requires this type of racist stratification and the mythology that those who are outside the hegemonic fold are incapable of hard work because it will cause too much of a strain on their "feeble-minded," "irrational" bodies. In other words, these narratives impose a particular reading of village affect: as lazy, fearful of outsiders, incompetent, and the like, the impure strains of Indian society that were holding it back. This kind of moral and affective impurity functions as an adequate moral foil to the technocratic zeal of Akshaya Patra, reproducing an urban-rural divide that sees NGO-based centralized urbanity as the solution to making everyday processes run smoothly, rationally, and efficiently in the village. This is one sense in which imagined narratives regarding village life, urbanity, and the like generate the conditions for what developmentalist sovereignty feels like and, therefore, the kinds of interventions that are made possible. Indeed, what Purushottam Sir is really illustrating is his own belief in the moral economy: efficiency is a moral good made possible only by state-led partnerships, which must be brought to the village as soon as possible.

To be clear, Purushottam Sir did not have any empirical basis for why villagers should be fearful after watching TV or should be exceptionally irresponsible in taking care of midday meals. In fact, the three women who worked at the school to make the midday meals, as I have indicated above, were deeply dedicated to the work they were doing. They took their jobs quite seriously, were enmeshed in a set of village-level social relations that actually added pressure on them to do their work well, and continued despite the fact they had not been paid.

I asked Purushottam about this fact and the fact that the women have not been paid for the work they are doing. He replied:

PURUSHOTTAM: The department will give . . . it has to be allotted by the Zilla Panchayat. They bill it at the Taluk level, that so many people should get their salaries. That goes to Zilla Panchayat. It has to be approved by the Zilla Panchayat and come back to Taluk Panchayat. From the Taluk Panchayat it goes to SBM [State Bank of Mysore]. SBM distributes it to the respective accounts. Because of all this process, it gets delayed. The system is like this. It is the same with our salaries.

ARJUN: You haven't got your salaries?

PURUSHOTTAM: We have. The Zilla Panchayat allots the money once every six months, for so many *crores*. The Taluk Panchayat spends that money for education. Thinking that it will be a problem because it's a huge amount for a lot of people, and because it will create pressure on elected bodies, teachers will not work if not given salaries. So they will give our salaries faster. This [midday meal scheme] is a recent development, so it gets a little delayed. We can't help it.

When faced with the actuality of the women's hard work, the fact that they come to work every day and still have not been paid, Purushottam is no longer able to rely on the stereotypical affective fields associated with villagers. Instead, he is forced to recognize the actual source of the problem: state-level centralized bureaucracy and inefficiency, the very same process that only days earlier he had been praising. Here, the women unhinge developmentalist sovereignty simply through the act of showing up to work without pay, something that subverts sovereign expectations of them and what sovereign expectation requires in order to justify centralization. For example, if the three women had stopped showing up because they had not been paid, it could have been used as a reason to move toward centralized meals: "See, these women won't show up to work. We knew it!" Unpaid or not, incompetence or incapacity would have been proven.

For the women, their particular position in relation to this bureaucratic functioning generated a number of interwoven affective strains. On the one hand, Bhagyamma, Jayamma, and Parvatamma were quite aware of the power imbalance that they faced and wilfully continued to voice their grievances against those in power:

SANJANA: Why are you working here despite not having got your salaries for so many months?
PARVATAMMA: We said the same! We refused to come. They say it is our wish.
BHAGYAMMA: We say that we will not come and we will not cook. They tell us to talk to the authorities who come. Don't work if they won't give you the salaries—otherwise work. No authority came. We didn't speak to anyone. We are simply working here.
BHAGYAMMA: We told the headmaster that we will not work if this continues. He said he'll take us to an office in Kanakapura to talk to them. But it's of no use if only three people go there and talk. The workers from all schools should come.

The women were very clearly aware that they had been wronged, that they should have gotten a salary, and that they should seek out the appropriate authorities in order to receive just and timely compensation. Here, the cooks clearly strained against the idea that this is how it must and should be, that there is no other possibility but to give in to a kind of fatalist affect produced by developmentalist sovereignty. They recognized the value of their labor and strategized ways to remove themselves from the strain of this work in the school, knowing that this might be the only way to get changes made.

But Bhagyamma also recognized that the problem could not be solved by just the three of them alone. Instead, she explained that the only way anything could change was through mass collective action; a collective straining against these injustices. Not just three people, but all the workers from all the schools, producing a collective affect that would reach in excess of any of their bodies or voices. Unfortunately, Bhagyamma's very precarity actually prevented this kind of collective action. Instead, because she knew she could not afford to leave work and to undertake the incredibly arduous task of organizing a worker's movement, she only mentioned it in passing. Still, she marked that there was a way to make change through collective strain, even if she simply could not mobilize it at the moment. This bodily resistance to the way it is and recognition of another possibility might be just enough to thwart being consumed by the regime of morality produced within and through developmentalist sovereignty.

I left at that moment, believing that these cooks would no longer be working the next time I came. And it was, in fact, quite a while before I was able to travel to Adavisandra again. When I did finally return to Adavisandra's school some twelve months later, the Akshaya Patra meals still had not arrived. Instead, the secondary school had now built a small kitchen for the midday meals, where Bhagyamma, Parvatamma, and Jayamma continued to cook. I asked Purushottam Sir why they never managed to get the Akshaya Patra meals, which he had made me believe was quite imminent in our previous conversation. He shrugged and told me that they had tried to get the Akshaya Patra meals but that unfortunately the organization had refused to come to Adavisandra because the school was too far into "the interior," just outside of the radius where they could deliver, a radius that covered the school just five kilometers away. The inevitable transition I had imagined just a year earlier was thwarted by distance itself, the push toward centralized development kept at bay by the physical constraints that had always been its most significant nemesis. The universalizing impulse was thwarted, yet again, by the perpetual problems of space and time.

I met the cooks one last time, and I asked them what they would do if the ISKCON food ever did come, a now more distant possibility than it had been before:

PARVATAMMA: We shall work as domestic help . . . or in our fields. . . .
BHAGYAMMA: What can we do? . . . We'll do coolie work. There are factories here. The factories are very far. We can't go there because we have to finish all house-chores and send our children to school. Either we'll work in our fields or go to work as coolies.

JAYAMMA: We'll go for other work then, labor work.

PARVATAMMA: We'll work with the silkworms, removing the cocoon, etc.

If they lost their jobs as cooks, they would fall back on their traditional occupations, working the land to make whatever income they could. These possibilities were mentioned with only a shrug of the shoulder, so constitutive of their everyday that they were not really worthy of too much attention or strain. For now, they had a job that gave them purpose, and if it ended, they would do what they had to do, as they always had done, and find a way to continue to live dignified lives in an age that they knew was and is difficult for them.

Conclusion

In conclusion, I would like to briefly turn back to the question of developmentalist moral sovereignty in relation to affective strain. Much affective scholarship has based its analysis on Spinoza's (2002) most famous definition, in which affects are related to "the affections of the body whereby the body's power of acting is increased or diminished." In this classic Spinozist definition, the affective is never divorced from the possibility for action. Here, I have sought to theorize and explore affective strain as one way of understanding the types of action that persist within moral regimes of developmentalist sovereignty; to show how regardless of the totalizing impulses of developmentalist morality, it can never truly achieve complete colonization because of the unexpected, unintentional excess that comes with straining to live a dignified, relational life.

Many have explained that in order to maintain itself, a nation-state must continuously discipline its citizenry and create the illusion that it has the sole authority to determine how injustice should be redressed. A citizenry must believe that the state is always working in its best interest and therefore holds a monopoly on what can or cannot be a legitimate moral intervention. The state, in other words, must be viewed as unilaterally benevolent and working toward the good of its people and must be the sole authority by which to determine legitimate moral claims. If not, then sovereign power might come totally unhinged. This is why, for example, the moral economy in India was meant to produce, more than anything else, a totalizing legitimacy regarding how the issue of children's welfare and malnutrition should be solved and who should solve it. This form of developmentalist morality seeks to emplace the idea that technocratic, centralized, efficient, and standardized solutions to the problem of poverty alleviation and food insecurity are the only solutions worth undertaking. At the same time, these types of solutions rely on masculinist, brahmanic Hindu, urban overvaluations, even implying that these forms of redress are "purer" and that those who fall out of these categories must be less valuable, less capable, and less pure.

I have argued here that the day-to-day strain of living relationally itself thwarts the totalizing colonizing impulse of developmentalist sovereignty precisely because it functions in excess of sovereign expectation. Affective strain, while sometimes valorized in many (neocolonial) liberal stories of bootstrap struggle and survival that enlist people into the perpetuation of their own disciplining in ways that allow for extraction, instead should be viewed through the prism of material relations that produce what is considered excess. The daily strain to lead a dignified ethical life—to continue working even if one isn't paid, to care about community in nondevelopmentalist terms, to believe in a future that could be different than one's present immobility, to refuse to dishonor one's own history, family, and community or see one's embodied practices as impure or valueless—cracks the enclosure of sovereign morality. In other words, the work of life and the work of care are always sites of potential, even inevitable, unhinging.

Affective strain does not always have to be explicit, and strain should not be interpreted as a case of counterhegemony, which tends to imply active and conscious challenges to sovereign power. Instead, strain and the excess it produces functions in far more subtle and less direct ways. Such strain gives us hope, perhaps because it reveals the futility of neocolonial control. As this chapter comes to an end, I wonder: What would sovereignty look and feel like if it was not premised on producing lives that required so much strain to persist, refuse, and exist with dignity?

Notes

1 One thousand rupees is approximately US$14. The official (and heavily disputed) international poverty line is US$1.90 per day.

2 But massive growth like that seen in India is unsustainable, and anxieties over slows in GDP catalyzed Modi's project to demonetize, a show of sovereign strength that quite literally took cash out of the hands of India's citizenry because it may or may not have been tainted by the sickness (*bimari*) of "corruption" (Dharia and Trisal 2017). The explicit message was, of course, that demonetization would restart India's economic development, filling loopholes

Arjun Shankar

that were preventing India from taking its rightful place in the geopolitical order. In reality, demonetization only continued the slow erosion of citizenship rights in postliberalization India for those most marginal in India today, continuing in a tradition of transferring "financial and developmental risk onto bodies whose economic precarity is deeply inflected by class, caste, region, religion, and gender" (Dharia and Trisal 2017).

3 For example, in 2017 the Global Hunger Index ranked India one hundredth among 119 "developing" countries, behind North Korea, Bangladesh, and Iraq. The index's ranking was based on four indicators—undernourishment, child mortality, child wasting, and child stunting—each of which focused India's human development problem on the Indian child.

4 The declaration begins with the line, "Whereas recognition of the inherent dignity and of the equal and inalienable rights of all members of the human family is the foundation of freedom, justice and peace in the world." Here, living the life of dignity becomes an inalienable right of all humans, though what this means in practice is contested terrain along considerations of economic, political, and sociocultural claims.

5 In 2015, Anand wrote that in India, "the first-ever exercise by the CBI [Central Bureau of Investigation] to map registered NGOs has disclosed that India has at least 31 lakh NGOs—more than double the number of schools in the country, 250 times the number of government hospitals, one NGO for 400 people as against one policeman for 709 people."

6 Bangalore, the urban context most pertinent to the discussion undertaken in this chapter, might be the best example of India's current development project, tripling in size and quadrupling in population in a ten-year period beginning in the late 1990s (Goldman 2011). While previously a small town in South India, best known for its weather and gardens, Bangalore's ascent was driven by the information technology sector, as both international and national IT corporations made it the hub for a new generation of technologists whose aspirations for mobility were tied to the global flow of data in a postdigital world. Fiber optic networks made information sharing ever more possible and, in turn, laid the foundation for Bangalore's reimagining as a "world-class city" (Goldman 2011).

7 Here, I am drawing from Walter Mignolo, who writes, "First, the logic of coloniality . . . went through successive and cumulative stages presented positively in the rhetoric of modernity: specifically, in the terms salvation, progress, development, modernization, and democracy. . . . This transformation of the rhetoric of salvation and the logic of control became prevalent during the period of the secular nation-state" (2011, 14).

8 Such sentiments interweave the affective with the economics of neoliberal governance, shaping a moral narrative that "combines the aspiration to self-realization with the claim of emotional suffering" (Illouz 2007, 4).

9 Here, I am referring to and drawing from Jodi Melamed's insights regarding racialized capitalism, in which she states, "To this end, one way to strengthen

racial capitalism as an activist hermeneutic is to use it to name and analyze the production of social separateness—the disjoining or deactiving of relations between human beings (and human and nature)—needed for capitalist expropriation to work. Ruth Wilson Gilmore suggests a similar understanding of racial capitalism as a technology of *antirelationality* (a technology reducing collective life to the relations that sustain neoliberal democratic capitalism) in her seminal definition of racism" (2011, 78).

10 Sattvic food is generally associated with Ayurvedic and Yoga literature and considered healthy and pure within many Hindu traditions. *Sattva* means "purity, wholesomeness, and virtue" in Sanskrit.

11 From the Akshaya Patra website: "All the kitchens of Akshaya Patra follow a standard process for preparing the mid-day meals. This process is charted out to ensure hygiene and quality of the cooked meal and also to adhere to the food safety standards. All the cooking equipment like cauldrons, trolleys, rice chutes and sambar/dal tanks, cutting boards, knives etc. are sterilised using steam before the cooking process begins. The vessels used in the kitchens are made of stainless steel of 304 grade and is best for cooking and handling food" (Akshaya Patra, "Our Kitchens," accessed April 12, 2022, https://www.akshayapatra.org/our-kitchens).

12 Kumar and Sarangapani chart the travels of this idea of quality into the education sector, writing, "As has been noted, since the 1960s onwards we find specific references to the term 'quality,' or rather the lack of it, and the need to ensure it in schools. The wider ethos was one in which the economic discourse of quality was acquiring precision and appeal in areas such as industrial production and marketing (Dooley 2000). Ideas of quality control and assurance through statistics-based monitoring laid the foundation for testing-based production with W. Edwards Deming's ideas of 'total quality management,' 'quality control,' and 'assurance' to ensure maximum efficiency and standards in manufactured goods" (2004, 41).

8

The Slaughterhouse after Surplus Value

ALEX BLANCHETTE

This chapter is situated in the pseudonymous town of Dixon, the center point of a Great Plains region inhabited by some fifteen thousand humans and seven million hogs. A company town that has been remade to maximize capitalist value across the industrial hog's life and death cycle, Dixon is the site of an experiment in vertical integration led by a company I call Dover Foods. This agribusiness corporation owns and controls every phase in the conception, birthing, raising, and killing of hogs with the aim of generating nineteen thousand radically uniform animals every day. They do so, as this chapter suggests, to better match hog bodies to automated machines and standardized labor processes—that is, augmenting the intensity of meatpacking workers' exploitation using slaughterhouse line speed increases. The American pig's body is violently shaped across its lifetime to further accelerate the labor and outlandish productivity of humans at its moment of death.

In late 2021, COVID-19 was still tearing through American slaughterhouses. Over 86,000 American slaughterhouse workers had been sickened; at least 423 had died. In the early days of the pandemic, industry commentators forecasted that meatpacking plants would either shut down or would revert to a model from the 1970s of slower kill line speeds and minimal cutting of hogs' bodies to better enable social distancing among workers (see Two Centuries of Dead Labor, below). A year later, none of that had happened. Shortly after the outbreaks, the president of the United States invoked the Defense Production Act for mass-produced meat. He declared people's lives to be expendable to secure the "critical infrastructure" of American animal killing, along with the votes of a white rural American populace that predatorily depends on these (primarily migrant) workers for their highly capitalized farms and businesses. Most slaughterhouses returned to full capacity. Some poultry and pork plants even lobbied to further increase their line speeds.

The pages that follow detail what was saved by the invocation of the Defense Production Act, a system that was already collapsing under the weight of its own interminable logic of compounding growth, uniformity, and rapidity. These pages further illustrate the paradoxical nature of late industrialism. Anthropocentric dominion over animal lives has paradoxically reached such extremes of control that no one in this system of killing appears capable of feeling sovereignty. And the inability to exhibit or even sense agency—beyond, that is, repetitiously intensifying century-old processes—by those who work within this system, including its ostensible architects, is only the tip of the iceberg. Public discourse has also entered a standstill as reformists call for governmental regulation, and corporations insist that they should be left to self-regulate. For all their differences, both positions insist on their rational capacities to be sovereign over these industrial capitalist processes. As American slaughter perennially explodes through interspecies biological limits, however, what seems clear is that capitalism's fixation on possessing human time and energy—or labor—cannot be reformed over the long run. I thus offer this chapter to give a portrait of just how unhinged systems of efficient human work have become, in the hope of convincing readers that the viable path is to abolish these institutions and see what else can arise.

Efficiency is still discussed in some economic circles as a matter of increasing sovereign control; in some outdated visions, industrial capitalist competition will gradually lead to an ever-more-rational use of human energy and nonhuman resources. However, in many late capitalist places, such as slaughterhouses, efficiency is itself out of control—and its increase offers nothing more than the intensification of violence against all bodies within.

Vertically Integrating Tendons

A few weeks after I first moved to Dixon, the town was awash with gossip about an event that had occurred in the slaughterhouse. I made no effort to follow up or confirm the details. It felt wrong to turn this incident into a piece of anthropological research, although it was impossible to avoid the local chatter as people tried to puzzle out the meaning of the act. The

Stockyard. Photograph by Sean Sprague.

rumor was that a young man had committed suicide in the slaughterhouse using a bolt gun. Bolt guns are used to euthanize large breeding animals on farms; that is not the usual way industrial pigs are slaughtered. Occasionally, hogs are injured in a truck on the way to the packinghouse and cannot walk. These nonambulatory hogs are shot in the head in the stockyards (see figure 8.1) and then rendered for pet food and biodiesel. The man must have got hold of the stockyard's bolt gun.

An elderly woman at a truck stop diner was the first to mention the incident to me. Her rhetorical question was the same that everyone else in town was asking: "Why would he do that . . . like that?" Many believed the act must have been a profound statement—that it was performative, a symbolic gesture—rather than a matter of opportunity in terms of a suicidal man finding himself with the means in hand. An inebriated former slaughterhouse employee at a bar, a few nights later, loudly recounted how he was abused by managers and then fired. He saw the form of the suicide as a tribute to the spirit of meatpacking work. "They treat people like they're pigs," he bellowed to everyone in earshot. This phrase is common in meatpacking communities, an expression that rolls off the tongue. Many slaughterhouse stories contain some variation of the phrase (see, e.g., LeDuff 2000). It claims that people working in slaughterhouses are expendable like hogs. The phrase's charge is that corporations do not afford workers special dignity as human beings.

This chapter argues that there is some truth to this slogan, though it is complicated: workers in vertically integrated systems are not disposable, but they are treated in ways that parallel the treatment of industrial pigs. In mid-2016, the social justice organization Oxfam America briefly made waves with its investigation into labor conditions in some of the largest American chicken plants. The report that received the most media attention was titled *No Relief: Denial of Bathroom Breaks in the Poultry Industry* (Oxfam America 2016). Oxfam investigators interviewed poultry workers who claimed that they were rarely allowed to step off the cut floor to use the bathroom (see also Ribas 2016). People were being humiliated on the line. They were forced to choose between urinating on themselves, not drinking liquids, or wearing diapers to work. The report offered a jarring image of industrial modernity in that key factors in the cheap price of chicken nuggets are diapers and urinary tract infections. The report and subsequent media commentaries pushed the poultry industry to adopt and follow its own best practices of employing additional workers to step onto the disassembly line as floaters and provide others with a few minutes' break. This is an important intervention given the acute and immediate needs of laborers in slaughterhouses. But there is also the issue that the system requires floaters in the first place, for what is remarkable in this case is how so-called efficiency in meat cutting is so out of control that corporations must solicit an official bathroom reliever position. The human bladder is a problem of production.

This chapter is about the still-evolving place of the human body in modern meat; it explores how human workers' and industrial hogs' corporeal forms have become newly entangled on the disassembly line. It traces how human physiologies are vertically integrated into the project of butchering nonhuman animals—how human and hog muscles are coproduced on the line—at a moment in which almost two hundred years of industrial refinement in slaughter has resulted in a system that operates at the limits of the working body. Meatpacking has often acted as a preview of forms of industrialism to come. Henry Ford (1923), for instance, claimed to take the idea of the assembly line from the 1890s Chicago meatpackers' disassembly line.

Alex Blanchette

What I want to suggest is that the slaughterhouse may still act as a site that forecasts the state of global industrialism, along with the changing value of capitalist human labor.

Every year or so, Dover Foods adds another venture to deepen its capitalization on the porcine species. Sometimes this extends the existing system's scale. In the early 2010s, for instance, it built an additional fifty finishing barns for meat hogs to accommodate growing average litter sizes and sow productivity. Other geographic modes of expansion include constructing new bacon, ham deboning, and processing plants in strategic locations across North and Central America, where labor costs are lower. A third, more intriguing form is Dover Foods' attempts to further industrialize materially different elements of hog physiology by rendering blood plasma or manufacturing biodiesel using hog fat. Dover Foods is searching for ways to increase the scope of its vertical integration of American animality and extract hidden forms of profit from within the porcine body.

During my first year of research in 2010, I expected to see the construction of a building or machine that would remake something like a porcine muscle or gland. Perhaps it would be some kind of biomedical harvesting process of heart valves for implantation into human beings (see Sharp 2013). Instead, Dover Foods announced that it was going to construct a health clinic for employees. During his speech at the public grand opening, Dover's chief executive framed this operation as an altruistic gift to the community. It was sorely needed. Most people believed it would benefit everyone in Dixon. It was a place where employees could seek medical care for themselves and their families. It would decrease the long waits at the struggling, overcrowded local rural hospital. The clinic would relieve pressure on the community's few existing doctors, especially at a moment—in the aftermath of the 2008 US recession—when the town was growing in population as working-class people came in from the coasts in desperate search of a paycheck. It was, as someone said, "a win-win solution." As an executive later recounted to me, "It is great when our needs and those of the community overlap and we get these opportunities."

I was, however, left perplexed about why workers' health was a key site of industrial expansion. I initially wrote it off without too much thought, plugging it into my settled habits of interpretation. I assumed that this could be figured as a typical industrial story of maintaining a reserve of able bodies for providing labor power to the slaughterhouse (see Marx 1992; Sunder Rajan 2007). The health clinic functions as a place where employees can be treated for nonwork illnesses such as a fever or strep throat. In terms of the corporation's bottom line, this could theoretically lead to fewer sick days by treating workers and their families promptly. A bit more nefariously, I figured the clinic would also function as a place where employees could receive rapid treatment for injuries that they suffered on the slaughterhouse trimming floor. Perhaps this would reduce an injury's severity, decreasing the number of days off and, concomitantly, the size of a workplace compensation claim to be paid by out of the corporation's insurance scheme. It felt perfectly sensible, though certainly no less disturbing, to think that a slaughterhouse merits its own hospital. And to be certain, the health clinic does provide these kinds of services in managing workers' bodies. From the community's perspective, it keeps people healthy. From the corporation's view, one could say that it maintains labor power in a remote town.

But it soon became clear that the situation was more complicated than this. The health clinic was operating in such a way that the new profit that the company aimed to unlock within the industrial pig was actually residing in its human employees' muscles and tendons. As I would learn while speaking with managers and reading newspaper stories, the clinic's primary purpose was to evaluate human bodies—and the differences across a single body—for their suitability for work on distinct parts of the disassembly line. Upon being hired, a person undergoes a series of tests that are far more extensive than a standard physical with X-rays. Potential workers at this clinic are asked to engage in forms of repetitive motion or to lift a progressively heavier series of weights from distinct angles and postures. Perhaps their range of motion for reaching is evaluated, or the strength of their pinch grip is being appraised. Each muscle group is separately evaluated, and the strongest segment of a person is then matched to a discrete cut floor motion. Thus, the corporation can gauge distinctions in the physical fitness of each body, assigning a given individual to the spot on the line that is most suited to their musculoskeletal state. In simple terms, this is done to decrease the probability that a person will be injured and file a compensation claim. More elaborately, it suggests how workers' bodies are becoming pools of potential value once the increasingly fast-moving disassembly line of cheap pork itself becomes a liability to corporate profits. Moreover, this arches beyond the standard capitalist terms of realizing profit through wage exploitation and surplus value—it operates in parallel to the postkill processing of hogs' distinct body parts, as workers are treated as differential physiologies. Disassembling industrial hog muscles is made more profitable by parsing differences in workers' bodies.

Alex Blanchette

The point of this chapter is not to offer a superficial critique of the health clinic, or even of corporate ergonomics efforts to profit by reducing injuries. It is clearly desirable to invest resources in limiting injuries on the line, regardless of the impetus.[1] Within the broader field of US meatpacking, ethnographers have found that many people truly are treated like disposable biologies and surplus lives to lower the price of meat (see Ribas 2016; Stuesse 2016). When a broader industry is quite literally premised on draining the "vital energies" of workers (see Vora 2015), even small efforts to maintain workers' bodies can initially feel progressive.[2] But I do want to reflect on what this health clinic suggests about the biology of labor in late industrialism. Workers in this slaughterhouse are not disposable; the management of their muscles has become a site of investment in a vertically integrated system. Workers are treated not like generic animals but instead as akin to one way I have been describing industrial pigs: as distinct and segmentable physiologies. What we are seeing here is how slaughterhouses are pushing outside of a standard labor theory of value whereby the cost of pig meat boils down to the amount of average social labor time exerted in its generation. Instead—or, perhaps better, in addition—it marks a situation where decades of effort to wring more value from porcine bodies are now doubling back to remake how the human body is marshaled as an industrial site to create new money.

What is the changing relation between pig bodies and human muscle? How have working human muscles become entangled with the state of hog flesh? For what this situation begins to suggest is that the industrial pig is paradoxically at its most vital—in terms of resisting human agency and will (cf. Bennett 2010)—only after its moment of death. This chapter develops by situating some slaughterhouse managers' claims that they have reached the maximum point of efficiency at which they are pushing the human body to its limits using machines, and are now dependent on additional pig standardization from the genetics and farming side to continue increasing automation and output. It elaborates the notion that factory farming is a dualistic biological system in which both vitality and capital determine managerial actions. Meanwhile, it juxtaposes these managerial words to workers' counterdiscourse of "breaking in" to describe an industrial system that transforms their bodies, muscle tissues, and hands via repetitive motion. The not-yet-perfect standardization of the pig results in managers feeling forced to increase the speed of the disassembly line in a way that pushes the limits of human biology; by doing so, this slaughter machine begins to destandardize human bodies.

[Upton] Sinclair's overdrawn prose notwithstanding, he effectively captured the endemic character of workplace dangers in the modern meatpacking industry.... Meatpacking's greatest danger was the way it progressively wore down the human body. Cold attacked lungs, salty brine solutions wore down flesh, and knives cut hands and limbs.... Yet the real dangers lay in the smaller incremental injuries.... [In a 1943 study,] one operative cutting up hogs had twenty-two knife wounds in one year; three with equivalent jobs in beef processing experienced a total of sixty-seven injuries, of which fifty-three were by cuts and lacerations. The job of these workers could be read in their hands!
—Roger Horowitz, "That Was a Dirty Job!"

One evening I was eating dinner at the home of a meatpacking worker named Sergio Chavez. We were discussing how he was recruited via relatives from Chihuahua (Mexico) to Dixon to work in the pork industry. Sergio's story was not premised on coming to town in desperate search of income; his is not the meatpacking tale of crossing the border for backbreaking labor as a matter of last resort (cf. Schlosser 2001; Stull and Broadway 2013). He was the scion of a family of businesspeople. The modest yet beautiful home where we were eating, in one of the affluent parts of Dixon where company managers live, could not have been the product of laboring on the cut floor alone. Sergio vaguely explained that his youthful leisure had spiraled out of control to the point at which he risked falling into danger in a northern Mexico on the verge of drug wars. His decision to leave was affirmed by his childhood friends who had become victims of violence between the Mexican government and the drug cartels, or of kidnappings for ransom. He seemed to be suggesting that his move across the US-Mexico border in the early 2000s was a self-imposed journey of moral rehabilitation to escape his youth. He claimed there was little worth remembering from his arrival except that it was snowing, he was living in a trailer, the place was barren, and he had work on breeding farms. "I came here to work," he explained, using a phrase echoed across conversations with laborers and even management. "This is only a place to work."

Within a few years of joining relatives in Dixon, however, Chavez was married and discovered a communitarian purpose in church, although he still described the town's overriding value using a motif of ascetic labor. He acquired a job in the slaughterhouse on the evening B-shift, from 3 p.m. until as late as 3 a.m., so he could spend the mornings with his young children. He cycled through various positions for the first two years. "The first sixty

8.2 Meatpacking plant. Photograph by Sean Sprague.

days were always a struggle," he said. "Every second was a fight. Every day was a rematch." Moving boxes of vacuum-packed meat across conveyor belts in shipping tore apart his upper back. The knife work of making one little slice across flesh five thousand times a day strained his hand muscles to the point where he once struggled to pick up a lime at Walmart after work. Working on the kill floor amid all the hot bodies was like being in a sauna; slicing parts of the loins on the refrigerated cut floor was an exercise in enduring bone-numbing cold (see figure 8.2).

Yet Sergio now spoke with masculine pride about this period of (self-) flagellation once his muscles and mentality had molded to the repetitive pain of the disassembly line. Each day he made the same motion of scraping blood and shit from ten thousand pigs' intestines, cleaning them out before passing them down the line for the next step in their treatment. Over the time prior to when we spoke, he must have run the tips of his thumbs over the surface of millions of intestines. He flipped over his hands on the table and nodded, grinning proudly, at the history of hard labor and sacrifice scarred into his thumbs. Repetitive motion was permanently etched into his thumbnails. The white of his thumbnails—the edge parts that usually begin at the tips of the fingers—went down to his cuticles. Over the years of scraping these hog intestines, his fingernails' shells had delaminated from the raw flesh that they were supposed to be protecting.

Upon seeing this proud gesture, one of Sergio's urbane younger friends chimed in across the table that he, too, wanted to try working at the slaughterhouse. "Why?" asked Sergio, in a flabbergasted tone. "I have to try it," insisted the man, nodding, as if he was convincing himself of his genuine desire. "So many people talk about it. I don't care if it's hard. I want to feel it." The slaughterhouse, for this physically fit friend, not unlike Sergio, was more than just a dependable blue-collar income. It was a test of character. As I understood this man's yearning to suffer, those sixty days—what others label the breaking-in period—were the basis for an embodied material experience that would help him share sensate bonds, and become part of a "sensory public," with Dixon's laboring populations.[3] In those fingernails and the histories of motion they indexed, this friend might have seen complicated forms of masculine mastery and will: over the grinding pace of slaughter that made many people quit, over the embodied sacrifices to support a family, and over being defined by one's past station in life. For my part, I have never gotten past how Sergio's fingernails hinted at the ways that the disassembly line—a 150-year-old capitalist technology that has intensified in speed over the years—was now moving so quickly that it made new bodies.

In terms of injury rates, the slaughterhouse has historically been one of the most dangerous places to work in the United States (Horowitz 2008; Human Rights Watch 2005). Most exposés of meatpacking feature the story of someone who has lost a limb or who has such severe carpal tunnel syndrome that they may never be able to work again. Ethnographic accounts from beef and chicken plants illustrate a picture of ergonomics and safety training as a bureaucratic chore during orientation week videos that tends to get ignored in practice (see, e.g., Pachirat 2011, 104–5; Striffler 2005, 129–33). Rare stories of someone's hand being ripped off by a machine would trickle out of the slaughterhouse. But these shocking injuries are almost red herrings. Dover Foods is not teeming with amputations and human death. As others note, the modern slaughterhouse is a story of mundane nicks, strains, and pulls that build over time until the person gives up (Horowitz 2008; Striffler 2005; Stull and Broadway 2013). A friend, an ex-"nurse" in the slaughterhouse who thought this position might help him train to become a real nurse, described to me a lexicon of classifying the escalating severity of routine violence in terms of the "flesh pokes," "slashes," "gashes," and "tendon cuts." His job was not to mend these wounds, "because there's only so much you can do in a place like that." His task was to sort cases and "paperwork" as he decided whether an injury could be fixed with Band-Aids and ointment, or if it would require a visit to the emergency room (and hence carry with it the threat of a compensation settlement).

In Sergio's fingernails, however, there are hints of another form of violence that is not an accidental injury caused by an exception, however systematic accidents may be when thousands of people work with sharp knives. This is a consequence of the line running normally. His fingernails point toward an embodied history of labor extraction etched into the surfaces, musculature, gait, and posture of Dixon's population. They indicate a population that has been biophysically molded by industrialization; this is a situation where the manipulation of porcine carcasses transforms the human body and, in turn, gives a cross-species meaning to managers' discourse that they manage a "biological system" in the slaughterhouse. Though less shocking than missing limbs—and Sergio's and others' masculine pride in their jobs makes it more morally ambiguous—I am haunted by impressions across interviews that no one knew how to control the packing plant, that this biological machine had become almost agentive and lively. If, as the labor historian Roger Horowitz (2008, 14) writes, the "job of these [packing] workers could be read in their hands," then what can Sergio's thumbnails tell us about the factory farm at the stage of the slaughterhouse? This is not meant as a story of exceptionalism, but rather of intensity—work always shapes bodies. Breeding-farm managers frequently had damaged knees from walking on concrete in rubber boots for many decades; wrist and back strains are common among office workers (see Jain 2006). What is striking about Sergio's fingernails, however, is the localized nature of the repetition that suggests how the slaughterhouse has refined its process to the point where it concentrates onto small parts of the body. Moreover, these motions are spread across populations such that each person's body becomes slightly different.

Breaking In

It is hard to remember the first time that I heard someone use the term "breaking in" (or, alternatively, "break-in") to describe the agonizing process of molding the human body to the disassembly line's machine-driven repetition. Every employee I met had a break-in story. Preparing new hires for this shock of pain—and emphasizing that it is a temporary ache—was part of the plant's orientation training and the origin of the term. The human resources department was trying to decrease the number of workers who show up for one week and never return. It was not unusual to hear rumors that the plant was hiring fifty new employees in a week during the peak of the late 2000s economic recession. The US Department of Labor's Occupational Safety and Health Administration (1993, 5), as part of its nonenforceable "voluntary ergonomics guidelines," developed in conjunction with the industry trade group the American Meat Institute, defines "break-in" as an initial period of decreased workload to "condition [employees'] muscle-tendon groups prior to working at full capacity." While some people recounted having a lighter workload on the line when they first started, breaking in was more typically narrated as a period of suffering and a process of learning how to reinhabit one's body once it is suffused with aches and pain.

Breaking in is an experience that can unite slaughterhouse workers from across the country. When I lived in a homeless shelter for new migrants to the area, I met a man from Minnesota who had grown up working in slaughterhouses and developed his own break-in remedies. Flexing stress balls after work, dipping swollen hands in ice baths, constant movement to keep from seizing up: these were home remedies that he taught new residents for overcoming the traumas of the line. Evenings in this shelter were often surreal, with people in too much pain to talk as they sat on couches and squeezed stress balls. Some managers—most of whom grew up in packing towns, took a job immediately after high school, and rose internally through the ranks—would proudly recount their own teenage experiences of sharp pain shooting through fingers, hands, and arms as if it was yesterday. Even the plant's senior vice president acknowledged the physical challenge of finding, shaping, and maintaining adequate bodies. "You're learning to become an athlete when you're not [an athlete]," he said, suggesting how hard it was to maintain modern packing in the face of a postindustrial North American populace without the required physical specialization to thrive in this kind of extreme environment.

I once saw a man who prided himself on his tough demeanor, an Eritrean refugee, curled up on the couch and fighting back tears as another man pried open and flexed his hands to keep them from seizing up. I overheard one new hire warn another about pain in the hands: "I can't take a shower; you can't even move a finger." Another woman, a roaming white Christian mystic, stayed in this shelter as she passed through town. These sorts of haunting sights of strained bodies, of people being treated, as she put it, "like the slaves of Judah," made her decide to stay in town and begin

Alex Blanchette

a mission after she saw a vision of "the Beast" (Satan) while driving her truck past the plant on her way out of town.

Alicia, a strong thirty-year-old who was originally from Chicago, began six long slaughterhouse years with the job of using enormous scissors to cut out part of the pigs' stomach for tripe (or "paunch," as she put it) on the humid kill floor, or "hot side." She narrated break-in as a deeply internal pain, as if she was being gradually torn apart:

> In the orientation classes, they have that break-in pain they tell you about. And you feel it. It's all in your body because you've never worked like that before. You're constantly moving, you're standing there on concrete. . . . It feels like you're flammable or something. Your bones really hurt. Your hands hurt. Your back hurts. Like sometimes I would get off a shift, because I worked on the kill floor for ten hours a night, and I couldn't sit down. I couldn't lie down in bed because my body was so sore. My back. I had to sit down on the couch for an hour before I could even lie down. It's just some kind of pain that you get that your body hasn't sensed before. It's this pain that your muscles are working more than ever, just something that you've never felt before. That's what they always say in the orientation classes.

Alicia described breaking in as a 24/7 pain that followed her home as her body was remade. Her suffering occurred most descriptively not as she wielded scissors on the kill floor but as she sat alone at home. As one of the anthropologist Steve Striffler's (2005, 129) coworkers on a chicken line described the consuming and almost addictive quality of the slaughterhouse, "As soon as I start hanging chickens I feel fine. It's like that is all my muscles know how to do. I am in constant pain when I am not at work." This is a radically manual labor in the sense that it forces all mental attention to the body and its senses; it is a novel form of embodiment for Alicia, "just something that you've never felt before." She described herself as doubly isolated by the disassembly line: unable to think of anything except her body's movements at work and unable to have a social life outside of work due to the pain's constancy. For Striffler (2005, 134), this "oppressive routine" left him so exhausted during two summers of undercover work that he could not even go get a haircut or otherwise "establish a viable routine beyond the factory gate."

The second step of some breaking-in narratives is the bodily release from the line's grasp and the overwhelming sociality that emerges. The slaughterhouse's senior vice president himself was not atypical when he claimed that, during his teenage years on the kill floor, the "work was always very hard, but you learned to also laugh. You are constantly talking with people for eight, nine, ten hours." Indeed, despite Alicia's recollections of breaking in, the majority of our two-hour interview concerned the pleasures of social life once you got "used to it. You learn to talk, work, talk." Describing the slaughterhouse as something between "a city that never sleeps" and a "high school," she asserted, "I had a community. I really liked it." Although she quit once she could not keep up with the line—which increased from sixteen thousand to nineteen thousand pigs per day while she was there—Alicia maintained her contacts to learn about the rumors and relationships on the cut floor. Once one gets past the sixty or so days of breaking in, a social world opens up in a way that many who spoke English or Spanish described as a joyful feeling of release prior to the onset of ensuing monotony.

For others, though they also described the release from the grip of pain as an initial period of liberation, this post–break-in sociality and boredom management could come to dominate. Many women complained about sexual harassment. A Burmese migrant whose job was to separate the semi-frozen trotter, or what he called the "wrist," of the pig and hang it on a hook spoke about the initial pain in his own wrists that blocked him from even noticing how many trotters he was handling. As the break-in pain receded and his feeble English and Spanish left him too shy to talk, he noticed that coworkers were entertaining themselves by taunting him as "a Chinese": "They call[ed] me *marrano* [pig/boar]." The only way to avoid racial harassment was to joke and appear to enjoy the labor process, he said: "To be like them . . . you have to pretend to be happy and talk about how it is good money." This forced display of emotion was necessary to make the job livable, but it also entailed a burden of having to perform socially on the line.

Theorizing the body politics of Fordist labor process in the early twentieth century—especially in terms of whether the (dis)assembly line could be redeemed for building a socialist future—the Italian Marxist Antonio Gramsci (1971, 295) analyzed proto-forms of breaking in. He was curious about whether industrial work could become ingrained in the body so that it would be as natural as writing with a pen. For Gramsci, however, the problem of Fordist production was the mental remainder: it was inhumane to make someone repeat the same task for hours on end without a higher social purpose beyond surplus value (see also Bell 1947; Buck-Morss 1992). It is a remarkable and disturbing reflection on the state of American society and social consciousness that today, to prompt public concern about slaughter work, social justice advocates need to investigate whether people are urinating on themselves. Back in the 1920s, even Henry Ford (1923) felt obliged to publicly respond to this kind of charge of dehumanizing mental abuse in a chapter titled "The Terror of the Machine," arguing that, "to a certain kind of mind," repetition is pleasurable (see Peña 1997). Such austere anthropologies—almost one hundred years later—still rationalize the work of (dis)assembly. Slaughter managers tended to deflect my criticisms of industrial violence using similar neo-Fordist notions that the full scope of human desires could find a place on the line. The ensuing examples, however, revealed a rather paltry set of human natures that can be accommodated by industrial killing. One told me, "The type of person who works on the cut floor is the type who is content with doing the same thing over and over," while "the type of person who does material handling is the type who likes to move." The ideology of labor being tacitly proposed here is that the workforce is one of simple minds and highly complex bodies.

But what Sergio Chavez's fingernails illustrate is the impossibility of bodies' ever fully adjusting to the pace of this killing machine. The third step of breaking in, that which arises from a molded body, seemed to stand outside standard genres of narration. After meeting Sergio, I asked others how the disassembly line was changing their bodies now that it moved at a rate of one hog every three seconds. Some men enthusiastically lifted up their T-shirts to reveal different patterns of muscular development etched across their backs, while others showed how one of their wrists, arms, or fingers differed from others in size or shape. In Sergio's grin I sensed a record of sacrifice for a better life—not just for monetary income but in terms of an honest way to make a living. For others, this third step was attached to a sense of fear. One woman, long after she stopped working at the plant, told me that the cold of the cut floor made her fearful of premature aging—that the years on the line had subtracted from her able-bodied life: "You can get arthritis early in life. I don't think I have it, but I don't know. My grandmother has it, so I was worried. My hands were always hurting . . . even after I quit." In patchy English, a skinny man originally from Burma seemed to suggest that the third step marked a race to either overcome or get off the line. "We're too weak to do the job," he said. "We need to build." I was not sure whether "building" meant that he must become physically stronger in order to resist permanent injury or, as he was doing at the moment when we spoke, learn English to get his general equivalency diploma and leave for other work. Minimally, this third stage of breaking in indicates a form of industrial capital that gets inside the body and gradually manifests in unendingly permanent transformations.

Two Centuries of Dead Labor

"Since the opening of the nineteenth century," writes the slaughterhouse historian Paula Young Lee (2008, 239), "the guiding imperative behind the slaughterhouse's creation was the extraction of animal slaughter from quotidian experience." It was a matter of controlling the public image of death (see also Pachirat 2011). In popular narratives, perhaps because of the invisibility of animal death, "the slaughterhouse system was completely 'modern,' a gigantic machine without narrative or history, perpetually regurgitating a product issued inside a moral vacuum" (Lee 2008, 3). Horowitz (2008, 13) notes that "our cultural sensibilities are shocked by the very presence of an industry given over to death," and it can become easy to neglect how mass killing is changing. Too often, journalists' reports on the slaughterhouse seem to presume that the violence—toward both pigs and people—has gone unchanged since the publication in 1906 of *The Jungle*, Upton Sinclair's vividly brutal pre–New Deal exposé. On the one hand, this is worth critically troubling: the form of killing animals is changing in history with technology and capital, bringing with it new kinds of impact on workers' bodies. On the other, tracing technological innovation and mutability risks underplaying the sheer degree of industrial intensity compounded into the slaughter machine over the past two centuries. For this system dates back to the innovations of mid-nineteenth-century Cincinnati; viewed from another perspective, there are almost two hundred years of industrial refinement bearing down on fingertips and wrists.

At the heart of the capitalist mass production of death is a tension: the fixity of the biological form of the hog—its legs, spine, and ribs always in the same rough relation to each other—enables extremely precise divisions of human labor around the carcass. Yet subtle variations within the contours of body parts—the fact that the pig is not fully standardized at scale in terms of the animals' weight, tendons, muscle distribution, or glands—can militate against full automation and the replacement of labor with machines. The perfectly standardized pig is far from a reality. The slaughterhouse requires upward of one thousand workers per shift to trim meat until it manifests the appearance of uniform pork.

In this sense, the scale and speed of the slaughter has increased in intensity over the twentieth century while the cut floor remains utterly dependent on human bodies, retinal perception, and on-the-fly judgment. Dover Foods' slaughterhouse was built with laser-sighted cut-assistance systems, machines that marble fat from the shoulders into tenderloins, and automated

Alex Blanchette

truck-loading devices. But the primary tools of the job remain—not entirely unlike those of earlier, nineteenth-century meatpacking—a motor-driven chain, conveyor belts, knives, and human hands and eyes that can adjust as they address subtle carcass differences.[4] While human judgment cannot be obviated entirely, relatively more uniform hog carcasses can simplify this work and allow increases in line speeds once there is greater predictability to the body parts moving down the line. A key point to underline here is that the pig's body is itself being shaped across its lifetime for increased rates of labor exploitation. The hog that enters the integrated slaughterhouse is not a raw material but a being whose bodily composition operates as a kind of biological technology for the extraction of value from human workers.

The origin of Dover Foods' slaughterhouse is not, however, *The Jungle*. Instead, it dates to 1967 and Iowa Beef Packers (IBP). Seeking to reduce well-paid line butchery to break the hold of unions and thus lower wages, IBP invented a new category: "boxed beef" (Broadway 1995; Horowitz 2006; Stull and Broadway 2013). As the company's founder said to *Newsweek*, "We've tried to take the skill out of every step" to produce cheap and uniform labor (quoted in Broadway 1995, 19). Rather than shipping entire sides of beef to regional butchers, who would then break down the carcasses into primal cuts such as tenderloins, IBP began dividing labor in the slaughterhouse around minute portions of the animal and vacuum packing the pieces for direct sale at grocery stores. After a series of failed worker strikes around older plants that tried to match IBP's competitive advantage—most famously, the Hormel strike in Minnesota (Rachleff 1993)—the result was a dismantling of union bargaining power, wages, and safety provisions across the United States. In 1982, IBP entered pork processing in Iowa using the same system (Broadway 1995). Dover Foods' slaughterhouse, which breaks almost twenty thousand pigs down into as many as eleven hundred product codes using upward of two thousand workers each day, is one of the many inheritors of IBP's dubious legacy.

As noted, the slaughterhouse has always been one of the most dangerous American spaces of labor. But as Horowitz (2008, 13) writes, "The kinds of dangers have changed, as have the location of the injuries that scar packing-house workers for the rest of their lives." In 1943, a study commissioned by the US Department of Labor found that accidents that cause absence from work in the slaughterhouse were double the national average for manufacturing (Horowitz 2008, 14). These were often injuries that maimed the worker in one fell swoop: amputating fingers on power saws or mangling arms in grinders. Unionization from 1943 until the 1970s changed this by enforcing safety protections on machines, slowing line speeds, and giving workers sick leave with pay to ensure that minor injuries would not become more serious. In seven years "the injury rate fell to 15.1 percent, one-third the 1943 level" (16). However, as packing companies such as IBP responded to workplace organizing, they found ways to deskill butchers; they used conveyor belts to coordinate across sections of the plant; and they broke down the tasks of killing and cutting animals to finer motions. By 1970, the slaughterhouse's injury rate was again at the 1943 level of almost 47 percent and was three times greater than the manufacturing average (16). These were new forms of injury, however, in that the accidents were less severe—requiring fewer sick days per incident—as cumulative strain replaced maiming.

Horowitz (2008, 18) notes that in the 1980s there was an "appalling collapse in working conditions . . . as meatpacking employment changed from a middle-class, blue-collar job to an employment of last resort." In 1979, meatpacking wages were 15 percent above the national average; by 1990, they had dropped down to 20 percent below wages in other manufacturing industries. In 1970, the Bureau of Labor Statistics began tracking repetitive motion disorders under the category of "industrial illness," and these incidences grew 442 percent between 1981 and 1991 (Horowitz 2008, 18). As health insurers pressured meat corporations to limit their worker's compensation claims, injuries causing lost days dropped 50 percent from 1991 to 2001. Packinghouses had begun to use the division of labor designed into their factories to reassign workers so they would not miss work because of strains. By 2001, the slaughterhouse was the leader in repetitive motion disorders, with 11,700 cases in a national workforce of 147,000, or thirty times higher than the industrial average. Yet its compensation claims still dropped significantly. In 2002, the Bureau of Labor Statistics, via bureaucratic magic, made the slaughterhouse "safer" by changing reporting rules in ways that made the category of "repeated trauma" disappear. Slaughterhouses no longer needed to report injuries as long as the resulting absence was restricted to the day the injury occurred; the nature of what constitutes "restricted work activity" changed, and relapses of prior injuries would not count as new cases for reporting (Horowitz 2008, 22). Eighty percent of industrial illnesses reported for slaughterhouses are now classified as "Other," and the reported injury rate fell by half between 2001 and 2003 when these rules went into effect (23). While reported cases and workdays off have decreased at a slower rate since then, the forms of report-ing for modern injuries make these statistics suspicious.

The point of Horowitz's analysis is that the form of violence in the slaughterhouse is changing from accidental amputations to chronic forms of muscle and nerve damage; it is shifting from sudden external trauma to slow internal bodily transformation. The slaughterhouse is one of the world's original industrial forms (see Hounshell 1984). It may now also be among the most precisely divided systems of labor, with hundreds of working motions divided around the finite body parts of a pig. The laboring movements of human muscles are being as finely physiologically divided as the sliced hog.

Biological System

The term *biological system* was one invoked by managers across almost all sites at Dover Foods that involve pigs—from artificial insemination to truck washes. Regardless, I was always perplexed by the tone of insistence with which slaughterhouse managers used the phrase in continuous quality improvement (CQI) classes.[5] I initially understood the phrase biological system in ways that resonate with theories derived from agrarian studies and geography: it was an expression of impediment or recalcitrance to human will and total industrialization; it suggests that there is an inherent unpredictability to engineering life relative to, say, metal or synthetic rubber (cf. Goodman, Sorj, and Wilkinson 1987; Goodman and Watts 1997). When a feed mill operator in these classes would ask why the rendering department could not predict how ground piglets would clog pipes, a manager would shrug and say, "Well, it's a biological system." When I overheard Dover Foods' chief executive ask managers on the farm side whether they could reproduce the low piglet mortality rates of 2010 in a biological system into the far future, the term made sense. But as one of the ur-forms of the industrial, the slaughterhouse might appear to be just a system filled with machines. The animal at this point—as dead, inert body parts—would seem to be least vital in terms of resisting the will of capital and human agency.

Yet manager after manager would point to surprising forms of variability in the dead carcass. The first was seasonality. Mosquito bites on pig carcasses during the summer could account for as much as a 3 percent decrease in carcass yields, while litter sizes and hog weights also shifted with the season. The second form of biological variation that slaughterhouse managers invoked was accidental short-term variation that, some argued, should be controllable. One barn's pen structure, workers' habits, and pig genetics can lead to additional abscesses or bruising on the carcass, which can change flesh yields. Alternatively, the company is always developing new processes to derive more value out of the pig parts. This means that rendering—the department that boils diseased pigs, floor trimmings, and excess offal for proteins, fats, and collagens (see Shukin 2009)—is constantly dealing with shifting quantities, ratios, and forms of biological materials. This variation can cause breakdowns to the boilers and pipes. Most fundamental, however, is long-term variation: the fact that the pig is not yet uniform enough to replace human laborers with automated machines. While the labor process employs conveyor belts to bring a new piece of the hog's carcass to a line worker every few seconds, most of the company's attempts to use laser-guided cut systems or meat separators were abandoned years ago. As the senior vice president at the plant stated, "I'm not one to believe that you'll ever have a machine that can separate muscles" because of their variation. When the task is to cut meat apart at the minute scale of hundreds of different pieces, the complexities in tendon, muscle, and bone placement will overwhelm any machine. Moreover, at the broad scale of nineteen or twenty thousand animals per day, even a set of two hundred carcasses that weigh ten pounds less than others would require human work-ers' manually cutting to adjust to their specificities.[6]

Dover Foods used manufacturing theory across its managerial divisions for three reasons. The training was designed to provide a shared statistical language for managers to communicate across production phases that are experientially distinct, such as genetic farms versus biodiesel transesteri-fication. These specific lessons in post–World War II Japanese manufac-turing theory were also a way to convey industrial control over the animal using the same terms favored by many of the company's investors and wholesalers in East Asia. Finally, CQI sessions could be grasped as a series of consciousness-raising exercises to militate against debilitating notions that the biological was a blockade to human will. As one manager who subscribed to CQI maxims insisted, "Variation is fine so long as it's predictable." One of the basic tasks of these courses was to teach managers how to measure the range of variation in fluctuations of a biological system for the purpose of identifying the most variegated links in the system from life to death.

The point of CQI is precisely that all forms of production are subject to "natural variation"—the crucial term in the philosophy. This is true whether one deals with a live pig, a human being's actions, an industrial disease, a tire, or a sheet of metal. This philosophy is comparable to a working, cap-italist version of so-called new materialism. In her book *Vibrant Matter*, Jane Bennett (2010) attempts to develop a vitality that is common to all inanimate things, from pencils to human flesh. As actants with a certain contingent agency in an assemblage that cannot be identified beforehand, her claim is that all things have a vital capacity "not only to impede or block

Alex Blanchette

the will and designs of humans but also to act as quasi agents or forces with trajectories, propensities, or tendencies of their own" (Bennett 2010, viii). The notion of "a life" (as opposed to "Life" in the abstract) is one that exceeds unified characterization, and "the aim is to articulate the elusive idea of a materiality that is itself heterogeneous, itself a differential of intensities, itself a life" (Bennett 2010, 57). We might say that vibrant matter is a proposition of radical ontological resistance to archetypal industrial standardization as an idea(l) and as an orientation—perhaps even resistance to the unity of form itself. Bennett argues that in "vital materialism there is no point of pure stillness, no indivisible atom that is not itself aquiver with virtual force" (57). Even metal has a vitality, "a (impersonal) life" (59), in that a hunk of metal is never composed of indistinguishable metal despite its appearance to the untrained human eye. Metal contains a "variegated topography" of imperfections and gaps at the "interfaces of grains" (59), something of which all actual metal workers are cognizant.

In a sense, CQI is designed to attune managers and industrial architects to the ontological notion that everything has its own shimmering singular vitality—"a life," or "natural variation"—whether it is a piglet, a knife, or a pork chop. But the similarities between the two end there. Vital materialism pushes beyond viewing the material world as "a passive environment or perhaps a recalcitrant context for human action" (Bennett 2010, 111). It strives to engage the irreducible multiplicities of a material world for the purpose, in part, of imagining new modes of political engagement with nonhuman artifacts, beings, and infrastructures that does not simply boil down to human will. It enables an orientation that human life—for better and for worse—is tied up with environmental forces whether one is on an urban street corner or hiking through a nature preserve (see also Chen 2012; Murphy 2017a). Continuous quality improvement aims to measure vital materiality on a quantitative plane to make the objects and subjects of production relatively less vital (or, what is the same, predictably vital). The "continuous" element of CQI accepts the ontological principle that standardized vitality is never total. The material world will always exceed engineering. In this sense, under the dictates of CQI, the pig cannot be a "machine" or "built to spec" in the popular understanding of that term. This is so not because of ontological differences among lively life, dead biology, and metallic motors but because no machine is a perfectly standardized machine. At the same moment, CQI's ambition is to make bioindustrialization more like our popular images of the standardized factory and perhaps, due to its reflexivity, more factory-like than any hitherto existing factory.

As the CQI course progressed over the next eight months, it became clear that I was misunderstanding the meaning of "biological system" as an abstraction for the integration of hog life and death. Under vertical integration, the shimmering "biological" can be interpreted as a potential source of innovation, and the deadening machinic "system" is the blockade to improvement (see Beldo 2017). As the plant's vice president put it, owning and controlling the pigs through "vertical integration ensures that we get a higher quality raw material coming in."[7] But such dependence on the pig indicates why the farm side of the operation had become intellectually dominant within the company, since paths of intensification were through the animal's body (see Blanchette 2020).

Variation in the vitality of animal carcasses could be seen as open-ended sources of possibility for industrial growth, albeit mostly outside of slaughterhouse managers' control. By contrast, all of those managers with whom I spoke discussed the extreme pressures they felt to keep the line moving. They presented themselves as controlled by the machine and narrated how one breakdown in the process of cutting animals would reverberate across the whole disassembly line. They could cite—with shifting values for any day—how much money the packing plant would lose in a minute when a piece of the line broke down. The figure often started at $1,000. Line maintenance workers, whom kill and cut workers often claimed had an easier job, discussed mental stress that made them want to quit their positions. Whenever the line's conveyor belts broke down, managers would scream out figures for how much the stoppage was costing the company as maintenance crews tried to replace parts or fuses. As one shipping manager put it, "We don't have a chain pushing us, but we have a clock. Every minute of the clock, you're losing twenty boxes [of meat]." A delay in the loading of boxes onto trucks destined for the port of Oakland, en route to an eighteen-day journey to Japan, would cascade back onto the cut floor once the freezers with reserve space were stuffed full.

The problem that became clear in talking to plant managers was their inability to imagine both the killing machine and the human body being subject to higher speeds. They felt that—in my words—they had reached the end of industrial time after many decades of refinement, when (dis)assembly is so perfectly worked out that it operates at the very limits of the inescapable human form. It was in talking to shipping managers—who deal with cardboard boxes and thus are least tethered to animal biology—that I realized it was partly the (machinic) system in "biological system" that is the key roadblock to realizing capitalist growth in this plant. "Those conveyors

Alex Blanchette

are currently maxed out," explained one shipping manager. "We've run lots of tests. There's only one speed." That is, through years of time-motion studies that increase the line's speed, and of decades of seeking to fragment processes even further to kill more hogs, the manager claimed he had identified the maximum speed for the average person to sort boxes and move them from conveyer to conveyer without threatening acute injuries.[8] Employees must scan, sort, and move boxes across conveyors that automatically load the boxes into trucks in batches graded by hog piece for a specific market. "There's a psychology to moving boxes," he explained after I told him stories about the pain-laden first two stages of break-in from the perspective of lifting fifty-pound boxes all day, "and people need to get past that." But he went on to state that "the maximum is ten boxes a minute" and said that the human body simply cannot go faster than that point on a consistent basis. This is a startling sense of the biological in "biological system" not only because this man cannot see the possibility of industrial intensification via machines. Once slaughter is consciously acknowledged to work at the exact limits of the human body, it is the shimmering variable vitality within each human physiological form that must be managed, measured, and contained. The result is a biological system in a fourth sense: one that includes two thousand human workers whose labor on pigs' carcasses remakes their bodies.

The End of Industrial Time

This outcome both resonates with and diverges from discussions concerning the state of humanity in industrial capitalism. The idea that human beings must be culturally industrialized in capitalist spaces is an old one. Edward P. Thompson (1967) illustrated how rural British conceptions of lived time were brought into alignment with early factory systems. Sigfried Giedion (1948) and Susan Buck-Morss (2000) described how art and aesthetic tastes of the early twentieth century were inseparable from industrial rationalities. Gramsci (1971) analyzed how Henry Ford's Sociological Department sought to construct new kinds of moral subjects alongside making cars, instilling staid domestic mannerisms into workers that would ensure that their diversions did not affect their ability to assemble vehicles (see Muehlebach and Shoshan 2012). Silvia Federici (2004) redescribed early modern European witch-hunting as a spectacular form of violence against women in ways that were designed to produce docile female subjects who would reproduce workers for capital. Aihwa Ong (1987), in a classic analysis of spirit possession on early Malaysian shop floors, demonstrated just how deeply

US dwellers' sense of the world was subtly engineered for them to tolerate the monotony of industrial work. These excavations of commonsense affects point to how the engineering of cultural sensibilities was necessary to make people willing and able to sell their time to industrial capitalists, to rent out their labor power for the enrichment of others, no matter how repetitive and boring the work.

Yet this is also more complicated than industrial capital requiring healthy physical bodies for the purposes of working the disassembly lines. As I noted, by 2010 a surplus of workers was available to Dover Foods as the aftermath of the 2008 financial crisis brought people in from the US coasts. Kaushik Sunder Rajan (2006, 2007), Joseph Dumit (2012a), and Melinda Cooper (2008) have done creative conceptual work to develop a notion of "surplus health" that is tethered to increasing the value of the human body as a market in the American biocapitalist present. From extending the life of Americans so that they consume more drugs, to constantly limiting what counts as a healthy body that does not need drugs, these scholars have theorized how the human body and health have shifted from being an "arm of capital" to "an industry in itself" (Sunder Rajan 2007). Human life, rather than labor alone, is the site of investment.

What I have been charting across this chapter is a kind of surplus health that is emerging through industrialization after there is little time or motion left to cut. The health clinic's series of tests and physicals for new employees are designed, one could say, to measure the vibrant matter that inheres in parts of each worker's irreducibly singular body. In those offices, Dover Foods is studying the varied state of working-class human embodiment in the United States—measuring how past or changing forms of labor, behavior, and lifestyle manifest within distinct workers' muscle groups. In the absence of the ability of corporations to refine machines, partly tied to variation in hog muscles, it is the human body that is being newly reindustrialized by matching it to an ideal motion or part of the line where it has the least chance of breaking down after breaking in. The health clinic brings states of human and hog muscles into novel forms of entanglement, instantiating emerging forms of industrial engineering at the interspecies conjunction.

What the biological system of the slaughterhouse underlines is how industrialism is not a finished project, with fixed logics, at the end of an era. It is still evolving to find new terrains and substances for extraction and will continue to do so until we collectively and deliberately construct another social and economic world. The anthropologist Kim Fortun (2012) has argued that we are not inhabiting a postindustrial world underpinned by novel and emergent forms of digital entrepreneurialism or financial accumulation—or, at least, the present is also a moment of late industrialism marked by worn-out infrastructures and paradigms of thought (see also Besky 2019). As bridges, chemical factories, and nuclear reactors increasingly go awry due to lack of maintenance or a changing climate, we are all at risk of experiencing industrialism in new ways as these systems more intimately harm life and health. Put differently, the waning phase of industrialism may be when we live with its effects most intimately. But the integration of human muscles and tendons as a dimension of capitalist meat and animality also suggests other modalities of late industrialism. This is a matter not of industrial exhaustion but of technics compounding in systems of raising and killing hogs to the point at which the central object of production has little room left for industrial expansion. This is a kind of late industrial efficiency that is, paradoxically, out of control. How corporations corral value from hog bodies as segmentable physiologies appears to be emerging as a template for finding value in the human body, pushing beyond classic capitalist frames of using humans as labor power and managing workers as a dimension of industrial swine. The speed and scale of the modern slaughterhouse—at the end of industrial time, when architects can no longer easily find ways to profitably refine the labor process—is turning slaughter into more of a biological system than ever before.

Notes

This chapter is reprinted from the 2020 book *Porkopolis*, edited and updated in light of the pandemic's effect on American slaughterhouses—including the one where this chapter takes place.

1   Moreover, these kinds of post-offer employment testing facilities are by no means unique to Dover Foods or the meatpacking industry. They appear to be ascendant in large companies in an era of high health care costs and overefficient industrial processes. In the wake of a failed 2021 unionization drive in an Amazon warehouse in Alabama, for instance, the company's head, Jeffrey Bezos, announced the initiation of a complex ergonomics program to lessen the endemic musculoskeletal traumas of its labor process (see Subin 2021).

2   For more on the politics of labor disposability in American farm work, see Guthman (2019).

3   Catherine Fennell (2011) has written on the topic of shared forms of "sensory publics" as modes of memory and collective politics with respect to the experience of good heat in low-income housing in Chicago.

4 For additional notes on this point, see Stull and Broadway (2013, 99).

5 Continuous quality improvement classes—a kind of statistics-heavy lean manufacturing program—were regularly taught to Dover Foods' senior managers across both the farm and slaughtering sides of the company. See below, and also Blanchette (2020), for more details on the impetus for these forms of cross-company pedagogy.

6 At the same time, we should be cautious about what is mystified by these company representatives' solitary focus on hogs and machines. What the COVID-19 pandemic has glaringly revealed, which has been far more severe in American relative to European meatpacking plants, is that depressed wages due to 1970s deskilling, union breaking, and racialization have further militated against technological investment. While there is nothing remotely approaching fully automated packing plants in Europe, the relatively higher wages in some of those countries have resulted in more reliance on machines in select parts of the process.

7 *Quality* in CQI, which this manager is here invoking, is synonymous with uniformity. Quality in this philosophy simply means decreases in process variation.

8 Note that this is not just a matter of quantity and accumulated weight over the eight-to-ten-hour shift. One could add more people if that was the case. Instead, if the conveyer is moving too quickly, the worker cannot read and scan the label for sorting. Alternatively, moving any faster could result in people being acutely hurt, beyond repetitive motion injuries, by boxes smashing into their hands.

Alex Blanchette

The Lung Is a Bird and a Fish

LOCHLANN JAIN

Writing:

POSITIONING THE SUBJECT, in which no air is placed on or beside a living morsel and hypotheses are tested regarding the relationship between them.

Born with entitlement, a human takes a breath. Just like each of the billions of mammals, ever, it immediately exacts another. To breathe is to never be satisfied: to demand air is human. There can be no redundancy and no substitution. Neither bread nor water, caviar nor cash, will do when air's presence is entreated. Denying air—could there be anything more simple and straightforward than air?—by some action or failure abjures another's animality and perhaps one's own humanity. Anticapitalist, breathing belies the whole idea of saving, let alone stockpiling.

Over an average life span, a human will take and take and take, a dozen or so times for each of 36 million minutes, until they have sipped some 265 million liters of air. Polo players pilfer extra. Factory owners purloin even more. A seventy-year-old will have puffed, sniffed, and snorted a football field–sized balloon of the stuff. A spherical football field, each, for six billion average humans. Each gives back, of course, but it's different downwind.

The humble mouth and nose apparatus conceals an ambitious scheme, considering the sheer weight of the human meat sustained by oxygen—on a global scale perhaps some 600 billion pounds of flesh. And the trifling perforations serve higher ambitions. Enabling smell, taste, affection, communication, drug delivery, and alimentation, they provide access to appreciation and repulsion of nearly every sort for the owner and those nearby. Not only the entry (and exit) point of physical worlds, the human visage enables (and

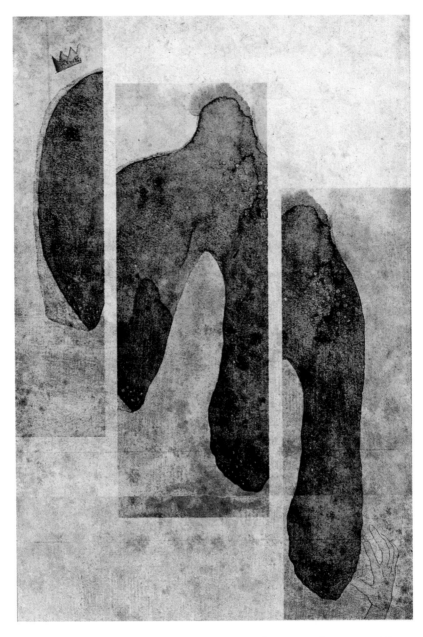

Lochlann Jain, *Organ King Blue*, 2020. Ink on paper with digital manipulation, 24 × 36 inches.

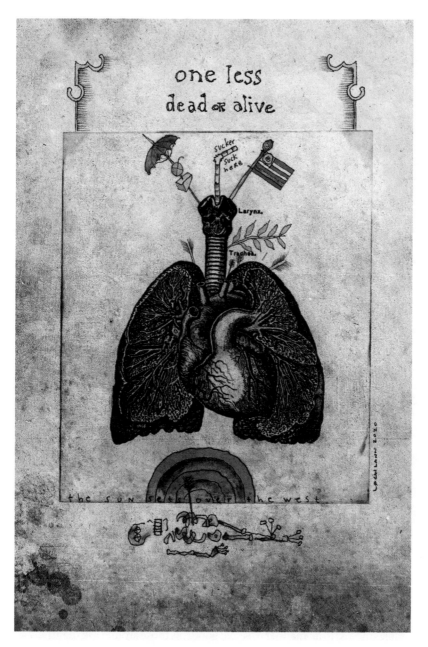

Inter2.2   Lochlann Jain, *Sucker Punch*, 2020. Inked lithograph on
paper, 24 × 36 inches.

Inter2.3   Lochlann Jain, *The Receiver*, 2020. Ink on paper, 24 × 36 inches.

disables) access to all manner of social goods, as those around ask themselves: Is that pie-hole handsome, are those teeth straight and white? Do you want to hire, or have a beer with, or lay one on that orifice? What of these maws?

Given the small size—a quarter-inch nostril aperture can sustain the splendor and mediocrity of an entire life—the chance of malfunction and the ease with which it can be disjointed or crushed surprises less than the rarity

Inter2.4   Lochlann Jain, *Boyle's Brief*, 2020. Pencil on paper, 24 × 36 inches.

Inter2.5   Lochlann Jain, *Sissy Boy with Geraniums*, 2020. Ink on paper, 20 × 18 inches.

of error. Most people never stomach a serious glitch—except, definitively, at the end. To be sure, a morass of statistics hints at the designed-in dangers: peanuts or lag screws caught in the airways; water, carbon monoxide, or phosphine inhaled neither by accident nor on purpose, but because there was nothing else there; homicide or suicide by chain or cushion; seizures involving errant tongues; asthma, emphysema, or allergies; pierogi speed-eating contests; marshmallow cheek-stuffing dares; viral cinnamon-swallowing YouTube challenges; capital punishment with ropes and gallows or trees; sex involving thongs, masks, and hoses. After that the list gets peculiar.

Bereavement aside, local conventions attend to the incongruities resulting from multipurpose human apertures. Slurpers of soup can be either gracious or uncouth depending on the soup's locale. Snoring library habitués and wheezy opera buffs beg for lenience, if only to save one's own sanity. Numerous dare-I-suffocate-my-loud-breather-husband quandaries litter the internet. The dinner table most highlights these unspoken customs, for here the competing wants of ventilation, communication, and ingestion most imperil each other. Indeed, a not insignificant number of people find their meal companion dead in the privacy of a locked restaurant toilet stall, having adjourned their humiliation if not the nonbreathing itself. The event even has a name, the "café coronary," since dinner companions may ignore or misrecognize the antics of a florid friend, not waving but choking, until they clatter to the floor—often, then, mistakenly identified as suffering a myocardial infarction and receiving disobliging (and nondislodging) CPR. The brain, in this case, in its last act of humanity, secretes an opioid to smother a choker's terror and disappointment as they recede from consciousness.

Like breathing, air is unobtrusive, effective, mysterious, and free. Air squats in random places. It hunkers; it drips; it seeps, absconds, and spurts. It communes and conveys, equally considerate of perfumes, pollutants, and pathogens. Free for the taking and easy to adulterate, it can evolve, still under the name *air*, still exchanged across time, flesh, space. And it took an age to figure it out. A history of the science and philosophy of breathing and its maintenance, namely the discovery of the air/lung relationship, required birds to take up residence in vacuum chambers with candles and plants, dog carcasses to be cut and piled up in the corners of Enlightenment laboratories, oxygen and nitrogen to be cashed out of the larger project of air, doctors and bystanders to devise and improvise devices to remove rooks and shillings from bronchial folds.

Made of negative space, imperative and imperiled like all negatives, air is either taken for granted or saturated in panic.

One guesses that early on the casual observer had noted that people and animals who ceased to respire would cease to be. Even still, late seventeenth-century Europeans obsessed over proving it: frogs, rabbits, and birds croaked without air and did so consistently and quickly. These scientists had happed upon the perfect event. Engineering the expiration of an animal could at once illustrate cause and effect, offer an expedient demonstration, and flaunt charismatic metal and glass instruments, and thus, these men elegantly inaugurated a new system of knowing called experimental science.

Still, the details of the air-animal intersection posed a mechanical and intractable problem, beyond the not insignificant difficulties of creating and maintaining an airless space. Look at the duck: the chest rises, air scuttles the vacuum, the chest falls, air emerges from the windbag. And so on. Sure, clogging that process led to paroxysms and seizures. Time to death could be counted on pocket watches and recorded using new forms of annotation. Indeed, yes. But *how* did the nourishment take place? Was it the air itself? Something in the air? Or was it the movement of the chest? How to caress the lung with air, but disallow the movement? Ligatures and sparrow-sized glass bulbs were fashioned. Observations were made. Convulsions were had. Illustrations were commissioned. Reports were written and printed and circulated. Witnesses were enlisted.

When remedies for drowning victims were proposed (hanging upside down, bellows in the anus), some objected on the grounds that saving a life required stealing it from God. Experimentalists in the 1600s found form as God's Father Christmas—glass goblets featuring keeling and swaying little animals constituted a gift that kept on giving. Historians devoted to linear progress narratives consider these experiments with their persistent deflation of animal lungs as the precursors to the inflation of others (human) with game-changing iron lungs and ventilators.

During an experiment of 1662, a "large and lusty frog" took center stage in Robert Boyle's exhibition. A frog that had "freely breathed" in a small glass receiver all of a sudden "did not appear by any motion of his throat or thorax (chest) to exercise respiration" (Boyle 1670, 2015). What had changed? The mere "exsuction of the air" from the chamber—no one had so much as touched the poor thing. Air seemed to be subject to manipulation. In 1668, John Mayow found that an animal accompanied by a candle suffocated twice as fast as an(other) animal on its own, and concluded (dare we say, again?) air is necessary for life. On the other hand, a pot of mint placed in the glass compartment could extend an(other) animal's life by minutes.

Robert Hooke, polymath and assistant to Robert Boyle, wondered if fresh air was not the issue at all. Life, he hypothesized, emanates from the movements of breathing. His contemporary, Richard Lower (1667), describes Hooke's experiment in "An account of making a dogg draw his breath exactly like a wind-broken horse, as it was devised and experimented by Dr. Richard Lower, with some of his instructive observations thereon." Lower writes,

> Hooke . . . carried out another experiment . . . on May 9, 1668. A brass tube was tied into the trachea of a dog and the animal was allowed to rebreathe into a large bladder attached to the tube. The report states "After about three or four minutes, the dog began to struggle violently, and to repeat his endeavors for breath very frequently. . . . Yet, after about six minutes, his strength failed a-pace . . . and then he began to be convulsed; and at the end of about eight minutes, we could see no signs of life."

Concluding that life required more than simply a breathing motion, Hooke designed a further experiment. This time he cut gills in the lower parts of the dog's lungs and blew a constant stream of air through the trachea such that air passed the lungs with no movement. The dog survived this experiment (though for how long?), thus enabling Hooke to reconfirm that air is necessary for life and recommit to "thoroughly discover the Genuine use of Respiration; and afterwards consider of what benefit this may be to Mankinde" (1667, 540).

The executions were pondered and repeated, hare by hare, chaffinch by robin. Just as certain equations or fables offer perfect building blocks, say, for a child's education, the demonstration of air's necessity by suffocating small animals advanced an ideal way to develop the then novel mode of scientific investigation. People could see for themselves science at work, as they thrilled at attempts to solve the ultimate life death enigma. A body had motion, squeaks, chirps, joy, fear. A spirit, it could be said. Then it did not.

A century later, the painter Joseph Wright of Derby represented assorted forms of witnessing in his painting *An Experiment on a Bird in the Air Pump* (1768). Towering majestically over a viewer in London's National Gallery, it portrays divergent human reactions to—or, more accurately, around—a pretty bird in mid-suffocation, perhaps a cockatoo shipped from a colony. Two lovers make oogly eyes, called away from the momentous struggle

Inter2.6   Joseph Wright, *An Experiment on a Bird in the Air Pump*, 1768. © The National Gallery, London.

before them. A boy cocks his head for a better look, while beside him a young man feels the seconds of a pocket watch ticking against his palm as he pensively looks on. An older man studies a brightly lit vase suspending some sort of specimen in liquid. Some critics identify this gray mass as a lung in reference to Wright's own asthma and labored attempts at breath. The lung as vanitas. The painter as bird.

Chiaroscuro illuminates most clearly two girls—one wide-eyed with concern for the bird, the other turned away entirely as a father-figure comforts and explains. The girls could not, could never have, attested to the science of the thing, its accuracy or reproducibility: penises, real or assumed, were required for such affirmations. (What if the girl had cocked her head, intently watching the experiment across the table from a teary-faced boy?) That aside, as a reflection of, or foil for, (childish?) compassion, these dismayed expressions substantiate, in a still image, the effect of passing time: a bird is in the timeless and yet urgent process of asphyxiation. It's a fancy bird, a lovely one, not dissimilar to the girls of subsequent films, themselves smothered and snuffed for something like pleasure or at least gratification.

Lochlann Jain

Birds, like humans, are not breathers. Birds, likes humans, are breathed within a pneumatic microcosm. The lung and its environs choreograph changes in volume and pressure in a system that creates something like a feeling of need. The need doesn't present in choice; rather, surfactants, vacuums, and chemical reactions systematically produce respiration—until, of course, they don't. They don't if they are blocked for whatever reason, and then, a feeling may encroach, an experience of a sovereign physiology—the panic, the frustration, or pleasure at having to rely on something so utterly banal as air and the absurd, generic process of respiration. People pent up in closed spaces know versions of this, the pure biological phenomenon with its specific chemical and physiological properties, suddenly situated, pitted against the spatial necessities of their conditions of work or capture or play: coal mines, ship holds, diving bells, chimneys, BDSM bondage, and the like making breathing, choking, suffocating, and drowning into a historical, infinite, event-by-event-by-event repetition.

Thus, the canary. A breather system, vibrant or besieged, so dear to European hearts and mines.

The bird is a lung.

The Lung Is a Fish

Consider the choker. Physiologically, the throat will grip a perfectly chargrilled bolus of ribeye in a drowning response meant to protect the lung and its job to enervate the brain. In a rather weighty conceptual flaw, the nonbreather's own body hermetically seals the trachea around the steak (or tofu).

An extremely odd, fragmented, but nevertheless distinguishable history attends the enigma of pending respiration with titles such as *A Dissertation on Suspended Respiration from Drowning, Hanging, and Suffocation: In which is recommended a different Mode of Treatment to any hitherto pointed Out* (Coleman 1791) and which describes numerous nonconsensual experiments involving drowned, hanged, and otherwise asphyxiated cats, dogs, rabbits, and small beings; this time the goal was life-saving. Once rendered unable to respire—in other words, incapable of receiving heat from the air into their blood—the animals underwent dissection and, in the case of this dissertation, were served as the pudding's proof for bloodletting as a treatment for the aforementioned modes of suffocation.

Dr. Samuel Gross, rendered immortal by Thomas Eakins and Alexander Calder (father of the twentieth-century mobile sculptor), if not his medical endeavors, wrote a monograph collating both fascinating and mundane cases of choking. *A Practical Treatise of Foreign Bodies in the Air-Passages* (Gross 1854) recounts numerous reports of objects that had been lodged in throats; their exact locations and styles of entrapment; the often fulsome, if not downright melodramatic, clutching and reeling macro- and microreactions to these happenings; and an array of tools for creative extraction. He asks, rhetorically:

> How many persons have perished, perhaps in an instant and in the midst of a hearty laugh, the recital of an amusing anecdote, or the utterance of a funny joke, from the interception at the glottis of a piece of meat, a crumb of bread, a morsel of cheese, or a bit of potato without suspicion, on the part of those around, of the real nature of the case! Many a coroner's inquest has been held upon the bodies of the victims of such accidents, and a verdict rendered that they died by the visitation of God, when the actual cause of death lay quietly and unobserved at the door of the windpipe of the deceased. (Clerf 1975, 1450)

In specifying a hitherto obscured medical enigma, the doctor also grasps the full uncanny concurrence: the animated raconteur precipitously rendered mute and red-faced by a newly fixed and foreign—of all banal things—French fry, the very thing meant to sustain and entertain, intended as a means of companionship and merriment, now turned assassin, destroying, quickly, but too slowly for the comfort of the gawking, paralyzed bystander, who instantly, in his dumb immobility, turns abetter. All rendered inscrutable to medical science and history by an oblivious coroner. How to even comprehend such a preternatural marvel: fifteen hundred miles of air conduits packed into a couple of square feet with an area the size of a tennis court, and spelled with an alchemical sensitivity to transfigure mere air—everyday empty space—into life itself. How to imagine that the magic of this most beguiling of organs could be stymied by such ridiculousness as a chunk of chocolate-covered bacon?

Snubbing the explanation of God's visitation, Gross gives mechanics a turn; he explores in great detail the geometry of throats and entrenched objects before considering known treatments: emetics, sneeze producers, iodine, leeches, castor oil, rhubarb, hog bean, upside-down hanging.

While the human form has remained somewhat constant, the foreign objects found in the airpipe are the very epitome of cultural specificity.

Lochlann Jain

A piece flown from a toy whip lodges itself in a child, a glass collar button relaxes into a bronchial fold and takes an interminable six months to smother its host, a brass atomizer tip holes up in a windpipe. Unremarkable crucifixes, cockleburs, fence staples, shoe buttons, shawl pins, diaper pins, and real and false molars all, somehow, dwelled in the long-gone air passages of long ago.

If Gross's efforts favored the chronicle, Chevalier Jackson was the true hero of those whose windpipes harbored damming foreign objects. A truly obsessed geographer of all things tracheal and thoracic, he found an "indescribable pleasure" in his work. He perfected his scope-and-prod design by retrieving objects a medical assistant inserted into a dog's throat (Capello 2012, 96). He kept, categorized, labeled, matted, titled, and framed the hundreds of objects he had collected from various locations in his patients in lieu of payment (the human subject had no choice in the matter). An entire drawer of jacks. Each accompanies notes on the procedure, including type of forceps (alligator, straight, rotation, side curve, etc.), "location in patient," complications, age, outcome. These fetishes now rest at the Mütter Museum of medical curiosities in Philadelphia.

Such adventures became the subject of his autobiography, one littered with admonitions against placing objects in the mouth to begin with. The book devotes a full two pages to women's brilliance and superior abilities; though he never married, he took pride in treating his assistants well. His inimitable fascinations struck a chord with readers, who made the work a bestseller in 1938.

Chevalier was unquestionably the most revered remover of foreign bodies. Eugene Willis Gudger (1866–1956), an obscure bibliographer of fish literature, was Hooke, line, and sinker the weirdest. Gudger, perhaps only marginally (self-)interested in respiration, was "always on the lookout for unusual phenomena wherein fishes are concerned" (1933, 573). Among his four hundred–odd articles, one finds a collation of cases gathered from around the world not only in 1926 and 1927, but also in 1933. Unusual indeed were the cases he collected for "Live Fishes Impacted in the Food and Air Passages of Men," "Live Fishes Impacted in the Pharynx of Man: An Addendum," and "More Live Fishes Impacted in the Throats of Men" (Gudger 1926, 1927, 1933).

Tallying case studies in which fish "jump down a man's throat" from medical journals and fishing magazines, he includes a random assortment of facts about the (usually) deceased person, the (usually) deceased fish, the (usually haphazard) attempts to save the person, the location,

Inter2.7   Chevalier Jackson with his collection of foreign objects.
Courtesy of the Chevalier Jackson Papers, Archives Center,
National Museum of American History, Smithsonian
Institution.

and the unique circumstances surrounding each "curious and interesting fatality." Accounts of the fish, the throats, and the audacious efforts to reinstate breath are of a factual, bibliographic nature only, bereft of even a perfunctory expression of sympathy, much like his own obituary: "At his request, the word 'ichthyologist' was carved on his tombstone" (Quinlan 1986).

A Nigerian woman placed a fish in her mouth while attending to the nets with both hands. When she collapsed, her "friends at once opened her mouth and endeavored to remove the obstruction; they failed and after five minutes all her convulsive movements ceased" (Gudger 1933, 534). The doctor "found a small fish, 3¼ inches long, wedged firmly down the trachea, with the snout lying transversely between the vocal cords. Minute spines on the dorsal surface and at the border of the gills effectually prevented its extraction upwards, and, indeed, the tail had already been pulled off by the victim's friends." In this instance, the deceased had been taken to a mortuary not to gather these incidentals, but to determine whether she was a witch. In the West, too, breath and the occult corresponded. In the ancient catch-22 of ordeal by water, a sinking body indicated a suspect's innocence; capital punishment awaited those who survived.

In other cases, death came more slowly. A toddler playing with a *pla lin ma* in Siam persisted for a full eleven hours after it "slipped into her throat" (Gudger 1933, 575). A child named Fiem underwent what must have been a somewhat brutal treatment after several hours of intimacy with an *Anabas testudineus*. With the air-blocking creature finally unwedged, the boy died in ten more minutes. The fish, one learns, survived.

In addition to fish chokers, knucklebone chokers, and hot dog chokers, one could compose other inventories. Wikipedia's list of famous chokers enumerates mostly men. Attila the Hun, Tennessee Williams, James Madison—plugged from the inside. Women, at least in the public record, seem to have been spurned in their breathing efforts from the outside. Most famously, Isadora Duncan was choked by her scarf trapped in the spokes of a car. (And then a litany of both notable and quotidian girlfriends suffocated by their men for anger or delight.) From the point of view of the subject, the details—the specific object caught in the throat, its precise location, which forceps might best attempt extraction—are superfluous. What matters is exactly what is not happening in the particular moment and when that not-happening might stop. At this moment, the sovereign brain's requirement for a chemical and the sovereign mind's requirement for comfort split in absolute terms, leaving the self to flounder amidst in a jag of violent, ineffectual, mortifying (albeit posted on YouTube) gagging.

If breathing has a history, it has no memory. Nonbreathing tracks a memory with no history. Everyone remembers or fears or could at least imagine the lodging of a fish in their own airpipe, its spines painfully lodged askew against the larynx; a button, its flat velvety plastic trapped just beyond the reach of a friend's long fingernails; or a masticated cracker-Camembert-Cabernet mass ineluctably sliding down the (very) wrong pipe.

If one hasn't experienced or witnessed an asphyxiation firsthand or has neglected to read Chevalier Jackson's blockbuster memoir, a few idiosyncratic obsessives have chronicled the events for a reader's entertainment and contemplation. But aside from this register of case studies that aim more toward locating general rules of checked respiration, coining ideas for prevention and treatment, or exhibiting morose entertainment, the story of instantaneous nonbreathing, generated through an aggregate of individuals, does not particularly inspire the sort of grand narrative required to make history. No, nonbreathing recedes, event by event, from obituary to memory, to a trace, to nothing itself.

The fish is a lung.

The Bird Is a Fish

Meanwhile, America, an economic and political project not tied to deep historical foodway customs, allied itself with the project of embedding new forms of harm in the breathways: fallout from hundreds of atmospheric nuclear bomb tests, torrents of leaded gas and other pollutants, clouds of tobacco smoke all propelled new kinds of breathing and nonbreathing subjects. How can you convince a population to accept, even celebrate as a national right and victory, the terms of their own suffocation? It's all about swagger, and since everyone knows it's uncouth to swagger with a paunch, the middle offers as good a place as any to start.

In 1953, as iron lungs were breathing some Americans while cigarettes asphyxiated others, that most infamous of un-Americans, Ethel Rosenberg, was killed in the electric chair for passing nuclear secrets to the USSR.

But 1954's activities aligned America, with a strange specificity, to the project of curtailed respiration. In 1954, the signing of the Interstate Highway Act, sold to citizens at the 1939 World's Fair by General Motors as a vision of liberation, had the result of injecting lead debris into virtually every American lung. In the all-out effort to market the sale (and only incidentally, dispersal) of leaded gas, atmospheric lead tripled between the 1927 advertisement "Ride with Ethyl in a high compression motor and get the thrill of a lifetime!!" (Dupont 1927) and 1954, when it was all but forgotten that Ethyl once signified a home-makeable harmless alcohol that could once power an automobile. Now it signified a plump thirty-seven-year-old traitor and a profitable leaded gas.

In 1954, with 45 percent of Americans smoking, the first major study linked "toasted" and "tasty" cigarettes to lung cancer, and the tobacco industry began the mass production of scientific controversy. And also, they launched the flip-top box, which jabbed through the breast pocket

Inter2.8   Norman Bel Geddes, Futurama Exhibit,
New York World's Fair, 1939. © The Estate of
Margaret Bourke-White/Norman Bel Geddes
Collection, Harry Ransom Humanities Re-
search Center, University of Texas at Austin.

but required the removal and display of the box and brand for all to see each time you wanted a fag. For the next half century, more Americans than not would witness themselves, their friends, or their relatives suffocate to death.

In 1954, the USSR exploded its first thermonuclear bomb, and the United States bungled the Castle Bravo nuclear test. Underestimating the force of its blast by two-thirds, the military contaminated seven thousand square miles of the South Pacific. A tuna boat, the *Lucky Dragon #5*, that had been outside the designated danger zone nevertheless shoveled piles

The advertisement reads:

TAKE A TIP FROM US

TO CHICAG[O]

ETHYL

WORLDS FAIR OR BU[ST]

THIS YEAR you need a *real* vacation. You need to breathe fresh air, see new places, and wash away your worries with comfortable, refreshing travel.

Even an old car can give you that kind of vacation if you do just one thing—give it Ethyl!

With Ethyl Gasoline you banish harmful knock, overheating and sluggish performance. You put *new life* into your car; bring back the youthful power that makes it *fun* to drive!

Whether you make week-end trips or cross the continent—

remember: *the next best thing to a brand new car is your present car with Ethyl.*

Even if you don't put dollars and cents value on the extra enjoyment and satisfaction, Ethyl will make savings in lessened repair bills that more than offset its small additional cost. Ethyl Gasoline Corporation, Chrysler Building, New York City.

Ethyl fluid contains lead. © E. G. C. 1933

GOING TO THE WORLD'S FAIR?

Be sure to visit the Ethyl Exhibit at the Century of Progress in Chicago. You'll find it in General Motors Building and will see with your own eyes why Ethyl makes *any* car run better and actually costs LESS by the year.

NEXT TIME STOP AT THE ETHYL PUMP

Inter2.9   Advertisement in *National Geographic* magazine, June 1933.

of radioactive ash off the decks and took two weeks to return to Japan. The return of the sick twenty-three-member crew rendered public what the United States had hitherto kept an airtight secret: that radiation sickness was real, and that its time-space footprint far exceeded that of the bomb blast. Still, the United States refused to disclose the composition of the fallout, citing issues of national security. Nevertheless, aboveground bomb tests continued in the American West for another ten years, spreading nuclear contamination across the country.

Castle Bravo nuclear test. Courtesy of the National Archive and Records Administration.

Ethel the pawn, many would agree, was captured and killed by a stereotype of American womanhood. Accused of typing, of all things, for her husband and brother as they conspired to give the Russians nuclear secrets. At the kitchen table, of all places, the hearth of the American family where togetherness and love were performed through SPAM! Alpha-Bits! Minute Rice! Tang!! A concocted story had her witnessing the tearing of a red, white, and blue Jell-O: imitation raspberry! box that, in true spy form, could be matched by two strangers carrying one apiece. This scenario became a last-ditch effort for the government to extract her husband's confession (for Julius, ultimately, communism trumped conjugal interests; he admitted nothing).

Ethel's story parallels the artifact of her downfall: "America's favorite dessert," "you can't be a kid without it," itself a story of America's infinite, breathless simulacra and better living through chemistry. A national self-definition relied on the ability—the right—to choose which color of animal hoof extract mixed with sugar and chemical flavoring would usher your

Inter2.11   Marlboro cigarette pack. Photo by
              Lochlann Jain.

offspring into American childhood. Meanwhile it would take the government another five decades to counsel those Americans that had grown up
in the 1950s and 1960s and drunk milk that they were at risk from fallout-
produced cancers. No wonder it took five shocks of two thousand volts for
this spy to perish. That is what sovereignty feels like.

Chevalier Jackson, ever advising on dangerous playthings, lived just long
enough to witness plastic-wrapped children executing new forms of suffocation. Plastic bags, introduced in 1959, soon displayed *Warning: this is not
a toy*. Plastic aims to arrest respiration, protecting the contents from air's
ability to corrode food and food-resembling products. The resulting spate of
limp and lifeless children indicated less an accidental side effect of packag-

Inter2.12 Ethel Rosenberg being taken
to trial, 1951. Bettmann via
Getty Images.

Inter2.13 Campbell's soup can. Photo
by Lochlann Jain.

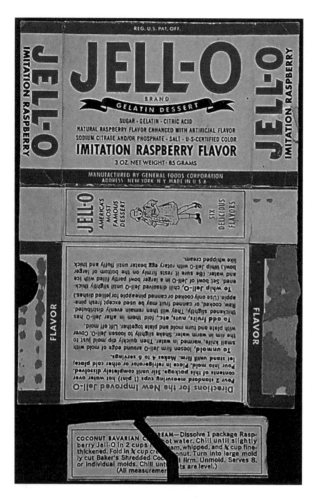

Inter2.14   Jell-O box exhibit used in the espionage trial
of Julius and Ethel Rosenberg and Morton
Sobell. Courtesy of the National Archive and
Records Administration.

ing than the real deal, a concentrated portent of the soon-to-be-ubiquitous
junk. Even DuPont (who, with GM and Standard Oil, also gifted us leaded
gas) advertised its product with children encased in the stuff: babies and
toddlers as glistening offerings. "Everything's at its best in Cellophane."
Perhaps truer if cellophane were soundproof.

A wrapper, as a hermetic seal, acts to preserve by stilling air's corrosive effects. As a hermeneutic seal, a package blusters and masquerades. Andy Warhol

Mom says
I'm so fresh
and so clean
(*sometimes*)—
she ought to
wrap me in
Cellophane
to keep me
that way.

Everything's at its best in Cellophane

· Cellophane keeps things clean
· Cellophane keeps things fresh
· Cellophane lets you see what you buy

DU PONT
Cellophane

DU PONT

BETTER THINGS FOR BETTER LIVING
...THROUGH CHEMISTRY

Watch "Du Pont Cavalcade Theater" on Television

Inter2.15 "Everything's at Its Best in Cellophane," 1956, series I, box 43, folder 33, E. I. du Pont de Nemours & Company Advertising Department records (accession 1803), Manuscripts and Archives Department, Hagley Museum and Library, Wilmington, Delaware.

apotheosized the effect, repeating tomato soup cans (not just any brand would do), murderous tuna fish cans (any middle-class housewife would do), and colorful Marilyns (not just any Marilyn) as well as mass-produced deaths: car crashes and electric chairs. Brought into the same orbit, these object sets absorbed other Americana as one and the same: the suburb needed the station wagon needed the gas but also the mother who needed the grocery store to quiet with sugar those children she'd been told (and believed) would make her whole and they occasionally did but mostly she wanted to suffocate them herself, and the tabloids could vulgarize the crashes and the electric chairs

INKHAM'S . PROVERBIAL . PHILOSOPHY. . . . .

Coming events cast their shadows before.

The feeling of utter listlessness, lack of energy, desire to be alone, or the "don't care" feeling, are all shadows of coming events. No woman should permit those symptoms to gain ground, for, being forewarned, she should be forearmed. *Lydia E. Pinkham's Vegetable Compound* will disperse all those shadows. It goes to the very root of all female complaints, renews the waning vitality, and invigorates the entire system. Surely such letters as this will support our claims:

"Reach for a vegetable instead of a sweet"

Inter2.16 Lydia Pinkham's Vegetable Compound, 1920. From the Stanford Research into the Impact of Tobacco Advertising collection (https://tobacco.stanford.edu/).

could punish the un-Americans and now the art collectors could join in the diversion and increase their share of the pie. Jasper Johns could be American Flags and bull's-eyes, and bull's-eyes could be Lucky Strikes and slimming, and Benjamin Kubelsky could be the Jell-O Program with Jack Benny and jiggles while Virginia Slims became tennis so that tennis could be women although not the Equal Rights Amendment but malignant all the same.

Advertising for one of the best-known patent medicines of the nineteenth century, Lydia E. Pinkham's Vegetable Compound hinted at women's propensity toward plumpness in middle age as a barely veiled threat— "coming events cast their shadow before"—and of course a promise: "Reach for a vegetable instead of a sweet." If this 1890s campaign rings familiar, it's because the entire thing, foreshadowing, tagline, and quote, was ripped off and used to sell Lucky Strike cigarettes. The threat of litigation from the candy industry amputated the slogan, but by then every American could join the dots: "Reach for a Lucky instead of a . . ." If Joseph Wright of Derby displayed a lung as vanitas, producers and consumers corroborated to turn America's cancer sticks into pure vanity.

Inter2.17   Lucky Strike ad, 1929. From the Stanford
             Research into the Impact of Tobacco
             Advertising collection (https://tobacco
             .stanford.edu/).

Contents eaten or inhaled, containers stick around. If someone squint-ing might confuse the palm-size red-and-white Marlboro cigarette box with a Campbell's soup can, the projects of breathing and eating could also be substituted, each industry vying for the same working- and middle-class American dollars.

For the purposes of "A Lung Is a Bird and a Fish," ideally Thomas Midgley Jr.'s expiration date would have been 1954, rather than ten years earlier. Midgley introduced two inventions that changed the world and

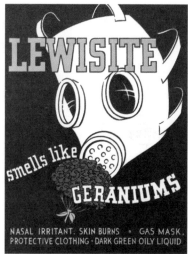

Inter2.18 Geraniums Lewisite Gas ad. Courtesy of the Detroit Historical Society.

Inter2.19 Gas Mask Lewisite Gas ad. Courtesy of the Otis Historical Archives, National Museum of Health and Medicine.

everyone in it. Alongside General Motors, he promoted his leaded gas, christened Ethyl, over the unprofitable use of ethanol, even as he himself, as well as others working to prototype the additive, suffered from severe lead poisoning. Freon, too, responsible for ozone depletion, was his, phased out only in 2020. He escaped both of these means of slow death, his soul departing his body with the help of one of his other inventions. A pulley system, designed to help him out of bed after a disabling bout of polio, strangled him, leading him to thoroughly discover the Genuine use of Respiration.

Note

Perpetual and repeated gratitude to Derek Simons, who read numerous drafts of the project, which, at base, is inspired by his capacious and generous approach to scholarship; Jackie Orr, who offered her cavalier brilliance; Owen Kraus, Maria McVarish, and Alexis Roworth, who read for substance and sense; Joseph Masco and Deborah Thomas, who devotedly lassoed butterflies to bring the volume to fruition; Richard McGrail, who brainstormed on the value of drawing to scholarship; and Hilary Thorsen, who tirelessly tracked down the means to gain permissions for the more arcane images.

PART III

Exclusion/
Embrace

i was dreaming when i wrote this
a mixtape for America

KRISTEN L. SIMMONS AND KAYA NAOMI WILLIAMS

Intro

"In my opinion," Kendrick Lamar says softly as the final track on his album *To Pimp a Butterfly* approaches its conclusion, "the only hope we kinda have left is music, and vibrations. A lot of people don't understand how important it is." The assertion comes close to the end of "Mortal Man," the just-over-twelve-minute track that closes out the critically acclaimed 2015 album. As the track concludes, Lamar places himself in conversation with the late musical legend Tupac Shakur. He does so using audio from a Swedish radio interview with Shakur that took place in 1994, two years before the artist was murdered. Lamar's claim that "the only hope we kinda have left is music, and vibrations" is posed as a response to Tupac's prophecy that the United States is headed toward a violent internal conflict with bloodshed on a scale most cannot now imagine. Tupac's theorizing of the internal contradictions of American democracy is effortlessly intersectional as he considers the effects of systemic poverty, structural racism, and state violence and reaches his inevitable conclusion: "I think America think we was just playing and it's gonna be some more playing, but it ain't gonna be no playing. It's gonna be murder. . . . It's gonna be like Nat Turner 1831 up in this motherfucker, you know?" 'Pac says. "It's gonna happen." "That's crazy," Kendrick responds, pauses, then suggests that in his opinion, the only hope we kinda have left is music.

And vibrations. This collaboratively written piece is an attempt to both theorize and perform the kind of vibrational work we believe is necessary

Lake Michigan. Photograph by Kaya Williams.

for academics across disciplines committed to creating the conditions of a good life within and beyond anti-Black settler colonial racial capitalism. We began this collaborative endeavor in 2015 as a project of thinking and writing together through music; a means of shaking loose the disciplinary practices that threaten to render our work lifeless and irrelevant to life. At the time, we were both graduate students in anthropology at the University of Chicago and finding it difficult to think and write our intellectual projects amid a thick atmosphere of violence at the university within which we were called to simultaneously play the roles of both victim and perpetrator of harm. The land on which the university stands; the legacies of genocide, slavery, imperialism, and theft in which all US universities are entangled but for which the University of Chicago has long been a node of power; the simple fact of working every day in spaces that were predominantly white and predominantly male, within an academic discipline shaped by settler colonialism and white supremacy: all threatened to suffocate when we had come intending to create. We began this project as performance and play—theorizing with music that played aloud as we spoke. Our first rehearsal was conceived as an experiment in refusal and in Afropessimistic theory: using the music as a vehicle to tarry awhile in what anti-Blackness and settler colonial violence feel like while refusing to search for hope or potentiality in suffering.[1] We called it a "Dark Side Mixtape," and we riffed with our favorite musical artists to unhinge freedom, escape, protest, and fugitivity from the optimisms those terms so often carry.

As we rehearse the mixtape in a written form, we sample and play with the ethnographic and institutional entanglements that bring us to these rehearsals with love and with a fierce sense of urgency. Think of it as something like liner notes to our unfolding mixtape for America. Like the making of any good compilation tape, it is done with love, and with a healthy disenchantment toward romantic narratives through which capitalism and white supremacy bind love with abuse. We seek to refuse linear narratives about individual self-possessed souls; we are thinking with Deborah Thomas on the imperative to engage with the connections forged through the pressures of violence in the wake of plantation slavery. Thomas (2016) suggests that attention to such pressures is best understood through quantum entanglement: vibration together across both space and time. As we dance from scene to scene, we are vibing with the other authors in this collection in a mutual refusal of sovereign self-possession and a reaching toward our shared needs and vulnerabilities. We aim here to address the many and multiple presents of racial violence in the United States, not by seeking causality or an accounting of harm but through an affective engagement with those entanglements not easily accounted for. As we move through this mixtape, we move through these forms of entanglement and simultaneity, allowing the music to disturb the connections we have been habituated not to feel. In this mixtape, Chance the Rapper and Walter Benjamin are easy contemporaries: *walked into Apple with cracked screens and told prophetic stories of freedom.*[2]

The text follows musical connections and other powerful vibrations as they encourage us to travel between home, academic institution, and field site, and to feel how those locations resonate and dissonate even when they are the same place. We use the collective plural in both our ethnographic and analytic writing to emphasize grammatically the ways in which we have never been individuals—to declare our consent not to be single beings (Gilbert, Sapp, and Tauber 2012; Moten 2017). The "we" voicing is an invitation into multiplicities and a call toward radical relationality, drawing upon not only who we claim but who we are claimed by. It is a refrain that reminds us that self-possession is not liberation, a signal to collective debt and collective power.

open correctional gates in higher deserts . . .

Driving to Standing Rock with a friend on Black Friday, the car piled high with donations; respirators and their corresponding cartridges spilling out of cheap plastic bags. We cross the state border into South Dakota and are promptly pulled over by police officers. We had already discussed this possibility, concerned with our visible Indigeneity and queerness after hearing stories of discrimination from others on their way to the camps. We haven't experienced such wanton racism in years as we do at rest stops and while getting dinner. We know that tensions are particularly high, with some local residents resentful of the number of individuals who have come to "Stand with Standing Rock." But we also know that these tensions exceed our time, and we wish the accrued murderous legacies and their contemporary forms wouldn't feel as visceral as they do when we see the flash of police lights. The officers flank the car and pepper us with questions—friendly words delivered in a less than friendly manner: "Goin' to Morton County to help out?" After they finish scanning the car, we pull back onto the road. Beyoncé's newest album, *Lemonade*, has been soundtracking the majority of the fifteen-hour drive anyway. It is natural and necessary to play "Freedom"; to hear what we couldn't articulate to one another in the moment, soothe the anxiety built up in our muscles and prepare for the militarized camp still hours ahead of us.

open correctional gates in higher deserts . . .

There are two facilities bearing the name High Desert State Prison, although the higher deserts contain much more than two correctional facilities. The Nevada High Desert complex is located in Indian Springs, thirty-five miles north of Las Vegas on Southern Paiute territory, not far from the reservation where we were raised. At 1,576,000 square feet and a capacity to hold 4,176 human bodies, it is the largest major institution in the Nevada Department of Corrections, though certainly not the largest correctional institution in the country. It stands next to Creech Air Force Base, which specializes in "remotely piloted aircraft systems": Predator and Reaper drones. Sixty miles to the north is the Nevada Test Site, which remains the most bombed place on earth, where 928 of 1,032 US nuclear tests occurred between 1951 and 1992. Initial tests were conducted in the Pacific but were found too costly to sustain. Nevada's proximity to the uranium industry in the Southwest allowed for shorter supply lines, and the Nevada Test Site was constructed in 1951. The profound violence of dispossession is found in the region's definition as a national sacrifice zone; the toxic legacies of atomic testing ensure its perpetual status as an experimental site for national capital investment: not wasting the wasted.

California's High Desert State Prison was one of twenty-nine state-run facilities cited when in 2006 the governor of California declared a state of emergency within the Department of Corrections due to prison overcrowding. California's rate of incarceration had been increasing exponentially since the early 1970s, mirroring national trends in mass incarceration that target poor people of color in particular. In 2011, the US Supreme Court ruled that incarceration in California's overcrowded prison system amounted to "cruel and unusual punishment" and ordered the state to reduce its prison population. In response, the state implemented a Public Safety Realignment program that moved people convicted of lower-level felonies (defined as nonviolent, nonsexual, and nonserious crimes) out of the overcrowded state prisons and into either county jails or parole supervision. Ruth Gilmore argues that incarceration in the United States serves as an instrument of dispossession, legalizing through criminal courts a process of stripping from those populations most heavily policed in the United States not only the right to private property but also control over "bodily habits, pastimes, relationships, and mobility" (2007, 12). National media made much of the "realignment" of many from prison to parole, which is a form of community-based supervision, warning that the problem of overcrowding was forcing California toward an opening of the correctional gates—a release of bodies presumed dangerous into the homes of those presumed to have a right to safety. Little attention was paid outside of criminal justice circles to the massive transfer as well of sentenced individuals from overcrowded facilities nonetheless designed for long-term captivity to county jails designed for short-term pretrial stays. Kelly Lytle Hernández reminds us that the first jail in what would become Los Angeles was built by settlers as a tool to eliminate Tongva people from "land, life, and society" in the region— today the LA County Jail continues this project with targets who are Black, poor, immigrant, and mad (Hernández 2017).

Kendrick's line on "Freedom" sets the connections between our projects all abuzz. The same seductive logics that allowed for the establishment of the Nevada Test Site and the expansion of the military industry in the region extend to the expansion and invisibility of the carceral industry. The figure of the desert as barren and hostile land secure in its remoteness, the scale of its perceived emptiness, and long traditions of conquest and genocide have crafted the region as a space that is ripe for radical engineering and experimentation, for projects of empire that operate in plain sight yet unseen. The same techniques of dehumanization and dispossession that fill jails, prisons, and parole rolls with Black and brown bodies also fill those

bodies with cancers; fed by radiation, stress, trauma, and chronic vulnerability to state violence and toxic ecologies alike.

And when they carve my name inside the concrete I hope it forever reads . . .

"It takes muscular political capacity," writes Ruth Wilson Gilmore, "to
realize widescale dispossession of people who have formal rights" (Hernández 2017). It takes something like a limber and muscular will, we think, to
move through and beyond the negative space of dispossession to something
else; to something to sit with and to something-to-be-done. This mixtape
is more than just a meditation on music—it is a rehearsal of the practices
of movement and stillness we wish to attend to and attune with as scholars: an attempt to carve into concrete our refusal to be captured in stone.

Music helps us to think with stillness and motion, both improvised
and enforced. On the one hand, Black and Indigenous bodies are arrested,
captured, held still; our histories and futures set in stone. "Fixed like dye,"
in the words of Frantz Fanon; Blackness experienced as a "crushing ob-
jecthood" producing muscular dreams (Fanon [1952] 2008). Indigeneity
experienced in the words of Jodi Byrd as "the site of already-doneness that
begins to linger as unwelcomed guest to the future" (2011, 20). Framed in
the logics of dispossession, Indians have always and already been a problem for the settler state. The "Indian Problem" Audra Simpson (2014, 19)
writes about is the existence of continued life (of any form) in the face of
an acquisitional and territorial desire *that then moves through time* to become, in liberal parlance, the "problem" of difference. Black studies turns
to fugitivity in search of liberation—finding refuge for self-possession in
a state of constant motion (Harney and Moten 2013; Roberts 2015). But
constant movement exhausts, and the energy to refuse capture is not
everywhere ready to hand (Povinelli 2011). And possession—of land or of
self—is a meager substitute for liberation. Thinking with music helps us
to consider what it might feel like to refuse the choice between fight and
flight, between motion and stillness, between stay and go. If this piece is a
mixtape, it is written in the style of *Lemonade*: a lyrical articulation of the
difficult decision to stay, set to the beat of all of our best reasons to leave.

This piece is a performance and a methodological intervention. Academic
production is too often individuated and stagnant: stand-alone articles and
books published on a schedule designed to maximize institutional ratings
and standardize the metrics of success. The collaboration we do here aims
to refuse the seduction of the ready-to-hand scripts for individual success and embrace entanglements with complex others. We believe those

entanglements—and the dedications to which they are anchored—are necessary. Our individual research projects are deeply entangled in communities and literatures beyond and opposed to the institution of the university. We are committed to the traditions of Black and Indigenous radical thought toward which our projects are oriented, even as we recognize with alarm the unfamiliarity with which those traditions approach one another. This is a work of uneasy collaboration: we write within a feeling of being already owed so much and a feeling of too much having already been taken, which, we are learning, are not the same feeling at all. We contribute to this work unevenly, lovingly, unwillingly, enthusiastically. We think slowly. We write in a hurry. Collaboration is a dance without a single tempo: it trips, it flows, it surprises, sometimes it hurts. In the dance of such collaboration we seek, as Fred Moten might suggest, to tap into "our common capacity, insofar as we are one another's means, to live beyond our means" (2013, 241).

In other words, in the writing of this piece, in the rehearsals that lie before it, we accrue debts to one another that cannot be accounted for, but can be and are felt.[3] Debts that rest on histories of violence, theft, and harm even as they rest in the immediate and seemingly individual decisions to put in work, to take a break, to lean on one another without knowing if the other can bear the load. This piece is also a rehearsal of our refusal to collect.

On days we're not feeling particularly loved or loving, or the pain of the world is screaming at us through various forms of social media, we hear Audre Lorde's echo: "What are the words you do not yet have?" (Lorde 1984, 41). What can happen when we put our nonsingular being with your nonsingular being? A cacophony, a symphony. Those "discordant and competing representations of diasporic arrivals and native lived experiences—that vie for hegemony within the discursive, cultural, and political processes of representation and identity that form the basis for . . . states of injury and biopolitics," as Jodi Byrd (2011, xiii) articulates. Honoring the relations and legacies that rest in our bones underneath tense muscles; creating a space for rehearsal that is always an incomplete, imperfect practice of movement. Rehearsal makes us stronger: toning and stretching. We've moved through rehearsals together in many spaces and forms, always returning to agitate, strengthen, check in. Decolonial praxis requires radical intimacy and both stillness and movement. Liberation requires improvisation, celebration, mourning.

In *The Economization of Life*, Michelle Murphy (2017b, 1) discusses how practices of quantification, so foundational to so many academic disciplines, have worked to "install economy as our collective environment" and asks how we might assemble life differently toward other futures. As this mixtape unfolds, we ask our readers to both travel and sit with us as we attempt to move through and shake loose the ready-at-hand narratives about Black and brown bodies that frame what has been taken from us as a matter of economy. We invite our readers to think and feel instead the irreparable harms and unrepayable debts that vibrate through the spaces we inhabit and shape the conditions of possibility for action within them. Sitting in this discomfort demands listening; an attunement to vibrations, to that which you cannot see but feel. We want to insist on this as a listening to Blackness—as we move through moments in Black American music, we hope to attune to the ways in which Indigenous and Black liberation alike depend upon liberation from anti-Blackness in particular.

Dis/Possession

everyone's missing . . .

The high clear falsetto of Tunde Olaniran's chorus fills our headphones as we run in the shadow of the Mississippi River through a neighborhood in New Orleans now commonly referred to as the Bywater by its many new young residents. Before the storm, the neighborhood was called the Upper Ninth Ward; in the years following Hurricane Katrina it has transformed from a majority-Black neighborhood of homeowners to a majority-white neighborhood of renters. In 2015, it is one of several frontiers of gentrification sparking conflict between New Orleans natives and transplants. We read in the local paper that so-called vandals have recently scrawled "Yuppies Go Home" on the windows of the St. Roch Market on St. Claude Avenue. The recently redeveloped former fish market continues to bear the name "market" but serves specialties, not staples: sushi, fresh oysters, gourmet coffee and pastries. Down the block, an equally unaffordable co-op grocery sells staples to those residents able to afford the sustainably sourced markup. For residents whose residence predates the storm, the area is something of a food desert.

The streets are quiet on this early-morning run; the only sounds are the music in our headphones, the deep vibrations of commercial ships navigating the Mississippi, and the uneven lively sound of our feet hitting broken pavement, tree root, pebble, and dirt. *Everyone's missing*, Tunde laments in falsetto, *but I'm still here*. His falsetto feels like desolation, like determination. We breathe in and the air around us feels heavy with humidity and with more than humidity. We feel as though the city's dead are running with us, as though we are inhaling a bit of them each time we take a ragged breath. When we return to Chicago, we carry those ghosts with us.

everyone's missing...

We moved to Chicago to pursue a PhD and found a conspicuous absent presence. Indigeneity is everywhere and nowhere—place names, monuments. It is colloquially known that Chicago, *shikaakwa*, means something like "smelly onion," or a place that smells. The city is the center of industry and capital in Illinois; the mascot of the state university here is (still) the Fighting Illini. Chicago's Stanley Cup–winning hockey team, the Blackhawks, covers the city's concrete walls and moving buses with images of disembodied Indigenous heads. The city seems to revel in stark juxtapositions: the violence of settlement, dispossession of Indigenous land, capitalist accumulation, racialized violence, and miles of preserved public access to the great lake. Chicago is a jewel on Lake Michigan. It is the most segregated city in America. What work is necessary when you enter a new ecology? When we fly (back) to Chicago, we have to reteach ourselves how to love the city: we listen to Chance the Rapper, BJ the Chicago Kid, Jamila Woods. *I know you think it's crazy there...*

We returned home to Chicago for graduate school and encountered a present absence. Black dispossession suffuses the white stone campus. The Midway Plaisance, site of the 1893 World's Columbian Exposition, once marked the border of the University of Chicago's campus: now it serves as an artery cutting through a campus expanding with an aura of manifest destiny through the historically Black South Side of the city. Signs along Fifty-Third Street welcome visitors to "downtown Hyde Park." Federal agents are on the street now and then: ATF agents arrive to help Chicago's police force fight the "carnage" while residents protest carnage at the hands of that same police force; the federal government responds to new protests of the same shit with the deployment of FBI, ATF, and DEA. *Please don't forget about Jason Van Dyke.* What work is possible as you lose your home? When we fly, drive, or ride the train (back) to Chicago, we always listen to "Homecoming" by Kanye West. *Do you think about me now and then?*

everyone's missing...

We see Tunde live at Reggies near State and Cermak in Chicago. We drive there from Hyde Park: a small carful of University of Chicago graduate students desperate to shake ourselves out of the rhythmic violence of campus life. We are seeking relief from the light percussion of campus "safety and security updates" in our email inboxes informing us of crimes within the University of Chicago Police Department's jurisdiction, and reassuring us that the victim(s) were individual(s) "not affiliated with the University"; the high-pitched crescendo of regular racialized "incidents" on campus, the loudest of which merit official statements delivered to our inbox in familiar stock language; the steady electronic hum of surveillance as one of the largest private police forces in the country patrols every block of the neighborhood stretching twenty blocks north of campus and ten blocks south, and from the campus's western edge to the lake; the irritating rumble of the particular patrol car that idles daily on the private street on which our grandmother has lived for the better part of a century, just outside her front window; the deep thrumming bass line that receives no mention in our inboxes but which we feel in the air on campus as we look around at subdued young faces and make careful, quiet deductions: suicides, frequent, almost always young students of color.

Traveling to Reggies recalls a story a friend told us about her orientation at the University of Chicago some decades prior. She was given a map of the city as part of her orientation packet, highlighting all of the places in Chicago a new student might like to explore. One such location, Chinatown, appeared to be just a few blocks north of Hyde Park on the map, so she decided to walk—realizing only after she had been walking a full hour that the map had simply redacted the thirty city blocks between the two neighborhoods as irrelevant to an incoming University of Chicago student. We are routinely advised upon matriculation to treat the surrounding areas as surround (Harney and Moten, 2013).

but i'm still here...

"Everything I love survives dispossession," writes Fred Moten (2013) in "The Subprime and the Beautiful." "Is therefore before dispossession." Before, as in prior, as in what precedes and also what awaits (Harney and Moten 2013). Reggies has two levels. We stand along the edge of the stairs for a better view but are drawn down to the floor and toward the stage by Tunde's opening act. This is our first time hearing the music of New Orleans native Dawn Richard, and the music instantly transports us, moves us, shakes us. We are on the floor at Reggies surrounded by the exuberant love of Dawn's Chicago-based fans. We are flying down Rampart Street at night along the edge of the French Quarter, breathing in the lights and sounds of revelry not our own. We are dancing on the edge of the bayou feeling cool rain on our bare skin and feeling the hair on our arms stand on end in anticipation of a coming storm. *Don't you know that I love playing in the rain, baby?* We will write our dissertations listening to Dawn Richard's album, pausing within it to sit with "LA (feat. Trombone Shorty)" on repeat. The chorus, *These LA streets are killing me,* colors our dreams.

In her introduction to *Ghostly Matters,* Avery Gordon describes haunting as "those singular yet repetitive instances when home becomes unfamiliar, when your bearings on the world lose direction, when the over-and-done-with comes alive, when what's been in your blind spot comes into view" (2008, xvi). She suggests attention to haunting—one might say attention to a feeling of being unhinged that is also a certain kind of ghostly *possession*—as essential to the production of knowledge about forms of dispossession and violence. Everything I love survives dispossession. *I can be the revenant.* Everything we love possesses us.

When Tunde comes on, we are still in Chicago and we are still in New Orleans, but we nonetheless find ourselves in Flint, Michigan, as well. The small midwestern city became a household name in places far afield from Michigan in the late 1980s after filmmaker and Flint native Michael Moore cast his hometown as the star of the documentary *Roger and Me,* which chronicled the economic devastation following General Motors' closing of the automobile plants that provided one of the only sources of stable employment in the region. Flint reprises its role as the site of the nation's unwilling but apparently acceptable human sacrifice in 2014 as the revelation hits national news that the emergency manager appointed to handle the municipality's financial crisis has saved the city money by poisoning its water. The country is outraged, but the people of Flint do not get the clean drinking water they are owed. "I'm from Flint, Michigan," Tunde announces to a cheering Chicago crowd. As he performs the track "Brown Boy," his voice seems to hit hardest on the word "refugee." *I'm every single thing you think of me, I'm a sinner, killer, drug-dealer, refugee.*

Love & Hate

Michael Kiwanuka's song "Love & Hate" plays in our headphones on repeat as we carefully pack swimsuit, cap, goggles, and towel into a light cloth backpack and prepare to leave the house. The pool is only three blocks away: that the over-seven-minute track has been playing on loop is the only indication that we are feeling apprehensive. We have been tense ever since arriving in Somerville, Massachusetts, where we will be living (again), despite youthful vows never to return. We understand in this return that the whiteness of Boston and its surrounding areas is more than just the young white men near Fenway Park who once threw stones at our car for sport as we waited, tense, at a red light. Today in Somerville we encounter welcoming smiles and friendly banter and white liberal generosity, and we do not wonder that it coexists so easily, familiarly, with the white racist hostility we encounter here too. The two are old lovers, and they seem to drive each other to extremes. We find ourselves catching our breath at the threshold of every new space we enter in anticipation of what we are never sure: overt racism perhaps, warm embrace equally likely. Neither feel entirely consensual. Both feel somewhat suffocating. Today is our first foray to the public pool. Our fear of less-than-easy access to this particular public space is based not only in the suspicion with which we have come to treat this entire metropolitan area but also in the knowledge of the history of public pools as a site of racialized exclusion in the United States. The fear is mostly, however, based in the embodied knowledge of our own desperate need to submerge.

We stand in the parking lot of the local elementary school, scanning the signs for directions to the pool entrance. The smell of hot concrete, the hum of generators, the vague whiff of chlorine indicates we are getting close, if not yet arrived at our relief. We stand in the parking lot of the elementary school and we stand as well on the pavement outside another public pool in another city on another day that feels like today. On that day we awake at the hour the pool opens, wasting no time in gathering our belongings and walking over. Stallings Pool is huge and outdoors and just a few blocks away from our home on Crete Street in New Orleans. Swimming in Stallings Pool under the warm summer sun in the hour before work begins is a form of morning worship, a grounding of our bodies and souls in the water. On this day it is also a prayer for relief. Perhaps there is no need to describe here which of our friends, family, or neighbors we had lost the night before. No need to offer you the particulars of the loss of a loved one to homicide, to suicide, or to some cause others will gloss in un/easy avoidance as "natural." Better to say simply that this was a morning on which the distinction between those ways of dying did not seem to us terribly important. We crossed the parking lot and approached the pool door with an air of quiet determination, were stopped at the doors by a teenage lifeguard who informed us that there were thunderstorms in the area, and that the pool could not open until the thunder was some miles away. Defeated, deflated, we sat on the concrete steps and wept, praying that the thunderstorms would at least bring rain.

Today we enter the school cautiously, making our way to the basement where we encounter a familiar municipal scene. A boy clad in lifeguard red smiles a familiar teenage welcome free of the antagonism and refusal we feared, holding instead only the resigned boredom of a child indoors on a sunny summer day. We submerge ourselves in the near-empty pool and swim to exhaustion, familiarizing ourselves as we do with the contours of this new place of refuge, making it our own. We walk happily back to our new home, "Love & Hate" still playing on repeat in our headphones. *I need something, give me something wonderful.* The music feels like water.

We first heard Michael Kiwanuka's music as the credits rolled on episode five of the Netflix series *Dear White People* (Simien 2017). We had been advised by a dear friend to turn off auto-play and enjoy the mixtape of the season's final credits; the opening chords of "Love & Hate" wash over us as the screen darkens on one of the show's most talked-about episodes. Directed by Barry Jenkins (director of the critically acclaimed *Moonlight*), the episode culminates with a white cop pulling a gun on a Black student at a campus party and ends with the student, Reggie, crying alone in his dorm room. We watched the whole series in just a few sittings, finding a kind of urgent relief of recognition in the show's portrayal of institutions of higher education. We consumed the show quickly, but we always sat with the soundtrack. *Love and hate / how much more are we supposed to tolerate . . .*

"I love this city," Jenkins's character Micah tells the girl he has just slept with in the director's breakout film *Medicine for Melancholy* (Jenkins 2008). "I mean I hate this city, but I love this city."

We know how he feels.

Do you know what it means to miss New Orleans?

When we fly from Chicago to Las Vegas for the holidays or for fieldwork we always book a window seat. Las Vegas is one of the fastest-growing cities in the country, and as we've grown, we've seen the city grid stretch and expand across the valley floor, creeping toward the mountains. There is a debate: Is Las Vegas (the Entertainment Capital of the World, Sin City) a mirror or a model for America? In *Addiction by Design: Machine Gambling in Las Vegas*, Natasha Dow Schüll argues that "running alongside the debate . . . is the question of whether to view the city as a shape-shifting marvel of human inventiveness and technological sophistication or as a dystopic instantiation of consumer capitalism" (2012, 7).

We book a window seat not because we delight, as many tourists do, in seeing the surreal image of the cartoon-colossal Las Vegas Strip—a glittering seam of lights in a desert valley or a closer view of tacky simulacra—New York, Luxor, Paris. No, we sit by the window to focus on the landscape; the gradation of color of different minerals: bluish greens into pale browns, shadowed curves of dry alluvial planes, black dots of sagebrush. We think this is what military jet operators from Nellis Air Force Base see too; we consider what this perceived emptiness has allowed. "Pink + White" by Frank Ocean is on repeat in our headphones—it feels like entering a warm bath, where there is no partition, you are one with the environs. *Kiss the earth that birthed you / you showed me love.*

When we return to Chicago for the holidays, we always make our way quickly to the shores of Lake Michigan. Not the lakefront downtown where tourists on motorized scooters snap selfies in front of this lake that resembles a quiet ocean. We approach the shore near Fortieth Street, where the city is building a prairie-land bird sanctuary and where young Black and tan teenagers from North Kenwood and Bronzeville go to skate and smoke weed amid the concrete and tall grasses. We stand there before an endless horizon holding gently the knowledge that the horizon is not endless, that we are looking toward Indiana and Michigan, that perhaps in clearer air we might see the silhouettes of those not-so-distant shores. Jamila Woods in our headphones on repeat, "LSD." *You gotta love me like I love the lake.* When we return to Chicago, we drive down Lake Shore Drive with the windows rolled down and the music blasting. As the torque of the turning car pulls our bodies like gravity toward the soft blue welcome of the lake, we think about Lochlann Jain's paradoxical joyrides against cancer, the cruel optimism of Lauren Berlant, and the muscular dreams of Frantz Fanon (Jain 2013; Berlant 2011a; Fanon 1961). We turn up the music and press harder on the gas.

Breathe till I evaporate / my whole body see through

In *Islands of Decolonial Love*, Leanne Simpson (2013) poses a project of vulnerability, looking toward the potential found in incoherence, or losing the cohesive self through deep entanglement with another cartography of inseverable relations with the land. We think about our capacities for loving a landscape that has been so irrevocably changed through infrastructures of settlement, land that is chemically and socially perceived as toxic or wasted, when breathing in deep to ground ourselves is opening ourselves to harm. We love it so much we ink it into our skins in our adopted city.

You gotta move it slowly / take and eat my body like it's holy . . .

We learn through the music of the Social Experiment to think decolonial love and Black love together and find ourselves resting in maternal love and divine grace. Donnie Trumpet and the Social Experiment's "Sunday Candy" celebrates the ensemble in its addition to the generations-long tradition of writing love songs to Black grandmothers. This is a surrender of the cohesive self to those many human others who lie before the self: a return to the unrepayable debt a child owes her mother, her grandmother, her ancestors. In the Black musical tradition it is both a song and a refrain, echoing from the gratitude of "Grandma's Hands" to the grace of "Sunday Candy" to the breaking and broken promises of "Hey Mama" written before and performed again and often after Kanye West loses his mother.

For Saidiya Hartman (2007), to *Lose Your Mother* is a collective condition. The theft of a homeland and the loss of a mother—a dispossession and also a haunting possession—create a world debt to Blackness as unrepayable as that which we owe our mothers. Our second rehearsal of this mixtape tuned to this frequency—that of a mother's love and the hatred of slavery—as a way to think through debts beyond accounting. We take love to be one grammar through which art and theory approach the unaccountable. We understand the structure of this grammar to be an open question in the anti-Black, pro-capital, settler colonial conditions in which we live and breathe. Our second rehearsal asked after love in the face of settler violence, love that entangles you with unrepayable debt, love as relations; love as conspiracy, as breathing together (Choy 2016). We considered these modulations of love in conversation with the artists we love, attending with them to the pain, the jarring vibrations of loving Blackness in a world structured by its hatred and captivity. We wanted to think with Kendrick, who jubilates "*i love myself*" on "i" only to turn and scream "*loving u is complicated*" into the mirror on "u." Thinking with love, we wanted to attend to the power of its energy and to the physical toll love takes on those who recognize Black and brown bodies as worthy of it. Love within what Harney and Moten call bad debt, "which is to say real debt, the debt that cannot be repaid, the debt at a distance, the debt without creditor, the black debt, the queer debt, the criminal debt. Excessive debt, debt for no reason, debt broken from credit, debt as its own principle" (2013, 61).

We are thinking now with Harney and Moten again of love's *hapticality*: "the feel that no individual can stand, and no state abide. The capacity to feel through others, for others to feel through you, for you to feel them feeling you" (2013, 61). In what remains of this rehearsal, we wish to wonder further after love's attunements to dis/possession; after the lessons we might learn from a mother's love in an ecology of bad debt: mothers whose chronic illnesses exist along, through, as part of capitalist development and extraction, mothers who survive, mothers who die, mothers who *smell like light, gas, water, electricity, rent.*

Loving u is complicated

The scene with which this piece began, Kendrick Lamar's resurrection of hip-hop legend Tupac Shakur, bears a haunting resemblance to another recent resurrection: the 2011 documentary *The Black Power Mixtape: 1967–1975*, created using footage taken by Swedish filmmakers in the late 1960s and early 1970s (Olsson 2011). In both resurrections, we witness an intergenerational encounter with Blackness. Both encounters stand out in the archive: moments in Black American history preserved by a European fetishization of Blackness—a toxic kind of love that nonetheless breathes life into forgotten places. In "Mortal Man," Kendrick suggests to the man who might have been his mentor that the only hope we kinda have left is music. 'Pac responds by suggesting that music is a kind of possession. "We ain't even really rapping," he says, "we just letting our dead homies tell stories for us." Strains of free jazz begin their slow crescendo toward the album's final notes, and Kendrick begins to read a poem written by one of his homies, "The Caterpillar and the Butterfly." The poem considers what Fred Moten has described as a kind of ontological unfairness in Blackness, casting the Black artist as both caterpillar and butterfly: hated and loved, strong and weak, ugly and beautiful, victim and messiah, one and the same. As the instrumentals reach their height and the poem reaches its conclusion, Kendrick asks Tupac what he thinks of that. This time, he does not offer himself a response. 'Pac? 'Pac!

In *The Black Power Mixtape* we are in Stokely Carmichael's mother's home, sometime in the late 1960s. It is just Stokely, his mother, and the Swedish film crew. The scene begins with Mrs. Carmichael telling the young Swedish interviewer that every time her son is arrested through his involvement with the Student Nonviolent Coordinating Committee, she dies "a thousand times." During a pause in the conversation, Stokely, crouched in the corner with arms folded protectively around his torso, tilts his head back and begins to unfurl, asking the filmmakers as he does if they'd like *him* to interview his mother. "Would you really?!" the young filmmaker exclaims in delight, and the microphone and equipment are quickly handed to Stokely, who is already seating himself next to his mother on the couch.

"Mrs. Carmichael," Stokely begins, laying one arm along the back of the couch and crossing one leg across the top of the other, "when you came to the United States with your children, where did you live?" Mrs. Carmichael leans away from her son just slightly as they speak. Her left hand is folded carefully across her lap, a seeming attempt to physically restrain the rest of her body from fidgeting in the discomfort she so obviously feels. As the interview continues you see her left hand slowly make its way up her right arm, squeezing tense muscles methodically as it moves until it comes to rest at the node of that tension at the base of her neck. Stokely is gentle but insistent as he pushes past her attempts at euphemization.

"What kind of neighborhood was it?" "What do you mean by the run-down side?" "How big was the place you lived in?" "And how many people lived there?" "How many is that altogether?" "And how was life in general for your children? Could they do most things other children in the United States could do? And did you have enough money to do those things?" "Why didn't they?" "Why didn't he make enough money?" "But there were other carpenters who lived better than your husband?" "And why didn't your husband?" "Why was he always the first to be laid off?" Finally, almost in defeat, Mrs. Carmichael says, "Because he was a Negro."

"Thank you," her son replies, and hands the microphone back to the Swedes.

Loving u is complicated

The free jazz that floats above Kendrick's voice in "Mortal Man" brings the conversation between Kendrick Lamar and Tupac Shakur into the room with Stokely Carmichael and his mother. It is the late 1960s still, it is the early 1970s still, and free jazz legend Sun Ra is rehearsing with his Arkestra, lecturing at the University of California–Berkeley and working on the film *Space Is the Place*. In each medium, the artist rehearses variations on a theme: there is no place for the Black man on earth; these terrestrial forms of politics will not free us; we must journey to a new planet; music can transport us there. What would Stokely Carmichael, who left the United States in 1969 under increasing threats and surveillance from the FBI-COINTELPRO, say to the assertion that there is no home for him here? Carmichael spent the last thirty years of his life in exile. He traveled often. Always on the move. *It's after the end of the world. Don't you know that yet?*[4]

Just Throw This at the End If I'm Too Late
for the Intro . . .

We float in a sensory deprivation tank in downtown Chicago after returning from Standing Rock. We had gone to be in good relation with other Indigenous nations and those more than human. We held close our own experiences with settler state violence: extraction and contamination. We needed to go, but the combination of frontline violence, camping in cold weather, and driving long distances in not-so-friendly swaths of the country has taken its toll on our bodies. Our friend urges us to take respite; they know we need our strength for what's ahead. We hear in the spaces around their speech: "You know what happens to women of color in the academy . . ."

We worry about feeling too much in the dark. The presidential election is fresh, and we are actively concerned for the safety of our friends and family across the country. What will happen when we mute the white noise? We are instructed to shower and cover any small open wounds (like paper cuts, not the other wounds) with Vaseline so that the salt does not sting us. A woman tells us to trust in relaxing our neck and shoulders, our heads will not submerge, we will not drown. We thought we might drive ourselves crazy with so much time and so many feelings. We live in excessive times.

We rehearse the mixtape between the summer of 2020 and the summer of 2021, matching the tempo to the moment and slowing it way down. These days we are not often able to submerge in water—we find ourselves submerged instead in an atmosphere thick with fear, hostility, and callous disregard. As always, everything and nothing has changed. We find ourselves thinking still and again with Christina Sharpe, who writes *In the Wake* of Fanon's work on breath in *Toward the African Revolution*. As "I can't breathe" echoes across the staccato rhythms of violent Black death and protest in solidarity with Black life; as an illness borne on breath claims lives along all-too-familiar lines of vulnerability, we ask with Sharpe, "Who can breathe free?" (2016, 112). We note with Fanon that "the individual's breathing is an observed breathing. It is combat breathing" (1969, 50). We rehearse this mixtape (again) in an atmosphere in which some people's breath comes a little bit harder than others. In an atmosphere where even assisted breathing is at capacity. An atmosphere in which our practices of care require that we manage our breath, distance, calculate risk. In which these practices of care are smothered in an atmosphere attuned to the policing of breath. We think, with Tim Choy, of the importance of breathing together. Of our need to conspire (Choy 2016). To work in ensemble, *in case i get shortness of breath.*

The invitation to contribute a version of the mixtape to *Sovereignty Unhinged* comes as we are feeling decidedly unsovereign, increasingly unhinged: we feel ourselves falling apart, unable to hang together. Ever more acutely attuned to our interdependence in shared atmosphere, we are therefore unnerved by declarations of soundness amid felt collapse. Our police departments sanction individual acts of violence, or fail to; our universities and departments sanction individuals charged with sexual harassment, or fail to; everywhere we turn we see individual bad apples cast out and canceled as institutions and structures declare themselves well and whole, or at least working on it. Never mind that the full phrase is "one bad apple can spoil the barrel." We dwell in doomed barrels feeling as loath to cast out the bad apples as we are to live with them. In other words, we find ourselves listening to a lot of Kanye West.

I know it's past visiting hours, but can I please bring her these flowers?

We are on the second floor of The Promontory, a restaurant, bar, and event venue in the "new downtown Hyde Park" that would be unrecognizable to our grandmother living just a few blocks away, if she ever went there anymore. The crowd is an interesting mix: some people affiliated with the University of Chicago and mostly Black people from farther south and west in the city out for a good time in a neighborhood decidedly more their vibe than downtown Chicago. We are here on the invitation of an acquaintance who is senior faculty at the University of Chicago—she knows the bouncer. We are skeptical of the invitation for so many reasons, tracking so many well-worn scripts: our companion is a white woman inviting us to a visibly Black event; she's a famous academic of the kind that the structure of this apple barrel makes quite dangerous; the venue is helping to gentrify the neighborhood. But we pay our cover fee and ascend the stairs, getting drinks and finding our way to a corner where we can just stand and listen together. It is an open mic night, and most of the performers are in their late teens. They're good. Their friends are all here to cheer them on. We find ourselves smiling as we listen to the cadence, the musicality, the irreverence, and hear echoes of Kanye vibrating through the vulnerable ethic of a new generation. As we rehearse this mixtape in the wake of the passing of our conspirator that night, in the wake of the passing of so many young Black people who find joy in remixing Kanye's style, the evening feels like a gift. We find ourselves haunted by this moment, drawn lovingly to this moment—and toward an infrequently cited Earthseed verse: "*there is no end / to what a living world / will demand of you.*"

The pandemic means that when our relatives are hospitalized with their preexisting health conditions, we are forced to confront the hospitals' infrastructure of care, which means one entrance, one exit, one visitor, and restricted visiting hours to reduce exposure to the vulnerable. The line starts an hour prior to being let in as heatwave temperatures hit the one hundred-teens, we hear guards saying, "We have to temp earlier cos they're tempin' too hot" and watch whiteness at work as white men yell angrily at the idea of having to wear a mask to enter a hospital and white women pull theirs down to passive-aggressively argue about the line on their cell phones. This is our highest daily exposure. Driving to the hospital means cutting across the Las Vegas Strip, the capitalist nightmare that had historically shuttered its properties for three months and famously refused to shelter the houseless; instead the city painted "socially distanced boxes" on the parking lot pavement. One day a Black Lives Matter march interrupts the typical flow of tourists, and we remember Fred Moten reminding us Nevada was once called the Mississippi of the West and that referential refrains can be a tool for a remembering and a reworlding.

Two words, Chi-town, raised me, crazy / so I live by two words: fuck you, pay me.

"Fuck sharing governance," Fred Moten and Stefano Harney argue in conversation with the University of California–based graduate student-led group Fuck You, Pay Us. "Fuck sharing governance, or the slightly more equitable distribution of extracted surplus; let's share needs." "The landscape of need," they add, "is dark and lovely" (Moten and Harney 2020). Every day it feels more and more delusional to work in ways that uphold the university structure. But we are reminded that not to do so would be to appear to fall apart. And that to appear to fall apart is to lose credibility, credit, and investors. Even Kanye loses money when he appears to really come undone. Perhaps we are thinking with Kanye now more than ever because he feels to us such a hyperbolic example of what the struggle for sovereignty feels like. Kanye is as free as he can possibly be, which is to say not free at all. He is singular, yet we have imbibed so much of him, shaped our own cadences and rhythms to his offerings. He is crazy, and so are we. *Woke up in my sympathy the cane-black Judas*. We think the alliterative ring of "Cancel Capitalism" strikes a clearer tone than "Cancel Kanye."

Must be love on the brain. Every version of this mixtape—written, performed, kept private, unfinished—vibes with a powerful, unromantic love. We love each other, of course, and the music: that's the easy part. But we are trying to think and feel with loves less easy but no less real. Love for anthropology: a discipline born as a military endeavor of indigenous dispossession and raised on a steady diet of scientific racism. Love for our friends and colleagues: our ride-or-die homies, duh, but also those colleagues, if not friends, who regularly dismiss, disrespect, belittle, and hurt us with the best of intentions and the worst of them. Love's gotten a bad rap—too many love songs tie love to romance, and romance is a white supremacist grammar. Forgive us if this goes astray, and please don't sue us if we've gone too fast. We are trying to think with Prince about loves both jubilant and violent; with potentialities both expansive and apocalyptic. To think with Rihanna about loves that hurt. We are still learning the rhythms and steps to think critically about the collective project of loving one another—which is to say loving ourselves—like Jamila Woods loves the lake, like Dawn Richard loves Louisiana, *like Kanye loves Kanye*.

Track List

(In order of citation—track lyrics in italics throughout the text)

INTRO

"Mortal Man"—Kendrick Lamar, *To Pimp a Butterfly*
"Blessings (Reprise)"—Chance the Rapper, *Coloring Book*
"Freedom" (feat. Kendrick Lamar)—Beyoncé, *Lemonade*

DIS/POSSESSION

"Everyone's Missing"—Tunde Olaniran, *Transgressor*
"Home"—BJ the Chicago Kid, *In My Mind*
"Ultralight Beam" (feat. Chance the Rapper)—Kanye West, *The Life of Pablo*
"Homecoming"—Kanye West, *Graduation*
"Hurricane"—Dawn Richard, *Redemption*
"LA" (feat. Trombone Shorty)—Dawn Richard, *Redemption*
"Miracle"—Tunde Olaniran, *Stranger*
"Brown Boy"—Tunde Olaniran, *The Second Transgression*

LOVE & HATE

"Love & Hate"—Michael Kiwanuka, *Love & Hate*
"Do You Know What It Means to Miss New Orleans?"—Louis Armstrong and Billie Holiday, soundtrack to *New Orleans*
"Pink + White"—Frank Ocean, *Blonde*
"LSD" (feat. Chance the Rapper)—Jamila Woods, *Heavn*
"Nights"—Frank Ocean, *Blonde*
"Sunday Candy"—Donnie Trumpet and the Social Experiment, *Surf*
"Grandma's Hands"—Bill Withers, *Just As I Am*
"Hey Mama"—Kanye West, *Late Registration*
"i"—Kendrick Lamar, *To Pimp a Butterfly*
"u"—Kendrick Lamar, *To Pimp a Butterfly*
"It's After the End of the World"—The Sun Ra Arkestra, *Space Is the Place*

(JUST THROW THIS AT THE END IF I'M TOO LATE FOR THE INTRO . . .)

"Late" and "Ultralight Beam"—Kanye West, *Late Registration*, *The Life of Pablo*
"Blessings"—Chance the Rapper, *Coloring Book*
"Roses"—Kanye West, *Late Registration*
"Two Words" (feat. Mos Def)—Kanye West, *The College Dropout*
"With You"—Noname, *Room 25*
"Love on the Brain"—Rihanna, *Anti*
"1999"—Prince, *1999*
"I Love Kanye"—Kanye West, *The Life of Pablo*

Notes

1 When we talk about rehearsal here, we are thinking with Stefano Harney and Fred Moten (2013, 107, 110), who use the concept to indicate both a jazz-improvisational relationship to writing and an openness to ongoing collaboration.

2 Throughout this text, we'll be citing lyrics from the music in a musical form of citation: as emphasis and within the flow of the piece, anticipating the listener and reader's recognition, demanding it. A full track list follows the piece, and the tracks are listed in the order in which they appear in the text, whether as explicit reference or lyrical hook. To help guide our reader through the mixtape, when citing lyrics, we italicize (see Benjamin [1927] 2002; Chance the Rapper, *Coloring Book*, self-released, 2016).

3 In "The Subprime and the Beautiful," Fred Moten characterizes Cedric Robinson's project in *Black Marxism* as seeking "to alert us to the radical resources that lie before the tradition, where 'before' indicates both what precedes and what awaits, animating our times with a fierce urgency" (Moten 2013). When we speak of before, we are thinking of this, and of the robust tradition in Black Atlantic studies of theorizing the prior.

4 Sun Ra, *Space Is the Place* (Evidence Records, 1974).

10

The Sovereignty of Vulnerability

DANILYN RUTHERFORD

In *The Beast and the Sovereign*, the late Jacques Derrida (2009) asked a remarkable question: What if sovereignty and vulnerability went hand in hand? What if the other others—the ones beyond the pale of citizenship and even humanity—were actually rulers of the realm? Sovereignty is only sovereignty to the extent it demands recognition. By virtue of this dynamic, the vulnerable can sometimes appear in an unexpected position of power. In this essay, I describe three very different ethnographic scenes in an effort to illuminate this paradox, which should lead us to wonder whether sovereignty can ever be pinned down.

One way of reading *The Beast and the Sovereign* is as a response to Giorgio Agamben, whose account of sovereignty posits a sheer opposition between the source of law and its target. Viewed as lacking reason and language, animals provide a perfect figure for what Agamben (1998) calls "bare life," that which is excluded from the law's protection since it is defined by the sheer fact of being alive. In the series of lectures compiled in the book, Derrida shows what happens to our understanding of sovereignty when the opposition between the human and the animal breaks down. One lecture focuses on the D. H. Lawrence poem "Snake," whose narrator is a man who goes to a well to fill his pitcher and finds that a snake has arrived before him. As the man waits for the snake to finish, he is caught between the "voices of his human education," which tell him to kill the creature, and the claim to hospitality that this "first comer" extends and demands. When the snake slithers back into its hole, the narrator's horror overcomes his hesitation.

He throws a log at the creature, then is flooded with remorse for having missed an appointment with this "lord of life" (Derrida 2009, 244). Note that it is not when the snake's face is visible but when the snake turns away and becomes subject to assault that the question of sovereignty arises. It is when the snake is most vulnerable that another order comes into focus, a realm both deeper and wider than that circumscribed by the order of human morality: an "underworld" ruled by "uncrowned kings." A new ethics arises in the aftermath of its violation. Life might not be so bare after all.

Something similar, I will argue, happens in the scenes I discuss. They unfold in contexts in which signs of recognition are idiosyncratic and uncertain. They involve what Louis Althusser (1971) called "bad subjects": figures that resist interpellation, that don't turn around when, say, a policeman yells, "Hey, you!" The first scene features the "Stone Age Papuans," described by their European colonizers as the most "primitive" natives in the Dutch East Indies. The other two feature severely disabled students and their advocates in a legislator's office and in a Santa Cruz–area school. I focus on moments when these "bad subjects" turn away and an alternative to the sovereignty on offer briefly comes into view.

I recognize the risks involved in bringing these "bad subjects" together. Rosemarie Garland Thomson (1997) has described how racism, colonialism, and ableism worked together in the nineteenth-century freak show to provide a foil for what she calls the "normate," a subject defined as able-bodied, white, and male. It's no accident that P. T. Barnum toured "General Tom Thumb" alongside "the Missing Link," and dubbed conjoined siblings "Siamese twins." What these performers have in common with one another is their positioning vis-à-vis an established form of sovereignty—one that operates by determining who counts as a political actor, and who does not. The same goes for the figures I describe. But I'm interested in understanding more than simply the reinforcement of existing hierarchies. My story is one of refusal and the forging of connections that leave differences intact. Unhinged from the state, caught in between what Masco and Thomas (introduction, this volume) call "exclusion" and "embrace," the strange and insistent power explored in the following pages undoes some of the distinctions through which humanity has been defined.

Full disclosure: one of these "bad subjects" is my severely disabled daughter. As such, part of this chapter charts corners of a social world that is very close to home. But let's start in Dutch New Guinea, where the year is 1938, and Police Commissioner J. P. van Eechoud is about to show a group of Papuans what happens when you shoot a gun.

Danilyn Rutherford

J. P. van Eechoud was midway through an expedition from the southern coast to the main lake in the Wissel Lake region when our first episode took place. He was on his way by foot to establish the first permanent post in the highlands of this distant corner of the Dutch East Indies. Van Eechoud was probably hungry. He was certainly troubled by fear of getting lost or stranded, given how hard it had been for his men and materials to get this far. So far, the Papuans' pity and interest in foreign trinkets had yielded the pigs and potatoes van Eechoud needed to feed his troops, but the stream was beginning to run dry. Van Eechoud had friends among the handful of highland leaders who had traveled with other officials. But he didn't have what he and his superiors hoped to acquire through this costly endeavor: that is, the Papuans' respect.

Van Eechoud and his men were armed, but arms do little good when the people they are supposed to frighten have no sense of what they are for. And so van Eechoud went to work.

> Behind a twenty-centimeter tree, an empty trekking drum was set. Five meters in front of the tree, I positioned myself with a carbine. Through gestures and by making noise, I tried to make it clear that the tree as well as the can would be bored through with a loud report. Full of tension, the group watched. I aimed, shot, and looked triumphantly to see the effect on their faces—but there were no more faces. With great leaps, some of the group had vanished into the forest, while others raced at full speed to the other side of the garden running, or so they thought, for their lives.
>
> If another shot had been fired, then the poor devils in their panic would have climbed over Mt Carsten. But we began to call reassuringly— at least it seemed to us reassuringly. Meanwhile, at least a half an hour went by before a couple of them dared to return, wavering and reluc- tant. Fear was again in their eyes when they looked at either me or the carbine. (van Eechoud 1953, 103)

"Come back!" van Eechoud calls to the Papuans in vain. Rulers, like rifles, need to be recognized to work. As a representative of Dutch sovereignty, van Eechoud was vulnerable not simply to the vagaries of his equipment, but also the vagaries of Papuan interests. Not only could these natives physically turn their backs on Dutch officials; they could turn their backs on the message they sought to convey. Following this incident, word spread among the Papuans. Soon villagers were greeting van Eechoud with the request that he shoot one of their pigs. Those who witnessed these performances apparently enjoyed the spectacle, and they seemed happy to trade with the foreigners when they passed by. But they showed little reverence for the Dutch East India Company—and little inclination to change much about the way they lived.

Van Eechoud wrote in a humorous vein, but his account reveals wider predicaments. People in this part of the highlands did not speak or understand Malay, the Indies lingua franca, nor did the Dutch have any grasp of the multiple languages the Papuans spoke. Van Eechoud wrote with confidence of the Papuans' panic, but he could only guess at what they felt or thought. Van Eechoud and his colleagues responded to this uncertainty by redoubling their efforts. Less than two decades later, the region was home to mission schools, trading posts, agricultural extension projects, and jails (see Rutherford 2015). Villagers learned from bitter experience what could happen when a soldier pulled a gun. I am not claiming that the Papuans had the resources to resist colonial encroachment, merely—and importantly— the capacity to put its agents to shame (see Rutherford 2009).

It isn't that hard to imagine how the colonized might turn the tables on their colonizers (see Rafael 1992; Rutherford 2003, 2009, 2018). It's harder to picture how severely disabled people might speak back to power. What does it mean for someone like my nonverbal and sometimes not even very responsive daughter to be a citizen? How can someone with no language with which to express an opinion contribute in any small way to the fashioning of the laws of the land?

Legislation Day

It was May 4, 2016, and I was in Representative Mike Ball's office on the second floor of the new wing of the California State House.[1] Starched shirt, bow tie, and an anchorman-worthy helmet of gray hair, Representative Ball was standing at the head of a long mahogany table. Crowded around were some angry-looking women, most in their mid-forties, white, like Representative Ball, well-groomed, well-bred, articulate, strident, effortlessly presentable in their expensive work-casual attire. "It's the Palo Alto delegation," our leader whispered to me as we crept into the room. A motley and far more diverse crew with our backpacks, sneakers, and sandals, the four of us representing Santa Cruz retreated to a leather couch by the window. I squeezed past the coffee table and wheeled Millie's wheelchair into position next to an office chair. I seated myself, carefully assessing whether Millie was in striking distance of the desk; it looked like there might be some tasty pieces of legislation sitting on it, which she would no doubt love to grab and chew.

It was a hot day, and it had already been a long one. We had spent the morning in a ballroom in a nearby hotel, with other delegates from community advisory councils from around the state. We had heard from a lobbyist, a legislator, special education administrators, and two mothers with their sons who had stolen the show, the first with a moving tribute in American Sign Language to his mother's courage, the second with a hilarious description of what being a smart kid with autism was like. We had lined up for meals. We had attempted to keep the children we had brought along with us occupied. Millie had sat on a regular conference chair, played with her stuffed jellyfish, and devoured her lunch and breakfast. She giggled when the crowd reacted to something a speaker said. She even clapped once or twice, a good thirty seconds after the rest of the applause had stopped.

We had come to Sacramento for Legislation Day, an event tacked onto the Special Education Liaison Administrators' Annual Conference. With Xiaona, Millie's cheerfully devoted aide, in tow, I'd driven over from Santa Cruz the day before, since the event began early and we wanted Millie to get a good night's sleep. In addition to Xiaona, who was born in China, others in the party included Lucia, our community advisory council's chair, a Latinx woman who was the parent of two emotionally disturbed teens, and Jennifer Smith, a white woman like me, who had just been hired as the director of special education oversight for area schools. By the time we arrived for our first appointment, we were late, and even though we had lingered in the ballroom so Millie could use the bathroom, she was agitated. As a staffer directed us into Mike Ball's office, she had whined angrily and contorted herself to nip her arm.

The woman who was talking kept on going. I know the type, I thought, taking in the pearl earrings, the expensive handbag, the tasteful makeup, the neatly trimmed eyebrows shaped into an arch. She spoke in the tones of the self-righteously aggrieved. She was telling us a horrific story. Her son—not with her—autistic but brilliant, had been removed from his school placement and transferred to a facility for the emotionally disturbed, where he was an easy mark for bullies. The month she had spent trying to get him moved. The lawyers she had called, her son's deepening depression, his talk of suicide, even though he was only in fourth grade. He'd been disruptive, they told him; now he was scarred for life.

These Palo Alto women were a class act—one taking over from another in a carefully choreographed recitation of the system's failures. Their testimony filled the room. None of us, by contrast, seemed likely to speak. Representative Ball had glanced over when we walked in, but at that point he was busy giving a little speech touting all the good things he'd already done for the special needs community. His most recent accomplishment came in the form of support for the recently passed "people first" amendment, which was basically an exercise in terminology cleansing—in all state documents, the phrase would henceforth be "people with disabilities" rather than "disabled people" or "students with disabilities" rather than "disabled students," as had been the case. During the Palo Alto mothers' tirade, he had listened sympathetically, concentrating, nodding, his mouth curved into a gentle frown. I began to wonder whether the Santa Cruz delegation would leave the state house without saying a word.

When the women were done, Mike Ball thanked them for their insights but made no promises, then turned to our corner of the room. Millie was getting noisier, and I worried for a second that someone was going to ask us to leave. Not sure what to say, Jennifer apologized for being late and explained who we were. I remembered the advice from the lobbyist—"Be brief, be brave, be gone"—and psyched myself up to open my mouth. (It's not surprising, given the way white privilege works in these settings, that Jennifer and I were the ones from our party who felt moved to speak.) But Representative Ball wasn't looking at me; he was looking at Millie, who was alternating between gnawing on her right arm and lunging at one of the Palo Alto ladies' purse straps. "This is Millie," I suddenly heard coming out of my mouth, followed, as is my wont, alas, by an enthusiastic, entirely unscripted bout of storytelling—about all the school districts she'd been through, and about how Santa Cruz had been the best place for Millie since everyone accepted her as she was. Scratch that, I thought to myself—I was supposed to be complaining—then I remembered our talking points. "But she hasn't had a speech therapist for the past three months." The room was silent as I spoke, all eyes trained on Millie. No one seemed to have noticed I was on verbal autopilot. Even as I corrected my course, inside I squirmed. I felt guilty for putting Millie through the discomfort she was clearly experiencing. I felt embarrassed to have her be the target of all this attention. When the representative closed the meeting a few minutes later, his remarks focused exclusively on Millie, on how brave we were in the face of her challenges, how committed he was to helping people just like us.

Danilyn Rutherford

This was not the way I imagined the meeting ending. I'd felt sheepish even mentioning Millie's brief interruption in services after hearing the horror story from Palo Alto. I'm competitive by nature, and some part of me might have relished the idea of scruffy Santa Cruz stealing the show. If so, that feeling evaporated the moment I had opened my mouth. And now I felt awful. I thought about the suicidal fourth grader, the frazzled mother, the unresponsive bureaucrats. I wouldn't want to be living this woman's life. Before we left, Representative Ball asked us to stay for photographs. His staffer pulled out a fancy camera, and we all handed over our iPhones: Representative Ball, with his politician smile, straight out of central casting; Millie, dress crumpled, eyes crossed, her expression blank. This is the sovereignty of vulnerability at work, I thought grimly. Millie had not engaged in rational critical debate, that form of public discourse Habermas (1991) saw as the legitimate basis of modern sovereignty. Rather, she had personified what Lauren Berlant (1997) has called infantile citizenship. Silent, she had spoken more loudly than vocal others. Her presence had had more of an effect than that of the Palo Alto delegation, at least at that moment—even though they no doubt had the resources to eventually push legislation through. Others would not have. I thought of a long list of people with cause to protest who would never get a hearing like the one we just had. The vulnerable can be sovereign, but only if they keep their mouths closed and what looks like suffering on display.

What happened in that office looked like American politics as usual, which, as Lee Edelman (2004) has argued, elevates the innocent—the children, the future generations—at the expense of those caught up in the pleasures and pains of contemporary life. But the moment felt peculiar, and it was—in a room where all other eyes were on him, Representative Ball sought out the recognition of my daughter, the person who was least likely to meet his gaze, to offer him gratitude, to give him the time of day. Her failure to respond seemed both to attract and to disturb him. Much as lowland Philippines worshippers use their pity for Christ to bridge the gulf that divides them from the dangerous and powerful deity, in pitying Millie, the legislator turned her into a more manageable interlocutor (see Cannell 1999). He made this "bad subject" into a better one by defining her as a beneficiary of his political largesse. Lobbying is one way in which individuals like my daughter can exercise sovereignty. But there are others. Let me take you to San Lorenzo Valley High School, where Millie is enrolled.

Sovereignty Meets Vulnerability:
Making Smoothies

It's 11:30 a.m., and I am in Millie's classroom. In the back are dividers that carve out four cubicles, each equipped to meet a student's needs. There are padded sleeping benches, diapers, medical supplies, boom boxes, computers, and fans. Millie's cubicle is the most crowded, thanks to her energetic aide: she has a desk with a lamp, a stuffed bear, and a mirror where she can see herself, with a photograph of the two of us near it. The action now is in the front of the room at the circular table where Millie's teacher holds group activities. Today the group is small; the speech therapist, a thirty-something blonde, is here for a session with Millie and her classmate, whom I'll call Liam.

This is, believe it or not, also a setting for the performance of sovereignty. Millie belongs to the ranks of the multiply disabled: she can't talk, she can't walk on her own, and her cognitive abilities are impossible to measure. She is a "defective speaker," someone who, by extension, might count as a "defective person," given how Western thinkers have associated humanity with language (see Goodwin 2004). More to the point, she is a defective future citizen: incapable of "rational critical debate."[2] And yet she's in school, like millions of other disabled children across the nation, partaking of an extensive menu of therapies and adapted activities meant to prepare her for effective participation in the sovereign "we." More modestly, in a neoliberal vein, there is talk of "life skills" and "self-care." I know, and Millie's aides, teacher, social worker, and therapists all know, that Millie will never live independently. But I'm told she'll have a job when she ages out of the system. Petting kittens at the animal shelter is the current frontrunner. Millie has gentle hands and a passion for the tactile. I love this idea. It shows just how far workfare can go.

I also love visiting Millie at school, but my presence that day brings up another way in which sovereignty is being performed. School is not just a good idea; it's mandatory, and parents whose children are truant can go to jail. It's also a right, and when it comes to special needs students the relationship between education and sovereignty is particularly tight. Enacted in 1975 and updated by Congress in 2004 and 2011, the Individuals with Disabilities Education Act guarantees "a free appropriate education in the least restrictive environment."[3] Parents who suspect their children are not receiving what they are owed can sue the school districts where they are enrolled. Families with money, cultural capital, and time to learn to work the system have won settlements worth hundreds of thousands of dollars

Danilyn Rutherford

to cover the cost of private treatment centers and schools. Remember the community advisory councils that gathered in Sacramento? The California Department of Education created these bodies to stem the tide of litigation: they provide "input and advisement" to their region's Special Education Local Plan Area, or SELPA, a unit in California's byzantine educational bureaucracy.[4] Each SELPA's administrators are responsible for ensuring that local services meet federal requirements: their job is to keep their region's school districts out of court.[5] The parents, teachers, and therapists who serve as members may work together toward this end, but they have different stakes in the system. The staff members in Millie's classroom always seem happy to see me. But I know, and they know, that the law is on my side. The staff represents the government, in this most governmental of endeavors, this remnant of the welfare state still in action. I potentially trump them, having the power to go federal and take actions that could cost the school district a fortune and these employees their jobs.

I ask for everyone's permission, then get out my iPad to videotape the session. Liam's aide, a pretty brunette with dimples and a sardonic laugh, wheels Liam over. Millie is already sitting, rocking gently, on a stool. Reclining in his wheelchair, Liam is beatific: glowing skin, light hair, eyes half closed, faintly smiling.[6] Liam's aide puts on his shoes while the speech therapist gets Millie started. There is a blender in the middle of the table, along with a gray-and-blue switching box and a red button. There is also an iPad in a powder-blue case. The speech therapist and Millie's aide sing a little song asking Millie her name; Millie hits the switch, and it says, "Millie." Then it's Liam's turn. His aide tilts his seat forward: five, four, three, two, one blast-off! Everyone laughs. Smoothie making has begun.

First the speech therapist goes over the recipe on the iPad, which Millie and Liam are supposed to hit in order to activate a voice conveying the next step. (Add the banana. Put in the water.) Then the students make the smoothie. With the speech therapist guiding their hands, Millie puts in the banana, and Liam puts in the water. "We're making a smoothie together," the speech therapist says. For anyone used to speech therapy among the severely disabled, this is pretty standard issue. This isn't Millie's first foray with a blender, and luckily this one isn't loud.

This is a scene filled with language. There are the words in the iPad—machine words that give voice to what Millie and Liam supposedly want to say. There are the many more words the speech therapist and the aides direct at Millie and Liam: "Here, friend, it's your turn!" "Way to go!" "Millie, you're going to be the next Rachael Ray." Then there are the words the three women put in Millie's and Liam's mouths. "She's like, 'I don't need your help.'" "So he's like, 'I know what to do with a banana.'" "This is an example of 'give me what I want.'" There are also the words the three staff members say to one another. "This was what, I think, like, asking him to touch the iPad, this is like four for four. I am really impressed." "Every time you tell her you're going to help her, then she does it herself." Sometimes these varieties get tossed together, as when the speech therapist talks through Liam to his aide.

> SPEECH THERAPIST (*to Liam*): Well, while Millie's doing her job, maybe Rachel will give you another bite.
> LIAM'S AIDE: I will!
> SPEECH THERAPIST: I bet she will.
> LIAM'S AIDE: I'm kind!

Finally, there is the language of Millie and Liam themselves. Liam sits back, head slightly cocked to one side, gently and rhythmically strumming a toy that's a bit like an overgrown abacus: wooden frame, metal wires, beads. Every now and then he lets out a high-pitched mewling sound. He also occasionally, and somewhat incongruously, shakes his head no. Perched upright, Millie is as busy as Liam is still: reaching forward, grabbing at the blender, flinging her arms around. Her vocalizations are equally idiosyncratic: there's a hum that seems to indicate interest—but who knows!—and another, verging on whining, that suggests complaint. Every so often, Millie abruptly flings her arms around her shoulders in an awkward embrace. It looks like she's hugging herself, but if you look closely, you can see that she's bringing her bicep up close to her mouth so she can take a bite. When Millie is frustrated or unhappy, she chews on her arm. Sometimes the only way to tell that Millie is sick is to look for marks.

I call these behaviors language, but there's no reason to think they are intentional. Millie's brain is a mystery—although we've picked out patterns, it's clear that much of what she does indicates an organ in overdrive, unable to modulate its circuitry, to communicate with other components, to accomplish such easily taken-for-granted tasks as proprioception, or gait, or the use of fine motor muscles to pick up a spoon. But this is why this scene is so illuminating of what turns bodily movements into speech. Elinor Ochs (2012) has reflected on how the "incompleteness" of language shapes the experience of those caught up in the flow of a conversation. "Language arcs towards the place where meaning may lie," Ochs (2012, 149) writes, quoting Toni Morrison to describe how interlocutors work together to create what will have been said (see also Goodwin 2004; Mead 1965).[7] Millie's speech therapy is characterized by the staff's insistence on the meaningfulness of gestures whose sources are far from clear. Language arcs toward a place of uncertainty: an extreme version of the contingency that dogs and fuels every interaction, every collaborative effort to make sense.

In this setting, the speech therapist has a claim to sovereignty: she sets the agenda and puts words into the students' mouths.[8] So do I, for all the reasons outlined above. And so does language, with all the force of a convention; as Martin Heidegger (1971) put it, "language speaks." But so do Millie and Liam, whose reactions determine whether the session will count as a success.[9] In the end, Liam earns an A in smoothie making. He hits the iPad or button within seconds of it being offered to him every time. Despite a promising start, Millie quickly loses interest. And yet when the smoothie is finished, she's all business, sucking down the purple drink through a straw, a death grip on her covered cup. The speech therapist and the aides make a joke of her recalcitrance. "She's like, this is what I want," quips Liam's aide. "I wanted everybody else to do all the work."[10] The typical speakers in this setting needed the illusion that they knew what their interlocutors had in mind. And yet the staff's gentle humor belies their awareness of horizons far more strange. If a conversation is a game of ping-pong, "defective speakers" have a habit of pocketing the ball. This is one way of thinking about sovereignty—as the power to take without returning, to turn one's back and face another world, and in doing so to compel a response.

Conclusion

Snakes don't command armies; disabled students don't run schools; and West Papuans have yet to emerge from colonial occupation. The small moments I have considered in this chapter raise a question. To put it bluntly, so what? Elizabeth Povinelli (2011) has described the alternative worlds—the "otherwises"—that can arise on the margins of neoliberal orders out of experiences of "carnality," her term for unregimented episodes of bodily life.[11] Recall the humming, the sideways glances, the rocking, and the biting with which Millie responded to the speech therapist's entreaties. These behaviors foreground aspects of discourse that we tend to overlook: the grain of voice, the pleasure of repetition, the fact that sign use always involves embodied minds.[12] I remember sitting on the floor in Millie's bedroom on a sunny Sunday afternoon, holding hands and rocking back and forth. She said, "Mmmm . . . haa," and I said, "Mmmm . . . haa" back. She laughed, then she did what she rarely does in other contexts: she repeated the noise I'd just made. In encounters with people like Millie, typical speakers are thrown off kilter. They find themselves inventing new conventions of bodily comportment, conjuring new frames, perhaps even new kingdoms, that shimmer in the imagination (see Ochs, Solomon, and Sterponi 2005).[13] It is in this sense that a being like Millie—or Lawrence's snake—can appear as a "lord of life." When Millie addresses me, I am interpellated from a place I cannot name.

What kind of "otherwise" might emerge if we came to recognize sovereignty in such fleeting moments? Perhaps something like the politics described by the feminist philosopher Eve Kittay (1999). Kittay criticizes liberal theories of justice for privileging equality. Instead, she insists on the fact of dependency: far more than language, it is the distinguishing mark of the human species, from our extended infancy to our protracted old age. Children, the disabled, and the elderly need care, but they may never be in a position to repay this gift. Care workers accept this imbalance because they identify with their charges; they can't walk away without doing violence to themselves. Kittay calls for a society in which care workers are justly compensated for entering into a relationship that is inherently unjust. Note the logic: the sovereign power at the heart of this system of justice resides with children, the disabled, and the elderly. The vulnerable make others vulnerable; they institute a web of obligations when they demand a response. Call it the force of collectivity; call it the spirit of the unrequited gift. This is not just a matter of diapers, bath chairs, and dishes. We all live in a state of vulnerability, a state of irrevocable debt.[14]

The Dutch official had a rifle and access to institutions that would transform the Papuans' homeland. The speech therapist had control over the words and the blender and could have put Millie back in her wheelchair and rolled her away. Yet they both sensed there was more to the story. Sovereignty is vulnerable, but vulnerability is also sovereign. Sovereignty is never as secure as it might seem. In these dark and troubled times, for those of us brave enough to face it, this insight can inspire something that feels a bit like hope.

Danilyn Rutherford

1   Mike Ball, along with the other names used in this section, are pseudonyms, as are the names given to Millie's classmates and the therapists and aides who worked with them, except for Xiaona, who wanted to be named here. Millie is Millie's real name.

2   She's not much of a neoliberal subject, either. Millie shows little signs of a capacity for entrepreneurial self-fashioning, little knack for maximizing utility by matching ends to means.

3   See Center for Parent Information and Resources, "IDEA—the Individuals with Disabilities Education Act," September 2017, http://www.parentcenterhub .org/repository/idea/.

4   For a useful explanation of community advisory councils, or CACs, and the bureaucracy they are part of, see "California Special Education Local Plan Areas," California Department of Education, accessed June 10, 2022, https:// www.cde.ca.gov/sp/se/as/caselpas.asp. See also "CAC: Community Advisory Committee of North Santa Cruz County SELPA," accessed June 10, 2022, https://santacruzcoe.org/wp-content/uploads/2021/07/new-cac-brochure-in -word.pdf.

5   See "California Special Education Local Plan Areas."

6   The last time I was here, he slept the whole time; I'm happy to see him awake.

7   Charles Goodwin (2004) describes how a stroke victim with aphasia used prosody, gesture, and his loved one's memories to tell a story using his interlocutors to articulate what he wanted to say.

8   In the incident reported by Ochs (2012), a therapist exerted herself forcefully, taking hold of her client's head to make him face her.

9   Their individualized educational plans set goals—like "make an appropriate choice between two options in eight out of ten trials"—which the school district is responsible for helping them meet.

10   In a similar spirit, the speech therapist turns to Liam with a paper towel she's just used to wipe the table. "Okay, Sir Liam. Can you help me throw it away?"

11   Povinelli distinguishes carnality from "corporeality," those dimensions of bodily experience regimented by social means. Carnality, in its underdetermined materiality, marks less the limits of discourse than the site where possible discourses meet. What Webb Keane (1996) calls the undetermined materiality of signs allows them to call to mind a multiplicity of meanings, multiple ways that objects can function semiotically and in doing so leave a mark. I began my work in West Papua by exploring just one of the imaginary worlds that emerged on the margins of Dutch and Indonesian state authority, attending to how Biaks, who belonged to one of the dominant coastal groups, foregrounded the materiality of language and its enactment. This tendency allowed Biaks to participate in Indonesian state institutions without becoming good Indonesian subjects, instead pursuing recognition from other scenes.

12 Those of us who spend time with Millie talk to her constantly in the normative ways illustrated in this session. But we also have conversations of a different sort. I'm just one of many; Millie has had fifteen caregivers over the past six years.

13 Ochs, Solomon, and Sterponi (2005) draw on Bourdieu to describe the conditions under which habitus can change. A crisis or a revolution can lead to the emergence of new modalities of bodily comportment. Day-to-day encounters with an autistic child, Ochs argues, can have the same effect.

14 We can extend Kittay's insight not just to speech therapy but also to sign use more generally. We do not converse as autonomous individuals, formulating ideas and intentions, then expressing them. We communicate as I communicate with Millie, grasping at meanings, offering responses, searching for a provisional sense of "what's happening here now." There is reaction, but never reciprocity. Millie owes her identity to people like me and her aides and speech therapists—just as I owe my identity in this fleeting moment of conversation to you.

11

The Condition of Our Condition

JOSEPH MASCO

What is the collective condition in the United States, at the end of the second decade of the twenty-first century? Formally, it is late 2018, two years into the Donald J. Trump presidency, an era of continuing war, of radical economic inequality, of racist, sexist, and xenophobic federal pronouncements, of voter suppression and minority rule, of climate change denial and administrative advocacy for toxic industries, of escalating police violence, mass incarceration, and high-ranking sexual predators, to name but a few immediate concerns. Mass media follows these issues largely in a predictable crisis mode, creating a competing agitation across newspapers, radio, television, and social media—collectively arguing for an unprecedented instability in national politics, marked as a divided nation, a corrupt White House, a covert foreign attack, a corporate conspiracy. This crisis narrative form assumes that recovery of a prior mode of politics is the necessary collective relief—assuming a counterrevolutionary posture and rejecting the need for a serious reevaluation of core logics, institutions, or practices in the United States (Masco 2017). However, none of these crises are fundamentally new to American life. There is, rather, a shocking explicitness to official antidemocratic desires in the contemporary moment, a breakdown in the long-standing cover-story languages of social care and inclusion, of coded dog-whistle politics, of tactical nods to the welfare state, social justice, and environmental protection. Historically rooted forms of racial, gender, and class violence in the United States are now consolidated in high office by a vocal advocate for an unmasked xenophobic white nationalism, an explicit patriarchy, and an oligarchy founded in petrochemical capitalism, finance capital, and contempt for the law. What, then, does the Trump moment say about the state of the American social contract or the vitality of democratic institutions in the United States?

What, in other words, is the condition of our condition?[1] Such a strange query necessarily requires further elaboration: Who is the assumed "us" in this condition? What is the environment under consideration? What counts as a condition?[2] Still, I like this formulation, as the doubling-up of a collective self-assessment—the *condition* of a condition—underscores that one is always already made by the world, that the forms of sovereignty that individuals desire are historical formations, always structured and limited by environmental forces, inherited infrastructures, long-term violences, and already established cultural imaginaries.[3] By assessing the condition of a condition, one attunes to qualities and intensities, recognizing the imbrication of lives, worlds, affects, and environments from one moment to the next; it is to give up on expectations of conceptual purity or newness in favor of attending to messy realities and fraught ongoing negotiations. To live in the United States has always been to experience the violent contradictions of an imperial order that speaks in the inclusive language of democracy and rule of law while practicing military action abroad and violent exclusions at home. It is also to navigate an ideological project that promises increasing mobility, security, and prosperity across the generations but does so through redlining, dispossession, and theft. This ideology is usually glossed as the American Dream or the expectation of a perpetual upward class mobility in the United States.

Belief in the American Dream is the definitional form of what Lauren Berlant (2011a) called "cruel optimism," an attachment to an ever-deferred positive potential. If today each group and generation of Americans is now nostalgic for a different historical era, one that brought their community closer to the American Dream (via increasing economic power, social movements, or channeling revolutionary energies), it is not just because of the radically unfinished nature of the American social contract. Such nostalgia in the twenty-first century also indexes that collective conditions are materially, measurably, changing: since 2001, precarity for most people has intensified across the domains of security, economy, and the environment, linking new structures of global warfare to turbulent boom-and-bust economic cycles to radical ecological disruption, each of which works unpredictably on a global, even planetary scale. The result is that while a few in the United States are experiencing a new gilded age of consolidated wealth and political power (and thus are insulated from, or directly profiting from,

Joseph Masco

the increasingly volatile conditions), the vast majority are experiencing the contractions of a social contract that is retreating from collective security, economic opportunity, and environmental protection.[4] This combination of military, financial, and ecological precarity—and the unpredictable compounding violences between them—are fomenting collective visions for many of an ever more unstable, violent, and exclusionary future to come, creating a powerful affectively charged space for, among other things, illiberal political recruitments.

According to the International Monetary Fund, the United States had the largest economy in the world in 2018, half again as large as that of the second biggest state, China.[5] The United States also maintained the world's largest military, with a budget greater than the next seven largest military states combined.[6] United States defense spending, at historical heights since 2002, received a big boost in the first year of the Trump administration alongside commitments to rebuilding the entire nuclear weapons triad of bombers, missiles, and submarines (projected at $1.2 trillion over the next three decades; see US Congressional Budget Office 2017). These numbers represent the standard definition of a global superpower—a nuclear state with unrivaled economic and military strength and thus seemingly maximal security and domestic resources. However, the 2018 military budget of $716 billion (which the Trump administration increased by $82 billion, or more than twice the entire budget of the US State Department), in combination with the first round of Trump-era tax cuts, left the United States with a $779 billion deficit for the year (see Hartung 2018; Stein 2018). This means that the numerical equivalent of the entire 2018 US defense budget was funded on credit, adding to the year-after-year, War on Terror deficit spending patterns that go back to 2001. The Watson Institute's Costs of War project estimates that between 2001 and 2018 the United States committed at least $5.9 trillion to the War on Terror—constituting an ongoing debt load that will frame all other budgetary decisions for the coming decades (Crawford 2018b). In any assessment of the state of domestic life in the United States, the scale, scope, and deficit funding of US wars around the world matters, not only in terms of recognizing the profound American investment in militarism and responsibility for global violence, but also in terms of the loss of life and the alternative worlds that might otherwise have been built.

Thus, the language of ultimate sovereignty—of superpower state status—masks a more complex reality in the United States, a country that continues to attempt to garrison the world via nearly eight hundred foreign military installations (Vine 2015) while aging domestic infrastructures are left largely unattended, receiving a comprehensive grade of D+ from the American Society of Civil Engineers (2017). There is, then, an older story than Trump, one founded in a post–Cold War commitment to unregulated neoliberalism and to warfare over welfare. Thus, the condition of our condition today is in part tied to a radical federal experiment in market fundamentalism and an equally radical imperialism, which in combination have worked to dramatically shrink the investments in and imaginations for domestic life since the early 1990s while amplifying the conditions of global violence (see Masco 2014). The compounding vulnerabilities enabled by this mode of rule are now ever-present in American life, remaking political imaginaries, distributing direct and structural violences, and loading up burdens on specific populations, generating a foreign and domestic body count that continues in 2018 as an awful, and astonishingly normalized, background condition, constituting a hyperviolent politics as usual.

In this chapter, I explore three areas that inflect the condition of our condition in the United States in 2018 and structure the affective terrain of sovereign agency in the twenty-first century: addiction, climate disruption, and minority rule. My interest is not only to document a shift in the material conditions of living in the twenty-first-century United States (see Masco 2020) but also to consider why the formal commitments of the Trump regime—an explicit defense of whiteness combined with antienvironmentalism and aggressive class consolidation—have such political power and currency at this historical moment. While each of these forms has a long history in the United States (i.e., there have been other racist presidents, other climate-change-denying or antienvironmental presidents, and other administrations that resisted the expansion of democratic institutions and social justice), the historical configuration of the Trump administration comes at a moment when the future cost of these political projects is so well documented and scientifically understood that it constitutes a suicidal project. Thus, my goal in this chapter is to assess the formal (not new, but now hyperexplicit) deployment of a suicidal whiteness in American life, one that is content to destroy the collective environment rather than embrace a sustainable multiracial vision of the future.

Sourcing Pain

In 2017, Philip Alston, the United Nations Special Rapporteur on Extreme Poverty and Human Rights, evaluated the daily conditions for the forty million (roughly one out of eight) Americans living in poverty. Finding the

Joseph Masco

United States an outlier among industrial countries for extreme wealth in-equality, lack of health care protections for the poor, and high child poverty, Alston documented many ways in which being poor is currently criminal-ized (via vagrancy laws, fines, and cash bail) and worsened by state forms of abandonment (i.e., lack of access to water, sanitation, and basic health care). Noting that, unlike most other industrialized nations, the United States has never accepted the idea that "economic and social rights are human rights," Alston sought to draw attention to how the poor are targeted across race and gender lines. Poverty in the United States, he notes, can produce recur-sive effects (appearance, lack of an address or phone number) that make it extremely challenging for individuals to find regular employment, even for those physically capable of doing so. It also rides on economic misfortune—for example, the vast elimination of wealth in the 2008 Great Recession (a product of deregulated banking and substantial corporate fraud)—and, of course, is exacerbated by sheer bad luck, from health problems to mental illness to injury to addiction. Alston (2017) concludes that "Americans can expect to live shorter and sicker lives" than in any other rich democracy. His portrait is of a contemporary America that is both hyperwealthy and hypercruel, a social order more committed to extracting resources from the poor than protecting basic human rights. The Trump administration's response to Alston's deeply troubling report was not to address the docu-mented suffering with new resources or regulatory help but rather to block future UN access to the United States and to cease participation in the UN human rights program altogether (Pilkington 2019). This reaction was consistent with a larger Trump administration rejection of human rights around the world, and a domestic policy aimed at punishing asylum seek-ers trying to enter the United States.

Alston's assessment reveals the intensifying effects of a long-term coun-terrevolutionary project in the United States, a half-century shift away from what was once a War on Poverty toward a War on Crime that has combined material abandonment with forms of social death, most clearly illustrated in both homelessness and mass incarceration.[7] Elizabeth Hinton has traced the rise of the prison industrial complex to the weaponization of certain War on Poverty programs from the 1960s, aimed at the new, largely Af-rican American, populations moving into northern cities from the South looking for industrial jobs. The inclusion in antipoverty legislation of laws on delinquency for juveniles, the creation of new crime databases, and the linkage of aid to law-and-order policing, according to Hinton (2016), infused welfare state programs with the very repressive tools (drug sentencing, and ultimately zero-tolerance and three-strikes laws) that created mass incarceration from the 1970s to today (see also Metzl 2011). Kaya Williams (2018) has shown how these techniques have generated current incarceration rates in Louisiana so high that the New Orleans jail, meant merely as a holding space for those awaiting trial, now routinely cages people for years who cannot pay cash bail and who have not been convicted of anything. These conditions endure because of a lack of state resources but also due to ongoing commitments to repressive policing, constituting a highly modern, institutionalized, and frequently extralegal form of social abandonment.

Hinton argues that the early linkage of welfare to policing at the start of the War on Poverty offered tools for domestic political repression (used directly by the Nixon and Reagan administrations and reinforced by three-strikes rules in the Clinton administration). Hinton summarizes how a few decades of this kind of law-and-order policing have changed incarceration rates in the United States:

> In the century between the end of the U.S. Civil War in 1865 and Johnson's call for the War on Crime, a total of 184,901 Americans entered state and federal prisons. During the two decades between the passage of the Law Enforcement Assistance Act and the launch of Reagan's War on Drugs, the country added 251,107 citizens to the prison system. The American carceral state has continued its rapid growth ever since, so that today 2.2 million citizens are behind bars—representing a 943 percent increase over the past half century. Home to the largest prison system on the planet, with a rate of incarceration that is five to ten times higher than that of comparable nations, the United States represents 5 percent of the world's population but holds 25 percent of its prisoners. (2016, 5)

Indelibly linked to mass incarceration, poverty rarely figures as a subject of national political concern in the contemporary United States in the twenty-first century, even as homeless populations have risen dramatically in American cities since the 2008 financial crash. Multigenerational poverty in urban and rural areas now characterizes financially distressed populations that Trump calls out to via promises of more law-and-order politics, anti-immigration campaigns, and "America First" promises. The financialization of policing in which fines, seizures, and cash bail strategies are not only financial life support for police but also modes of bodily capture in often highly racialized terms have been continually refined in the twenty-first century and now move targeted populations into jails and prisons, creating large nonvoting blocks of the past and present incarcerated. Here the recursivity of poverty

Joseph Masco

and policing creates a compounding violence that informs an industrial prison system that also functions as a direct form of voter suppression.

But in 2018 Americans are not only the most incarcerated on planet Earth, they are also the most drugged. In the Trump era, the United States consumed 80 percent of the world's opioids (McGreal 2018, xiv). The Centers for Disease Control (Scholl et al. 2019) reports that over seventy thousand died in the United States of drug overdoses in 2017 alone, 67 percent of which were opioids. The overdose and death rates have increased exponentially since the late 1990s when pharmaceutical companies, notably Purdue Pharma, started a wide-ranging campaign to convince doctors and patients that their new opioid, oxycodone, was not addictive. The result, documented in detail by Chris McGreal (2018), has been a staggering crisis of addiction and death. From 1999 to 2017, there were 702,568 overdose deaths in the United States, 399,230 involving opioids (Scholl et al. 2019). The death toll from opioids is now greater than the number of Americans killed in World War II, and approaching the number of people killed by US War on Terror campaigns in Iraq, Afghanistan, and Pakistan since 2001 (see Crawford 2018a).

The story of Purdue Pharma, and its famous art philanthropist family owners, the Sacklers, is an emblematic story of corporate exploitation in the twenty-first-century United States (see Keefe 2017). Purdue Pharma was not simply following the industry trend of seeking to expand markets by treating the risk of a disease occurring rather than actual symptoms (see Dumit 2012b). Rather, company executives set out to create a new expectation for pain treatment, then produced new addictions by pushing opioid prescriptions, and then marketed drug treatments for the various symptoms connected to those addictions—extracting profits at every turn. Purdue Pharma launched a national campaign in the 1990s around the proposition that there was an epidemic of untreated pain in the United States and then offered a new supposedly nonaddictive drug—oxycodone—to treat it. The campaign focused on veterans and the elderly, and targeted working-class areas of the country—places where manual labor (the coal mining regions of West Virginia, Kentucky, and Tennessee, as well as postindustrial areas of Ohio and Maine) maintained masses of aging, injured, and sore bodies. Individuals in these regions were recruited to addiction by new pain centers promoting the virtue of a safe new pain-relief drug and providing free samples and connections to doctors that could prescribe oxycodone (McGreal 2018). The creation of a mass addicted population through prescribed medications is now acknowledged by all: a federally declared opioid crisis has produced new rules for prescription, as well as a growing infrastructure of Narcan anti-overdose medications (in schools, public libraries, fire stations, and street corners) in regions suffering frequent overdose emergencies. The demographic effects of opioids over the past decade in the United States remain truly staggering, creating a war-zone-scale death rate, as well as a vast number of current and former addicts negotiating continuing pain, lost livelihoods, and ongoing psychological struggles (Jones et al. 2018).

Anne Case and Angus Deaton (2015) have statistically documented the first decline in life expectancy for non–college educated, white populations in the United States in over a century, a drop not currently found in any other industrialized country. Tracking the evolution of the current epidemic since 1999, Case and Deaton detail a reduction in life expectancy that is tied to the combined toll of drug overdoses, alcoholism, and suicides, as well as declines in overall health, mental health, and quality of life—featuring chronic pain among the white working class. In a follow-up report, Case and Deaton (2017) labeled these "deaths of despair" and articulated a radically stressed life condition as the basis for chronic pain, substance abuse, and suicides. While not offering a detailed analysis of the origins of this stress or of whiteness (see Metzl 2019), Case and Deaton suggest that the disruptive force of globalization, the loss of union-protected jobs, and changes in family dynamics are creating increasing pressures on this segment of the US population. The ideology of the American Dream, with its deep historical ties to the promotion of whiteness, promises that life, and quality of life, will improve in the United States across generations, as it did for some but not all populations through much of the twentieth century. Case and Deaton document, then, not only a shift in life expectancy but also a foundational challenge to a central ideology in American life, one that has always relied on a radically undemocratic, raced and classed mode of priority in who should have access to class mobility. George Lipsitz (2006) famously called this a "possessive investment in whiteness"—naming the multitudinous ways that white supremacy is located in wealth accumulation, jobs, educational opportunities, and housing, and reinforced by law (see also Rothstein 2018). What, then, is the source of the current mass addiction within the self-identified white working class—what could explain such a massive and desperate turn to opioids, alcohol, and suicide?

Whiteness is a foundational project of political power in the United States, an invention of settler-immigrants seeking a financial advantage, constituting a ferocious mode of social control (see Allen 2012). It relies on counterformations but also is continually reinvented through the absorption of new immigrant groups. Whiteness is then an imaginary field, one

Joseph Masco

that works to produce reactionary formations through violent exclusions (see Anderson 2016). What is at stake in 2018 is not only the condition of specific bodies self-identifying as white but what they are willing to do in defense of that structural whiteness. Jonathan Metzl (2019) argues, from a strictly biomedical point of view, that there are some in the United States that are literally dying of whiteness, refusing health care if it is perceived to come from an African American president while fighting regulations on guns (even though most gun deaths are home suicides). In his interviews with men predominantly from Missouri, Tennessee, and Kansas, Metzl found injured and sick citizens that refused federal help, performing a self-sacrificial defense of white privilege knowing full well that it meant for them a shorter, more painful life. This is a suicidal form of white sovereignty—a kamikaze necropolitics. Metzl quantifies the biological costs of committing to whiteness, offering a biomedical calculation of the literal life-shortening effects of whiteness in the twenty-first century.

Trump was able to identify and capture this population by speaking in a language of white restoration—of "Making America Great Again"—while also identifying who was to blame for a reduced quality of life: immigrants, welfare recipients, China, and so on. Indeed, Trump's singular political skill in the 2016 election was to generate a false nostalgia for an imagined lost white advantage among just enough voters to capture the electoral college, embracing racial resentment as the organizing principle of his politics. Trump's affective recruitment focused on generating rage, but rage not at specific injuries, which would require a context, diagnosis, and analysis (and that would then produce very different policies than those pursued by his administration). Rather, he directed rage at an imagined and projective theft of the power, pleasure, and enjoyment historically connected to whiteness. The twist in this Trumpian promissory note is that Trump's actual policies make more vulnerable the very populations being appealed to through this overt call to whiteness, constituting a world that is ever more dangerous financially, militarily, and environmentally. The negative metrics proliferate accordingly, but consider just this point: in 2017–19, 4.1 million children participated in active shooter lockdowns in schools. This creates a new kind of nervous system in American youth tied to the idea of a sudden murderous assault in the classroom, a fear not of Soviet nuclear weapons like their grandparents were taught in school (see Masco 2014), but rather of suicidal white men with guns (Rich and Cox 2018).

Importantly, Trumpian politics do not ask, where did this pain come from? There is no serious interrogation of the origins of suffering across race and class lines. Trumpian politics merely serves up racial aggrievement as the answer to decades of neoliberal economic policies and unrestrained militarism, modes of extraction and abandonment that ride on top of infrastructural neglect and the mounting climatic costs of petrochemical emissions. Trumpian politics transforms investments in a collective life organized for increasing health and security into an imagined attack on those committed to maintaining a perceived racial superiority, creating for those invested in whiteness a fear of a multiracial egalitarian future. This is a cynical code-switch that allows the causes of contemporary domestic suffering to remain unchallenged at the federal level, inevitably exacerbating distress (both psychic and material) as an intensifying American condition, adding to the ocean of untreated pain across all American demographics.

On Planetary-Scale Stress

In October 2018, the Intergovernmental Panel on Climate Change (IPCC) released its latest report detailing the effects of a 1.5°C rise in atmospheric temperatures (notably less than the standard 2°C consensus threshold on climate disruption used in all prior reports). It was a response to island nations, who are the most immediately vulnerable to rising sea levels from accelerating climate change. The report predicted radical changes in the environment at this lower temperature threshold, projecting extreme weather events (heat waves, storms, coastal floods), sea level rise and flooding of coastal cities worldwide, a wide range of health effects, negative changes in air quality, disruptions in crops and food production—the list goes on and on (IPCC 2018). However, the IPCC also revealed that there would be huge environmental advantages in reducing the projected temperature rise from greenhouse gas emissions by as little as .5°C. In the end, the report was horrifying because it reset the timetable for severe climatic disruption events from distant generations to 2030. Based on some six thousand scientific reports and approved by 195 nation-states, the IPCC study represents the consensus of international science and is directed at mobilizing a collective response to the impacts of greenhouse gases on the global environment. A few weeks after the IPCC report was released, the U.S. Global Change Research Program—mobilizing US domestic science and focused solely on conditions within the United States—issued its Fourth National Climate Assessment (USGCRP 2018). Concurring with the IPCC, the USGCRP concluded that climate change was already impacting every aspect of American life, from increasing extreme weather events, to water quality and availability, to biodiversity loss, and projected accelerating climate disruptions. It focused particularly on the built environment, concluding that "climate change and extreme weather events are expected to increasingly disrupt our Nation's energy and transportation systems, threatening more frequent and longer-lasting power outages, fuel shortages, and service disruptions, with cascading impacts on other critical sectors" (USGCRP 2018, 17). In chart after chart, the report moves from the projected future consequences of greenhouse gas emissions to recent anthropogenic events, linking hurricanes on the Gulf Coast to drought in the Rockies to heavy rains in the Midwest to tidal flooding in the Southeast to coral bleaching in the Pacific Islands to megafires on the West Coast and to storm damage in the Caribbean. In short, every ecological relation and built infrastructure located in US territories is already under stress from global warming, and intensifications of these dynamics are projected under every expert mitigation scenario into a distant future: the question is not whether Americans inhabit a new condition but rather the intensities of that condition from region to region, year to year, person to person, organism to organism.

Climate assessments are part of an ever more detailed scientific documentation of anthropogenic global warming, a key part of international governance of greenhouse-gas emissions. They uniformly issue an unprecedented call to collective security, one exceeding the international mobilizations at the height of the Cold War over the danger of nuclear war (which remains the other great existential danger of the twenty-first century). Importantly, the shifts in atmosphere, in weather, in heat and cold, in rain and illness, will put new stresses on all beings, amplifying the embodied conditions of late industrial, neoliberal modernity discussed in the previous section on pain and addiction. Indeed, it is difficult to account for how life inside a rapidly changing environment affects individuals directly, how an increasingly unstable ecological condition comes to matter in terms of psyches, well-being, and sensory regimes. The condition of our condition is, from the point of view of the global environment, now technically unstable, a fact that should activate political sensibilities, governance regimes, social sympathies, and modes of care.

President Trump, however, called global warming a hoax and ran for office as a vocal advocate for coal—the single most damaging carbon emitter. Thus, his administration is aggressively antienvironmental, rejecting any responsibility for responding to anthropogenic environmental damage while waging an all-out war on climate science itself. Indeed, Trump has committed the federal government to intensifying the consumption of fossil fuels and has made a point of raising taxes on green energy options, like wind and solar. The Fourth National Climate Assessment concluded that if nothing were done to reduce emissions, the US costs by the end of the century would be at least $440 billion per year. This financial calculation signals a vast reduction in the future quality of life for all in the United States, including the forced migration of populations because of flooding, drought, and fires, the loss of biodiversity, damage to food production, and increased illness. What are we to make of a political project that cannot respond to scientific depictions of insecurity of this magnitude and intensity, one that literally, avowedly, and publicly prefers to protect petrochemical profits over life itself?

As president, Trump announced the United States would not participate in the Paris Climate Agreement, called for more coal plants, and placed petrochemical industry representatives in key positions throughout the Environmental Protection Agency and the Department of the Interior. A key goal in Trump's administration has been to dismantle the scientific expertise and regulatory tools for climate change mitigation. Activities include, but are not limited to, overturning higher mileage standards for automobiles, eliminating rules on methane emissions for oil and gas companies, reducing clean water standards, shrinking national parks and protected areas, rejecting bans on neurotoxic pesticides, changing the regulatory status of copper, lead, and coal dust . . . the list is very long, and it collectively affects air, land, water, ocean, ecosystems, endangered species, and national parks (see Popovich, Albeck-Ripka, and Pierre-Louis 2018). The Environmental Data and Governance Initiative (EDGI 2018) has documented the elimination of climate change discussions and environmental monitoring data from federal websites under Trump, the forced exodus of environmental scientists from key roles in regulatory agencies, and a significant national drop in enforcement of environmental regulations in 2018. As one might predict, the lack of enforcement of environmental regulations on petrochemical industries produced a 3.4 percent spike in carbon emissions in 2018, after years of steady reductions (Mooney and Dennis 2019).

Thus, the condition of our condition in 2018 involves a vast scientific assessment of radically deteriorating environmental conditions caused by petrochemical industrial activity, which require concerted state and international action to resolve, yet these conditions are being met by a presidential administration that not only denies the existence of the problem but is energetically pursuing precisely the policies and activities that would ensure the very worst-case scenario. This is a suicidal form of governance,

Joseph Masco

one that literally chooses petrochemical profits over lives and futures and recruits a subset of voters to the necropolitical pleasure of environmental disregard and destruction. Given that the United States is the largest historical emitter of greenhouse gases, the Trump administration has revealed an ideological and even libidinal relation to the environment, one that seeks to reestablish the idea that extraction and consumption are limitless processes, even as people everywhere are experiencing new environmental extremes. When combined with the activities of the War on Terror since 2001, which involved ongoing wars on several continents and, in 2017, the deployment of special operations forces to a record 149 countries (Turse 2017), the United States in 2018 is a, perhaps the, leading exporter of global violence, a rogue state by any definition of the term. What should citizen-subjects now make of the fact that the foundational racism at the center of the American project has hit a historical public inflection point in the Trump administration, one that is synchronous with the expansive global ambitions of the War on Terror (now approaching its third decade) and the accelerating petrochemically driven effects of planetary-scale climate disruption?

The Long Counterrevolution

It is important to point out that President Trump has never held the support of 50 percent of the US population. He won the electoral college, a hedge built into the US Constitution against a straight popular vote, a concession to the debate over slavery in the eighteenth century. The Trump era has also exposed a wide-ranging right-wing commitment to minority rule, an inversion of democratic order in which having the most votes does not lead to possessing political power. In the twenty-first century, minority rule has become an increasingly overt and determining element of US politics, part of a long-term strategic project by a few billionaires that has sought to hack democratic institutions on behalf of narrow class and extractive industry interests. Nancy MacLean (2017) has documented how the antiwar and civil rights campaigns of the 1960s energized a subset of very wealthy far-right activists to seek a defense of wealth and whiteness against the power of the popular vote, civil rights, and taxation. Their public project was to create a set of think tanks, political alliances, and bureaucratic instruments that could provide an intellectual and political infrastructure in support of extreme wealth consolidation. This multidecade project merged a neoliberal ideology of free markets with an increasingly powerful media project (first on talk radio, then Fox News, and now social media) in support of key industries (particularly petrochemical and military-industrial). Importantly, as MacLean (2017, xx) notes, its proponents were less interested in shaping public opinion than in shaping the rules of the game in the American political context; that is, to make the mechanisms of the American political machine work inherently for their class interests.

In other words, this counterrevolutionary political project relies fundamentally on stealth, on hiding its core commitments and using techniques of distraction. With the Voting Rights Act of 1965, the political momentum in the United States turned toward a democratic order based for the first time in American history on each adult having a vote, regardless of race, class, or gender. Jane Meyer (2016) has explored the covert politics of right-wing billionaires, tracking how the Koch, Scaife, Olin, Bradley, and other dynastic families have influenced the mechanisms of democratic order since the 1970s, supporting a wide range of projects designed to change the instruments of democracy, using front groups to hide agendas as well as sources of funding (what she calls "dark money"). Part of a long-term strategic effort to fight the expansion of the welfare state, voting rights, and environmental protections, this multifaceted right-wing movement has been methodical in building political institutions, counteruniversities, policy and funding groups, and mechanisms for cultivating potential elected officials, all designed to fight government spending, regulatory oversight, and civil rights, and to push for greater tax breaks. MacLean (2017) describes this overall project as a systematic effort to limit democracy—a way of managing state and federal policy to maintain the power of key industries and consolidate wealth against civil rights and environmental protections. Increasingly, this political project has relied on a profound rejection of technoscientific expertise as the basis for public policy, a commitment to generating an alternative world of pseudo-facts as well as strategic zones of unknowability, for a world that can be made more compliant with political projects. A key moment in this project was the Republican revolution of 1994, led by Newt Gingrich, which brought not only a hyperpartisan approach to congressional politics but also involved shutting down little-known but important agencies, such as the Office of Technology Assessment, that were charged with doing nonpartisan technical studies of complex issues for Congress. Gingrich wanted the facts for debate to be produced not by technical experts but by privately funded nongovernmental groups—that is, ideologically committed think tanks and lobbyists—and so he sought to eliminate nonpartisan technical expertise throughout government. Big oil accelerated its climate denial projects at precisely this early post–Cold War moment, moving to contest in public what company scientists had already documented in their laboratories about the destructive effects of petrochemical emissions on the global climate (Oreskes and Conway 2010).

In short, through a variety of mechanisms and across a spectrum of corporate interests, the oligarchic counterrevolution has been an astonishingly successful political movement, one that has helped shift the United States over the past forty years into levels of inequality last seen in the gilded age of the nineteenth century. It is important to see this not just as politics as usual but rather as a formal response to voting rights, antiwar protests, and the rise of the environmental movement. The mid-twentieth-century idea of an egalitarian, peaceful society living within an ecologically sustainable economy has been met with an extremely well-funded counterproject, one that seeks to reduce the power of government to manage collective security in support of unregulated property rights. But here we might pause to ask: What happened to all that revolutionary energy, the coalitions of people across race, gender, and class lines that sought to activate the democratic language of the state into collective action across the twentieth century—mobilizing against war, for healthy environment, for racial, gender, and sexual equality?

Let's pause to consider three structural changes informing American youth in the twenty-first century that are an important backdrop to the condition of our condition in 2018: (1) the end of the military draft, which not only created a contract army but also helped transform a growing generational political resistance to war into a celebratory military culture largely indifferent to permanent war; (2) the growth of the industrial prison system, which physically captured young Black and brown bodies on a massively disproportionate scale, curtailing generations of social justice activism and distorting voting blocs; and (3) the rise of student debt since the end of the Cold War, which has financially captured young adults on an unprecedented scale. It is impossible to have sovereign agency if one is under military contract, in jail, or carrying so much debt that many low-paying fields of social activism and service become simply untenable. And now, after the highly raced addiction regimes of the 1980s (cocaine) and the 2010s (opioids), drugs are also having the effect of countering activist and revolutionary energies on a societal level. Pain is usually a motivator for political mobilization, but only if the body is physically able. The opioid epidemic has revealed a vast population of voters and potential activists across the United States captured in an everyday circuit of pain and medication. For many, the only activism that is possible is to send a guaranteed disruptor to Washington, DC, to break things. From these vantage points, the vitality of democratic sensibilities in the United States in 2018 is informed by the long-term strategic efforts by a narrow class interest to limit and contain political imaginaries, as well as by the new modes of physical, financial, and psychological capture (in terms of youth, race, gender, and class).

Conversely, however, the power of the president as both executive and commander in chief has expanded to engage emergency conditions across finance and counterterror, creating new domains of collective life that are not regulated or subject to democratic review. It is not coincidental that two of the most radical presidencies in the past century have both come into office having lost the popular vote: George W. Bush was installed by a Supreme Court decision (having lost both the national vote and, on a full nonbinding recount, the electoral college as well in 2000), while Donald Trump lost the popular vote by close to three million. Consider the profound decisions made by these presidents—Bush to declare a global War on Terror (what some in the military now call the "forever war"), and Trump to pull the United States out of international agreements on nuclear weapons and climate change and to eliminate environmental protections across industries. Thus, we have a historic situation in the twenty-first century: the most consequential decisions of our moment, those with multigenerational and even planetary-scale effects, have been enabled by US presidents with the weakest claims to political legitimacy.

What is remarkable about Trump, however, is that he has removed so much of the stealth from the right-wing politics of the past forty years. He is saying explicitly that which was formally coded, arguing explicitly for whiteness, for less democracy, for extraction, and for patriarchy. There is a chance, then, that his presidency will reveal the weaknesses and assumptions of the US political system in a new way, allowing effective corrections in the name of increased democratic process. There have already been mass protests over specific policies that could galvanize a new kind of political sensibility in the United States. Trump's effort to eliminate the eight-year record of the Obama administration on environmental protection, for example, should be understood up front as a form of voter nullification, a racist project that rides almost entirely on an assumed white privilege (fueled by many of the old counterrevolutionary alliances in the fossil fuel industries). In short, Trump is attempting to energize a political project increasingly endangered due to demographic change, changing environmental realities, and financial instability by violently reasserting the terms of white rule (see Coates 2017).

The explicitness of Trump's racism, misogyny, and class formation has provoked large and varied public protests (from the Black Lives Matters campaign against police violence to the #MeToo movement's campaign against sexual harassment and assault) and energized a major shift in Congress in the fall 2018 elections. This is why the Trump administration's national campaign to use imagined voter fraud to restrict voting access is so important. It is a de facto acknowledgment that minority rule is the current political agenda of both Trump and the Republican Party. On many of the important issues in 2018—the environment, health care, reproductive rights, taxes, gun regulation, corporate accountability, war—there is a substantial public consensus that can only be overcome via democracy reduction techniques. What Trump has ultimately revealed is an all-or-nothing political commitment among a very narrow class interest to control the future, one that will destroy the environment to support petrochemical interests, one that will privilege billionaires over the lives of hundreds of millions of citizens, one that will use deception and covert techniques to maintain political control. But it is also quite possible that in a few years the overtness of the Trump moment—its cruelty, its illiberalism, and its promotion of plutocratic interests—will have produced its opposite; namely, a newly galvanized commitment to the collective commons, one that requires political and corporate oversight and that not only protects the right to vote but recognizes the necessity of a healthier political, geopolitical, and ecological environment.

At the end of 2018, however, all signs are uncertain: as of this writing, Trump has shut down the federal government because he could not get funding for an expansive wall on the border with Mexico—holding the federal government hostage for ideological purposes while abusing refugees and asylum seekers from the south. There are also corruption investigations into his family businesses and into many members of his cabinet and federal appointees. There is a special prosecutor examining the Trump election campaign for corruption and for accepting help from foreign powers (notably Russia). There is increasing talk of impeachment, of indictment, of a possible presidential resignation. Still, one needs to ask why Trump as a figure was so recognizable to some 62 million voters in 2016, why a person whose chief claim to public life rested in denying that the existing two-term president was actually born in the United States and thus legitimate, who also claimed that climate change was a hoax and promised a rejuvenated whiteness at the moment Barack Obama had broken through the ultimate racial ceiling in American politics. Why was such a person plausible for high public office to a substantial portion of the electorate? I have argued that the condition of our condition in 2018 involves negotiating a suicidal whiteness that is confronting its potential finitude and defending its holdings using all available tools, finding its advocates, its instruments, its enemies, and its audience.

But this twenty-first-century form of white supremacy should be contextualized by another historical revelation: it is now abundantly clear that all conditions—even climatic ones—are subject to direct modification: people can alter the quality of the air, the composition of polar ice, the height of the oceans. Thus, the condition of our condition, circa 2018, is an index of the forms of agency that people choose to acknowledge and activate while negotiating industrial aftermaths and the recruitments of the historical moment—to illiberal politics, to vengeful electoral strategies, and to necropolitical pleasures or to something else. Antiracism, ecological protection, gender equality, and a capacity to imagine a world without war are all modes of world-making that remain readily available, and even potentially vibrant modes of collective life. The Trump administration's revelation of an explicit, well-funded, and powerful plutocratic project to make the world more unequal, more polluted, and more violent is thus an invitation to articulate an alternative politics and with it an alternative future community. The unhinged sovereignty of the contemporary American moment has stripped the public sphere of the alibis, deceptions, and codes that for generations have sutured the language of free markets, national defense, and voter fraud to a racial project that is literally transforming the atmosphere—chemically, biologically, and affectively (see Sharpe 2016). The pain documented in this essay (across addiction, environmental disruption, financial distress) has material origins that can be addressed rather than exploited but, of course, that would require a reinvestment in an all-but-lost political vocabulary, including terms like the public interest, equality, and peace. Thus, the question in the United States today concerns what the counter-counterrevolution might produce given the distortions, disinformations, and institutional captures of so much of official political culture. Indeed, it demands support for a vision of collective life that is decolonial, committed to nonviolence, and actually democratic—about, in other words, a future condition of our condition.

Joseph Masco

1 A condition is always both material and temporal, an ever-evolving state of being that is an assessment of intensities, vulnerabilities, pleasures, and suffering. In this chapter, I am interested in thinking from a particular standpoint in time about US politics to understand the longevity and mutability of serious problem sets in American life. For example, in late 2018, the COVID-19 global pandemic did not yet exist (but would ultimately result in over one million US deaths), Trump had not yet been impeached by the US House of Representatives once, let alone twice, and supporters of Trump had not yet tried to reject the results of the 2020 election via a nationwide campaign that culminated in a violent attack on Congress to prevent the presidential vote from being certified. What is foreseeable—even thinkable—at any given moment is part of one's condition, a point that Octavia Butler explores directly in *Parable of the Sower*. This chapter is set in the fall of 2018 as a hinge moment in American politics. Thus, it recognizes a moment filled with opposed political possibilities—a deepening authoritarianism filled with racist callouts and science denialism or the intensification of a collective rejection of such antidemocratic projects.

2 My understanding of a "condition" has been developed via long-term collaboration (and a forthcoming book) with Tim Choy, Jake Kosek, and Michelle Murphy on environmental emergency. I am grateful for their support and engagement. In this chapter, I am specifically interested in how a society understands/apprehends structural changes in economic, political, and psychic life that work on so vast a scale that they are primarily experienced or rendered visible via a sudden contraction of public abilities to imagine a collective futurity. I am also interested in identifying the tactics and techniques being used to exploit intensifying physical and psychic distress as a means of consolidating political and economic power.

3 This line is based on a curious lyric from the Mickey Newbury song popularized by Kenny Rogers and the First Edition in 1968, titled "Just Dropped In (To See What Condition My Condition Was In)." That year was also a year of war, economic and racial inequality, and environmental degradation, much like our moment. The song offers a paradoxical view, simultaneously referencing the need for a fix while evoking the status of rehab. It is a drug culture reference evoking a kind of nonsovereignty that needs further definition and that rejects any pure state of being. It suggests that the narrator needs help understanding their experience and is interested in assessing intensities and qualities of being.

4 See Hooper et al. (2018) for an assessment of the lack of generational class mobility, the consolidation of wealth in the top 1 percent, and the declining purchasing power of most Americans over the last half century.

5 See International Monetary Fund, DataMapper, "GDP, Current Prices," accessed April 15, 2022, https://www.imf.org/external/datamapper/NGDPD@WEO/OEMDC/ADVEC/WEOWORLD.

6   See National Priorities Project, "Military Spending in the United States," accessed April 15, 2022, https://www.nationalpriorities.org/campaigns/military-spending-united-states/.

7   See Cunningham (2019) for a discussion of water shutoffs and housing seizures in Detroit following the 2008 Great Recession and the appointment of an emergency manager.

Joseph Masco

Afterword

MICHAEL RALPH

As long as there is breath in my body, I will do what I can.
—Congressman John Lewis, 1940–2020

This volume is jazz: it interrupts, plays with, elides, riffs on, and reconstitutes normative frameworks for sovereignty.

This afterword is rather modest by comparison. If the volume is a primer on sovereignty, this afterword is something like the upside-down answers in the back. That is to say, the afterword teases out some of the threads that stitch these pieces together and highlights some key features of sovereignty the contributors reference and riff on in their virtuoso adaptations.

In this regard, the most productive place to sit and listen involves the breath required for life—for struggle (Jain, interlude 2). For it is not possible to make music without accounting for the breath that sets the tone and marks the pace.

The reference to jazz is neither accidental nor incidental. This artistic form was born during the long eighteenth century—a period roughly stretching from the latter part of the seventeenth century to the first part of the nineteenth (from around the time of the Treaty of Westphalia to the abolition of the slave trade in Britain and the US and the Napoleonic Wars). More to the point, jazz is bound up in the contradictions of sovereignty.

The history of jazz emerges from the history of policing. At Congo Square in New Orleans, where jazz was invented, enslaved people sold produce, animals, and handmade items on Sundays—the Sabbath day, the only time in a grueling work week they were afforded some respite. Congo

Square was also notorious as a haven for maroons (Africans who escaped slavery to forge their own lifestyles and settlements, from the Spanish *cimarrón*, meaning wild or savage), most notably the legendary maroon leader Bras-Coupé, whose descendants are credited with having invented jazz (Wagner 2019, 2009).

As formerly enslaved people visited close friends and kin at the Congo Square limes, law enforcement officials developed techniques of surveillance. Consequently, jazz music was, from its inception, a fugitive art form conceived under the close watch of police. In fact, this context marks the site for an important origin of policing in the ad hoc militias property-owning white men formed to recover freed people they conceived as stolen property. This scenario is thus a reminder that policing has long been concerned with both managing populations and safeguarding property.

During the #BLM protests that spread like wildfire throughout the United States after Minneapolis police killed the unarmed African American George Floyd on May 25, 2020, long-standing critiques about mass incarceration and police abuse pushed a plea familiar to abolitionists into commercial journalism and casual conversation.

"Defund the Police."

It is a fascinating and captivating demand because it distills the two essential features of policing: finance and violence (or, it *would be* "violence" except that concept refers to the excessive or illegitimate use of force). Prosecutors and judges indifferent to police killings of unarmed African Americans frame the use of force by police as always inherently legitimate. Oppressed people call it "state violence"; the privileged, "law and order." This is America.

In the days following Derek Chauvin's murder of George Floyd, corporations churned out press releases declaring their support for #BlackLivesMatter, and affluent allies and academics debated the texts they preferred to include on antiracism reading lists while low-income and working-class African Americans (women, in particular) spent even more time doing what they had been doing for the past decade, especially during the reign of Trump: sharing strategies for building wealth and acquiring expertise in firearms. In other words, "defund the police" hooks into the priorities of rank-and-file African Americans about how to defend the value of their lives in terms of what life means as a precious resource. This is what makes life "matter" and what matters in how we discuss policing.

In other words, low-income and working-class Black people realize the conversation about why Black lives matter is a debate about sovereignty:

Michael Ralph

about the value of Black lives in practical terms. They also realize that the value of life is tied to the forms of policing and militarism used to defend lives—or to take lives. This means the value of life is central to the history of policing in the same way that it is central to the history of insurance: together, the history of finance and violence.

It is perhaps no surprise that police departments and law enforcement officials sometimes contract insurance policies worth millions of dollars they can use to pay settlements on the rare occasions that they are successfully sued for having used extralegal force to injure or kill someone. Chicago may be battling a deficit of more than $838 million, but it spent over half a billion dollars on settlements for police abuse in the past decade (including more than $113 million in 2018). Minneapolis—where Chauvin killed Floyd—spent $20 million on a single settlement in 2017.

Police precincts sometimes use bonds—what some call "police brutality bonds"—to make settlement payments: claiming that million-dollar settlements drain their budgets, law enforcement officials take capital from investors who profit from discourses about cities that are well managed and amenable to development by affluent demographics. But since taxpayers fund law enforcement agencies, we are ultimately the ones who pay for police misconduct. These partnerships let police evade accountability while financial firms generate record profits.

This relationship between finance and violence defines the long eighteenth century that has given us normative frameworks for sovereignty. From the eighteenth century forward, US economic growth was fueled by marine insurance (through which merchants secured cargo—including enslaved people—shipped to these shores); fire insurance (to secure homes); and life insurance (to secure lives, as well as those of the enslaved people merchants grew their wealth by renting out after the slave trade was outlawed in 1808). The era that fostered the birth of insurance to secure cherished assets witnessed the birth of policing to safeguard commerce and to protect property—including slave patrols made up initially of white slaveholders who banded together as armed militias to recover stolen property in the form of African people who escaped slavery to secure their freedom.

If law enforcement was defined in large measure by antebellum slave patrols, the US armed forces derived from efforts to contain a different sort of adversary likewise conceived as a threat to national security.

The US Army was born from explicit efforts to dispossess and exterminate Indigenous people. After the Revolutionary War, public concern about the limits of state power forced the Continental Army to disband. Yet the state pursued a persistent interest in displacing the prior inhabitants of what is now the United States by passing the Militia Act of 1792 (and then 1795). The Continental Army was succeeded by the Regular Army, succeeded by the Legion of the United States, until in 1796 it became known thereafter as the US Army.

With the Naval Act of 1794, the US Navy consolidated a state project to subdue African pirates who interrupted US commerce. Alongside these events, insurance was used to secure the value of property and other assets and to grow capital, while police, militia, military—as security forces—subdued perceived threats to law and order, protecting assets while eliminating obstacles to capital growth.

Capital is not a thing—it is a relationship. It entails an agreement by financial institutions that a person or corporate entity has exclusive access to an asset and that the state—that is, the police or military—will punish unauthorized access to it. The state does the most to protect the people with the largest capital investments, leaving people with the least capital invested to fend for themselves. Thus, the counterpart to insurance is mutual aid: the community funds and projects people used before the birth of the formal insurance industry (and still use when they are denied access to it).

"Defund the police" is an explicit effort to mobilize medical experts, therapists, teachers, activists, scholars, and social workers rather than outsourcing the complicated task of running society to law enforcement officials who believe they can solve social problems without bothering to study them.

"Defund the police" is a call to revisit the capital relations that have created what economists call "moral hazard": police paid to brutalize—for Tupac Shakur, "beat"—African Americans, gender-nonconforming people, and members of other despised groups. The fact that we are forced to subsidize our own subjugation adds insult to injury and financial liability.

"Defund the police" is part of a broader recognition that reforms make it too easy for police departments and insurance companies to make a killing.

But "defund the police" is also a deliberate attempt to reshape the parameters of sovereignty—to cancel the forms of finance and violence on which it is premised to free up a collective effervescence that could inaugurate a new political moment.

This is what sovereignty feels like.

As such, this volume dwells in the artistic spirit that some used to conceive jazz while others pioneered new forms of policing. Can insurgency be a vibe (Simmons and Williams, chapter 9)? The eighteenth-century French philosopher Denis Diderot proposed a different way to understand where ideas come from and where they go than the notion of "enlightenment" that ultimately became hegemonic. Against the focus on reflection that defined the Enlightenment, Diderot was interested in how ideas reverberate, in what our editors call "new possibilities for juxtaposition" (Welcome, interlude 1): a sensibility that makes it easier to see how we connect through time and space (Thomas, chapter 3) and to appreciate the porous boundaries between people and other living organisms (Jain, interlude 2; Blanchette, chapter 8).

Bras-Coupé, legal name Squire, earned his alias when he lost a limb fleeing the police (*bras*, French for "arm"; *coupé*, the past participle of "cut"). How does a different orientation to ability prepare us for a different relationship to leadership and thus help transform sovereignty (Rutherford, chapter 10), "creating," as our editors put it, "a modern subject that is neither sovereign nor in control but rather one that attempts to navigate both physically and psychically a wildly contingent world and its distributed violences—and does their best every day to make it work" (Mankekar and Gupta, introduction)?

Thus jazz is the governing metaphor for this primer on sovereignty. It speaks to the innovation (García, chapter 2) and underscores the breathing techniques—the breathing space—crucial to establishing autonomy, hatching plans, building community, and tackling the predicament of sovereignty.

This is a long-winded way of saying that no concept is better suited than breath to help us make sense of sovereignty in the long eighteenth century.

In the first instance, this is because breath is neither free nor effortless. Until it was outlawed in Britain in the eighteenth century—and even after, as the tragic fates of Eric Garner and George Floyd have revealed—suffocating someone suspected of a crime was a pervasive technique of punishment. The protocol could be instituted when the accused remained silent in the face of an accusation and consisted of laying a wooden or metal slab on top of the person until a confession was forthcoming or the accused simply died (Carby 2020).

Punishing the people most victimized by the normative frameworks for sovereignty and forms of capital that dominated the long eighteenth century by snatching the air from their lungs accords with the assault on the environment and other living organisms that defined the alleged formation of civil society from a primordial state of nature. For this reason, it is intriguing that Hobbes spent a lot of time debating the science of air in a bizarre yet fitting parallel to his political philosophy.

Hobbes's greatest nemesis was not another social contract theorist but a scientist, Robert Boyle, who pioneered the air pump. Hobbes was vexed by Boyle's creation and routinely wrote articles questioning his methods as well as the implications of his newfangled science (Shapin and Schaffer 2017). Hobbes could scarcely imagine that the double-sided air pump was a parable concerning the growing reach of state sovereignty and its capacity to steal breath from inhabitants of newly forged nation-states.

But the focus of this volume is not on these familiar events and conventions. Instead, the scholars assembled here are interested in a different kind of leadership—one modeled in this volume, where a range of skills, insights, talents, and perspectives are introduced to tackle a familiar problem from unusual yet illuminating angles. Thus, rather than sovereignty, as conceived in normative frameworks, this volume issues forth an appreciation for mutual aid where we each share our distinct skills and expertise with the collective (Shankar, chapter 7) in the spirit of reciprocity.

The aforementioned maroon societies are arguably the paradigmatic example of mutual aid. Yet it is crucial to consider that the explicit language of mutual aid has been the rallying cry of social movements from #Occupy-WallStreet to the Arab-Spring-that-was-also-an-African-Spring to #BLM.

Mutual aid cannot escape normative frameworks of sovereignty; in fact, the forms of organizing we develop are implicated in them (Winegar, chapter 1; Bonilla, chapter 4). Political recognition in prevailing frameworks of sovereignty relies on the consensus of privileged actors; more specifically, it involves ritual protocols for anointing polities—and certain actors within them—as members of a political community (Thomas, chapter 3).

In revisiting the politics that inspire and animate this intervention, we are prompted to interrogate another domain dominated by sanctioned authorities—the academy. In the face of the "disciplinary practices that threaten to render our work lifeless and irrelevant to life" (Simmons and Williams, chapter 9), we might revisit familiar customs to define anthropology not merely as a discipline but as a framework.

To the extent that anthropology is the study of human society, every social practice or institution deserves as much consideration as any other. Anthropologists particularly concerned with carving out a market niche distinct from other disciplines narrow the focus to a signature method that is currently more pervasive in anthropology than in other academic disciplines: ethnography. But ethnography cannot be conflated with anthropology for obvious reasons. Police officers conduct ethnographies, as do corporations and the armed forces—no credible anthropologist would consider these investigations comparable to the discipline's most influential and highly regarded scholarship. Further, it is worth noting that anthropological training involves taking seriously every social practice. It also involves taking seriously every remnant of social life: every conceivable form of evidence that people generate about human society. Anthropology is arguably the only field that entertains the detritus of society in its breadth and fullness. From that perspective, what makes anthropology distinct is how it treats evidence. Anthropologists are concerned with the discrepancy between how people narrate a context and how we understand that context to be organized at a structural level.

Works now regarded as crucial to anthropological theory have called for decolonizing the discipline and increasingly demand that we develop abolitionist frameworks (Shange 2019). From one perspective, this project was inaugurated in the long eighteenth-century moment that gave us normative frameworks for sovereignty.

Immanuel Kant famously theorized anthropology "from a pragmatic point of view," but he did not conduct original research in that vein. A more influential touchstone for the birth of anthropology in tandem with normative frameworks for sovereignty—the project to collect a broad range of data about the people and polities that define our shared world—might be the Société des Observateures de l'Homme (Society for the Investigators of Man), founded in 1800.

The Société summoned "the profound metaphysician and the practicing physician, the historian and the voyager, he who studies the spirit of languages" to abandon "all passion, all prejudice" (Stocking 1968) in favor of a comparative study of diverse contexts. This project would ultimately involve collecting and cataloguing plants and animals—later, classifying and ranking people. Importantly, Carl Linnaeus, most known for his elaborate taxonomies of living organisms, contested a strict division between people and animals, insisting the former belonged in the latter category. Recall, this hierarchy had even informed Hobbes's theory of civil compact from the proverbial state of nature—it was this act that, Hobbes believed, raised human beings from the level of beasts. Of course, whether all human beings had been raised above that level is precisely what would be debated—and, by the nineteenth century, craniometry, clinical examination, statistics, and a range of scientific enterprises would become concerned with establishing and ranking "types of mankind" (Nott and Gliddon 1854).

Normative frameworks for sovereignty did not alleviate this problem but compounded it, precisely because the privileged status of being regarded as a sovereign person or polity has never been based on an objective assessment. Rather, sovereignty consists of quasi-mystical ritual protocols for establishing a person or polity as deserving of membership in an elite community. And that status can only be conferred by privileged members of the favored group. In its inception, North Atlantic sovereignty was a way of recognizing membership in God's kingdom. During the long eighteenth century, sovereignty became a way for privileged actors to determine which peoples and polities had earned the right to participate in the diplomatic protocols and forms of exchange that defined civil society—people and polities that had successfully navigated the path to Civil Society from the State of Nature.

Where anthropology is concerned, two events occurring within the French Empire coterminous with the Société have particular relevance for the discipline.

The first is the revolution in Saint-Domingue (1791–1803) that delivered the world's first republic composed of formerly enslaved people. The uprising began with communion, with the ritual slaughter of a black pig as a testament to the complex ecological system (Blanchette, chapter 8) through which African peoples defined their plight. The long eighteenth century occasioned leaps in industry, but this act invoked a different framework for causality (Rutherford, chapter 10) and thus a different politics. Makandal, one of the leaders of the revolution, was an herbalist famed for poisoning plantation owners, yet he was also a veterinarian and viewed the care of animals as crucial to the community to which he and his comrades belonged. Thus, the political vision of the revolutionaries in Haiti offers an appreciation for the breath that ties all living organisms together and a potent critique of the liberal humanism that unduly privileges possessive individualism.

The other crucial event from the French Empire with bearing on anthropology is Napoleon's invasion of Egypt in 1798. Along with thousands of troops, Napoleon brought hundreds of artists, surveyors, and cartographers who cataloged and captured Egyptian monuments and texts, while also producing ethnographic accounts of the occupation, which lasted until 1801. The most illuminating account of the moment was written by the Somali-Egyptian native anthropologist Abd al-Rahman al-Jabarti. From a family of intellectuals, al-Jabarti ([1798] 2006) detailed the economic initiatives and diplomatic strategies Napoleon mobilized to secure rule in Egypt, including donning customary attire to ingratiate himself with regional authorities. Unlike the stale accounts of timeless people that are too often the coin of the realm in introductory courses in anthropology, al-Jabarti masterfully weaves diplomacy and militarism with economic and political considerations in a deft work of anthropology that highlights the

Michael Ralph

discrepancy this afterword and book consider to be the defining feature of our critical intervention.

Thus, more than offering a definitive take on normative frameworks for sovereignty, this volume helps to explain why they are so often inadequate, incomplete, and unsatisfying. What's more, we offer insights about how people transform their contexts and reimagine possibilities that were utterly unfathomable to the architects of the institutions they refuse to let keep them captive. *This is what sovereignty feels like*—in the spirit of Congo Square we return, with bated breath, to that awesome sense of what we share—the experience that makes us who we are.

References

Abel, Elizabeth. 2014. "Skin, Flesh, and the Affective Wrinkles of Civil Rights Photography." In *Feeling Photography*, edited by Elspeth H. Brown and Thy Phu, 93–124. Durham, NC: Duke University Press.

Acurio, Gastón. 2008. *500 años de fusión: La historia, los ingredientes y la nueva propuesta de la cocina peruana*. Lima: El Comercio.

Acurio, Gastón. 2009. "Gastón Acurio: 'Cooking Is Combined with Moral Principles.'" *Power of Culture*, March. http://www.krachtvancultuur.nl/en/current/2009/march/gaston-acurio.html.

Acurio, Gastón. 2016. "La fragilidad." Facebook, October 22, 8 a.m. https://m.facebook.com/gastonacurio/posts/la-fragilidad-la-cocina-encuentra-su-fuente-en-el-amor-el-mismo-amor-que-hizo-de/10154697324993130/.

Acurio, Gastón. 2018. "Can Home Cooking Change the World?" TED en Español en NYC, April. https://www.ted.com/talks/gaston_acurio_can_home_cooking_change_the_world?language=en.

Adorno, Theodor. (1946) 2001. *The Culture Industry*. New York: Routledge.

Adorno, Theodor, and Max Horkheimer. (1944) 2007. *The Dialectic of Enlightenment*. Stanford, CA: Stanford University Press.

Agamben, Giorgio. 1998. *Homo Sacer: Sovereign Power and Bare Life*. Translated by Daniel Heller-Roazen. Stanford, CA: Stanford University Press.

Agamben, Giorgio. 1999. *Potentialities*. Translated and edited by Daniel Heller-Roazen. Stanford, CA: Stanford University Press.

Agamben, Giorgio. 2005. *State of Exception*. Translated by Kevin Attell. Chicago: University of Chicago Press.

Aguirre, Carlos, and Paulo Drinot. 2017. *The Peculiar Revolution: Rethinking the Peruvian Experiment under Military Rule*. Austin: University of Texas Press.

Ahmed, Sara. 2004. "Affective Economies." *Social Text* 22 (2): 117–39.

Ahmed, Sara. 2010. "Happy Objects." In *The Affect Theory Reader*, edited by Melissa Gregg and Gregory J. Seigworth, 29–51. Durham, NC: Duke University Press.

Ahmed, Sara. 2015. *The Cultural Politics of Emotion*. New York: Routledge.

Ahmed, Sara, Claudia Castada, Anne-Marie Fortier, and Mimi Sheller. 2003. "Introduction: Uprootings/Regroundings: Questions of Home and Migration." In *Uprootings/Regroundings: Questions of Home and Migration*, edited by Sara Ahmed, Claudia Castada, Anne-Marie Fortier, and Mimi Sheller, 1–15. Oxford: Berg.

Akomfrah, John. 2018. "Artist Conversation: John Akomfrah." Interview by Fawz Kabra. *Ocula*, July 5. https://ocula.com/magazine/conversations/john-akomfrah/.

Akshaya Patra. 2008. "Obama's Accolade for Akshaya Patra." *Bangalore Mirror*, December 12. https://www.prlog.org/11056494-obamas-accolade-for-akshaya-patra.html.

Aleinikoff, T. Alexander. 2002. *Semblances of Sovereignty: The Constitution, the State, and American Citizenship*. Cambridge, MA: Harvard University Press.

Alfred, Taiaiake. 2002. "Sovereignty." In *A Companion to American Indian History*, edited by Philip J. Deloria and Neal Salisbury, 460–74. Malden, MA: Blackwell.

al-Jabarti, Abd al-Rahman bin Hasan bin Burhan al-Din. (1798) 2006. *Napoleon in Egypt: Al-Jabarti's Chronicle of the French Invasion*. Princeton, NJ: Markus Weiner.

Allen, Theodore W. 2012. *The Invention of the White Race*. 2 vols. New York: Verso.

Allison, Anne. 2013. *Precarious Japan*. Durham, NC: Duke University Press.

Alston, Philip. 2017. "Statement on Visit to the USA, by Professor Philip Alston, United Nations Special Rapporteur on Extreme Poverty and Human Rights." United Nations Human Rights, Office of the High Commissioner, December 15. https://www.ohchr.org/en/statements/2017/12/statement-visit-usa-professor-philip-alston-united-nations-special-rapporteur.

Altamirano Rua, Teófilo, and Eric Altamirano Girao. 2019. *La nueva cocina peruana: En la era del cambio climático, la contaminación ambiental, las migraciones y la masculinización*. Lima: CreaLibros.

Althusser, Louis. 1971. "Ideology and Ideological State Apparatuses (Notes towards an Investigation)." In *Lenin and Philosophy*, 127–88. London: New Left.

American Society of Civil Engineers. 2017. *Report Card for America's Infrastructure*. https://www.infrastructurereportcard.org.

Amnesty International. 2011. "Jamaica: A Long Road to Justice? Human Rights Violations under the State of Emergency." London: Amnesty International.

Anand, Utkarsh. 2015. "India Has 31 Lakh NGOs, More than Double the Number of Schools." *Indian Express*, August 1.

Anderson, Carol. 2016. *White Rage: The Unspoken Truth of Our Racial Divide*. New York: Bloomsbury USA.

Aneesh, A. 2006. *Virtual Migration: The Programming of Globalization*. Durham, NC: Duke University Press.

Aneesh, A. 2015. *Neutral Accent: How Language, Labor, and Life Become Global*. Durham, NC: Duke University Press.

Apega. 2013. *El boom gastronómico peruano al 2013*. Lima: Apega.

Appadurai, Arjun. 2013. *The Future as Cultural Fact: Essays on the Global Condition*. New York: Verso.

Appelbaum, Nancy, Anne Macpherson, and Karin Alejandra Rosemblatt. 2003. *Race and Nation in Modern Latin America*. Chapel Hill: University of North Carolina Press.

Arendt, Hannah. 1968. *The Human Condition*. Chicago: University of Chicago Press.

Armbrust, Walter. 2009. "Long Live the Patriarchy: Love in the Time of 'Abd al-Wahhab." *History Compass* 7 (1): 251–81.

Armbrust, Walter. 2019. *Martyrs and Tricksters: An Ethnography of the Egyptian Revolution*. Princeton, NJ: Princeton University Press.

Azoulay, Ariella. 2008. *The Civil Contract*. New York: Zone.

Bal, Mieke. 1992. "Telling, Showing, Showing Off." *Critical Inquiry* 18 (3): 556–94.

Balkan, Osman. 2015. "Till Death Do Us Depart: Repatriation, Burial, and the Necropolitical Work of Turkish Funeral Funds in Germany." In *Muslims in the UK and Europe*, edited by Yasir Suleiman, 19–28. Cambridge: Cambridge University Press.

Barker, Joanne. 2005. "For Whom Sovereignty Matters." In *Sovereignty Matters: Locations of Contestation and Possibility in Indigenous Struggles for Self-Determination*, edited by Joanne Barker, 1–31. Lincoln: University of Nebraska Press.

Bartelson, Jens. 1995. *A Genealogy of Sovereignty*. Cambridge: Cambridge University Press.

Bataille, Georges. (1991) 2017. *The Accursed Share: An Essay on General Economy*, vols. 2 and 3. Translated by Robert Hurley. New York: Zone Books.

Bear, Laura, Karen Ho, Anna Lowenhaupt Tsing, and Sylvia Yanagisako. 2015. "Generating Capitalism." Theorizing the Contemporary, *Fieldsights*, March 30. http://www.culanth.org/fieldsights/650-generating-capitalism.

Beldo, Les. 2017. "Metabolic Labor: Broiler Chickens and the Exploitation of Vitality." *Environmental Humanities* 9 (1): 108–28.

Bell, Daniel. 1947. "The Study of Man: Adjusting Men to Machines." *Commentary Magazine*, January.

Benjamin, Walter. (1927) 2002. *The Arcades Project*. Translated by Howard Eiland. Cambridge, MA: Belknap.

Benjamin, Walter. (1935) 2008. *The Work of Art in the Age of Mechanical Reproduction*. Translated by J. A. Underwood. London: Penguin Classics.

Bennett, Jane. 2010. *Vibrant Matter: A Political Ecology of Things*. Durham, NC: Duke University Press.

Bergson, Henri. (1889) 2001. *Time and Free Will: An Essay on the Immediate Data of Consciousness*. Translated by F. L. Pogson. Mineola, NY: Dover.

Berlant, Lauren. 1997. *The Queen of America Goes to Washington City*. Durham, NC: Duke University Press.

Berlant, Lauren. 2007. "Slow Death (Sovereignty, Obesity, Lateral Agency)." *Critical Inquiry* 33 (Summer): 754–80.

Berlant, Lauren. 2011a. *Cruel Optimism*. Durham, NC: Duke University Press.

Berlant, Lauren. 2011b. "A Properly Political Concept of Love: Three Approaches in Ten Pages." *Cultural Anthropology* 26 (4): 683–91.

Berlant, Lauren. 2016. "The Commons: Infrastructures for Troubling Times." *Environment and Planning D: Society and Space* 34 (3): 393–419.

Besky, Sarah. 2019. "Exhaustion and Endurance in Sick Landscapes: Cheap Tea and the Work of Monoculture in the Dooars, India." In *How Nature Works: Rethinking Labor on a Troubled Planet*, edited by Sarah Besky and Alex Blanchette, 23–40. Albuquerque: SAR Press/University of New Mexico Press.

Besson, Jean. 2002. *Martha Brae's Two Histories: European Expansion and Caribbean Culture-Building in Jamaica*. Chapel Hill: University of North Carolina Press.

Biehl, João, and Peter Locke, eds. 2017. *Unfinished: The Anthropology of Becoming*. Durham, NC: Duke University Press.

Bilgrami, Akeel. 2014. *Secularism, Identity, and Enchantment*. Cambridge, MA: Harvard University Press.

Biolsi, Thomas. 2005. "Imagined Geographies: Sovereignty, Indigenous Space, and American Indian Struggle." *American Ethnologist* 32 (2): 239–59.

Birchfield, Lauren, and Jessica Corsi. 2010. "The Right to Life Is the Right to Food: People's Union for Civil Liberties v. Union of India & Others." *Human Rights Brief* 17 (3): 15–18.

Blanchette, Alex. 2020. *Porkopolis: American Animality, Standardized Life, and the Factory Farm*. Durham, NC: Duke University Press.

Bloch, Maurice, and Jonathan Parry. 1982. *Death and the Regeneration of Life*. Cambridge: Cambridge University Press.

Bodin, Jean. (1576) 1992. *On Sovereignty (Four Chapters from The Six Books of the Commonwealth)*. Cambridge: Cambridge University Press.

Bohardt, Meghan. 2014. "Peru's 'Gastronomic Boom': Critical Perspectives on Elite Gastronomy and Social Food Justice." MA thesis, University of Illinois at Urbana-Champaign.

Bonilla, Yarimar. 2015. *Non-sovereign Futures: French Caribbean Politics in the Wake of Disenchantment*. Chicago: University of Chicago Press.

Bonilla, Yarimar. 2017. "Unsettling Sovereignty." *Cultural Anthropology* 32 (2): 330–39.

Bonilla, Yarimar. 2018. "Trump's False Claims about Puerto Rico Are Insulting. But They Reveal a Deeper Truth." *Washington Post*, September 14.

Bonilla, Yarimar. 2020a. "The Coloniality of Disaster: Race, Empire, and the Temporal Logics of Emergency in Puerto Rico, USA." *Political Geography* 78 (April). https://doi.org/10.1016/j.polgeo.2020.102181.

Bonilla, Yarimar. 2020b. "Drive Through Covid-19 Protests in Puerto Rico." April 15, YouTube video, 6:29. https://www.youtube.com/watch?v=XcpRdWoV9bU.

Bornstein, Erica. 2012. *Disquieting Gifts: Humanitarianism in New Delhi*. Stanford, CA: Stanford University Press.

Bornstein, Erica, and Aradhana Sharma. 2016. "The Righteous and the Rightful: The Technomoral Politics of NGOs, Social Movements, and the State of India." *American Ethnologist* 43 (1): 76–90.

Bourdieu, Pierre. 1984. *Distinction: A Social Critique of the Judgement of Taste*. Translated by Richard Nice. Cambridge, MA: Harvard University Press.

Boyle, Robert. 1670. "New Pneumatical Experiments about Respiration." *Philosophical Transactions of the Royal Society of London* 5 (62): 2011–31.

Broadway, Michael. 1995. "From City to Countryside: Recent Changes in the Structure and Location of the Meat- and Fish-Processing Industries." In *Any Way You Cut It: Meat Processing and Small-Town America*, edited by Donald D. Stull, Michael J. Broadway, and David Griffith, 17–41. Lawrence: University Press of Kansas.

Brown, Vincent. 2008. *The Reaper's Garden: Death and Power in the World of Atlantic Slavery*. Cambridge, MA: Harvard University Press.

Browne, Simone. 2015. *Dark Matters: On the Surveillance of Blackness*. Durham, NC: Duke University Press.

Bruchac, Margaret M. 2018. *Savage Kin: Indigenous Informants and American Anthropologists*. Tucson: University of Arizona Press.

Buck-Morss, Susan. 1992. "Aesthetics and Anaesthetics: Walter Benjamin's Artwork Essay Reconsidered." *October* 62 (Autumn): 3–41.

Buck-Morss, Susan. 2000. "Hegel and Haiti." *Critical Inquiry* 26 (4): 821–66.

Butler, Judith. 1993. "Endangered/Endangering: Schematic Racism and White Paranoia." In *Reading Rodney King/Reading Urban Uprising*, edited by Robert Gooding-Williams, 15–22. New York: Routledge.

Butler, Judith. 2016. *Frames of War: When Is Life Grievable?* New York: Verso.

Butler, Octavia. 1993. *Parable of the Sower*. New York: Four Walls Eight Windows.

Byrd, Jodi. 2011. *The Transit of Empire: Indigenous Critiques of Colonialism*. Minneapolis: University of Minnesota Press.

Campt, Tina M. 2017. *Listening to Images*. Durham, NC: Duke University Press.

Campt, Tina M. 2019. "Black Visuality and the Practice of Refusal." *Women and Performance: A Journal of Feminist Theory* 29 (1): 79–87.

Cannell, Fenella. 1999. *Power and Intimacy in the Christian Philippines*. Cambridge: Cambridge University Press.

Capello, Mary. 2012. *Swallow: Foreign Bodies, Their Ingestion, Inspiration, and the Curious Doctor Who Extracted Them*. New York: New Press.

Carby, Hazel. 2019. *Imperial Intimacies: A Tale of Two Islands*. New York: Verso.

Carby, Hazel. 2020. "Peine forte et dure." *London Review of Books* 42 (15).

Carnegie, Charles. 1987. "Is Family Land an Institution?" In *Afro-Caribbean Villages in Historical Perspective*, edited by Charles Carnegie, 83–99. Kingston: African-Caribbean Institute of Jamaica.

Case, Anne, and Angus Deaton. 2015. "Rising Morbidity and Mortality in Midlife among White Non-Hispanic Americans in the 21st Century." *PNAS* 112 (49): 15078–83.

Case, Anne, and Angus Deaton. 2017. "Mortality and Morbidity in the 21st Century." *Brookings Papers on Economic Activity* (Spring): 397–476.

Casino City Press. 2018. "Casino City Press Releases 2018 Indian Gaming Industry Report: Indian Gaming Reaches All-Time High of $31.5 Billion." GlobeNewswire News Room, October 3. http://www.globenewswire.com/news-release/2018/10/03/1600517/0/en/Casino-City-Press-Releases-2018-Indian-Gaming-Industry-Report-Indian-Gaming-Reaches-All-Time-High-of-31-5-Billion.html.

Cassidy, John. 2020. "Trump's Coronavirus Response Has Single-Handedly Created a New Federalism." *New Yorker*, April 14. https://www.newyorker.com/news/our-columnists/trump-has-single-handedly-created-a-new-federalism.

Cattelino, Jessica R. 2007. "Florida Seminole Gaming and Local Sovereign Interdependency." In *Beyond Red Power: Rethinking Twentieth-Century American Indian Politics*, edited by Daniel Cobb and Loretta Fowler, 262–79. Santa Fe, NM: School of American Research Press.

Cattelino, Jessica R. 2008. *High Stakes: Florida Seminole Gaming and Sovereignty*. Durham, NC: Duke University Press.

Césaire, Aimé. (1955) 1972. *Discourse on Colonialism*. Translated by Joan Pinkham. New York: Monthly Review Press.

Charles, Chris. 2004. "Political Identity and Criminal Violence in Jamaica: The Garrison Community of August Town and the 2002 Election." *Social and Economic Studies* 53 (2): 31–74.

Charney, Paul. 2001. *Indian Society in the Valley of Lima, Peru, 1532–1824*. Lanham, MD: Rowman and Littlefield.

Chen, Mel Y. 2012. *Animacies: Biopolitics, Racial Mattering, and Queer Affect*. Durham, NC: Duke University Press.

Chiu Werner, Alexander. 2012. "La marca Mistura." *Diario Gestión*, August 27. https://gestion.pe/blog/anunciasluegoexistes/2012/08/la-marca-mistura.html.

Choy, Timothy. 2011. *Ecologies of Comparison: An Ethnography of Endangerment in Hong Kong*. Durham, NC: Duke University Press.

Choy, Timothy. 2016. "Distribution." *Fieldsights*, January 21. https://culanth.org/fieldsights/distribution.

Chua, Jocelyn Lim. 2014. *In Pursuit of the Good Life: Aspiration and Suicide in Globalizing South India*. Berkeley: University of California Press.

Churumuri. 2017. "If Akshaya Patra's 'Sattvic' Food Is Good for Kids, Why Isn't It OK for the Poor?" *Churumuri* (blog), April 3. https://churumuri.blog/2017/04/03/should-there-be-onions-and-garlic-in-cheap-food-for-the-poor-or-should-it-be-sattvic/.

Clerf, L. H. 1975. "Historical Aspects of Foreign Bodies in the Air and Food Passages." *Southern Medical Journal* 68 (11): 1449–54.

Coates, Ta-Nehisi. 2017. "The First White President." *Atlantic*, October.

Cobb, Amanda J. 2005. "Understanding Tribal Sovereignty: Definitions, Conceptualizations, and Interpretations." *American Studies/Indigenous Studies Today* 46, no. 1 (3/4): 115–32.

Cogorno, Gilda, and Pilar Ortiz de Zevallos. 2018. *La Lima que encontró Pizarro*. Lima: Taurus.

Cohen, Alice. 2012. "Rescaling Environmental Governance: Watersheds as Boundary Objects at the Intersection of Science, Neoliberalism, and Participation." *Environment and Planning A* 44 (9): 2207–24.

Cole, Teju. 2016. *Known and Strange Things: Essays*. New York: Random House.

Coleman, Edward. 1791. *A Dissertation on Suspended Respiration from Drowning, Hanging, and Suffocation: In which is recommended a different Mode of Treatment to any hitherto pointed Out*. London: Printed for J. Johnson.

Colley, Brook. 2018. *Power in the Telling: Grand Ronde, Warm Springs, and Intertribal Relations in the Casino Era*. Seattle: University of Washington Press.

Comisión de la Verdad y Reconciliación (CVR). 2004. *Hatun Willakuy: Versión Abreviada del Informe Final de la Comisión de la Verdad y Reconciliación, Perú*. Lima: Corporación Gráfica.

Coombes, Annie E., ed. 2006. *Rethinking Settler Colonialism: History and Memory in Australia, Canada, Aotearoa New Zealand and South Africa*. Manchester: Manchester University Press.

Cooper, Melinda. 2008. *Life as Surplus: Biotechnology and Capitalism in the Neoliberal Era*. Seattle: University of Washington Press.

Coulthard, Glen Sean. 2014. *Red Skin, White Masks: Rejecting the Colonial Politics of Recognition*. Minneapolis: University of Minnesota Press.

Crawford, Neta. 2018a. "Human Cost of the Post-9/11 Wars: Lethality and the Need for Transparency." *Costs of War*, November. https://watson.brown.edu/costsofwar/papers/2018/human-cost-post-911-wars-lethality-and-need-transparency.

Crawford, Neta. 2018b. "United States Budgetary Costs of the Post-9/11 Wars through FY2019: $5.9 Trillion Spent and Obligated." *Costs of War*, November 14. https://watson.brown.edu/costsofwar/papers/2018/united-states-budgetary-costs-post-911-wars-through-fy2019-59-trillion-spent-and.

Cunningham, Molly. 2019. "Detroit Can't Wait: Love and War at the Brink of Municipal Death (An Ethnographic Accounting of Emergency)." PhD diss., Department of Anthropology, University of Chicago.

Cusicanqui, Silvia Rivera. 1987. *"Oppressed but Not Defeated": Peasant Struggles among the Aymara and Qhechwa in Bolivia, 1900–1980*. Geneva: United Nations Research Institute for Social Development.

Cusicanqui, Silvia Rivera. 2007. "Everything Is Up for Discussion: A 40th Anniversary Conversation with Silvia Rivera Cusicanqui." Interview by Linda Farthing. *NACLA Report on the Americas* 40 (4): 4–9.

CVR. 2004. *Hatun Willakuy: Versión abreviada del informe final de la Comisión de la Verdad y Reconciliación, Perú*. Lima: Corporación Gráfica.

Das, Veena. 2006. *Life and Words: Violence and the Descent into the Ordinary*. Berkeley: University of California Press.

Dave, Naisargi. 2016. "Love and Other Injustices: On Indifference to Difference." Humanities Futures, Franklin Humanities Institute, Duke University.

de la Cadena, Marisol. 2000. *Indigenous Mestizos: The Politics of Race and Culture in Cuzco, Peru, 1919–1991*. Durham, NC: Duke University Press.

de la Cadena, Marisol. 2010. "Indigenous Cosmopolitics in the Andes: Conceptual Reflections beyond 'Politics.'" *Cultural Anthropology* 25 (2): 334–70.

De Leon, Jason. 2018. "The Indecisive Moment: Photoethnography on the Undocumented Migration Trail." In *Photography and Migration*, edited by Tanya Sheehan. London: Routledge.

Deleuze, Gilles. 1990. *The Logic of Sense*. Translated by Mark Lester and Charles Stivale. New York: Columbia University Press.

Deleuze, Gilles. 1995. *Difference and Repetition*. Translated by Paul Patton. New York: Columbia University Press.

Deloria, Vine. 1979. "Self-Determination and the Concept of Sovereignty." In *Economic Development in American Indian Reservations*, edited by Roxanne Dunbar Ortiz, 22–28. Albuquerque: University of New Mexico Native American Studies.

del Pino, Ponciano, and José Carlos Agüero. 2014. *Cada uno, un lugar de memoria: Fundamentos conceptual del lugar de la memoria, la tolerancia y la inclusión social*. Lima: LUM.

del Pino, Ponciano, and Caroline Yezer. 2013. *Las formas del recuerdo: Etnografías de la violencia política en el Perú*. Lima: IEP-IFEA.

Dennison, Jean. 2012. *Colonial Entanglement: Constituting a Twenty-First-Century Osage Nation*. Chapel Hill: University of North Carolina Press.

Derrida, Jacques. 2006. *Specters of Marx: The State of the Debt, the Work of Mourning, and the New International.* Translated by Peggy Kamuf. New York: Routledge.

Derrida, Jacques. 2009. *The Beast and the Sovereign.* Translated by Geoffrey Bennington. Chicago: University of Chicago Press.

Desmond, Jane. 1999. *Staging Tourism: Bodies on Display from Waikiki to Sea World.* Chicago: University of Chicago Press.

Dharia, Namita, and Nishita Trisal. 2017. "Introduction: Anthropology in the Age of Executive Orders." Hot Spots, *Fieldsights,* September 27. https://culanth.org/fieldsights/1199-introduction-anthropology-in-the-age-of-executive-orders.

Diaz, Vicente M. 2015. "No Island Is an Island." In *Native Studies Keywords,* edited by Stephanie Nohelani Tevas, Andrea Smith, and Michelle Raheja, 90–108. Tucson: University of Arizona Press.

Dijkshoorn, L., B. M. Ursing, and J. B. Ursing. 2000. "Strain, Clone and Species: Comments on Three Basic Concepts of Bacteriology." *Journal of Medical Microbiology* 49 (5): 397–401.

Dillard, Cynthia B. 2016. "We Are Still Here: Declarations of Love and Sovereignty in Black Life under Siege." *Educational Studies* 52 (3): 201–5.

Drinot, Paulo. 2009. "For Whom the Eye Cries: Memory, Monumentality, and the Ontologies of Violence in Peru." *Journal of Latin American Cultural Studies* 18 (1): 15–32.

Drinot, Paulo. 2017. "Remembering Velasco: Contested Memories of the Revolutionary Government of the Armed Forces." In *The Peculiar Revolution: Rethinking the Peruvian Experiment under Military Rule,* edited by Carlos Aguirre and Paulo Drinot, 95–119. Austin: University of Texas Press.

Dumit, Joseph. 2012a. "The Biomarx Experiment." In *Lively Capital: Biotechnologies, Ethics, and Governance in Global Markets,* edited by Kaushik Sunder Rajan, 45–92. Durham, NC: Duke University Press.

Dumit, Joseph. 2012b. *Drugs for Life.* Durham, NC: Duke University Press.

DuPont. 1927. "Ride with Ethyl in a high compression motor and get the thrill of a lifetime!!" Advertisement, *National Geographic,* September.

Edelman, Lee. 2004. *No Future: Queer Theory and the Death Drive.* Durham, NC: Duke University Press.

EDGI. 2018. "A Sheep in the Closet: The Erosion of Enforcement at the EPA." Environmental Data and Governance Initiative. https://envirodatagov.org/wp-content/uploads/2018/11/Sheep-in-the-Closet.pdf.

Escobar, Arturo. 1995. *Encountering Development: The Making and Unmaking of the Third World.* Princeton, NJ: Princeton University Press.

Estes, Nick. 2019. *Our History Is the Future: Standing Rock versus the Dakota Access Pipeline, and the Long Tradition of Indigenous Resistance.* London: Verso.

Evans, Brad, and Julian Reid. 2014. *Resilient Life: The Art of Living Dangerously.* Cambridge: Polity.

Falcón, Sylvanna. 2018. "Intersectionality and the Arts: Counterpublic Memory-Making in Postconflict Peru." *International Journal of Transitional Justice* 12 (1): 26–44.

Fanon, Frantz. 1961. *The Wretched of the Earth.* Translated by Richard Philcox. New York: Grove.

Fanon, Frantz. 1969. *Toward the African Revolution*. Translated by Haakon Chevalier. New York: Grove.

Fanon, Frantz. (1952) 2008. *Black Skin, White Masks*. Translated by Richard Philcox. New York: Grove.

Fassin, Didier. 2012. *Humanitarian Reason: A Moral History of the Present*. Berkeley: University of California Press.

Favero, Paulo. 2005. *India Dreams: Cultural Identity among Young Middle-Class Men in New Delhi*. Stockholm: Department of Social Anthropology, Stockholm University.

Federici, Silvia. 2004. *Caliban and the Witch: Women, the Body, and Primitive Accumulation*. New York: Autonomedia.

Feldman, Allen. 2015. *Archives of the Insensible: Of War, Photopolitics, and Dead Memory*. Chicago: University of Chicago Press.

Feldman, Joseph. 2012. "Exhibiting Conflict: History and Politics at the Museo de la Memoria de ANFASEP in Ayacucho, Peru." *Anthropological Quarterly* 85 (2): 487–518.

Feldman, Joseph. 2019. "Memory as Persuasion: Historical Discourse and Moral Messages at Peru's Place of Memory, Tolerance, and Social Inclusion." In *Museums and Sites of Persuasion: Politics, Memory and Human Rights*, edited by Joyce Apsel and Amy Sodaro, 133–50. New York: Routledge.

Fennell, Catherine. 2011. "'Project Heat' and Sensory Politics in Redeveloping Chicago Public Housing." *Ethnography* 12 (1): 40–64.

Ferguson, James, and Akhil Gupta. 2002. "Spatializing States: Toward an Ethnography of Neoliberal Governmentality." *American Ethnologist* 29 (4): 981–1002.

Ferreira da Silva, Denise. 2007. *Toward a Global Idea of Race*. Minneapolis: University of Minnesota Press.

Ferreira da Silva, Denise. 2017. "1 (life) ÷ 0 (blackness) = ∞ - ∞ or ∞/∞: On Matter Beyond the Equation of Value." *E-flux Journal*, no. 79 (February). https://www.e-flux.com/journal/79/94686/1-life-0-blackness-or-on-matter-beyond-the-equation-of-value/.

Fineman, Martha Albertson. 2004. *The Autonomy Myth: A Theory of Dependency*. New York: New Press.

Fischer, Sybille. 2004. *Modernity Disavowed: Haiti and the Cultures of Slavery in the Age of Revolution*. Durham, NC: Duke University Press.

Fleetwood, Nicole R. 2011. *Troubling Vision: Performance, Visuality, and Blackness*. Chicago: University of Chicago Press.

Ford, Henry. 1923. *My Life and Work*. Scotts Valley, CA: Createspace.

Fortun, Kim. 2012. "Ethnography in Late Industrialism." *Cultural Anthropology* 27 (3): 446–64.

Franco, Jean. 2013. *Cruel Modernity*. Durham, NC: Duke University Press.

Fraser, Nancy, and Linda Gordon. 1994. "A Genealogy of Dependency: Tracing a Keyword of the U.S. Welfare State." *Signs: Journal of Women in Culture and Society* 19 (21): 309–36.

Fuller, Christopher J. 2011a. "The Modern Transformation of an Old Elite: The Case of the Tamil Brahmans." In *A Companion to the Anthropology of India*, edited by Isabelle Clark-Decès, 80–98. Chichester, UK: Wiley-Blackwell.

Fuller, Christopher J. 2011b. "Timepass and Boredom in Modern India." *Anthropology of This Century*, no. 1 (May). http://aotcpress.com/articles/timepass-boredom/.

Gandolfo, Daniella. 2009. *The City at Its Limits: Taboo, Transgression, and Urban Renewal in Lima*. Chicago: University of Chicago Press.

Ganti, Tejaswini. 2014. "Neoliberalism." *Annual Review of Anthropology* 43:89–104.

Garayar, Carlos, Luis Jochamowitz, Sandro Patrucco, and Eduardo Jahnsen. 1997. *La hacienda en el Perú: Historia y leyenda*. Lima: Ediciones Peisa, Banco Latino.

García, María Elena. 2005. *Making Indigenous Citizens: Identity, Development, and Multicultural Activism in Peru*. Stanford, CA: Stanford University Press.

García, María Elena. 2010. "Super Guinea Pigs?" *Anthropology Now* 2 (2): 22–32.

García, María Elena. 2013. "The Taste of Conquest: Colonialism, Cosmopolitics, and the Dark Side of Peru's Gastronomic Boom." *Journal of Latin American and Caribbean Anthropology* 18 (3): 505–24.

García, María Elena. 2021. *Gastropolitics and the Specter of Race: Stories of Capital, Culture, and Coloniality in Peru*. Berkeley: University of California Press.

Garland Thomson, Rosemarie. 1997. *Extraordinary Bodies: Figuring Physical Disability in American Culture and Literature*. New York: Columbia University Press.

Gary, Ja'Tovia. 2018. "A Care Ethic." AD&A Museum UCSB, July 26, YouTube video, 1:19:45. https://www.youtube.com/watch?v=GZwVuvU-4Qg.

Geertz, Clifford. (1973) 2017. *The Interpretation of Cultures*. New York: Basic Books.

Getachew, Adom. 2019. *Worldmaking after Empire: The Rise and Fall of Self-Determination*. Princeton, NJ: Princeton University Press.

Ghassem-Fachandi, Parvis. 2010. "On the Politics of Disgust in Gujarat." *South Asian History and Culture* 1 (4): 557–76.

Ghosh, Amitav. 2016. *The Great Derangement: Climate Change and the Unthinkable*. Chicago: University of Chicago Press.

Gibson-Graham, J. K. 2006. *The End of Capitalism (As We Knew It): A Feminist Critique of Political Economy*. Minneapolis: University of Minnesota Press.

Giedion, Sigfried. 1948. *Mechanization Takes Command: A Contribution to Anonymous History*. London: Oxford University Press.

Gilbert, S. F., J. Sapp, and A. I. Tauber. 2012. "A Symbiotic View of Life: We Have Never Been Individuals." *Quarterly Review of Biology* 87 (4): 325–41.

Gilio-Whitaker, Dina. 2019. *As Long as Grass Grows: The Indigenous Fight for Environmental Justice, from Colonization to Standing Rock*. Boston: Beacon.

Gilmore, Ruth Wilson. 2007. *Golden Gulag: Prisons, Surplus, Crisis, and Opposition in Globalizing California*. Berkeley: University of California Press.

Gilroy, Paul. 2000. *Against Race: Imagining Political Culture beyond the Color Line*. Cambridge, MA: Harvard University Press.

Ginocchio Balcázar, Luis. 2012. *Pequeña agricultura y gastronomía: Oportunidades y desafíos*. Lima: Apega.

Ginsburg, Faye. 1995. "The Parallax Effect: The Impact of Aboriginal Media on Ethnographic Film." *Visual Anthropology Review* 11 (2): 64–76.

Glenn, Evelyn Nakano. 1992. "From Servitude to Service Work: Historical Continuities in the Racial Division of Paid Reproductive Labor." *Signs* 18 (1): 1–43.

Glissant, Édouard. 1997. *Poetics of Relation*. Translated by Betsy Wing. Ann Arbor: University of Michigan Press.

Goldman, Michael. 2011. "Speculating on the Next World City." In *Worlding Cities: Asian Experiments and the Art of Being Global*, edited by Aihwa Ong and Ananya Roy, 229–58. Boston: Wiley Blackwell.

Goldstein, Alyosha. 2016. "Promises Are Over: Puerto Rico and the Ends of Decolonization." *Theory and Event* 19 (4). https://muse.jhu.edu/article/633271.

Goodman, David, Bernardo Sorj, and John Wilkinson. 1987. *From Farming to Biotechnology: A Theory of Agro-industrial Development*. New York: Blackwell.

Goodman, David, and Michael Watts, eds. 1997. *Globalising Food: Agrarian Questions and Global Restructuring*. New York: Routledge.

Goodwin, Charles. 2004. "A Competent Speaker Who Can't Speak: The Social Life of Aphasia." *Journal of Linguistic Anthropology* 14 (2): 151–70.

Gordillo, Gastón. 2011. "Resonance and the Egyptian Revolution." *Critical Legal Thinking* (blog), February 22. http://criticallegalthinking.com/2011/02/22/resonance-and-the-egyptian-revolution/.

Gordon, Avery. 2008. *Ghostly Matters: Haunting and the Sociological Imagination*. Minneapolis: University of Minnesota Press.

Govindrajan, Radhika. 2021. "Labors of Love: On the Political Economies and Ethics of Bovine Politics in Himalayan India." *Cultural Anthropology* 36 (2): 193–21.

Gramsci, Antonio. 1971. "Americanism and Fordism." In *Selections from the Prison Notebooks*, translated and edited by Quintin Hoare and Geoffrey Nowell Smith, 277–318. New York: International.

Gray, Obika. 1991. *Radicalism and Social Change in Jamaica, 1960–1972*. Knoxville: University of Tennessee Press.

Gray, Obika. 2004. *Demeaned but Empowered: The Social Power of the Urban Poor in Jamaica*. Mona: University of the West Indies Press.

Greenberg, Jessica. 2014. *After the Revolution: Youth, Democracy, and the Politics of Disappointment in Serbia*. Stanford, CA: Stanford University Press.

Gregg, Melissa, and Gregory J. Seigworth, eds. 2010. *The Affect Theory Reader*. Durham, NC: Duke University Press.

Gross, Samuel D. 1854. *A Practical Treatise on Foreign Bodies in the Air-Passages*. Philadelphia: Blanchard and Lea.

Gudger, E. W. 1926. "Live Fishes Impacted in the Food and Air Passages of Man." *Archives of Pathology* 2 (September): 355.

Gudger, E. W. 1927. "Live Fishes Impacted in the Pharynx of Man: An Addendum." *Archives of Pathology* 4 (September): 36.

Gudger, E. W. 1933. "More Live Fishes Impacted in the Throats of Men." *American Journal of Surgery* 22 (3): 573–75.

Guerrero, Andrés. 1997. "The Construction of a Ventriloquist's Image: Liberal Discourse and the 'Miserable Indian Race' in Late 19th-Century Ecuador." *Journal of Latin American Studies* 29 (3): 555–90.

Gunther, Juan. 1992. "Las ciudades hablan." In *500 años después: El nuevo rostro del Perú*, edited by Hugo Guerra Arteaga, Alejandro Miró Quesada Cisneros, and Bernardo Roca Rey, 57–71. Perú: Nuevas Ideas.

Gupta, Akhil. 2012. *Red Tape: Bureaucracy, Structural Violence, and Poverty in India*. Durham, NC: Duke University Press.

Gupta, Akhil, and Aradhana Sharma. 2006. "Globalization and Postcolonial States." *Current Anthropology* 47 (2): 277–307.

Habermas, Jürgen. 1991. *The Structural Transformation of the Public Sphere: An Inquiry into the Categories of Bourgeois Society*. Translated by Thomas Burger. Cambridge, MA: MIT Press.

Hage, Ghassan. 2003. *Against Paranoid Nationalism: Searching for Hope in a Shrinking Society*. Sydney: Pluto.

Hale, Charles. 2002. "Does Multiculturalism Menace? Governance, Cultural Rights and the Politics of Identity in Guatemala." *Journal of Latin American Studies* 34 (3): 485–524.

Hale, Charles. 2004. "Rethinking Indigenous Politics in the Era of the 'Indio Permitido.'" *NACLA: Report on the Americas* 38 (2): 16–21.

Hale, Charles. 2005. "Neoliberal Multiculturalism: The Remaking of Cultural Rights and Racial Dominance in Central America." *Political and Legal Anthropology Review* 28 (1): 10–28.

Hale, Charles, and Rosamel Millaman. 2006. "Cultural Agency and Political Struggle in the Era of Indio Permitido." In *Cultural Agency in the Americas*, edited by Doris Sommer, 281–301. Durham, NC: Duke University Press.

Hall, Arthur. 2010. "Give Us Our Dead Boys, Say Residents." *Jamaica Gleaner*, June 1. http://jamaica-gleaner.com/gleaner/20100601/lead/lead2.html.

Hamilton, Jennifer A. 2009. *Indigeneity in the Courtroom: Law, Culture, and the Production of Difference in North American Courts*. New York: Routledge.

Hansen, Thomas Blom, and Finn Stepputat. 2006. "Sovereignty Revisited." *Annual Review of Anthropology* 35:295–315.

Hardt, Michael. 1999. "Affective Labor." *Boundary 2* 26 (2): 89–100.

Hardt, Michael. 2011. "For Love or Money." *Cultural Anthropology* 26 (4): 676–82.

Harmon, Alexandra. 2010. *Rich Indians: Native People and the Problem of Wealth in American History*. Chapel Hill: University of North Carolina Press.

Harney, Stefano, and Fred Moten. 2013. *The Undercommons: Fugitive Planning and Black Study*. New York: Autonomedia.

Harring, Sidney L. 2002. "Indian Law, Sovereignty, and State Law: Native People and the Law." In *A Companion to American Indian History*, edited by Philip J. Deloria and Neal Salisbury, 441–59. Malden, MA: Blackwell.

Harriott, Anthony, ed. 2004. *Understanding Crime in Jamaica: New Challenges for Public Policy*. Mona: University of the West Indies Press.

Harriott, Anthony. 2008. *Organized Crime and Politics in Jamaica: Breaking the Nexus*. Kingston: Canoe.

Hartman, Saidiya. 1997. *Scenes of Subjection: Terror, Slavery, and Self-Making in Nineteenth-Century America*. Oxford: Oxford University Press.

Hartman, Saidiya. 2007. *Lose Your Mother: A Journey along the Atlantic Slave Route*. New York: Farrar, Straus and Giroux.

Hartung, William. 2018. "How the Pentagon Devours the Budget." *TomDispatch*, February 27. https://www.tomdispatch.com/william-hartung-the-pentagon-budget-as-corporate-welfare-for-weapons-makers/.

Haug, Wolfgang Fritz. 1986. *Critique of Commodity Aesthetics: Appearance, Sexuality, and Advertising in Capitalist Society*. Translated by Robert Bock. New York: Polity.

Hau'ofa, Epeli. 1993. "Our Sea of Islands." In *A New Oceania: Rediscovering Our Sea of Islands*, edited by Vijay Naidu, Eric Waddell, and Epeli Hau'ofa, 2–16. Suva: School of Social and Economic Development, University of the South Pacific.

Heidegger, Martin. 1971. *Poetry, Language, Thought*. Translated by Albert Hofstadter. New York: Harper and Row.

Hernández, Kelly Lytle. 2017. *City of Inmates: Conquest, Rebellion, and the Rise of Human Caging in Los Angeles, 1771–1965*. Chapel Hill: University of North Carolina Press.

Highmore, Ben. 2010. "Bitter after Taste: Affect, Food, and Social Aesthetics." In *The Affect Theory Reader*, edited by Melissa Gregg and Gregory J. Seigworth, 118–37. Durham, NC: Duke University Press.

Hinostroza, Rodolfo. 2006. *Primicias de cocina peruana*. León, Spain: Everest.

Hinsley, Francis Harry. 1986. *Sovereignty*. 2nd ed. Cambridge: Cambridge University Press.

Hinton, Elizabeth. 2016. *From the War on Poverty to the War on Crime: The Making of Mass Incarceration in America*. Cambridge, MA: Harvard University Press.

Holland, Sharon. 2000. *Raising the Dead: Readings of Death and (Black) Subjectivity*. Durham, NC: Duke University Press.

Hooke, Robert. 1667. "An account of an experiment made by M. Hook [sic], of preserving animals alive by blowing through their lungs with bellows." *Philosophical Transactions of the Royal Society of London* 2:539–40.

hooks, bell. 2000. *All about Love: New Visions*. New York: Doubleday.

Hooper, Peter, Matthew Luzetti, Brett Ryan, Justin Weidner, Torsten Slok, and Rajsekhar Bhattacharyya. 2018. *U.S. Income and Wealth Inequality*. New York: Deutsche Bank Research.

Horowitz, Roger. 2006. *Putting Meat on the American Table: Taste, Technology, Transformation*. Baltimore, MD: Johns Hopkins University Press.

Horowitz, Roger. 2008. "'That Was a Dirty Job!': Technology and Workplace Hazards in Meatpacking over the Long Twentieth Century." *Labor* 5 (2): 13–25.

Hounshell, David. 1984. *From the American System to Mass Production, 1800–1932: The Development of Manufacturing Technology in the United States*. Baltimore, MD: Johns Hopkins University Press.

Human Rights Watch. 2005. *Blood, Sweat, and Fear: Workers' Rights in U.S. Meat and Poultry Plants*. Report. https://www.hrw.org/report/2005/01/24/blood-sweat-and -fear/workers-rights-us-meat-and-poultry-plants#.

Hume, Yanique. 2018. "Death and the Construction of Social Space: Land, Kinship and Identity in the Jamaican Mortuary Cycle." In *Passages and Afterwords: Anthropological Perspectives on Death in the Caribbean*, edited by Maarit Forde and Yanique Hume, 109–38. Durham, NC: Duke University Press.

Hurston, Zora Neale. (1938) 1990. *Tell My Horse: Voodoo and Life in Haiti and Jamaica*. New York: Perennial Library.

Illouz, Eva. 2007. *Cold Intimacies: The Making of Emotional Capitalism*. Malden, MA: Polity.

Ingersoll, Karin Amimoto. 2016. *Waves of Knowing: A Seascape Epistemology*. Durham, NC: Duke University Press.

IPCC. 2018. "Summary for Policymakers." In *Special Report: Global Warming of 1.5°C.* Geneva: Intergovernmental Panel on Climate Change.

Jackson, Chevalier. 1938. *The Life of Chevalier Jackson: An Autobiography.* New York: Macmillan.

Jackson, John. 2010. "On Ethnographic Sincerity." *Current Anthropology* 51 (S2): S279–87.

Jackson, John L., Jr. 2013. *Thin Description.* Cambridge, MA: Harvard University Press.

Jackson, Vicki C. 1997. "Seminole Tribe, the Eleventh Amendment, and the Potential Evisceration of Ex Parte Young." *New York University Law Review* 72 (3): 495–546.

Jaffe, Rivke. 2013. "The Hybrid State: Crime and Citizenship in Urban Jamaica." *American Ethnologist* 40 (4): 734–48.

Jain, Lochlann. 2006. *Injury: The Politics of Product Design and Safety Law in the United States.* Princeton, NJ: Princeton University Press.

Jain, Lochlann. 2013. *Malignant: How Cancer Becomes Us.* Berkeley: University of California Press.

Jamaica Gleaner. 2010a. "Autopsy Nightmare, Says Observer." June 17. https://www .jamaica-gleaner.com/gleaner/20100617/lead/lead4.html.

Jamaica Gleaner. 2010b. "Echoes from the Morgue." June 20, A8.

Jamaica Gleaner. 2010c. "Hitches in Tivoli Autopsies." June 15. https://www.jamaica -gleaner.com/power/20208.

Jamaica Gleaner. 2017. "Training Ja's New Leaders in Forensic Pathology—Children of Late Philanthropist G. Raymond Chang Honour His Legacy." July 16. https:// jamaica-gleaner.com/print/671513.

Jamaica Gleaner. 2018. "Editorial: Need Deeper Analysis of States of Emergency." September 26. https://jamaica-gleaner.com/article/commentary/20180926/editorial -need-deeper-analysis-states-emergency.

Jeffrey, Craig. 2010. *Timepass: Youth, Class and the Politics of Waiting.* Stanford, CA: Stanford University Press.

Jenkins, Barry, dir. 2008. *Medicine for Melancholy.* IFC Films.

Jones, Mark R., Omar Viswanath, Jacquelin Peck, Alan D. Kaye, Jatinder S. Gill, and Thomas T. Simopoulos. 2018. "A Brief History of the Opioid Epidemic and Strategies for Pain Medicine." *Pain Therapy* 7 (1): 13–21.

Kaplan, Caren. 2003. "Transporting the Subject: Technologies of Mobility and Location in an Era of Globalization." In *Uprootings/Regroundings: Questions of Home and Migration,* edited by Sara Ahmed, Claudia Castaneda, Anne-Marie Fortier, and Mimi Sheller, 207–24. London: Berg.

Karuka, Manu. 2019. *Empire's Tracks: Indigenous Nations, Chinese Workers, and the Transcontinental Railroad.* Berkeley: University of California Press.

Kaufman, Sharon R., and Lynn M. Morgan. 2005. "The Anthropology of the Beginnings and Ends of Life." *Annual Review of Anthropology* 34:317–41.

Keane, Webb. 1996. *Signs of Recognition.* Berkeley: University of California Press.

Keefe, Patrick Radden. 2017. "The Family That Built an Empire of Pain." *New Yorker,* October 30.

Kempadoo, Roshini. 2008. "Amendments: A Fictional Re-imagining of the Trinidad Archive." *Journal of Media Practice* 9 (2): 87–99.

Kenner, Alison. 2018. *Breathtaking: Asthma Care in a Time of Climate Change*. Minneapolis: University of Minnesota Press.

Ketchley, Neil. 2017. *Egypt in a Time of Revolution: Contentious Politics and the Arab Spring*. Cambridge: Cambridge University Press.

King, Tiffany Lethabo. 2019. *The Black Shoals: Offshore Formations of Black and Native Studies*. Durham, NC: Duke University Press.

Kirwan, Laura, and Daniel McCool. 2001. "Negotiated Water Settlements: Environmentalists and American Indians." In *Trusteeship in Change toward Tribal Autonomy in Resource Management*, edited by Richmond Clow and Imre Sutton, 265–80. Boulder: University Press of Colorado.

Kittay, Eve Feder. 1999. *Love's Labor: Essays on Women, Equality, and Dependency*. New York: Routledge.

Klinenberg, Eric. 2001. "Bodies That Don't Matter: Death and Dereliction in Chicago." *Body and Society* 7 (2–3): 121–36.

Klinenberg, Eric. 2002. *Heat Wave: A Social Autopsy of Disaster in Chicago*. Chicago: University of Chicago Press.

Kollenda, Heidi. 2019. "From Farm to Table: Productive Alliances as a Pathway to Inclusive Development in Peru." *Anthropology of Food* 14. https://www.bloomberg.com/news/articles/2016-10-19/latin-america-s-best-chef-will-open-a-restaurant-at-the-top-of-the-world.

Kumar, Krishna, and Padma Sarangapani. 2004. "History of the Quality Debate." *Contemporary Education Dialogue* 2 (1): 30–52.

Laski, Harold J. 1917. *Studies in the Problem of Sovereignty*. New Haven, CT: Yale University Press.

LeDuff, Charlie. 2000. "At a Slaughterhouse, Some Things Never Die." *New York Times*, June 16.

Lee, Paula Young. 2008. *Meat, Modernity, and the Rise of the Slaughterhouse*. Lebanon, NH: University of New Hampshire Press.

Lewis, Courtney. 2019. *Sovereign Entrepreneurs: Cherokee Small-Business Owners and the Making of Economic Sovereignty*. Chapel Hill: University of North Carolina Press.

Lipsitz, George. 2006. *The Possessive Investment in Whiteness*. Philadelphia: Temple University Press.

Livingston, Julie. 2008. "Disgust, Bodily Aesthetics and the Ethic of Being Human in Botswana." *Africa* 78 (2): 288–307.

Lorde, Audre. 1980. *The Cancer Journals*. San Francisco: Aunt Lute.

Lorde, Audre. 1984. *Sister Outsider: Essays and Speeches*. Trumansburg, NY: Crossing.

Lowe, Lisa. 1996. *Immigrant Acts: On Asian American Cultural Politics*. Durham, NC: Duke University Press.

Lower, Richard. 1667. "An account of making a dogg [*sic*] draw his breath exactly like a wind-broken, horse as it was devised and experimented by Dr. Richard Lower; with some of his instructive observations thereon." *Philosophical Transactions of the Royal Society of London* 2 (28): 544–46.

Lugones, Maria. 2007. "Heterosexualism and the Colonial/Modern Gender System." *Hypatia* 22 (1): 186–219.

Maaka, Roger, and Augie Fleras. 2005. *The Politics of Indigeneity: Challenging the State in Canada and Aotearoa New Zealand*. Dunedin, New Zealand: University of Otago Press.

MacLean, Nancy. 2017. *Democracy in Chains*. New York: Viking.

Malmström, Maria Frederika. 2019. *The Streets Are Talking to Me: Affective Fragments in Sisi's Egypt*. Oakland: University of California Press.

Mankekar, Purnima. 2004. "Dangerous Desires: Television and Erotics in Late Twentieth-Century India." *Journal of Asian Studies* 63 (2): 403–31.

Mankekar, Purnima. 2015. *Unsettling India: Affect, Temporality, Transnationality*. Durham, NC: Duke University Press.

Mankekar, Purnima, and Akhil Gupta. 2016. "Intimate Encounters: Affective Labor in Call Centers." *Positions* 24 (1): 17–43.

Mankekar, Purnima, and Akhil Gupta. 2017. "Future Tense: Capital, Labor, and Technology in a Service Industry (The 2017 Lewis Henry Morgan Lecture)." *HAU: Journal of Ethnographic Theory* 7 (3): 67–87.

Mankekar, Purnima, and Akhil Gupta. 2019. "The Missed Period: Disjunctive Temporalities and the Work of Capital in an Indian BPO." *American Ethnologist* 46 (4): 1–12.

Mankekar, Purnima, and Akhil Gupta. Forthcoming. *Future Tense: Capital, Labor, and Technology in India's BPO Industry*. Durham, NC: Duke University Press.

Mann, Steve. 2004. "'Sousveillance': Inverse Surveillance in Multimedia Imaging." In *Multimedia '04: Proceedings of the 12th Annual ACM International Conference on Multimedia*, 620–27. New York: Association for Computing Machinery. https://doi.org/10.1145/1027527.1027673.

Marca Perú. 2011. "Documental Marca Perú 2011." May 12, YouTube video, 14:59. https://www.youtube.com/watch?v=8joXlwKMkrk.

Marcus, Sara. 2019. "'Time Enough, but None to Spare': The Indispensable Temporalities of Charles Chesnutt's *The Marrow of Tradition*." *American Literature* 91 (1): 31–58.

Markell, Patchen. 2003. *Bound by Recognition*. Princeton, NJ: Princeton University Press.

Marshall, Josh. 2020. "PPE and Ventilators Becomes Patronage in Trump's Hands." *Talking Points Memo*, April 9. https://talkingpointsmemo.com/edblog/ppe-and-ventilators-becomes-patronage-in-trumps-hands.

Martel, James. 2008. "Amo: Volo ut Sis: Love, Willing and Arendt's Reluctant Embrace of Sovereignty." *Philosophy and Social Criticism* 34 (3): 287–313.

Martínez Mercado, Eliván. 2020. "Puerto Rico Never Set Up an Information Network to Gather Data on COVID-19." *Centro de Periodismo Investigativo*, May 4. https://periodismoinvestigativo.com/2020/05/puerto-rico-never-set-up-an-information-network-to-gather-data-on-covid-19/.

Martuccelli, Danilo. 2015. *Lima y sus arenas: Poderes sociales y jerarquías culturales*. Lima: Biblioteca Nacional del Perú.

Marx, Karl. 1992. *Capital: A Critique of Political Economy*, vol. 1. Translated by Ben Fowkes. London: Penguin Classics.

Masco, Joseph. 2014. *The Theater of Operations: National Security Affect from the Cold War to the War on Terror*. Durham, NC: Duke University Press.

Masco, Joseph. 2017. "The Crisis in Crisis." *Current Anthropology* 58 (Suppl. 15): S65–S76.

Masco, Joseph. 2020. *The Future of Fallout and Other Episodes in Radioactive World-Making*. Durham, NC: Duke University Press.

Massad, Joseph. 2013. "Love, Fear, and the Arab Spring." *Public Culture* 26 (1): 127–52.

Massey, Doreen. 1994. *Space, Place, and Gender*. Minneapolis: University of Minnesota Press.

Massumi, Brian, ed. 1993. *The Politics of Everyday Fear*. Minneapolis: University of Minnesota Press.

Massumi, Brian. 2002. *Parables for the Virtual: Movement, Affect, Sensation*. Durham, NC: Duke University Press.

Matos Mar, José. 1984. *Desborde popular y crisis del estado: El nuevo rostro del Perú en la década de 1980*. Lima: IEP.

Mayer, Enrique. 2009. *Ugly Stories of the Peruvian Agrarian Reform*. Durham, NC: Duke University Press.

Mayer, Jane. 2016. *Dark Money*. New York: Anchor.

Mazza, Ed. 2020. "Jared Kushner Ripped for Saying 'Our Stockpile' Isn't Meant for States to Use." *HuffPost*, April 3. https://www.huffpost.com/entry/jared-kushner-stockpile_n_5e86dca8c5b6a949183425ca.

Mazzarella, William. 2010. "Beautiful Balloon: The Digital Divide and the Charisma of New Media in India." *American Ethnologist* 37 (4): 783–804.

Mazzei, Patricia. 2020. "Puerto Rico Lags Behind Everywhere Else in US in Virus Testing." *New York Times*, April 21. https://www.nytimes.com/2020/04/21/us/puerto-rico-coronavirus.html.

Mbembe, Achille. 2003. "Necropolitics." *Public Culture* 15 (1): 11–40.

Mbembe, Achille. 2019. *Necropolitics*. Durham, NC: Duke University Press.

McGranahan, Carol. 2016. "Theorizing Refusal: An Introduction." *Cultural Anthropology* 31 (3): 319–25.

McGreal, Chris. 2018. *American Overdose: The Opioid Tragedy in Three Acts*. New York: Public Affairs.

Mead, George Herbert. 1965. "Self." In *The Social Psychology of George Herbert Mead*, edited by Anselm Strauss, 199–246. Chicago: University of Chicago Press.

Melamed, Jodi. 2011. *Represent and Destroy: Rationalizing Violence in the New Racial Capitalism*. Minneapolis: University of Minnesota Press.

Melgarejo, Víctor. 2019. "Apega: 'Mistura 2019 será fuera de Lima.'" *Gestión*, January 14.

Menninghaus, Winfried. 2003. *Disgust: The Theory and History of a Strong Sensation*. Albany: State University of New York Press.

Metcalf, Peter, and Richard Huntington. 1991. *Celebrations of Death: The Anthropology of Mortuary Ritual*. 2nd ed. Cambridge: Cambridge University Press.

Metzl, Jonathan. 2011. *The Protest Psychosis: How Schizophrenia Became a Black Disease*. Boston: Beacon.

Metzl, Jonathan. 2019. *Dying of Whiteness: How the Politics of Racial Resentment Is Killing America's Heartland*. New York: Basic Books.

Mignolo, Walter. 2011. *The Darker Side of Modernity: Global Futures, Decolonial Options*. Durham, NC: Duke University Press.

Miller, William Ian. 1997. *The Anatomy of Disgust*. Cambridge, MA: Harvard University Press.

Milton, Cynthia. 2014. *Art from a Fractured Past: Memory and Truth-Telling in Post-Shining Path Peru*. Durham, NC: Duke University Press.

Milton, Cynthia. 2018. *Conflicted Memory: Military Cultural Interventions and the Human Rights Era in Peru*. Madison: University of Wisconsin Press.

Mines, Diane, and Nicolas Yazgi. 2010. *Village Matters: Relocating Villages in the Contemporary Anthropology of India*. Oxford: Oxford University Press.

Mirchandani, Kiran. 2012. *Phone Clones: Authenticity Work in the Transnational Service Economy*. Ithaca, NY: Cornell University Press.

Mirzoeff, Nicholas. 2011. *The Right to Look: A Counterhistory of Visuality*. Durham, NC: Duke University Press.

Miyazaki, Hirokazu. 2005. "From Sugar Cane to 'Swords': Hope and the Extensibility of the Gift in Fiji." *Journal of the Royal Anthropological Institute* 11 (2): 277–95.

Mooney, Chris, and Brady Dennis. 2019. "U.S. Greenhouse Gas Emissions Spiked in 2018—and It Couldn't Happen at a Worse Time." *Washington Post*, January 8.

Moreton-Robinson, Aileen. 2007. "Introduction." In *Sovereign Subjects: Indigenous Sovereignty Matters*, edited by Aileen Moreton-Robinson, 1–11. Crows Nest, Australia: Allen and Unwin.

Morrison, Toni. 1994. *The Nobel Lecture in Literature, 1993*. New York: Alfred A. Knopf.

Mosse, David. 2008. "Epilogue: The Cultural Politics of Water: A Comparative Perspective." *Journal of Southern African Studies* 34 (4): 939–48.

Moten, Fred. 2013. "The Subprime and the Beautiful." *African Identities* 11 (2): 237–45.

Moten, Fred. 2017. *Black and Blur*. Durham, NC: Duke University Press.

Moten, Fred, and Stefano Harney. 2020. "The University, Last Words." July 9, YouTube video, 1:55:25. https://www.youtube.com/watch?v=zqWMejD_XU8.

Muehlebach, Andrea, and Nitzan Shoshan. 2012. "Post-Fordist Affect: Introduction." *Anthropological Quarterly* 85 (2): 317–43.

Munroe, Trevor. 1972. *The Politics of Constitutional Democratization, 1944–1962*. Mona: Institute for Social and Economic Research, University of the West Indies.

Murphy, Michelle. 2017a. "Alterlife and Decolonial Chemical Relations." *Cultural Anthropology* 32 (4): 494–503.

Murphy, Michelle. 2017b. *The Economization of Life*. Durham, NC: Duke University Press.

Nadasdy, Paul. 2017. *Sovereignty's Entailments: First Nation State Formation in the Yukon*. Toronto: University of Toronto Press.

Nadeem, Shehzad. 2013. *Dead Ringers: How Outsourcing Is Changing the Way Indians Understand Themselves*. Princeton, NJ: Princeton University Press.

Nott, Josiah, and Samuel Gliddon. 1854. *Types of Mankind: Or, Ethnological Researches Based Upon the Ancient Monuments, Paintings, Sculptures, and Crania of Races, and Upon Their Natural, Geographical, Philological and Biblical History*. Philadelphia: J. B. Lippincott, Grambo & Co.

Nouvet, Elysee. 2014. "Some Carry On, Some Stay in Bed: (In)convenient Affects and Agency in Neoliberal Nicaragua." *Cultural Anthropology* 29 (1): 80–102.

Nussbaum, Martha. 2010. *From Disgust to Humanity: Sexual Orientation and Constitutional Law*. Oxford: Oxford University Press.

Occupational Safety and Health Administration. 1993. "Ergonomics Program Management Guidelines for Meatpacking Plants." OSHA 3123. https://www.osha.gov/Publications/OSHA3123.

Ochs, Elinor. 2012. "Experiencing Language." *Anthropological Theory* 12 (2): 142–60.

Ochs, Elinor, Olga Solomon, and Laura Sterponi. 2005. "Limitations and Transformations of Habitus in Child-Directed Communication." *Discourse Studies* 7 (4–5): 546–83.

Ogden, Laura. 2011. *Swamplife: People, Gators, and Mangroves Entangled in the Everglades*. Minneapolis: University of Minnesota Press.

Olsson, Göran. 2011. *The Black Power Mixtape: 1967–1975*. Louverture Films.

Ong, Aihwa. 1987. *Spirits of Resistance and Capitalist Discipline: Factory Women in Malaysia*. Albany: State University of New York Press.

Ong, Aihwa. 2006. *Neoliberalism as Exception: Mutations in Citizenship and Sovereignty*. Durham, NC: Duke University Press.

Oreskes, Naomi, and Eric Conway. 2010. *Merchants of Doubt*. Boston: Bloomsbury.

Ortner, Sherry. 1995a. "The Case of the Disappearing Shamans, or No Individualism, No Relationalism." *Ethos* 23 (3): 355–90.

Ortner, Sherry. 1995b. "Resistance and the Project of Ethnographic Refusal." *Comparative Studies in Society and History* 37 (1): 173–93.

Oxfam America. 2016. *No Relief: Denial of Bathroom Breaks in the Poultry Industry*. Oxfam Report, May 9. https://www.oxfamamerica.org/explore/research-publications/no-relief/.

Pacheco Velez, Cesar. 1985. *Memoria y utopía de la vieja Lima*. Lima: Universidad del Pacífico.

Pachirat, Timothy. 2011. *Every Twelve Seconds: Industrialized Slaughter and the Politics of Sight*. New Haven, CT: Yale University Press.

Packer, George. 2020. "We Are Living in a Failed State." *Atlantic*, June.

Padios, Jan. 2018. *A Nation on the Line: Call Centers as Postcolonial Predicaments in the Philippines*. Durham, NC: Duke University Press.

Palma, Ricardo. 1923. *Tradiciones peruanas*. Madrid: Calpe.

Palumbo-Liu, David. 1999. *Asian/American: Historical Crossings of a Racial Frontier*. Stanford, CA: Stanford University Press.

Parker, David. 1998a. "Civilizing the City of Kings: Hygiene and Housing in Lima, Peru." In *Cities of Hope: People, Protests, and Progress in Urbanizing Latin America, 1870–1930*, edited by Ronn Pineo and James A. Baer, 153–78. Boulder, CO: Westview.

Parker, David. 1998b. *The Idea of the Middle Class: White-Collar Workers and Peruvian Society, 1900–1950*. University Park: Pennsylvania State University Press.

Patel, Reena. 2010. *Working the Night Shift: Women in India's Call Center Industry*. Stanford, CA: Stanford University Press.

Peña, Devon Gerardo. 1997. *The Terror of the Machine: Technology, Work, Gender, and Ecology on the U.S.-Mexico Border*. Austin: Center for Mexican American Studies, University of Texas.

Pérez, Patricia, dir. 2011. *Mistura: The Power of Food*. Lima: Chiwake Films.

Pérez, Patricia, dir. 2014. *Buscando a Gastón*. Lima: Chiwake Films.

Peru. n.d. "The Generation with a Cause." *New York Times.* https://www.nytimes.com
/paidpost/peru/the-generation-with-a-cause.html.

Pilkington, Ed. 2019. "US Halts Cooperation with UN on Potential Human Rights
Violations." *Guardian*, January 4.

Plakias, Alexandra. 2013. "The Good and the Gross." *Ethical Theory and Moral Practice* 16 (2): 261–78.

Poovey, Mary. 1998. *A History of the Modern Fact: Problems of Knowledge in the Sciences of Wealth and Society.* Chicago: University of Chicago Press.

Popovich, Nadja, Livia Albeck-Ripka, and Kendra Pierre-Louis. 2018. "78 Environmental Rules on the Way Out under Trump." *New York Times*, December 28.

Portocarrero Maisch, Gonzalo. 2003. "Memorias del Velasquismo." In *Batallas por la
memoria: Antagonismos de la promesa peruana*, edited by Marita Hamann, Santiago López Maguíña, Gonzalo Portocarrero Maisch, and Víctor Vich. Lima: Red
para el Desarrollo de las Ciencias Sociales en el Perú.

Portocarrero Maisch, Gonzalo. 2007. *Racismo y mestizaje y otros ensayos.* Lima: Fondo
Editorial del Congreso del Perú.

Portocarrero Maisch, Gonzalo, ed. 2013. *Sombras coloniales y globalización en el Perú
de hoy.* Lima: Fondo Editorial, Pontificia Universidad Católica del Perú, Universidad del Pacífico and IEP.

Povinelli, Elizabeth A. 2002. *The Cunning of Recognition: Indigenous Alterities
and the Making of Australian Multiculturalism.* Durham, NC: Duke University Press.

Povinelli, Elizabeth A. 2006. *The Empire of Love: Toward a Theory of Intimacy, Genealogy, and Carnality.* Durham, NC: Duke University Press.

Povinelli, Elizabeth. 2011. *Economies of Abandonment.* Durham, NC: Duke University
Press.

Powell, Dana E. 2018. *Landscapes of Power: Politics of Energy in the Navajo Nation.*
Durham, NC: Duke University Press.

Protzel, Javier. 2011. *Lima imaginada.* Lima: Universidad de Lima, Fondo Editorial.

Quijano, Aníbal. 2000. "Coloniality of Power, Eurocentrism, and Latin America."
Nepantla: Views from the South 1 (3): 533–80.

Quinlan Crittenden, Janet. 1986. "Gudger, Eugene Willis." *NCPedia.* https://www
.ncpedia.org/biography/gudger-eugene-willis.

Rachleff, Peter J. 1993. *Hard-Pressed in the Heartland: The Hormel Strike and the Future
of the Labor Movement.* Boston: South End.

Rafael, Vicente L. 1992. *Contracting Colonialism: Translation and Christian Conversion in Tagalog under Early Spanish Rule.* Durham, NC: Duke University Press.

Ralph, Michael. 2015. *Forensics of Capital.* Chicago: University of Chicago Press.

Rao, Mohith M. 2017. "What Leaves Bengaluru's Washing Machines Ends Up in Its
Lakes, and Dinner Plates." *The Hindu*, June 10. https://www.thehindu.com/sci-tech
/energy-and-environment/more-than-a-bit-of-froth/article18936458.ece.

Ribas, Vanesa. 2016. *On the Line: Slaughterhouse Lives and the Making of the New
South.* Berkeley: University of California Press.

Rich, Steven, and John Woodrow Cox. 2018. "What If Someone Was Shooting?"
Washington Post, December 26.

Rifkin, Mark. 2009. "Indigenizing Agamben: Rethinking Sovereignty in Light of the 'Peculiar' Status of Native Peoples." *Cultural Critique*, no. 73 (Fall): 88–124.

Risling Baldy, Cutcha, and Melanie K. Yazzie, eds. 2018. "Indigenous Peoples and the Politics of Water." Special issue, *Decolonization: Indigeneity, Education and Society* 7 (1).

Roberts, Neil. 2015. *Freedom as Marronage*. Chicago: University of Chicago Press.

Rojas-Perez, Isaías. 2017. *Mourning Remains: State Atrocity, Exhumations, and Governing the Disappeared in Peru's Postwar Andes*. Stanford, CA: Stanford University Press.

Rosenthal, E. Lee, Paige Menking, and Mae-Gilene Begay. 2020. "Fighting the COVID-19 Merciless Monster: Lives on the Line—Community Health Representatives' Roles in the Pandemic Battle on the Navajo Nation." *Journal of Ambulatory Care Management* 43 (4): 301–5.

Roshini Kempadoo. 2016. "Spectres in the Postcolonies: Reimagining Violence and Resistance." In *Visualising Slavery: Art across the African Diaspora*, edited by Hannah Durkin and Celeste-Marie Bernier, 48–61. Liverpool: Liverpool University Press.

Rothstein, Richard. 2018. *The Color of Law: A Forgotten History of How Our Government Segregated America*. New York: Liveright.

RPP Noticias. 2019. "'La revolución y la tierra' ya es el documental más visto de la historia del cine peruano." October 30. https://rpp.pe/cine/peru/la-revolucion-y-la-tierra -se-convirtio-en-el-documental-mas-visto-del-cine-peruano-noticia-1227088.

Rutherford, Danilyn. 2003. *Raiding the Land of the Foreigners: The Limits of the Nation on an Indonesian Frontier*. Princeton, NJ: Princeton University Press.

Rutherford, Danilyn. 2009. "Sympathy, State-Building, and the Experience of Empire." *Cultural Anthropology* 24 (1): 1–32.

Rutherford, Danilyn. 2012. *Laughing at Leviathan: Sovereignty and Audience in West Papua*. Chicago: University of Chicago Press.

Rutherford, Danilyn. 2015. "Demonstrating the Stone-Age in Dutch New Guinea." In *From "Stone Age" to "Real-Time": Exploring Papuan Temporalities, Mobilities, and Religiosities*, edited by Martin Slama and Jenny Munroe, 39–58. Canberra: ANU Press.

Rutherford, Danilyn. 2018. *Living in the Stone Age: Reflections on the Origins of a Colonial Fantasy*. Chicago: University of Chicago Press.

Saad, Reem. 2012. "The Egyptian Revolution: A Triumph of Poetry." *American Ethnologist* 39 (1): 63–66.

Sabea, Hanan. 2011. "'A Time Out of Time': Tahrir, the Political, and the Imaginary in the Context of the January 25th Revolution in Egypt." Hot Spot, *Fieldsights*, May 9. https://culanth.org/fieldsights/a-time-out-of-time-tahrir-the-political-and -the-imaginary-in-the-context-of-the-january-25th-revolution-in-egypt.

Salazar Bondy, Sebastián. 1964. *Lima la horrible*. Lima: Ediciones PEISA.

Saldaña-Portillo, María Josefina. 2003. *The Revolutionary Imagination in the Americas and the Age of Development*. Durham, NC: Duke University Press.

Salecl, Renata. 1998. *(Per)versions of Love and Hate*. London: Verso.

Sanders, James. 2014. *The Vanguard of the Atlantic World: Creating Modernity, Nation, and Democracy in Nineteenth-Century Latin America*. Durham, NC: Duke University Press.

Sandoval, Chela. 2000. *Methodology of the Oppressed*. Minneapolis: University of Minnesota Press.

Sanger, David E., Zolan Kanno-Youngs, and Nicholas Kulish. 2020. "A Ventilator Stockpile, with One Hitch: Thousands Do Not Work." *New York Times*, April 1. https://www.nytimes.com/2020/04/01/us/politics/coronavirus-ventilators.html.

Sanjinés, Javier. 2004. *Mestizaje Upside-Down: Aesthetic Politics in Modern Bolivia*. Pittsburgh: University of Pittsburgh Press.

Schlosser, Eric. 2001. *Fast Food Nation: The Dark Side of the All-American Meal*. New York: Perennial.

Schmidt, Jeremy J. 2017. *Water: Abundance, Scarcity, and Security in the Age of Humanity*. New York: New York University Press.

Schmidt, Jeremy J., and Nathanial Matthews. 2017. *Global Challenges in Water Governance: Environments, Economies, Societies*. Cham: Palgrave Macmillan.

Scholl, L., P. Seth, M. Kariisa, N. Wilson, and G. Baldwin. 2019. "Drug and Opioid-Involved Overdose Deaths—United States, 2013–2017." *MMWR* 67 (5152): 1419–27.

Schüll, Natasha Dow. 2012. *Addiction by Design: Machine Gambling in Las Vegas*. Princeton, NJ: Princeton University Press.

Schuster, Caroline. 2015. "Your Family and Friends Are Collateral: Microfinance and the Social." Theorizing the Contemporary, *Fieldsights*, March 30. https://culanth.org/fieldsights/your-family-and-friends-are-collateral-microfinance-and-the-social.

Schwirtz, Michael. 2020. "The 1,000-Bed Comfort Was Supposed to Aid New York. It Has 20 Patients." *New York Times*, April 2; updated September 6, 2021. https://www.nytimes.com/2020/04/02/nyregion/ny-coronavirus-usns-comfort.html.

Scott, David. 2007. "Preface: Soul Captives Are Free." *Small Axe* 11 (2): v–x.

Sedgwick, Eve Kosofsky. 2003. *Touching Feeling: Affect, Pedagogy, Performativity*. Durham, NC: Duke University Press.

Seremetakis, C. Nadia. 1990. "The Ethics of Antiphony: The Social Construction of Pain, Gender, and Power in the Southern Peloponnese." *Ethos* 18 (4): 481–511.

Shange, Savannah. 2019. *Progressive Dystopia: Abolition, Antiblackness, and Schooling in San Francisco*. Durham, NC: Duke University Press.

Shapin, Steve, and Simon Schaffer. 2017. *Leviathan and the Air Pump: Hobbes, Boyle, and the Experimental Life*. Princeton, NJ: Princeton University Press.

Sharp, Lesley. 2013. *The Transplant Imaginary: Mechanical Hearts, Animal Parts, and Moral Thinking in Highly Experimental Science*. Berkeley: University of California Press.

Sharpe, Christina. 2016. *In the Wake: On Blackness and Being*. Durham, NC: Duke University Press.

Shore, Jim, and Jerry C. Straus. 1990. "The Seminole Water Rights Compact and the Seminole Indian Land Claims Settlement Act of 1987." *Journal of Land Use and Environmental Law* 6 (1): 1–24.

Shoshan, Nitzan. 2016. *The Management of Hate: Nation, Affect, and the Governance of Right-Wing Extremism in Germany*. Princeton, NJ: Princeton University Press.

Shukin, Nicole. 2009. *Animal Capital: Rendering Life in Biopolitical Times*. Minneapolis: University of Minnesota Press.

Siegel, James T. 1998. *A New Criminal Type in Jakarta: Counter-revolution Today.* Durham, NC: Duke University Press.

Simien, Justin, dir. 2017. *Dear White People.* Lionsgate.

Simpson, Audra. 2007. "On Ethnographic Refusal: Indigeneity, 'Voice,' and Colonial Citizenship." *Junctures* 9 (December): 67–80.

Simpson, Audra. 2014. *Mohawk Interruptus.* Durham, NC: Duke University Press.

Simpson, Leanne. 2013. *Islands of Decolonial Love.* Winnepeg: ARP.

Sinclair, Upton. (1906) 2006. *The Jungle.* London: Penguin Classics.

Sloterdijk, Peter. 2009. *Terror from the Air.* Cambridge, MA: MIT Press.

Sobo, Elisa. 1993. *One Blood: The Jamaican Body.* Albany: State University of New York Press.

Speed, Shannon. 2019. *Incarcerated Stories: Indigenous Women Migrants and Violence in the Settler-Capitalist State.* Chapel Hill: University of North Carolina Press.

Spillers, Hortense J. 1987. "Mama's Baby, Papa's Maybe: An American Grammar Book." *diacritics* 17 (2): 65–81.

Spinoza, Baruch. 2002. *Spinoza: The Complete Works.* Translated by Samuel Shirley and others. Indianapolis, IN: Hackett.

Staiger, Janet, Anne Cvetkovich, and Ann Reynolds, eds. 2010. *Political Emotions: New Agendas in Communication.* New York: Routledge.

Stein, Jeff. 2018. "U.S. Military Budget Inches Closer to $1 Trillion Mark, as Concerns over Federal Deficit Grow." *Washington Post*, June 19.

Stepan, Nancy Leys. 1991. *The Hour of Eugenics: Race, Gender, and Nation in Latin America.* Ithaca, NY: Cornell University Press.

Stevenson, Lisa. 2014. *Life beside Itself: Imagining Care in the Canadian Arctic.* Berkeley: University of California Press.

Stocking, George W., Jr. 1968. *Race, Culture, and Evolution: Essays in the History of Anthropology.* Chicago: University of Chicago Press.

Striffler, Steve. 2005. *Chicken: The Dangerous Transformation of America's Favorite Food.* New Haven, CT: Yale University Press.

Stuesse, Angela. 2016. *Scratching Out a Living: Latinos, Race, and Work in the Deep South.* Berkeley: University of California Press.

Stull, Donald D., and Michael J. Broadway. 2013. *Slaughterhouse Blues: The Meat and Poultry Industry in North America.* Belmont, CA: Thomson/Wadsworth.

Sturm, Circe. 2017. "Reflections on the Anthropology of Sovereignty and Settler Colonialism: Lessons from Native North America." *Cultural Anthropology* 32 (3): 340–48.

Stutzman, Ronald. 1981. "El Mestizaje: An All-Inclusive Ideology of Exclusion." In *Cultural Transformations and Ethnicity in Modern Ecuador*, edited by Norm E. Whitten Jr., 45–94. Urbana: University of Illinois Press.

Subin, Samantha. 2021. "Jeff Bezos Is Obsessed with a Common Amazon Warehouse Injury." CNBC @ Work, April 25. https://www.cnbc.com/2021/04/25/jeff-bezos-is-obsessed-with-a-common-amazon-warehouse-injury-.html.

Sunder Rajan, Kaushik, ed. 2006. *Biocapital: The Constitution of Postgenomic Life.* Durham, NC: Duke University Press.

Sunder Rajan, Kaushik. 2007. "Experimental Values: Indian Clinical Trials and Surplus Health." *New Left Review* 45 (May–June): 67–88.

Sutton, Imre. 2001. "Tribes and States: A Political Geography of Indian Environmental Jurisdiction." In *Trusteeship in Change: Toward Tribal Autonomy in Resource Management*, edited by Richmond Clow and Imre Sutton, 239–63. Boulder: University Press of Colorado.

Sze, Julie, ed. 2018. *Sustainability: Approaches to Environmental Justice and Social Power*. New York: NYU Press.

Takaki, Ronald. 1998. *Strangers from a Different Shore: A History of Asian Americans*. New York: Little, Brown.

TallBear, Kim. 2016. "The US-Dakota War and Failed Settler Kinship." *Anthropology News*, November. https://anthrosource.onlinelibrary.wiley.com/doi/10.1111/AN.137.

Taylor, Charles. 1994. "The Politics of Recognition." In *Multiculturalism: Examining the Politics of Recognition*, edited by Amy Gutmann, 25–74. Princeton, NJ: Princeton University Press.

Thomas, Deborah A. 2004. *Modern Blackness: Nationalism, Globalization and the Politics of Culture in Jamaica*. Durham, NC: Duke University Press.

Thomas, Deborah A. 2011. *Exceptional Violence: Embodied Citizenship in Transnational Jamaica*. Durham, NC: Duke University Press.

Thomas, Deborah A. 2013. "Caribbean Studies, Archive Building, and the Problem of Violence." *Small Axe* 2 (41): 27–42.

Thomas, Deborah A. 2016. "Time and the Otherwise: Plantations, Garrisons, and Being Human in the Caribbean." *Anthropological Theory* 16 (2–3): 177–200.

Thomas, Deborah A. 2019. *Political Life in the Wake of the Plantation: Sovereignty, Witnessing, Repair*. Durham, NC: Duke University Press.

Thompson, Edward P. 1967. "Time, Work-Discipline, and Industrial Capitalism." *Past and Present*, no. 38 (December): 56–97.

Thrift, Nigel. 2004. "Intensities of Feeling: Towards a Spatial Politics of Affect." *Geografiska Annaler* 86 B (1): 57–78.

Ticktin, Miriam. 2006. "Where Ethics and Politics Meet: The Violence of Humanitarianism in France." *American Ethnologist* 33 (1): 33–49.

Trask, Haunani Kay. 1999. *From a Native Daughter: Colonialism and Sovereignty in Hawai'i*. Honolulu: University of Hawai'i Press.

Trioullot, Michel-Rolph. 1991. "Anthropology and the Savage Slot: The Poetics and Politics of Otherness." In *Recapturing Anthropology: Working in the Present*, edited by Richard Fox, 17–44. Santa Fe: SAR Press.

Tronto, Joan C. 1993. *Moral Boundaries: A Political Argument for an Ethic of Care*. New York: Routledge.

Tsing, Anna. 2015. *The Mushroom at the End of the World: On the Possibility of Life in Capitalist Ruins*. Princeton, NJ: Princeton University Press.

Turner, Victor. 1977. *The Ritual Process: Structure and Anti-structure*. Ithaca, NY: Cornell University Press.

Turse, Nick. 2017. "Donald Trump's First Year Sets Record for U.S. Special Ops." *TomDispatch*, December 14. https://tomdispatch.com/nick-turse-a-wider-world-of-war/.

US Congressional Budget Office. 2017. *Approaches for Managing the Costs of U.S. Nuclear Forces, 2017–2046*. Washington, DC: Congressional Budget Office.

USGCRP. 2018. *Impacts, Risk and Adaptation in the United States: Fourth National Climate Assessment*, vol. 2. *Report-in-Brief.* Washington, DC: U.S. Global Change Research Program.

Valderrama, Mariano. 2016. *Cuál es el futuro de la gastronomía peruana?* Lima: Apega.

van Eechoud, J. P. K. 1953. *Met Kapmes en Kompas Door Nieuw-Guinea.* Amsterdam: Uitgeverij van H. C. de Boer, Jr.

Vatan, Florence. 2013. "The Lure of Disgust: Musil and Kolnai." *Germanic Review: Literature, Culture, Theory* 88 (1): 28–46.

Verdery, Katherine. 1998. *The Political Lives of Dead Bodies.* Durham, NC: Duke University Press.

Vico, Giambattista. 1948. *The New Science of Giambattista Vico.* Translated by Thomas Goddard Bergin and Max Harold Fisch. Ithaca, NY: Cornell University Press.

Vine, David. 2015. *Base Nation: How U.S. Military Bases Abroad Harm America and the World.* New York: Metropolitan.

Vora, Kalindi. 2015. *Life Support: Biocapital and the New History of Outsourced Labor.* Minneapolis: University of Minnesota Press.

Wade, Peter. 2010. *Race and Ethnicity in Latin America.* London: Pluto.

Wade, Peter. 2017. *Degrees of Mixture, Degrees of Freedom: Genomics, Multiculturalism, and Race in Latin America.* Durham, NC: Duke University Press.

Wagner, Bryan. 2009. *Disturbing the Peace: Black Culture and the Police Power after Slavery.* Cambridge, MA: Harvard University Press.

Wagner, Bryan. 2019. *The Life and Legend of Bras Coupé: The Fugitive Slave Who Fought the Law, Ruled the Swamp, Danced at Congo Square, Invented Jazz, and Died for Love.* Baton Rouge: Louisiana State University Press.

Wall Street Journal. 2020. "Class of 2020 Job Seekers May Be 'Walking into a Hurricane.'" Video, April 29. https://www.wsj.com/video/class-of-2020-job-seekers-may-be-walking-into-a-hurricane/D54FC13E-FE9A-4C00-860C-E359C7541085.html.

Walters, Jonah. 2019. "Puerto Rican Politics Will Never Be the Same: An Interview with Yarimar Bonilla." *Jacobin*, August 2. https://www.jacobinmag.com/2019/08/puerto-rico-ricardo-rossello-governor-unrest.

Weber, Max. (1905) 2002. *The Protestant Ethic and the Spirit of Capitalism.* Edited and translated by Peter Baehr and Gordon C. Wells. London: Penguin Classics.

Weheliye, Alex. 2014. *Habeas Viscus: Racializing Assemblages, Biopolitics, and Black Feminist Theories of the Human.* Durham, NC: Duke University Press.

Weinberg, Tanya. 2002. "Seminoles Hail Project to Improve Canal System on Reservation." *South Florida Sun-Sentinel*, January 16. https://www.sun-sentinel.com/news/fl-xpm-2002-01-16-0201160136-story.html.

Weismantel, Mary. 2001. *Cholas y Pishtacos: Stories of Race and Sex in the Andes.* Chicago: University of Chicago Press.

Werner, Erica, and Tom Hamburger. 2020. "White House and Congress Clash over Liability Protections for Businesses as Firms Cautiously Weigh Virus Reopening Plans." *Washington Post*, May 3. https://www.washingtonpost.com/us-policy/2020/05/03/congress-coronavirus-legal-liability/.

Wickstrom, Stefanie, and Philip D. Young, eds. 2014. *Mestizaje and Globalization: Transformations of Identity and Power.* Tucson: University of Arizona Press.

Wilkins, David E., and Tsianina K. Lomawaima. 2001. *Uneven Ground: American Indian Sovereignty and Federal Law.* Norman: University of Oklahoma Press.

Wilkinson, Francis. 2019. "Gavin Newsom Declares California a 'Nation-State.'" *Bloomberg,* April 9. https://www.bloomberg.com/opinion/articles/2020-04-09/california-declares-independence-from-trump-s-coronavirus-plans.

Williams, Kaya. 2018. "Until They Are Free: Dreamworlds of Captivity in New Orleans Jail Reform." PhD diss., Department of Anthropology, University of Chicago.

Williams, Robert, Jr. 2005. *Like a Loaded Weapon: The Rehnquist Court, Indian Rights, and the Legal History of Racism in America.* Minneapolis: University of Minnesota Press.

Willis, Paul. 2017. *Learning to Labour: How Working Class Kids Get Working Class Jobs.* New York: Columbia University Press.

Winegar, Jessica. 2012. "The Privilege of Revolution: Gender, Class, Space, and Affect in Egypt." *American Ethnologist* 39 (1): 62–65.

Winegar, Jessica. 2015. "A Civilized Revolution: Aesthetics and Political Action in Egypt." *American Ethnologist* 43 (4): 609–22.

Witter, Errol. 2013. *Public Defender in His Interim Report to Parliament (Concerning Investigations into the Conduct of the Security Forces during the State of Emergency Declared May, 2010).* Kingston: Office of the Public Defender.

Wolfe, Patrick. 2013. "The Settler Complex: An Introduction." *American Indian Culture and Research Journal* 37 (2): 1–22.

Wright, Fiona. 2016. "Palestine, My Love: The Ethico-politics of Love and Mourning in Jewish Israel Solidarity Activism." *American Ethnologist* 43 (1): 130–43.

Wynter, Sylvia. 2003. "Unsettling the Coloniality of Being/Power/Truth/Freedom." CR: *The New Centennial Review* 3 (3): 257–337.

Yazzie, Melanie, and Cutcha Risling Baldy. 2018. "Introduction: Indigenous Peoples and the Politics of Water." *Decolonization: Indigeneity, Education and Society* 7 (1): 1–18.

Young, Iris Marion. 2001. "Two Concepts of Self-Determination." In *Human Rights: Concepts, Contests, Contingencies,* edited by Austin Sarat and Thomas Kearns, 25–44. Ann Arbor: University of Michigan Press.

Zournazi, Mary, and Ghassan Hage. 2002. "'On the Side of Life': Joy and the Capacity of Being." In *Hope: New Philosophies for Change,* edited by Mary Zournazi, 150–71. London: Routledge.

Zournazi, Mary, and Brian Massumi. 2002. "Navigating Movements." In *Hope: New Philosophies for Change,* edited by Mary Zournazi, 210–43. London: Routledge.

Contributors

Alex Blanchette is associate professor of anthropology and environmental studies at Tufts University. His scholarship examines shifting conditions of animal life, capitalism, and the place of industrial work in the contemporary postindustrial United States. He is the coeditor for *How Nature Works: Rethinking Labor on a Troubled Planet* (2019) and the author of *Porkopolis: American Animality, Standardized Life, and the Factory Farm* (Duke University Press, 2020).

Yarimar Bonilla is the director of the Center for Puerto Rican Studies at Hunter College. She is also a professor in the Department of Africana, Puerto Rican and Latino Studies at Hunter College and in the PhD program in anthropology at the Graduate Center of the City University of New York. She is the author of *Non-sovereign Futures: French Caribbean Politics in the Wake of Disenchantment* (2015) and coeditor of *Aftershocks of Disaster: Puerto Rico Before and After the Storm* (2019) and *Trouillot Remixed: The Michel-Rolph Trouillot Reader* (Duke University Press, 2021).

Jessica Cattelino studies everyday political processes and imaginations in rural and urban America, with emphasis on Indigenous sovereignty, gender, environment, and economy. She is author of *High Stakes: Florida Seminole Gaming and Sovereignty* (Duke University Press, 2008). Cattelino's book-in-progress examines ways that people are tied to one another through water, in the Florida Everglades and beyond. She also conducts research about gender and everyday household water use in Los Angeles and about LA's Indigenous waters. She is a UCLA professor of anthropology and faculty affiliate in American Indian Studies.

María Elena García is professor in the Comparative History of Ideas Department at the University of Washington in Seattle. García's work explores the politics of race, Indigeneity, violence, and more-than-human life in contemporary Peru. Her most recent book, *Gastropolitics and the Specter of Race: Stories of Capital, Culture, and Coloniality in Peru* (2021), examines the transformation of Peru into a leading global culinary destination, focusing in particular on the ways this "gastronomic revolution" remains haunted by long histories of race and coloniality. García also pays attention to the guinea pig (or cuy) in this story, exploring the significant boom in cuy production over the past two decades. Her next project, *Landscapes of Death: Political Violence beyond the Human in the Peruvian Andes*, considers the impact of political and racial violence on human and more-than-human lives and bodies in Peru.

Akhil Gupta is past president of the American Anthropological Association, professor of anthropology at UCLA, and director of UCLA's Center for India and South Asia (CISA). Gupta is a sociocultural anthropologist working on questions of transnational capitalism, infrastructure, and corruption. His research on BPOs and call centers in India since 2009 (with Purnima Mankekar) was the subject of the Morgan Lectures in 2017, and has resulted in the manuscript *Future Tense: Capital, Labor, and Technology in a Service Industry* (with Purnima Mankekar). His research projects have led him from studying agriculture to state development agencies to multinational corporations. Gupta is interested in the themes of contemporary capitalism, development, postcoloniality, globalization, and the state. Gupta is the author of *Postcolonial Developments* (1998), and editor of *Culture, Power, Place* (1997), *Anthropological Locations* (1997), *The Anthropology of the State* (2006), and *The State in India after Liberalization* (2010). His book *Red Tape: Bureaucracy, Structural Violence, and Poverty in India* (Duke University Press, 2012), was awarded the Coomaraswamy Prize by the Association for Asian Studies. His most recent full-length publications are *The Promise of Infrastructure* (edited with Nikhil Anand and Hannah Appel, Duke University Press, 2018) and *The Anthropology of Corruption* (special issue of *Current Anthropology* edited with Sarah Muir, 2018).

Lochlann Jain is an award-winning author and professor of anthropology at Stanford University and Visiting Chair of Global Health and Social Medicine at King's College London. His work aims to unsettle some of the deeply held assumptions about objectivity that underlie the history of medical research. Jain is the author of *Injury* (2006), *Malignant: How Cancer Becomes Us* (2013), and a book of drawings, *Things That Art: A Graphic Menagerie of Enchanting Curiosity* (2019). Jain is currently working on two books. The first develops the concept of The WetNet, which refers to fluid bonding among humans and animals in ways that create pathways for the transmission of pathogens. Specifically, midcentury bioscientific practices such as blood transfusion and vaccine development and testing involved exchanges in human and animal effluvia, the risks of which have largely been disavowed. Jain's current book project elucidates the concept of The WetNet through a history of the hepatitis B virus and the development of the first hepatitis B vaccine. The second project, *The Lung Is a Bird and a Fish*, investigates, in prose and art works, a cultural history of drowning from 1750 to the present.

Purnima Mankekar is a professor in the Departments of Anthropology and Asian American Studies at UCLA, with a joint appointment in the Department of Film, Television and Digital Media. Her areas of expertise are theories of affect; digital media and virtual anthropology; transnational cultural and media studies; feminist anthropology and ethnography; cross-cultural perspectives on temporality and futurity; South

Asian and South Asian American studies; and critical race and ethnic studies. Her most recent book was *Unsettling India: Affect, Temporality, Transnationality* (Duke University Press, 2015). She is currently finishing a monograph with Akhil Gupta on affective labor and futurity in the information technology–enabled services industry, and her next ethnographic project is on algorithmic worlds and governance in India. She is also working on a book project on digital media, race, and intimacy. Trained as a cultural anthropologist, Mankekar has conducted interdisciplinary research on television, film, and digital media, and on publics/public cultures with a focus on the politics of affect. She is the author of *Screening Culture, Viewing Politics* (Duke University Press, 1999) and *Unsettling India: Affect, Temporality, Transnationality*. Her coedited books include *Caste and Outcast* (coedited with Gordon Chang and Akhil Gupta, 2002) and *Media, Erotics, and Transnational Asia* (coedited with Louisa Schein, Duke University Press, 2013). She has been awarded a Mellon Postdoctoral Fellowship at Duke University (1997–98); a Bunting Fellowship at the Radcliffe Institute for Advanced Study, Harvard University (2000–2001); a Stanford University Humanities Center fellowship (2005–6); and senior research fellowship at the Asia Research Institute, National University of Singapore (2013).

Joseph Masco is a professor of anthropology and science studies at the University of Chicago. His work considers the logics, affects, and futurities supporting technological revolution and the long-term US investment in militarism, as well as the cumulative effects of petrochemical capitalism and nuclear nationalism on collective life. He is the author of *The Nuclear Borderlands: The Manhattan Project in Post–Cold War New Mexico* (which won the J. I. Staley Prize and the Rachel Carson Prize, and was cowinner of the Robert K. Merton Prize) and two books with Duke University Press: *The Theater of Operations: National Security Affect from the Cold War to the War on Terror* (2014) and, most recently, *The Future of Fallout, and Other Episodes in Radioactive World-Making* (2021).

Michael Ralph is chair of the Department of Afro-American Studies at Howard University and teaches in the School of Medicine at New York University. Michael is the recipient of fellowships from the Andrew W. Mellon Foundation, Woodrow Wilson Foundation, Social Science Research Council, National Science Foundation, and the Institute for Advanced Study in Princeton, as well as Harvard University's Charles Warren Center for Studies in US History and the W. E. B. Dubois Fellowship. His 2015 book *Forensics of Capital* demonstrates that the social profile of an individual or country is a credit profile as well as a forensic profile. Ralph is now completing three graphic books. *Basketball IQ* (forthcoming in 2023) is about the game inside the game, insisting that basketball is conceptual—involving complicated plays and strategy, teamwork and timing—especially for players with storied legacies who have pioneered their own original theoretical contributions. *Before 13th* (forthcoming in 2023)—narrated by Ida B. Wells and Frederick Douglass—draws upon original archival research to challenge the widespread notion that leasing prison inmates to private corporations begins with the Thirteenth Amendment, demonstrating instead that it began several decades prior, with an experiment to have white inmates farm hemp at the Kentucky penitentiary. *Fishing* (forthcoming in 2023) draws on several years of ethnographic and historical research among incarcerated peoples to demonstrate that ingenuity cannot be incarcerated, using images of inmates using improvised threads, or "fishing," to share objects with each other.

Danilyn Rutherford is the president of the Wenner-Gren Foundation and the author of three books: *Raiding the Land of the Foreigners: The Limits of the Nation on an Indonesian Frontier* (2003), *Laughing at Leviathan: Sovereignty and Audience in West Papua* (2012), and *Living in the Stone Age: Reflections on the Origins of a Colonial Category* (2018). Her research has long focused on the disputed Indonesian half of New Guinea and has involved fieldwork and archival research in West Papua and the Netherlands. She has also written essays on topics ranging from kinship to money to global warming to ethics and epistemology within anthropology. She is currently completing an ethnographic memoir on cognitive mystery and the making of her daughter's social world.

Arjun Shankar is an assistant professor of culture and politics at Georgetown University. His research draws from theories in globalization and development, digital and visual ethnography, critical race and postcolonial theory, and curiosity studies. In his current book project, *Brown Saviors and Their Others*, he takes India's burgeoning help economy, specifically the education NGO sector, as a site from which to interrogate how colonial, racial, and caste capitalism undergird transnational and digitized NGO work in contemporary global India. As a methodologist, Shankar has been interested in developing decolonial, participatory visual methodologies. He has primarily focused on the neocolonial politics of representation, global circulation, and reception of the impoverished and suffering child figure and offers new multimodal methods as alternatives to these paradigms. He is also interested in multimodal evaluation and publishing, asking questions regarding the possibilities that might accompany nontextual knowledge production. Toward this end, he is a current coeditor of the multimodal section of *American Anthropologist*. Finally, he is an advocate for curiosity studies and coeditor of a book, *Curiosity Studies* (with Perry Zurn, 2020), an emerging interdisciplinary field that challenges us to think anew about scholarly production, pedagogic praxis, and the political role of the academician.

Kristen L. Simmons is a doctoral student in the Department of Anthropology at the University of Chicago. Her work engages toxicity and settler colonialism in the American West. Conducting ethnographic fieldwork in the Mojave Desert, she tracks multiple "energy" projects in development.

Deborah A. Thomas is the R. Jean Brownlee Professor of Anthropology and the director of the Center for Experimental Ethnography at the University of Pennsylvania. She is also a research associate with the Visual Identities in Art and Design Research Centre at the University of Johannesburg. Her recent book, *Political Life in the Wake of the Plantation: Sovereignty, Witnessing, Repair*, was awarded the Gordon K. and Sybil Lewis Book Award from the Caribbean Studies Association in 2021 and the Senior Book Prize from the American Ethnological Society in 2020, and was also the runner-up for the Gregory Bateson Prize in the same year. She is also the author of *Exceptional Violence: Embodied Citizenship in Transnational Jamaica* (2011) and

Modern Blackness: Nationalism, Globalization, and the Politics of Culture in Jamaica (2004), and is coeditor of the volume *Globalization and Race* (2006). Thomas codirected and coproduced the documentary films *Bad Friday* and *Four Days in May*, and she is the cocurator of a multimedia installation titled *Bearing Witness: Four Days in West Kingston*, which opened at the Penn Museum in November 2017. From 2016 to 2020, Thomas was the editor in chief of *American Anthropologist*, the flagship journal of the American Anthropological Association. Prior to Thomas's life as an academic, she was a professional dancer with the New York–based Urban Bush Women.

Leniqueca A. Welcome is an anthropologist and a designer by training. She is currently an assistant professor of anthropology and international relations at George Washington University. Her research in the Caribbean explores the entangled processes of racialization, gendering, and criminalization in Trinidad while speculating on the emergence of a world where life is unconditionally precious. Her work, informed by Black feminist theory, combines more traditional ethnographic methods with photography and collaging.

Kaya Naomi Williams is an assistant professor of anthropology at Barnard College. Her current work engages ethnographically with efforts by policymakers, lawyers, organizers, and other city residents to shape the future of New Orleans's municipal jail. Kaya's research on local incarceration focuses not on the practice of confinement itself but on the daily work of the individuals and communities whose labor seeks to fundamentally change American responses to crime. The work raises questions about the cultural, economic, and affective investments that produce incarceration in the United States as a supposedly intractable problem.

Jessica Winegar is professor of anthropology and Middle East and North African studies at Northwestern University. She is the author of numerous articles on visual culture and politics in the Middle East that have appeared in publications such as *American Ethnologist, Cultural Anthropology, Anthropological Quarterly, Middle East Journal of Culture and Communication, Review of Middle East Studies, Critical Interventions, Contemporary Practices, Middle East Report, Jadaliyya*, and *ArteEast*. Her book *Creative Reckonings: The Politics of Art and Culture in Contemporary Egypt* (2006) won the Albert Hourani Award for best book in Middle East studies and the Arnold Rubin Award for best book on African arts. She is also the coauthor, with Lara Deeb, of *Anthropology's Politics: Disciplining the Middle East* (2015).

Index

abandonment, 14–15

abolition: frameworks for, 303; of slavery, 54

accountability: change and, 21; mediation and, 85, 86; parameters of, 73, 77

action, collective, 180

activism, 2, 19, 31, 42, 94

Acurio, Gastón, 45, 46, 48, 50–51, 66, 70nn23–24, 70n26; agricultural producers addressed by, 59–60, 61; as benevolent patriarch, 54, 56, 63; on Mistura, 58; TED talk of, 64, 65

Acurio family, 69n12

Adams, Akanni "Dole," 105, 106

Adavisandra, India, 16, 162, 167, 170, 177–81

addiction, 124, 197, 283–84, 291

Addiction by Design (Schüll), 253

advertisement, 228, 233, 234, 235, 236

Afropessimism, 242–43

Agamben, Giorgio, 116, 131, 132, 138nn14–15, 160n3, 160n8, 263

agency, 2, 7, 8, 116

agrarian reform, 51, 52–53, 54, 55

agricultural producers, 56; Acurio addressing, 59–60, 61; beautifying, 57; masculinization of, 62

Ahmed, Sara, 47, 54, 65, 66, 67

aid, 88; mutual, 300, 302; spoiled, 91

air, 211, 217, 219

airlines, 121–22

Akomfrah, John, 99, 109n6

Akshaya Patra (NGO), 163, 166–67, 170, 180; factory, 171–77; standardization of, 171–72, 184n11

Aleinikoff, T. Alexander, 160n5

alliances, chef-producer, 55, 60, 61, 69n14

Allison, Anne, 119

Alston, Philip, 280–81

alternative politics, 294

Althusser, Louis, 264

Amazon, 209n1

American Dream, 278, 284

American Meat Institute, 196

ammu (uncle), 37

Amnesty International, 80

Andean panpipe (*zampolla*), 45

anthropology, 99, 302–3, 304

anti-Blackness, 242, 243

antiphony, 73, 86

antirelationality, 168, 183n9

Apega (Peruvian Society of Gastronomy), 56, 57, 59, 69n18

Arendt, Hannah, 30, 32, 42

Arima, Trinidad, 103

Army, US, 299–300

aspirations, 123–24, 125, 126, 136n5, 175

assumptions, shedding, 108

asthma, 10–11, 220

Astrid y Gastón (restaurant), 50–51, 55, 56, 64, 65, 68n10

"authorized Indian, the" (*el indio permitido*), 58, 59

automation, 200–201

autonomy, 5, 119, 135, 140; interdependency and, 141–46, 159; privileging, 161n9; Seminole Tribe, 147

autopsies: protocol for, 79–80; social, 85

bacterial strain, 169

"bad subjects," 264, 269

bags, plastic, 230, 232

Bangalore, India, 162, 166, 171, 173, 175–76, 183n6

Barker, Joanne, 161n10

Bataille, Georges, 4–5, 72, 74

beach, 107, 108

Bearing Witness (installation), 78

Beast and the Sovereign, The (Derrida), 263

beef, boxed, 201

being, 4, 5, 131

Bell, Deanne M., 78

belonging, 118, 119

benevolent patriarch (*el buen patrón*), 54, 56, 63

Bengaluru, India, 114, 117, 120–21, 137n10

Benjamin, Walter, 243

Bennett, Jane, 204–5

Berlant, Lauren, 7, 8, 23n5, 30, 269, 278

Beyoncé, 244

Bezos, Jeffery, 209n1

Biaks, 275n11

Big Cypress Reservation, Seminole, 139–40, 153, 154–55

Big Cypress Water Conservation Plan, 152, 156

binaries, of power, 131

biological system, slaughterhouse as, 203–7, 209

Biolsi, Thomas, 160n5

bird: as fish, 226–36; lung as, 218–21

Black Lives Matter, 260, 293, 298–99

Black Marxism (Robinson), 262n3

Blackness, 246, 248, 256

Black Power Mixtape, The (documentary), 256

Blanchette, Alex, 17

bodies, 17, 71, 78–79, 80, 85, 107; breaking in, 195–99; identification of, 81; labor and limits of, 188, 190; labor shaping, 195, 199; maintenance of, 191; Massumi on, 133; strain on, 168

Bodin, Jean, 160n2

bolt gun, 187

bonds, 299

Bonilla, Yarimar, 5, 8, 11, 13–14

borders, 115, 192

boundaries, 10, 30, 157

boxed beef, 201

Boyle, Robert, 218, 219, 301–2

Boyle's Brief (artwork), 215

BPO (Business Process Outsourcing), 114, 115

branding, 47

Bras-Coupé, 301

breath, 10, 11, 211, 217–19, 258, 297, 301

Brown, Vincent, 76

Buck-Morss, Susan, 207

Buendía, 69n15

buen patrón, el (benevolent patriarch), 54, 56, 63

bullet holes, 106

burdens: of scale, 171; social, 198

Bureau of Indian Affairs, US, 147, 158

Bureau of Labor Statistics, US, 202

burnout, 126, 132, 135

Bush, George W., 292

Business Process Outsourcing (BPO), 114, 115; gender and, 137n7, 137n11; spatiotemporalities of, 117–21

Butler, Octavia, 1–2, 9, 10, 14, 17, 18, 21, 22–23, 295n1

Byrd, Jodi, 246, 247

Bywater, New Orleans, 248

California State House, 266

Callao, Peru, 64

call centers, 15, 113, 114

camera, 107, 108

Campbell's soup, 231, 233

Campt, Tina, 108n2

canals, 55–56, 139, 154

Can Bou Play Foundation, 103, 104–5

capacitación (training), 62

capital, 60, 300, 301

capitalism, 5, 7; dis/enchantment and, 138n13; extractive, 67; path of, 135; petrochemical, 16, 277, 287–89; racialized, 183n9

care, 182, 274; burden of, 94; economies of, 165; failure of, 95

Carmichael, Stokely, 256, 257

carnality, 273, 275n11

Casa Hacienda Moreyra, 53, 54, 69n11; Astrid y Gastón in, 50–51; Mayer on, 52; periodization of, 55–56

Case, Anna, 284

casino gaming, 140, 141, 146, 152; compacts, 148, 150–51; interdependency in, 147; litigation for, 149–51

caste system, 118–19, 172

Castle Bravo nuclear test, 227–28, 229

Cattelino, Jessica, 15, 16

death, 5, 13, 23n5; disavowal and, 83–86;
    forensics of, 77–82; mass-produced, 233;
    mediation and, 72–73; sovereign, 71;
    witnessing and, 73–77
Deaton, Angus, 284
debates, COVID-19, 93–94
debt, 247, 248, 255, 291
declaration, of love, 29–30
decompartmentalization, 157
defective citizens, 270
Defense Production Act, US, 185–86
deficiencies, 177
Deleuze, Gilles, 134
Deloria, Philip, 47
Deloria, Vine, Jr., 143–44
Delta Tech Park, Bengaluru, 117, 118
Deming, Edward, 172, 184n12
demonetization, 182n2
Dennison, Jean, 143
Department of Education, US, 88
Department of Labor, US, 196, 201
dependency, 142–43
Derrida, Jacques, 134, 263
Desmond, Jane, 60
development, complex, 136
developmentalism, 4; paradoxes of, 164–71;
    regimes of, 170; risk and, 176–77; sover-
    eignty and, 167, 169; unhinging, 175
dialogue, 60
Diderot, Denis, 300–301
digitalization, of labor, 115
dignity, 40, 182, 183n4, 187–88
disability, 264, 266, 267, 268, 270
disappointment, 29
disavowal, death and, 83–86
discipline, 181
disenchantment, 138n13
disgust, 41; boundaries and, 30; of Indigenous
    people, 53; for Muslim Brotherhood,
    33–36; politics and, 29–31; protests sus-
    tained by, 31–33
disgust (*qaraf*), 31, 34
dispositions, 83–84
dispossession, 246, 248–51
*Dissertation on Suspended Respiration from
    Drowning, Hanging, and Suffocation, A*
    (Coleman), 221
diversity, 60, 64
Diwali, 101
dog, 48, 219, 223
domination, 3, 145
dons, 77–78
draft, military, 291

drainage, 154, 156
Drinot, Paulo, 53
drowning, 218, 221
drugs, 1, 2, 20, 208, 283–84
duck, 218
Duncan, Isadora, 225
DuPont, 232
duppy, 74–75, 77
duration, of labor, 134
Dutch New Guinea, 264, 265–66
duty, 119–20, 129, 130

earthquake, 8, 13, 80, 88, 91, 92
East Port of Spain, Trinidad, 97, 100, 101,
    108n1
Economization of Life, The (Murphy),
    247–48
economy: Bengaluru, 120–21; of care, 165;
    Egyptian, 34; of India, 164, 182n2; moral,
    174, 175, 181
ecosystem, 140, 156
Edelman, Lee, 269
EDGI (Environmental Data and Governance
    Initiative), 288
Eechoud, J. P. van, 264, 265–66
efficiency, 166, 167, 178, 186, 191
Egypt, 12, 27–28, 32–33, 38, 304
embodied knowledge, 170
emergency, 71, 85
emotions, 29, 41
empathy, 129
emplacement, 114, 115, 123
enchantment, 125, 138n13
enlightenment, 301
entanglements, 246–47
entitlement, 211
Environmental Data and Governance Initia-
    tive (EDGI), 288
environmental history, 158
errors, witnessing, 102
Escobar, Arturo, 62
Estes, Nick, 145, 146, 159
ethical frameworks, 129–30
ethnography, 2–3, 22, 302
Ethyl, 226, 228, 236
Everglades, Florida, 15–16, 139–40, 152, 156
Everglades Agricultural Area, 157
"Everything's at Its Best in Cellophane"
    (advertisement), 233
Ewidah, Boulos, 38
exclusion, 9, 20, 72
expansion, slaughterhouse, 189
experimental science, 218–19

net, social safety, 94
Nevada Test Site, 244, 245
Newbury, Mickey, 295n3
New Orleans, 248, 250, 252, 297–98, 305
NGOs (nongovernmental organizations), 163, 165–66
night, 122, 123, 134
nine-night (funerary ritual), 74–75
Nixon, Richard, 282
Noguera, Pedro de, 51
nondomination, 152
nongovernmental organizations (NGOs), 163, 165–66, 183n5
nonrecognition, 19
nonsovereign death, 13
No Relief (report), 188
normate, 264
nose, 211, 214
nostalgia, 9–10, 47, 278
nuclear test, 227–28, 229
nurse, 194–95
Nussbaum, Martha, 31

Obama, Barack, 90, 167, 292, 293
obligations, 75, 94, 129, 164, 169–70
occult, 225
Occupational Safety and Health Administration, US Department of Labor, 196
Oceania, 154
Ochs, Elinor, 272, 275n8, 276n13
Office of Technology Assessment, 290
Ong, Aihwa, 207–8
On Potentiality (Agamben), 116
opioid, 283–84, 291
opportunity, 14–15, 59
optimism, cruel, 278
organ implants, 189
Organ King Blue (artwork), 212
Ortner, Sherry, 137n6
otherness, 4, 18, 19
"otherwises," 273, 274
Our History Is the Future (Estes), 145
Oxfam America, 188
oxygen, 211

packaging, 230, 232
pain, 73–74, 291, 294; break in, 196, 197; chronic, 113, 202–3; liberation from, 198; sourcing, 280–86
Palo Alto, California, 266, 268, 269
pandemic. *See* COVID-19
pantry, 52
Papuans, 264, 265–66

Parable of the Sower (Butler), 1–2, 9, 10, 14, 17, 21, 22–23, 295n1
Parables for the Virtual (Massumi), 133
paradoxes: of developmentalism, 164–71; of industrialism, 186
Paris Climate Agreement, 288
path, of capitalism, 135
pathologists, forensic, 78, 79, 82
patience, 127
patriarchy, 37
pensioners, 127
People's National Party, Jamaica, 83
People's Union for Civil Liberties v. the Union of India & Others, 165
performance: of Peru, 45–46; of sovereignty, 270
periodization, of Casa Hacienda Moreyra, 55–56
Peru: Callao, 64; Lima, 48, 49, 56, 59, 69n16; as love story, 68n4; performing, 45–46
Peru, Nebraska, 45
peruanidad (Peruvianness), 47
Peruvian cuisine, 12–13, 66–67
Peruvianness (*peruanidad*), 47
Peruvian Society of Gastronomy (Apega), 56, 57, 59, 69n18
Peruvian Truth and Reconciliation Commission (CVR), 48, 50
petrochemical capitalism, 16, 277, 287–89
philanthropy, 148
photocollage, 14, 98–100, 109n5. *See also specific works*
photography, 97, 108
pigs, 17, 185, 187, 188, 189, 191, 200
pilot, 121
Pinkham, Lydia, 234
pisco sour, 51
Place of Memory, Tolerance and Social Inclusion (museum), 50
plantation, 71, 72
plastic bags, 230, 232
pluralism, 149–50, 243
police, 102–3, 297; defunding, 298, 300; operation, 85; private, 250; violence, 6–7
political cartoons, 34, 35
political modernity, 71–72
political vocabulary, 294
politics, 9, 12, 17, 289–90; alternative, 294; erasure in, 13; in Jamaica, 77–78, 83, 84; love and disgust in, 29–31; of memory, 50; racial, 18–19
Pollanen, Michael, 79, 80–82
pool, 252, 253

Trumpet, Donnie, 255
truth, 77, 101–2
Tsing, Anna, 128
Tunde, Olaniran, 248, 249, 250, 251
turnabout, 151
Twitter, 34

uncle (*ammu*), 37
uniformity, 210n7
unions, 201–2
United South and Eastern Tribes, 149
United States (US), 20–21; military, 279, 291; poverty, 280–83; Puerto Rico and, 90–91. *See also specific topics*
Universal Declaration of Human Rights, 165, 183n4
University of Chicago, 242, 249–50, 259
unpaid salaries, 178–79
unpredictability, foregrounding, 8
upward mobility, 113, 121, 175
urbanity, 178
US Sugar Corporation, 139, 148
utilitarianism, 169
utilities, 127
Uttar Pradesh, India, 124

values, moral, 167
variability, in pigs, 203–4, 206
Vegetable Compound, 234
Velasco Alvarado, Juan, 49, 50, 51, 52, 53–54, 55, 69n13
ventilators, 91
ventriloquist representation, 63
vertical integration, slaughterhouse, 186–91, 206
Vibrant Matter (Bennett), 204–5
vibrations, 241–42
vignettes, 100
violence, 13, 67, 83, 141, 277, 289; anti-Black police, 6–7; distributed, 15; fast and slow, 22; finance and, 298, 299; historical, 11; justifying, 41; normative, 2, 4; routine, 194–95; sexual, 123
vitality, 130–31, 134–35, 205, 206
vital materialism, 205
vocabulary, political, 294
vote, popular, 292
Voting Rights Act, US (1965), 290
vulnerability, 20, 114, 127–33, 254, 263, 274

wading, 96
Wading in the Thick (photocollage), 14
wages, 162–63, 178–79, 210n6
wake, 86
wall, 293
Wall Street Journal, 91
wardship, 147
Warhol, Andy, 232–33
"Wasicu" (fat taker), 161n12
water, 15, 16, 92, 158–59; in Big Cypress Reservation, 154–55; C&SF Project for, 156–57; decompartmentalization of, 157; flow of, 139–40; movement of, 153; Seminole Tribe managing, 152–53
Water Management District, South Florida, 139
Water Resource Management Department, Seminole Tribe, 152–53
watersheds, 157–58, 159
Wedderburn, Junior "Gabu," 78
weddings, 117
Welcome, Leniqueca A., 14
welfare, 271, 281, 282
Werner, Alexander Chiu, 58
West, Kanye, 259, 260, 261
West Kingston, Jamaica, 13, 73, 76–77, 83
West Kingston Commission of Enquiry, 80, 87n9
wheelchair, 266–67
whip (*chicote*), 63
whiteness, 21, 280, 284–85, 286, 293, 294
white supremacy, 242, 284, 294
Williams, Kaya, 18–19, 282
Winegar, Jessica, 7, 11, 12
witnessing, 98, 100; death and, 73–77; errors, 102; images employed for, 97; surveillance and, 84; Thomas on, 108n3
Witter, Errol, 78
Wolfe, Patrick, 47
Woods, Jamila, 249, 254, 261
Wright, Fiona, 42
Wright, Joseph, 219–20, 234

Young, Iris Marion, 142, 159, 160n6
Yukon First Nation, 161n11
yuyanapaq ("to remember"), 50

zampolla (Andean panpipe), 45
Zilla Panchayat, 178
zombies, 75–76
zosos (zones of special operation), 85